The European Union **How does it work?**

The New European Union Series

Series Editors: John Peterson and Helen Wallace

The European Union is both the most successful modern experiment in international cooperation and a daunting analytical challenge to students of politics, economics, history and law, and the social sciences. The EU of the twenty-first century will be fundamentally different from its earlier permutations, as monetary union, eastern enlargement, a new defence role, and globalization all create pressures for a more complex, differentiated, and a truly new European Union.

The New European Union series brings together the expertise of leading scholars writing on major aspects of EU politics for an international readership.

The series offers lively, accessible, reader-friendly, and research-based textbooks on:

Policy-Making in the European Union

The Institutions of the European Union

Origins and Evolution of the European Union

The Member States of the European Union

International Relations and the European Union

The European Union: How does it work?

The European Union

How does it work?

SECOND EDITION

Elizabeth Bomberg, John Peterson, and Alexander Stubb

OXFORD
UNIVERSITY PRESS

OXFORD
UNIVERSITY PRESS

Great Clarendon Street, Oxford OX2 6DP

Oxford University Press is a department of the University of Oxford.
It furthers the University's objective of excellence in research, scholarship,
and education by publishing worldwide in

Oxford New York

Auckland Cape Town Dar es Salaam Hong Kong Karachi
Kuala Lumpur Madrid Melbourne Mexico City Nairobi
New Delhi Shanghai Taipei Toronto

With offices in

Argentina Austria Brazil Chile Czech Republic France Greece
Guatemala Hungary Italy Japan Poland Portugal Singapore
South Korea Switzerland Thailand Turkey Ukraine Vietnam

Oxford is a registered trade mark of Oxford University Press
in the UK and in certain other countries

Published in the United States
by Oxford University Press Inc., New York

British Library Cataloguing in Publication Data

Data available

Library of Congress Cataloging in Publication Data

The European Union—how does it work?—2nd ed. / [edited by] Elizabeth
Bomberg, John Peterson, and Alexander Stubb.
        p. cm.—(The new European Union series)
   Includes bibliographical references and index.
   ISBN 978–0–19–920639–1
1. European Union.   I. Bomberg, Elizabeth E.   II. Peterson, John, 1958-
III. Stubb, Alexander C-G.
   JN30.E9417 2003
   341.242'2—dc22

                                                          2007037570

Typeset by Laserwords Private Limited, Chennai, India
Printed in Great Britain
on acid-free paper by
Ashford Colour Press Ltd, Gosport, Hampshire

ISBN 978–0–19–920639–1

10 9 8 7 6 5 4 3 2

■ PREFACE AND ACKNOWLEDGEMENTS

Change is a constant. That is one of the themes of this book and it certainly applies to the EU since we published the first edition of this volume in 2003. At that time, we were grappling with an EU of 15 diverse states and a population of 380 million. Today our task is even more daunting. Since publication of the first edition, the EU has expanded its members to 27, its population to nearly 500 million, and its land mass has increased by 25 per cent. The EU's size is not the only thing to expand. Today the EU is involved in an even greater array of policy areas, or involved in existing ones more intensely. Its engagement with the outside world has changed too, often in unexpected ways. What the EU does, how it does it, and with what consequences, have all altered or intensified in some (usually significant) way.

We have tried to reflect these changes in our revised edition. In addition to updating significantly each individual chapter (five years is a long time in EU affairs), we've altered the book's organization and overall content. First, we've added several entirely new chapters, including one dedicated to the EU's fastest developing policy area: in Chapter 7 John Occhipinti introduces the EU's internal security policy, which extends to issues of immigration, asylum, cross-border crime, and terrorism. A new chapter by Neil MacCormick wrestles with the big issues of democratic government by focusing on big constitutional questions (does the EU have a constitution? does it need one to be democratic? does anybody care?). Next, instead of a separate chapter on the enlargement process, Graham Avery (Chapter 9) looks more generally at EU expansion and the Union's evolving relationship with its neighbours. Finally, rather than including a separate chapter on policy-making, we've woven an analysis of the policy-making process into chapters on EU policies (Chapter 6), institutions (Chapter 3), and constitutionalism and democracy (Chapter 8).

Even more important is what we have *not* changed. Our core mission remains the same: to produce a clear, concise, truly introductory text for students and the curious general reader. No previous experience required. We know the EU is important; we demonstrate why and how in the next chapters. We also know it can be made both comprehensible and interesting. Our aim is to show how. If we succeed, it is in great part due to our all-star team of contributors, editors, support and publishing staff.

First, the contributors. One of the book's most distinctive and strongest qualities is its blend of academic and practitioner authors. All of the chapters were either co-authored or reviewed by both an academic and practitioner. We thank our team of authors for working to make this blend workable and even enjoyable. A special thanks to the co-authors of the *first* edition's Chapter 3 (Laura Cram and David Martin) and Chapter 10 (Michael E Smith). Their co-authored first-edition chapters, while significantly updated and revised, have served as the basis for the current edition's Chapters 3 and 10.

A second batch of thanks goes to the editorial and production team. In Edinburgh the editorial assistance offered by Louise Maythorne (University of Edinburgh) was tremendous. Louise read through almost every chapter, seeking clarification, offering sound advice, catching errors. She also helped compile and update the references and glossary—no mean feat in itself. Alex Stubb would like to thank his able assistants—Leigh Garner, Lauri Tierala, and especially Henrik Ruso—for their invaluable help.

We owe a very special thanks to series editor Helen Wallace, who offered not only excellent substantive guidance but also unflagging and essential encouragement. Thanks also to the production team at OUP, especially Ruth Anderson who demonstrated great patience and skill in seeing the project through.

Thirdly, our readers. The real advantage of a second edition is that we are able to benefit from the feedback from the first. We've profited enormously from comments offered by reviewers of the first edition, by practitioners in Brussels (special thanks to Michael Shackleton of the European Parliament and Ron Asmus of the German Marshall Fund), and by the many EU studies colleagues who have used this book in their teaching. An extremely useful range of comments, criticisms, and suggestions came directly from 'end users' themselves—including students using the first edition in their courses at the University of Edinburgh and College of Europe.

Most of the serious editing of text was performed while two of us (Bomberg and Peterson) were visiting scholars in Spring 2007 at the Institute of Governmental Studies, University of California Berkeley. We are immensely grateful for the logistical support, collegiality, and peaceful space offered there. Director Jack Citrin and administrator Liz Wiener made our stay especially productive, and we owe them a great deal. We would also like to thank friends and family in California and Vermont for graciously allowing their dining tables to be converted to work desks for the editing stages of this book.

Finally, amidst all the tumultuous change that marks scholarship on EU, one 'constant' most gratefully acknowledged is the support offered by the editors' families. Like last time, but more so: we could not have done it without you.

Elizabeth Bomberg, John Peterson, and Alexander Stubb

▌ GUIDED TOUR OF TEXTBOOK FEATURES

This text is enriched with a range of learning tools to help you navigate the text material and reinforce your knowledge of the European Union. This guided tour shows you how to get the most out of your textbook package.

Chapter Overviews

Chapter Overviews at the beginning of every chapter set the scene for upcoming themes and issues to be discussed and indicate the scope of coverage within each chapter topic.

Boxes

A number of topics benefit from further explanation or exploration in a way that does not disrupt the flow of the main text. Throughout the book boxes provide you with extra information on particular topics to complement your understanding of the main chapter text.

Discussion Questions

A set of carefully devised questions has been provided to help you assess your comprehension of core themes, and may also be used as the basis of seminar discussion and coursework.

Further Reading

To take your learning further, reading lists have been provided as a guide to find out more about the issues raised within each chapter topic and to help you locate the key academic literature in the field.

Web Links

At the end of most chapters you will find an annotated summary of useful websites that will be instrumental in further research.

Glossary Terms

Key terms appear in colour in the text and are defined in a glossary at the end of the text to aid you in exam revision.

▌ GUIDED TOUR OF THE ONLINE RESOURCE CENTRE

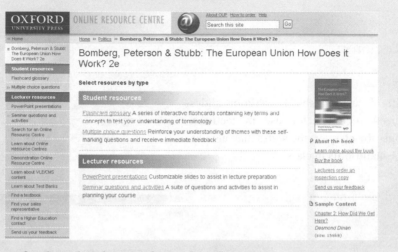

www.oxfordtextbooks.co.uk/orc/bomberg2e/

The Online Resource Centre that accompanies this book provides students and lecturers with ready-to-use teaching and learning materials.

For Students

Flashcard Glossary

A series of interactive flashcards containing key terms and concepts have been provided to test your understanding of terminology.

Multiple Choice Questions

The best way to reinforce your understanding of European Union Politics is through frequent and cumulative revision. A bank of self-marking multiple choice questions has been provided for each chapter of the text, and includes instant feedback on your answers to help strengthen your knowledge.

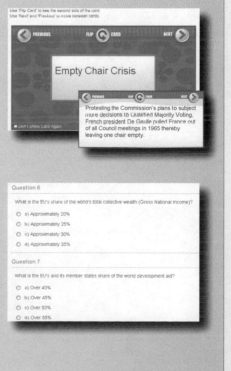

For Lecturers

PowerPoint Slides

A suite of customizable PowerPoint slides has been included for use in lectures. Arranged by chapter, the slides may also be used as hand-outs in class.

Why Study the EU?

- Understanding European politics
- Practical relevance
- Analytical significance
- Globalisation and integration
- EU as a political puzzle

Seminar Questions

A suite of questions has been provided to encourage class debate and reinforce understanding of key chapter themes.

Bomberg, Peterson & Stubb: The European Union How Does It Work?

Chapter 1

Discussion Questions

1. Which theory best describes the integration process of the EU? Why?
2. Why is the EU considered an "experiment in motion"?
3. The EU is said to have an expanding scope but limited capacity. Why is that the case? Do you think that is true?
4. How might the EU become more important or less important in the future of Europe?
5. Why do we care how integration occurs?

▮ OUTLINE CONTENTS

DETAILED CONTENTS — xiii

LIST OF FIGURES — xix

LIST OF BOXES — xx

LIST OF TABLES — xxii

LIST OF ABBREVIATIONS AND ACRONYMS — xxiii

LIST OF CONTRIBUTORS — xxvii

MAP: THE EXPANDING EUROPEAN UNION — xxviii

PART I   Background

1   Introduction — 3
    Elizabeth Bomberg, Alexander Stubb, and John Peterson

2   How Did We Get Here? — 22
    Desmond Dinan

PART II   Major Actors

3   The EU's Institutions — 45
    Elizabeth Bomberg and Alexander Stubb

4   Member States — 71
    Brigid Laffan and Alexander Stubb

5   Organized Interests and Lobbying — 92
    Rory Watson and Michael Shackleton

PART III   Policies and Policy-making

6   Key Policies — 115
    Alberta Sbragia and Francesco Stolfi

7   A Secure Europe? Internal Security Policies — 138
    John D. Occhipinti

8   Constitutionalism and Democracy in the EU — 159
    Neil MacCormick

PART IV   **The EU and the Wider World**

9   EU Expansion and Wider Europe   179
     Graham Avery

10   The EU as a Global Actor   201
     John Peterson

11   Conclusion   222
     John Peterson, Elizabeth Bomberg, and Alexander Stubb

APPENDIX: CHRONOLOGY OF EUROPEAN INTEGRATION   235
GLOSSARY   239
REFERENCES   245
INDEX   257

▌DETAILED CONTENTS

LIST OF FIGURES   xix

LIST OF BOXES   xx

LIST OF TABLES   xxii

LIST OF ABBREVIATIONS AND ACRONYMS   xxiii

LIST OF CONTRIBUTORS   xxvii

MAP: THE EXPANDING EUROPEAN UNION   xxviii

PART I Background

1 Introduction   3

Studying the EU   4

   Why Bother?   6

Understanding the EU: Theory and Conceptual Tools   10

   International Relations Approaches   11

   A Comparative Politics Approach   12

   A Public Policy Approach   12

   A Sociological/Cultural Approach   13

Themes   14

   Experimentation and Change   15

   Power-sharing and Consensus   15

   Scope and Capacity   17

Chapter Layout   18

DISCUSSION QUESTIONS   **19**

FURTHER READING   **19**

WEB LINKS   **20**

2 How Did We Get Here?   22

Introduction   23

Post-War Settlement   24

   Schuman Plan   26

   European Defence Community   27

   European Community   28

Consolidating the European Community   31
    Crisis and Compromise   33
    EC after De Gaulle   33
    Difficult Decade   34
The Emerging European Union   35
    Economic and Monetary Union   36
    Maastricht and Beyond   36
    Post-Cold War Enlargement and Constitution Building   38
Conclusion   39
DISCUSSION QUESTIONS   **40**
FURTHER READING   **40**
WEB LINKS   **41**

PART II   Major Actors

3   The EU's Institutions   **45**
Institutions in Treaty and Practice   46
    European Commission   46
    Council of Ministers   50
    European Council (of Heads of State and Government)   57
    European Parliament   58
    European Court of Justice   61
Why Institutions Matter   64
    Experimentation and Change   64
    Power-sharing and Consensus   66
    Scope and Capacity   67
Conclusion   68
DISCUSSION QUESTIONS   **69**
FURTHER READING   **69**
WEB LINKS   **70**

4   Member States   **71**
Introduction   72
Six Determining Features   73
    Entry Date   73
    Size   76
    Wealth   78
    State Structure   80

Economic Ideology   81
Integration Preference   81
Member States in Action   84
Managing EU Business   86
Explaining Member States' Engagement   86
Conclusion   88
DISCUSSION QUESTIONS   **89**
FURTHER READING   **89**
WEB LINKS   **91**

5   **Organized Interests and Lobbying**   **92**
Introduction   93
Types of Actor   94
Private Economic Interests   94
Public Interest Bodies   95
Governmental Actors   96
The Media in Brussels   98
The Rise of Organized Interests   98
Organized Interests at Work   100
Lobbying the Commission   101
Lobbying the European Parliament   103
Successful Lobbying   105
Conclusion   108
DISCUSSION QUESTIONS   **109**
FURTHER READING   **110**
WEB LINKS   **110**

PART III   **Policies and Policy-making**

6   **Key Policies**   **115**
Introduction   116
Key Features of EU Policies   118
Differences between National and EU Policies   118
The Primacy of Economic Integration   123
Market-building Policies   124
Competition Policy   125
Commercial (Trade) Policy   126

Economic and Monetary Union (EMU)   126
Market-correcting and -cushioning Policies   128
    Common Agricultural Policy (CAP)   128
    Cohesion Policy   128
    Environmental and Social Regulation   132
Comparing EU Policy Types   133
Conclusion   134
DISCUSSION QUESTIONS   **135**
FURTHER READING   **136**
WEB LINKS   **136**

7   A Secure Europe? Internal Security Policies   **138**
Introduction   139
Development of the Third Pillar   140
    Early Years   140
    The Amsterdam Era   142
Crime-Fighting and Counter-Terrorism   145
    Institutions   146
    Criminal Law and Counter-Terrorism   148
Border Management   151
    Immigration and Schengen   151
    Visa Policy   152
    Illegal Immigration   152
    Asylum and Refugee Policy   155
Conclusion   156
DISCUSSION QUESTIONS   **157**
FURTHER READING   **158**
WEB LINKS   **158**

8   Constitutionalism and Democracy in the EU   **159**
Introduction: Constitutionalism and Democracy   160
Constitutionalism without a Constitution?   161
    The EU's Constitutional Charter   163
    Rights   164
    Separation of Powers, Checks, and Balances   166
Constitutionalism in the EU   167
Is Democracy Possible in the EU?   169
    Supranational Democracy in the Community Pillar 169
    Intergovernmentalism and the Council   171
    European Democracy: Competing Views   173

Conclusion 174
DISCUSSION QUESTIONS **175**
FURTHER READING **175**
WEB LINKS **176**

PART IV   The EU and the Wider World

9   EU Expansion and Wider Europe **179**
Introduction 180
    Widening Versus Deepening 180
    The Transformative Power of Enlargement 182
    An Institutional Paradox 182
How the EU has Expanded 184
    Why Countries Want to Join 187
    Recent Enlargements 187
Countries on the Way to EU Membership 189
    Balkan Countries 189
    Turkey 192
    The Forgotten Enlargement 193
Wider Europe 194
    European Neighbourhood Policy 194
What Limits for the EU? 195
    What Frontiers? 195
    What is Europe? 196
Conclusion 199
DISCUSSION QUESTIONS **199**
FURTHER READING **199**
WEB LINKS **200**

10   The EU as a Global Actor **201**
Introducing European Foreign Policy 202
    Development 203
    The Basics 204
A National 'System' of Foreign Policies 206
The Community System 208
    Commercial (Trade) Policy 208
    Aid and Development 208
    Externalizing 'Internal' Policies 211
The EU System 213

The Common Foreign and Security Policy 213
A European Security and Defence Policy? 215
Theorizing the EU as a Global Actor 216
Conclusion 218
DISCUSSION QUESTIONS **219**
FURTHER READING **219**
WEB LINKS **220**

11 Conclusion **222**
Introduction 223
Three Themes 223
Experimentation and Change 223
Sharing Power and Seeking Consensus 224
Scope and Capacity 225
Explaining the EU 226
International Relations Approaches 226
A Comparative Politics Approach 227
A Public Policy Approach 228
A Sociological/Cultural Approach 229
Where do We Go from Here? 229
Debating the Future of Europe 230
How *Will* it Work? 231
Conclusion 233

APPENDIX: CHRONOLOGY OF EUROPEAN INTEGRATION 235
GLOSSARY 239
REFERENCES 245
INDEX 257

▌ LIST OF FIGURES

Prelims	Map	The Expanding European Union	xxviii
1.1		The three pillars of the European Union	5
4.1		'Onion' chart of EU enlargements	74
6.1		Breakdown of EU spending, 2006	129
9.1		Map: European Neighbourhood Policy	191
10.1		Funding for EC Humanitarian Aid by region in 2005	211

▌ LIST OF BOXES

1.1	What's in a name	4
1.2	The three pillars of the European Union	5
1.3	The practical significance of the EU	7
1.4	Constitutional Treaty or Reform Treaty?	9
1.5	Key concepts and terms	10
1.6	The Treaties	16
1.7	Lost in interpretation?	18
2.1	Interpreting European integration	23
2.2	Key concepts and terms	25
2.3	How it really works: Rhetoric versus reality in the Schuman Plan	27
2.4	Compared to what? Regional and economic integration	30
2.5	How it really works: British accession and competing visions of Europe	32
3.1	How it really works: Who initiates policy?	51
3.2	Sample Council agenda	52
3.3	How it really works: Reaching decisions in the Council	56
3.4	How the European Parliament 'squeezes' power	59
3.5	Key concepts and terms: Legislative procedures	60
3.6	Compared to what? The ECJ and the US Supreme Court	63
3.7	How it really works: Turf wars!	65
3.8	Other institutional bodies	66
3.9	Enlargement's institutional impact	68
4.1	Key concepts and terms	72
4.2	How it really works: Intergovernmental Conferences	84
4.3	How it really works: Decision gridlock?	88
5.1	Key concepts and terms	93
5.2	Compared to what? Lobbying in Brussels and Washington	97
5.3	EPACA code of conduct	104
5.4	How it really works: Lobbying and the REACH Regulation on Chemicals	106

6.1	Key concepts and terms	117
6.2	How it Really Works: Budget bargaining	119
6.3	The policy competencies of the EU	121
6.4	The policy process: Three modes	122
6.5	How it really works: 'Goldplating' and EU policy	125
7.1	Key concepts and terms	140
7.2	How it really works: Policy-making in JHA	143
7.3	Transatlantic cooperation	144
7.4	Hague Programme	145
7.5	Compared to what? Europol and the Federal Bureau of Investigation (FBI)	147
7.6	Compared to what? Counter-terrorism: the EU and US	149
7.7	White and black visa lists	153
8.1	Key concepts	161
8.2	How it really work(ed): The European 'Constitutional Convention'	162
8.3	Compared to what? Two kinds of 'Convention'	165
8.4	How it really works: The European Arrest Warrant (EAW)	172
9.1	Key concepts and terms	180
9.2	Criteria for membership	183
9.3	Chronology of enlargement	185
9.4	The path to membership	186
9.5	Compared to what? EU and NATO—a double race to membership	188
9.6	How it really works: Joining the EU singly or together	190
9.7	Other Europeans	197
10.1	How it really works: Commercial (trade) policy	209
10.2	How it really works: The EU and Russia	210
10.3	How it really works: Making foreign policy decisions	214
10.4	Compared to what? The European Security Strategy	217

∎ LIST OF TABLES

1.1	Theories of European integration and the EU	14
3.1	The institutions: Treaty reform and conferred powers	48
3.2	Voting in the Council of Ministers	54
4.1	Clusters of member states and candidate countries by size	77
4.2	Member states' gross domestic product in 2005	79
4.3	Support for EU membership	82
5.1	Overview of organized interests in the EU	94
6.1	Compared to what? EU and national budgets compared	119
6.2	CAP spending breakdown	130
6.3	Poor regions	130
6.4	Policy types in the EU	134
10.1	European foreign policy: Three systems	206

ABBREVIATIONS AND ACRONYMS

ACP	African, Caribbean, and Pacific
APEC	Asia Pacific Economic Cooperation
ASEAN	Association of South-east Asian Nations
BEUC	Bureau Européen des Union de Consommateurs (European Consumers Organization)
CAP	Common Agricultural Policy
CEPOL	European Police College
CFSP	Common Foreign and Security Policy
CIA	Central Intelligence Agency (US)
COPA	Committee of Professional Agriculture Organizations
CoR	Committee of the Regions and Local Authorities
COREPER	Committee of Permanent Representatives
DG	Directorate-General (European Commission)
EAW	European Arrest Warrant
EC	European Community
ECAS	European Citizen Action Service
ECB	European Central Bank
ECHO	European Community Humanitarian Office
ECHR	European Convention on Human Rights
ECJ	European Court of Justice
ECOFIN	(Council of) Economic and Finance Ministers
ECSC	European Coal and Steel Community
EDC	European Defence Community
EDF	European Development Fund
EEA	European Economic Area
EEC	European Economic Community
EEW	European Evidence Warrant
EFTA	European Free Trade Association
EMU	Economic and Monetary Union
EMS	European Monetary System
ENP	European Neighbourhood Policy
EP	European Parliament
EPACA	European Public Affairs Consultancies Association

EPC	European Political Cooperation
ERF	European Refugee Fund
ERM	Exchange Rate Mechanism
ESC	Economic and Social Committee
ESDP	European Security and Defence Policy
ESS	European Security Strategy
ETUC	European Trades Union Confederation
EU	European Union
EURATOM	European Atomic Energy Community
FBI	Federal Bureau of Investigation (US)
FD	Framework Decision
FRG	Federal Republic of Germany
FTA	Free Trade Area
FYROM	Former Yugoslav Republic of Macedonia
GAERC	General Affairs and External Relations Council
GATT	General Agreement on Tariffs and Trade
GDP	Gross Domestic Product
GMOs	Genetically Modified Organisms
GNP	Gross National Product
IGC	Intergovernmental Conference
IO	International Organization
IR	International Relations
JHA	Justice and Home Affairs
MEP	Member of the European Parliament
MEPP	Middle East Peace Process
MFA	Minister for Foreign Affairs
NAFTA	North American Free Trade Agreement
NATO	North Atlantic Treaty Organization
NGO	Non-governmental Organization
NSS	National Security Strategy
OEEC	Organization for European Economic Cooperation
OMC	Open Method of Coordination
OSCE	Organization for Security and Cooperation in Europe (formerly CSCE)
PCTF	Police Chiefs Task Force
PNR	Passenger Name Record
QMV	Qualified Majority Voting
REACH	Registration, Evaluation, Authorization, and Restriction of Chemicals
SAP	Stability and Association Process
SCIFA	Strategic Committee on Immigration, Frontiers, and Asylum

SEA	Single European Act
SGP	Stability and Growth Pact
SIS	Schengen Information System
SME	Small and Medium-sized Enterprise
TEC	Treaty establishing the European Community
TEU	Treaty on European Union
UK	United Kingdom
UN	United Nations
UNICE	Union of Industrial and Employers' Confederations of Europe
US	United States
VIS	Visa Information System
VWP	Visa Waiver Program (US)
WEU	Western European Union
WTO	World Trade Organization
WWF	World Wide Fund for Nature

■ LIST OF CONTRIBUTORS

GRAHAM AVERY	St Antony's College, Oxford
ELIZABETH BOMBERG	University of Edinburgh
DESMOND DINAN	George Mason University
BRIGID LAFFAN	University College Dublin
SIR NEIL MACCORMICK	University of Edinburgh
JOHN D. OCCHIPINTI	Canisius College, Buffalo, New York
JOHN PETERSON	University of Edinburgh
ALBERTA SBRAGIA	University of Pittsburgh
MICHAEL SHACKLETON	European Parliament Secretariat
FRANCESCO STOLFI	University College, Dublin
ALEXANDER STUBB	Minister for Foreign Affairs of Finland
RORY WATSON	Freelance journalist, Brussels

The Expanding European Union

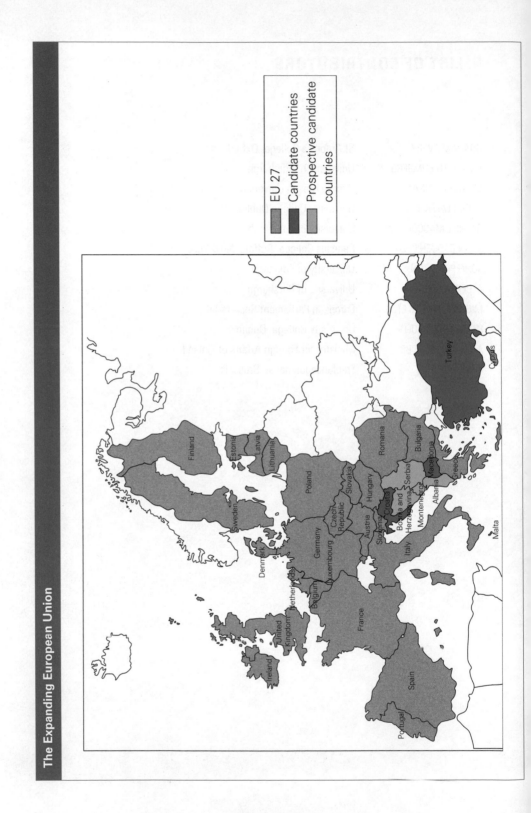

EU 27
Candidate countries
Prospective candidate countries

PART I

Background

CHAPTER 1

Introduction

Elizabeth Bomberg, Alexander Stubb, and John Peterson

Studying the EU	4	Experimentation and Change	15
Why Bother?	6	Power-sharing and Consensus	15
Understanding the EU: Theory and		Scope and Capacity	17
Conceptual Tools	10	Chapter Layout	18
International Relations Approaches	11		
A Comparative Politics Approach	12	DISCUSSION QUESTIONS	19
A Public Policy Approach	12	FURTHER READING	19
A Sociological/Cultural Approach	13	WEB LINKS	20
Themes	14		

▌ Chapter Overview

Understanding how the European Union (EU) works is not easy, but it is well worth the effort. This introductory chapter sets out the reasons—both practical and analytical—for studying the European Union. It then introduces some of the main conceptual approaches to understanding this unique institution, how it functions, and why. Finally, the chapter sets forth three broad themes that will tie together our analysis of the European Union and how it works.

Studying the EU

In 2007 the European Union celebrated its fiftieth birthday. Assessments of its state of health varied enormously, from the familiar hand-wringing 'Europe is dead' to the considerably more upbeat 'Europe's golden moment'. That the EU can elicit such diametrically opposite diagnoses is nothing new. It is an absolutely distinctive creation, varied and complex enough to invite wildly contrasting interpretations of the sort generated by blind men feeling different parts of an elephant (and extrapolating about the entire beast; see Puchala 1972). The aim of this book is to provide the knowledge and insights that will enable readers to make their own interpretation of the EU and how it works.

The European Union is not easy to grasp. To the uninitiated, its institutions seem remote, its remit unclear, its actions complex, and its policies perplexing. Such perplexity is understandable. To begin with, the EU defies simple categorization: it combines the attributes of a state with those of a traditional international organization, yet it closely resembles neither (see Box 1.1). Its development is shaped by an increasing number of players: 27 member governments, five EU institutions (with legal status, many more without it), and almost countless private interests, experts, foreign actors, and citizen groups all converge to influence what the EU is and what it does. 'What the EU does' has also expanded enormously since its origins in the 1950s. Originally concerned narrowly with free trade in coal and steel, its policy remit has expanded to cover agricultural, monetary, regional, environmental, social, immigration, foreign, and security policy, and the list does not stop there (see Box 1.2).

This task expansion—especially into areas traditionally seen as the responsibility of elected national governments—has meant that debates about the EU are increasingly wrapped up in larger debates about sovereignty, democracy, and the future of the nation-state. Studying European integration therefore means studying a lot more than

---

BOX 1.1	What's in a name

Even the question of what to call the EU can cause confusion. The European Union was originally established as the European Economic Community (EEC, colloquially known as the Common Market) by the 1957 Treaty of Rome. The name was shortened to European Community (EC) in 1992. The 1992 Maastricht Treaty created the European Union, which is made up of the EC as well as two other 'pillars' of cooperation in the areas of common and foreign policy and Justice and Home Affairs. We use the label European Community to refer to the organization in the pre-Maastricht period (see, especially, Chapter 2), but 'European Union' to refer to all periods—and the activities of all pillars—thereafter. Legal purists may object—formally, for instance, there is no such thing as 'EU law' or an 'EU budget', only Community law or the Community budget—but for simplicity's sake we use 'EU' as a kind of shorthand.

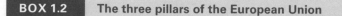

BOX 1.2	The three pillars of the European Union

The activities of the EU were divided into three areas or 'pillars' by the 1992 Maastricht Treaty. When (and if) the 2007 Reform Treaty comes into force, the pillars will be collapsed into one common institutional structure, which most closely resembles the old pillar I (European Community) and gives the EU a single legal personality.

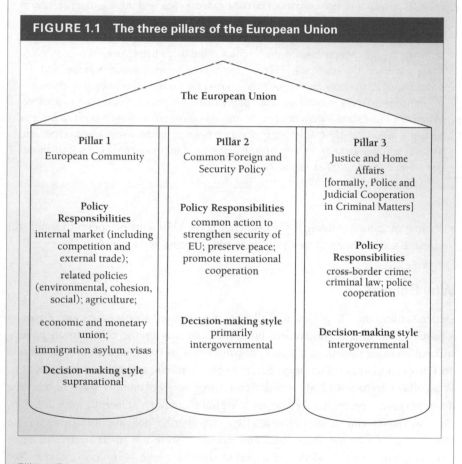

FIGURE 1.1   The three pillars of the European Union

The European Union

Pillar 1
European Community

Policy Responsibilities
internal market (including competition and external trade);
related policies (environmental, cohesion, social); agriculture;
economic and monetary union;
immigration asylum, visas

Decision-making style
supranational

Pillar 2
Common Foreign and Security Policy

Policy Responsibilities
common action to strengthen security of EU; preserve peace; promote international cooperation

Decision-making style
primarily intergovernmental

Pillar 3
Justice and Home Affairs
[formally, Police and Judicial Cooperation in Criminal Matters]

Policy Responsibilities
cross-border crime; criminal law; police cooperation

Decision-making style
intergovernmental

Pillar 1: European Communities
The first pillar is the busiest, incorporating what was previously the European Community and including the vast majority of EU responsibilities. It covers internal market policies as well as agriculture and competition policy. It also covers most immigration and asylum policies, and economic and monetary union. In this pillar the EU's common institutions (Commission, Council, Court, and Parliament) can act largely (never entirely) independently of the national governments.

Pillar 2: Common Foreign and Security Policy
In the second pillar, member states attempt to forge common positions and take joint action on foreign and security affairs. Decision-making is primarily intergovernmental (that is, between governments); neither the European Parliament nor the Court of Justice have much direct influence.

Pillar 3: Justice and Home Affairs (formally called Police and Judicial Cooperation in Criminal Matters)
The objective of the third pillar is to increase cooperation in the area of internal security, including the fight against international crime and the drugs trade. As in Pillar 2, decision-making in Pillar 3 is essentially intergovernmental. Common action is loose, and the unanimity of 27 member governments is required for virtually all important decisions.

Sometimes Treaty reforms can shift policy responsibility from one pillar to another. When this occurs, the nature of decision-making power can also shift significantly. For instance, when the 1997 Amsterdam Treaty moved policy on visas, immigration, and **asylum** from the third to the first pillar, it signalled a shift towards more supranational decisions in this area (see Chapter 7).

a single organization. Adding to the challenge is the EU's tendency never to stand still for long. It seems always in motion, constantly changing and expanding.

Why Bother?

Understanding the EU is thus a challenge, but one well worth taking on. First, on a purely practical level, no student of politics can make sense of European politics without knowing something about an organization that has daily and powerful effects on European (and non-European) governments, **markets**, and citizens (see Box 1.3). What other international body would or could, in a matter of months, issue far-reaching decisions governing: animal welfare, mobile phones, imports of illegally logged timber, caps on carbon emissions, university fees, cross-border policing, and peace in the Middle East? Of course these rules and decisions were not made overnight; most were negotiated and decided over a period stretching into years, not months. Not all had immediate or even perceptible impact: in foreign policy, especially, the EU finds it much easier to talk than to act. Nor were these decisions easily reached: they were the result of negotiations amongst an astonishing array of actors across regional, national, even international borders. Yet, however derived, EU decisions frequently have a significant impact on prosperity and peace in Europe and beyond.

Secondly, students of politics, economics, law, and international relations are interested in the EU not just because of its practical relevance, but also because of its analytical significance: it represents the most advanced experiment ever in multilateral cooperation and political **integration** (see Box 1.5)—the 'process whereby political actors in several distinct national settings are persuaded to shift their loyalties,

---

BOX 1.3   The practical significance of the EU

The EU's practical impact is felt in several areas including:

- Legislation: It is estimated that over 50 per cent of domestic legislation of the Union's member states originates in or is linked to EU legislation (see Chapter 6).

- Currency: In 2002 twelve national currencies—some dating back 600 years—ceased to be legal tender and were replaced by the euro. By 2008, 15 countries and over 300 million consumers used this single currency.

- Wealth: The EU's collective wealth (Gross National Income) accounts for about 30 per cent of the world's total.

- Market: The EU now regulates a market of nearly 500 million consumers, around 40 per cent more than the US.

- Trade: Not counting intra-EU trade, the EU's share of world trade (imports and exports) exceeds that of the US, accounting for around 20 per cent of all global trade.

- Aid: The EU and its member states are the world's largest donors of development aid, accounting for over 55 per cent. They are also the world's largest importers of goods from less developed countries (see Chapter 10).

While the wisdom or desirability of EU policies and actions is hotly contested, few would deny their practical importance.

Figures available from the websites of Commission, DG Trade,

- http://ec.europa.eu/economy_finance/euro/our_currency_en.htm

- http://ec.europa.eu/economy_finance/index_en.htm

- http://trade.ec.europa.eu/doclib/docs/2006/september/tradoc_122531.pdf

and from the World Trade Organization http://stat.wto.org/CountryProfiles/E25_e.htm

---

expectations and political activities toward a new center' (Haas 1958: 16). Thus, understanding the EU helps us to frame questions about the future of the nation-state, the prospects for international cooperation, the effects of globalization (see Box 1.5), and the proper role of governments in advanced industrial societies. Put another way, much of what makes the EU challenging to study—its dynamic character, complexity, and expanding activities—also makes it fascinating. Rather than avoid these attributes, we use them as themes to glue together our analysis (see below).

Finally, the EU fascinates because it represents a political puzzle. On one hand it has been enormously successful. EU governments and institutions have transformed it from a common market of six countries into a peaceful, integrated Union of 27 with a population of close to 500 million. It is the world's largest trading block, accounting for over 20 per cent of global trade with a combined Gross Domestic Product (GDP) considerably larger than that of the United States (US) (see Box 1.3). It has its own currency and a fledgling common foreign policy. A queue of applicants waits at its borders.

Yet what often seems like a growing number of citizens express disillusionment with the EU, and not just in the traditionally more 'sceptical' states such as the United Kingdom (UK). In 2005 citizens in two founding countries—France and the Netherlands—soundly rejected a Constitutional Treaty designed to make the EU more efficient and bring it closer to its citizens (see Box 1.4). 'Brussels bureaucrats' make easy targets for almost every ill, and populist parties often gain popular success through EU-bashing. Voter turnout in European Parliament elections has fallen with each election. EU institutions—the European Commission, the Council of Ministers (representing national governments), and even the directly elected Parliament—are viewed as increasingly remote and shrouded in secrecy, or just not worth bothering about. The EU certainly is not a well-understood body, and it is difficult even for diligent students to see just how (or if) the EU works.

In this book we address the practical question: 'how does it work?': who are the main actors, what are the main processes, dynamics, and explanations for what the EU does, and how it does it? But we also want to address the more rhetorical question: 'how (in the world) does it work?!' How can such a massive, complex, unwieldy amalgam of states, institutions, lobbyists, languages, traditions, legal codes, etc. possibly do much of the governing of Europe? More practically, why have sovereign states agreed to relinquish part of their sovereignty (see Box 1.5)? With what implications? Why do policies emerge looking as they do? Why did the EU develop the way it did and where is it likely to go from here? Why does it elicit such strong demonstrations of support and antipathy? Our main goal is to address these questions in a lively and comprehensible way.

We employ several devices to help us to achieve that goal. This book is largely written by experts with either research, teaching, or policy-making experience (some with all three). Many of its chapters are co-authored by an academic and practitioner to illustrate both how the EU works and how to make sense of it. Students need to understand both the formal 'textbook' rules of EU practice (what the Treaties say; what the legislation stipulates) but also how it 'really' works (how are the Treaties interpreted; what informal rules guide action). We capture this dual dynamic through a series of boxes (entitled 'How it really works'). These boxes illustrate how a particular actor, policy, or process actually works, regardless of what the formal rules are.

The book also seeks to make the EU more comprehensible by placing its institutions, structures, or policies in a comparative perspective. Most chapters include a 'Compared to what?' box which compares EU institutions, practices, or processes with their counterparts inside the member states or outside the EU. The intent is to help students better to understand the EU by underlining how it is like—or unlike—other systems of governance (see Box 1.5), and in what ways it is unique. More generally, the book is seasoned throughout with vignettes or other boxes which draw students into the substance of the chapter through real-life examples or illustrations. Finally, most chapters offer a 'Key concept' box that defines important terms, and each also provides guides to further reading and useful Internet sites. All these features are designed to achieve our overall aim: to bring the EU to life for our readers.

BOX 1.4	Constitutional Treaty or Reform Treaty?

The Constitutional Treaty, the result of a special Convention on the Future of Europe (see Chapter 8), was unanimously endorsed and signed by national EU leaders in 2004. The Treaty comprised three basic elements: institutional reform, a Charter of Fundamental Rights, and the consolidation of existing treaties. The primary institutional measures (see also Table 3.1) included:

- increased majority voting on the Council of Ministers (where each member state is represented), readjusted more closely to reflect member states' populations;

- more legislative powers for the European Parliament;

- a full-time president of the European Council (where heads of state and government are represented). This post would replace the six-month presidency that rotates between member states;

- a smaller European Commission; and

- a new EU minister of foreign affairs.

The second section of the Treaty codified a Charter of Fundamental Rights (a wide-ranging statement of 'rights, freedoms, principles' including the right to life, the right to free expression, and the right to strike; see Chapter 8).

The third part (by far the longest) consisted of a consolidated and amended version of all previous treaties. In addition, the Treaty established a constitution in name for the first time (it formally gave the Union a 'legal personality'). At the same time it provided an exit clause for states wishing to leave the Union. Designed to streamline and bring the EU closer to its citizens, the Treaty ended up stretching to 300 pages of text, not all of them comprehensible. (Thus the French government's decision to post copies of the entire text to all voters in advance of France's referendum was not a successful 'vote yes' strategy.)

Treaty change requires ratification by all member states. By mid-2007 eighteen of the 27 had ratified the Treaty. But voters in two founding member states—France and the Netherlands—had rejected the Treaty in referenda held in 2005. An alternative solution had to be found. In early 2007, several member states, led by Germany, sought to revive the Constitution. A 'road map' for its future was put to EU leaders at a European summit in June 2007.

European leaders thus agreed on a 'Reform Treaty' which changed the name and structure of the Constitution, stripped out all references to constitutional symbols such as a European flag or anthem, and (for example) renamed the EU Foreign Minister as its 'High Representative'. But the new Treaty maintained the bulk of the substance of the Constitutional Treaty. The Reform Treaty has two parts. The first is called Treaty on European Union, and contains all the basic aims, principles, and instruments of the EU. The second part is called Treaty on the functioning of the EU. It contains all EU policies. So, did we get a Constitution or a Reform Treaty? Well, actually a reformed treaty with constitutional elements.

BOX 1.5	Key concepts and terms (listed alphabetically)

Globalization is the idea that the world is becoming increasingly interconnected and interdependent because of increasing flows of trade, ideas, people, and capital. Globalization is usually presented as reducing the autonomy of individual states, although whether its impact is essentially positive or negative, inevitable or controllable, are hotly-debated questions.

Governance means 'established patterns of rule without an overall ruler'. Even though there is no government, the EU undertakes the sort of activities that governments traditionally have done. The EU is thus said to be a system of governance without a government (or an opposition).

Integration is the process whereby sovereign states relinquish (surrender or pool) national sovereignty to maximize their collective power and interests.

Intergovernmentalism is a process or condition whereby decisions are reached by specifically defined cooperation between or among governments. Formally, at least, sovereignty is not relinquished. The term intergovernmentalism is usually contrasted with supranationalism.

Multilevel governance is often used to describe the EU. It means a system in which power is shared between the supranational, national, and subnational levels. The term also suggests that there is a fair bit of interaction and coordination of political actors across those levels. How they interact and with what effect helps determine the shape of European integration.

Sovereignty refers to the ultimate authority over people and territory. It is sometimes broken down into internal (law-making authority within a territory) and external (international recognition). Opinions vary as to whether state sovereignty is 'surrendered' or merely 'shared' in the context of the EU.

Supranationalism means above states or nations; that is, decisions are made by a process or institution that is largely (but never entirely) independent of national governments. The subject governments (in the case of the EU, the member state governments) are then obliged to accept these decisions. The European Court of Justice (Chapter 3) is a supranational institution. The term supranationalism is usually contrasted with intergovernmentalism.

Understanding the EU: Theory and Conceptual Tools

When studying anything as complex as the European Union, we need conceptual tools to guide us. A theory or model simplifies reality and allows us to see relationships between the things we observe. Scholars trying to understand the EU employ different theories developed in the study of international relations, comparative politics, sociology, and public policy. Each theory seeks to explain different developments, episodes, and dynamics of EU politics and European integration. Just as there is no single explanation for events, so there is no one theory of EU politics. We offer here brief synopses of leading theoretical frameworks or approaches. Our aim is not to present or apply these approaches or theories with all their nuances, nor to privilege one over the others. We aim to pull out for the reader the key assumptions and insights offered by each. The following chapters will then use these insights to elaborate and explain their particular topic.

International Relations Approaches

Several classic theories of integration draw from international relations theory. They are concerned primarily with explaining the broad development of European integration: that is, how and why nations choose to form European institutions, and who or what determines the shape and speed of the integration process.

One of the earliest theories of European integration was **neofunctionalism** which was developed primarily by Ernst Haas in the 1960s to explain the development of the European Coal and Steel Community (ECSC) and the European Economic Community (EEC), the predecessors of the EU. Haas and others were concerned with explaining how a merger of economic activity in specific economic sectors (say, coal and steel) across borders could 'spill over' and provoke wider economic integration in related areas (Haas 1958; 1964; Lindberg and Scheingold 1970). More ambitiously, neofunctionalists believed that this economic integration would produce political integration and the creation of common, integrated **supranational** institutions to accelerate this process. ('Supranational' here means transcending national borders, interests, and powers; see Box 1.5). Finally, according to neofunctionalists, interests and loyalties would gradually shift from the national to the supranational level.

Early neofunctionalist theory seemed to explain well the initial successes of European integration, but its uni-directional logic (integration could only go forward) was heavily criticized when European integration appeared to stagnate and even to reverse in the late 1960s and 1970s (Rosamond 2005). Dissatisfaction with neofunctionalism led to the development of alternative theoretical models, especially **liberal intergovernmentalism**.

Most closely associated with Andrew Moravcsik (1993; 1998) liberal intergovernmentalism builds on the work of international relations scholars and historians who reject the notion that national governments do not control European integration (see Hoffmann 1995; Milward 1992; Schimmelfennig 2004). Marshalling impressive historical evidence, liberal intergovernmentalists argue that major choices—what Peterson (1995) calls 'history making decisions'—reflect the preferences of national governments rather than supranational organizations. Each state's preferences reflect the balance of their domestic economic interests. The outcomes of EU negotiation are the result of intergovernmental bargaining, that is, bargaining between sovereign national governments (see Box 1.5). Any subsequent delegation to supranational institutions is calculated, rational, and circumscribed. In short, national governments are the dominant actors in shaping integration, and they are in control: 'governments first define a set of interests, then bargain among themselves to realize those interests' (Moravcsik 1993: 481).

A Comparative Politics Approach

Analysts drawing on comparative politics approaches have challenged the primacy of the state in shaping European integration and the EU. Foremost among these approaches is new institutionalism, which emphasizes the importance of institutions in shaping or even determining government preferences. In the EU context, institutionalism demonstrates how the EU's common institutions (Commission, Council, Parliament, or Court) are more than impartial arbiters in the policy-making process: they are key players with their own agendas and priorities (Armstrong and Bulmer 1998; Pollack 2004). For new institutionalists, 'institutions' refer not only to institutions traditionally defined—executives, parliaments, courts—but also to values, accepted standards, and informal conventions that govern social exchanges between actors. These values affect or 'frame' the way actors perceive the choices open to them. So, for example, the informal rules or practices (say the unwritten goal of seeking consensus whenever possible) can mould the behaviour of national government representatives in ways that governments neither plan nor control.

A second insight of new institutionalist analyses is the concept of 'path dependency': the notion that once a particular decision or path is chosen, 'it is very difficult to get back on the rejected path' (Krasner 1984: 225). Path dependency means that it is hard to change policy—such as an expensive Common Agricultural Policy—even when it outlives its usefulness. The 'sunk costs' (time and resources already invested) of agreeing a policy in the first place are often considerable, and the idea of starting again on a long, time-consuming, and expensive process of agreeing a new policy are resisted for that reason (see Pierson 1996).

A Public Policy Approach

A third theoretical approach useful to those studying the EU is the policy networks framework (see Peterson 2004). Unlike neofunctionalism or liberal intergovernmentalism, this approach does not tell us much about the policy bargains struck between national governments, nor the history-making decisions (such as treaty reform) that set the broad direction of European integration. But network analysis is useful in uncovering the nitty-gritty, behind-the-scenes negotiation and exchange that can shape policies at a day-to-day level. A policy network is 'a cluster of actors, each of which has an interest or stake in a given EU policy sector and the capacity to help determine policy success or failure' (Peterson and Bomberg 1999: 8). Policy networks at the EU level usually bring together institutional actors (from the Commission, Council, Parliament) and other stakeholders such as representatives of private firms, public interest groups, technical or scientific experts and, perhaps above all, national officials. Networks lack hierarchy (there is no one actor in charge) and instead depend on resource exchange. That means that participants need to bring to Brussels (or Strasbourg) some valued resource with which to bargain: information, ideas, finances, constitutional-legal power, or political legitimacy. According to network analysts, bargaining and resource exchange among these actors—rather than strictly intergovernmental bargaining—determine the shape of actual EU policies.

A Sociological/Cultural Approach

An increasingly popular conceptual approach that cuts across multiple theories is constructivism, a school drawing on cultural and sociological studies and recent developments in International Relations (IR) theory. It is a strikingly diverse school, but at its core is an attempt to focus attention on the 'social construction' of the collective rules and norms that guide political behaviour (Eilstrup-Sangiovanni 2006: 393). At its most radical, a constructivist approach argues that reality does not exist outside human interpretation or language. In the study of the EU, however, a less radical or abstract form of social constructivism is prevalent.

Above all, constructivists seek to go beyond a rationalist approach to understanding the EU. The latter assumes pre-set and rational interests and identities; political actors (say, national representatives) weigh the costs and benefits of actions, and make decisions based on those calculations. Constructivists argue instead that EU political actors' positions and even identities are shaped not (only) by the rational pursuit of national or self-interest but by the bargaining process itself, especially the pressure to conform or reach consensus (see Lewis 2003: 99).

Constructivism can and has been coupled with the theories of integration introduced above. Like neofunctionalism, constructivism focuses our attention on socialization, transfers of loyalty, and the process whereby actors redefine their interests as a result of interaction within European institutions (Haas 2001). Similarly, constructivism complements the new institutionalism's emphasis on norms and ideas. Along with institutionalists, social constructivists suggest that informal rules and norms (such as reciprocity or the desire to show 'goodwill') can shape (or even determine) political actors' behaviour (Checkel 2006; Lewis 2003).

While most would agree that ideas or norms are important in some way (see, especially, Chapters 3 and 4), it is extremely difficult to show that abstract ideas or norms actually cause a change in behaviour as many constructivists argue. Construct-ivists often can correlate ideas with behaviour, but have trouble proving that ideas matter more than interests (Aspinwall and Schneider 2000; Checkel 2004). Thus, constructivism does not offer a theory for understanding the EU as much as it draws our attention to insights that might be missed by other theories.

Each of these approaches has its own assumptions, strengths, and weaknesses (see Table 1.1; Nelsen and Stubb 2003). No one theory can explain everything treated in this book. But each school introduced here offers different insights into different,

TABLE 1.1 Theories of European integration and the EU			
Theory/ Approach	Proponents/ Major Work	Assumptions	Shortcoming/ Criticisms
Neofunc-tionalism	Haas 1958	Supranational institutions crucial; spillover drives integration	Can't explain stagnation
Liberal inter-govern-mentalism	Moravscik 1998	Member states control European integration	Too state-centric; neglects day-to-day policy-making
New institutionalism	Bulmer 1998; Pierson 1996	Institutions matter; Path dependency	Overemphasizes power of the EU's institutions
Policy networks	Peterson 1995	Resource exchange within networks shapes policy	Cannot explain big decisions
Social constructivism	Checkel 2004 Risse 2004	Ideas matter; interests constructed, not pre-determined	Methodological weaknesses

key features of the EU: how integration evolves; the way policies are made, and the role of different actors in this process. Students need not master all these theories to use this book. Rather, these theoretical insights—and their application in subsequent chapters—are meant to encourage the reader to begin thinking about theory and its role in helping us to understand and evaluate European integration and EU politics.

Themes

To help the reader make sense of the EU this text is held together by three common themes. Each highlights a key, distinctive feature of the EU as:

1. An 'experiment in motion', an ongoing process without a clear end-state;
2. A system of shared power characterized by growing complexity and an increasing number of players;
3. An organization with an expanding scope, but limited capacity.

We introduce each of these themes below.

Experimentation and Change

Since its conception in the early 1950s, European integration has been an ongoing process without a clear *finalité*, or end-state. In one sense its development has been a functional step-by step process: integration in one area has led to pressures to integrate in others. As neofunctionalists would point out, the Union has developed from a free trade area to a customs union; from a customs union to a single market; and from a single market to an economic and monetary union. This development, however, has been neither smooth, automatic, nor predetermined. Rather, integration and the EU's development has progressed in fits and starts, the result of constant experimentation, problem-solving, and trial and error. European foreign policy, from failed attempts of the 1950s to the creation of a European Security and Defence Policy (ESDP) in the last decade, is a good example of this evolution. With no agreed end goal (such as a 'United States of Europe'), the EU's actors have reacted to immediate problems, but they have done so neither coherently nor predictably.

The nature and intensity of change are also varied. Constitutional change has taken place through Intergovernmental Conferences (IGCs)—special negotiations in which government representatives come together to hammer out agreements to alter the EU's guiding treaties. The first (resulting in the Treaty of Paris, 1951) created the European Coal and Steel Community made up of six states. More recently, the Constitutional Treaty (signed in 2004 but never ratified) or its successor, the so-called Reform Treaty (of 2007), were designed to serve an EU of 30 or more (see Box 1.4; 1.6). Less spectacularly, legislative change has taken place through thousands of EU directives and regulations. Finally, the EU's institutions, especially the European Commission and Court of Justice, have themselves acted as instigators of change, and have expanded the powers of the Union throughout its history. The point is that change is a constant in the EU. This book will explore its main sources and implications.

Power-sharing and Consensus

Our second theme concerns power and how it is shared between different actors and across layers of government. The EU policy-making system lacks a clear nexus of power: there is no 'EU government' in the traditional sense of the term. Instead, power is dispersed across a range of actors and levels of governance (regional, national, and supranational). Deciding which actors should do what, and at what level of governance, is a matter of ongoing debate within the EU. The principle of constitutionalism (see Chapter 8) is meant to address this issue, but debates about constitutional power and authority continue.

The three most important sets of actors are the member states, institutions, and organized interests. Certainly, much about the evolution of the EU has been determined by the member states themselves, and, in particular, their different approaches to

> ### BOX 1.6 The Treaties
>
> When practitioners and academics use the term 'the Treaties', they are referring to the collection of founding treaties and their subsequent revisions. The founding treaties include the Treaty of Paris (signed in 1951, establishing the European Coal and Steel Community) and two Treaties of Rome, 1957, one establishing the European Atomic Energy Community (Euratom), the other the European Economic Community. The ECSC became void in July 2002. The Euratom treaty never amounted to much. But the Treaty of Rome (signed in 1957) establishing the EEC became absolutely central. It has been substantially revised in the:
>
> - Single European Act (signed in 1986),
> - Maastricht Treaty (or Treaty on European Union, signed in 1992),
> - Amsterdam Treaty (signed in 1997), and the
> - Nice Treaty (signed in 2001).
>
> As Box 1.1 explained, the intergovernmental conference leading up to the Maastricht Treaty not only revised the Treaty of Rome (it is now formally called the Treaty establishing the European Community) but it also established the broader Treaty on European Union (TEU or Maastricht Treaty, 1992) which included two new pillars or areas of activity on foreign policy and JHA (see Box 1.2). The two core Treaties (at least until the Reform Treaty combines them) are thus the Treaty Establishing the European Community (TEC) which covers the first pillar, and the Treaty on European Union (TEU) which covers the second and third pillars of EU activity.
>
> These two key treaties, as revised in Amsterdam and Nice, form the basic toolkit of ministers, Commissioners, parliamentarians, and civil servants dealing with EU matters. Each piece of legislation is based on one of these treaty articles (of which there are nearly 700). The Treaties have grown increasingly long and complex. To improve the presentation and facilitate the reading of the Treaties, the articles were renumbered in the Amsterdam IGC of 1997. But the Treaties are hardly an easy read. Even many legal scholars would agree that the language borders on the incomprehensible. The 2004 Constitutional Treaty was intended to simplify the existing texts and make them more readable, but arguably it did neither (although it did reduce the number of articles from 700 to 450). Its successor, the 2007 Reform Treaty, marked another attempt to give the EU constitutional simplicity, although the term 'Constitution' was nowhere to be found. Presumably, it will remain a term that dares not speak its name in Brussels for many years to come.

integration. Some member states want deeper integration, others do not, and this division continues to shape the speed and form of the integration process. Meanwhile, EU institutions have shaped the EU's development as they vie for power with the member states, as well as among themselves. Finally, organized interests—including representatives of subnational levels of governance, private interests, citizens groups—now play an increasing role.

Part of what makes the EU unique—and certainly different from its member states—is that these actors exist in a complex web where there are established patterns of interaction but no overall 'ruler' or government or even dominant actor. Instead, actors must bargain and share power in an effort to reach an agreement acceptable to all, or at least most. This dynamic has been captured in the term multilevel governance (see Box 1.5), which suggests a system of overlapping and shared powers between actors on the regional, national, and supranational levels (Hooghe and Marks 2001). EU governance is thus an exercise in sharing power between states and institutions, and seeking consensus across different levels of governance. Coming to grips with this unique distribution of power is a key task of this book.

Scope and Capacity

Our final theme concerns the expanding remit of the EU, and its ability to cope with it. The EU has undergone continuous (in a phrase used by insiders) 'widening and deepening'. The widening of its membership has been astonishing. It has grown from a comfortable club of six member states (Germany, France, Italy, the Netherlands, Belgium, and Luxembourg) to nine (UK, Denmark, and Ireland joined in 1973), to twelve (Greece in 1981; Portugal and Spain in 1986) to fifteen (Austria, Finland, and Sweden joined in 1995). Then in 2004 the EU jumped to 25 following the accession of ten mainly central and eastern states. The accession of Bulgaria and Romania in 2007 took the EU to 27 with additional candidates, including Turkey, knocking on the door. The institutional, political, economic, and even linguistic challenges this enlargement poses are immense (see Box 1.7).

The EU has also 'deepened' in the sense that the member states have decided to pool sovereignty in an increasing number of policy areas, including, most dramatically, in the sensitive area of Justice and Home Affairs (JHA) (see Chapter 7). This robust policy development has meant that the EU is managing tasks that have traditionally been the exclusive preserve of the nation-state. At the same time the EU continues its attempt to dispose of its image as an 'economic giant, but a political dwarf'. The Union is trying to stamp its authority on the international scene through its leadership on issues such as climate change, or the development of a Common Foreign and Security Policy (CFSP), which, according to the Treaties, 'might in time lead to a common defence'. These developments have challenged the EU's 'capacity'—its practical and political ability to realize its ambitions. While the EU has taken on more members and more tasks, its institutional and political development has not kept pace. This mismatch—between the EU's ambitions on one hand and its institutional and political capacity on the other—raises questions about the EU's future and ability to adapt. It also represents the third theme of the volume.

> **BOX 1.7**   **Lost in interpretation?**
>
> With the addition of Irish as an official language in 2007, the EU boasted 23 official languages:
>
> Bulgarian, Czech, Danish, Dutch, English, Estonian, Finnish, French, German, Greek, Irish, Hungarian, Italian, Latvian, Lithuanian, Maltese, Polish, Portuguese, Romanian, Slovak, Slovene, Spanish and Swedish.
>
> The EU's translation service is the largest in the world by far (over twice the size of the UN's) and the cost of translation and interpretation is over €800m a year (Commission 2007c). In Parliament alone, where interpreters in soundproof boxes attempt to translate words such as gobbledegook (the word doesn't exist in Polish), and avoid confusing frozen semen with seamen (as occurred in one parliamentary debate), the cost and potential confusion is immense. But being able to communicate with your electors and fellow representatives in your own language is also seen as a fundamental right. After all, it is difficult for EU citizens to feel close to an institution which does not operate—at least officially—in their own language. In practice, most of the work of the EU is carried out in just three languages, English, French, and German. Meanwhile, the rising cost of translation and interpretation has had one positive effect—it has forced practitioners to limit official texts to under fifteen pages.
>
> Commission (2007b; 2007c), *National Geographic* (2005)

Taken together these three themes address:

* how the EU has developed and why (experimentation and change);
* who are the main players and how do they interact (power-sharing and consensus);
* what the EU does, and how it does it (scope and capabilities).

These three themes provide the glue necessary to hold together our investigation of the EU and how it works.

Chapter Layout

Any book on European integration that aims to be at all comprehensive is bound to cover a lot of ground, both theoretical and practical. In explaining how the EU works it is necessary to look at the historical background of European integration, the major actors involved, the key policies and their impact, and the EU's global presence. The book's layout reflects this logic. Chapter 2 tells us 'how we got here' by providing a concise historical overview of the EU's development. The next section (Chapters 3–5) focuses on the major actors: the EU's common institutions, the member states, and organized interests such as business groups and non-governmental organizations (NGOs). Section III focuses on policy and process. It provides an expert overview of key economic and related policies (Chapter 6), the newer area of JHA (Chapter 7), and the wider constitutional issues arising from these policy processes (Chapter 8). Chapters in the last section examine the EU's relations with the wider world. Chapter 9 covers EU enlargement and its policy towards states in its geographical neighbourhood, whereas Chapter 10 explores the EU's growing role as a global actor. A conclusion draws together the main themes of the volume and ponders how the EU might work in the future.

?

DISCUSSION QUESTIONS

1. The EU can be seen as one of the most successful modern experiments in international cooperation, yet it often seems increasingly unpopular amongst its citizens. Why?

2. Which theory appears to offer the most compelling account of recent developments in European integration?

→

FURTHER READING

Some of the key themes introduced in this chapter are inspired by leading general broad studies of the EU including Hooghe and Marks (2001), Scharpf (1999), Wallace, Wallace, and Pollack (2005) and Weiler (1999). Nelsen and Stubb (2003) feature a collection of seminal works on European integration theory and practice. Holmes (2001) provides a collection of 'Eurosceptical' readings while Leonard and Leonard (2001) counter with their 'Pro-European Reader'. An excellent and comprehensive overview of key perspectives, works, and theories is provided by Jørgensen *et al.* (2006). A useful summary and overview of different theoretical approaches is offered by Eilstrup-Sangiovanni's collection (2006). For an incisive survey of these different theories applied to the EU, see Rosamond (1999). To explore in more depth some of the key theoretical approaches, see Haas (1958) on neofunctionalism; Milward (1992) and Moravcsik (1998) on liberal intergovernmentalism; Armstrong and Bulmer (1998), Pollack (2004), or Meunier and McNamara (2007) on new institutionalism; Peterson (2004) on policy networks; and Checkel (2006) on constructivism.

Armstrong, K., and Bulmer, S. (1998), *The Governance of the Single European Market* (Manchester and New York: Manchester University Press).

Checkel, J. (2006), 'Constructivism and EU Politics' in Jørgensen, K. E., Pollack, M. and Rosamond, B. (eds), *Handbook of European Union Politics* (London: Sage): 57–76.

Eilstrup-Sangiovanni, M. (2006), 'The Constructivist Turn in European Integration Studies' in M. Eilstrup-Sangiovanni (ed.), *Debates on European Integration. A Reader* (London: Palgrave).

Haas, E. (1958), *The Uniting of Europe: Political, Social, and Economic Forces* (Stanford, CA: Stanford University Press).

Haas, E. (2001), 'Does Constructivism Subsume Neo-functionalism?' in T. Christiansen, K. E. Jørgensen, and A. Weiner, *The Social Construction of Europe* (London and Thousand Oaks, CA: Sage): 22–31.

Holmes, M. (ed.) (2001), *The Eurosceptical Reader, 2nd edn* (Basingstoke: Palgrave).

Hooghe, L., and Marks, G. (2001), *Multi-level Governance and European Integration* (Lanham and Oxford: Rowman & Littlefield Publishers, Inc.).

Jørgensen, K. E., Pollack, M., and Rosamond, B. (eds.) (2006), *Handbook of European Union Politics* (London and Thousand Oaks, CA: Sage).

Leonard, D., and Leonard, M. (eds.) (2001), *The Pro-European Reader* (Basingstoke: Palgrave).

Meunier, S., and McNamara K. (eds.) (2007), *Making History. European Integration and Institutional Change at Fifty* (Oxford and New York: Oxford University Press).

Milward, A. (1992), *The European Rescue of the Nation-state* (London and Berkeley: Routledge and University of California Press).

Moravcsik, A. (1998), *The Choice for Europe: Social Purpose and State Power From Messina to Maastricht* (Ithaca, NY and London: Cornell University Press and UCL Press).

Nelsen, B., and Stubb, A. (eds.) (2003), *The European Union: Readings on the Theory and Practice of European Integration*, 3rd edn. (Boulder: Lynne Rienner and Basingstoke: Palgrave).

Peterson, J. (2004), 'Policy Networks', in A. Wiener and T. Diez, *European Integration Theory* (Oxford and New York: Oxford University Press): 117–33.

Pollack, M. (2004), 'New Institutionalism' in A. Wiener and T. Diez, *European Integration Theory* (Oxford and New York: Oxford University Press): 137–56.

Rosamond, B. (1999), *Theories of European Integration* (London and New York: Palgrave).

Scharpf, F. W. (1999), *Governing in Europe: Effective and Democratic?* (Oxford and New York: Oxford University Press).

Wallace, H., Wallace, W., and Pollack, M. (eds.) (2005), *Policy-making in the European Union*, 5th edn. (Oxford and New York: Oxford University Press).

WEB LINKS

The EU's official website 'The European Union online' (http://europa.eu.) is a very valuable starting point. It provides further links to wide variety of official sites on EU policies, institutions, legislation, treaties, and current debates.

Precisely because the EU's website is so large, the Europa—Information Services website provides a nice index of where to find answers on the Europa website (http://europa.eu/geninfo/info/guide/index_en.htm).

You can also use the web to access the *Official Journal* (OJ) which is updated daily in several languages. The OJ is the authoritative and formal source for information on EU legislation, case law, parliamentary questions, and documents of public interest (http://eur-lex.europa.eu/).

For pithier reporting, the *Economist* (www.economist.com) provides useful general articles, while *European Voice* (www.europeanvoice.com) offers insider coverage of EU policies and news.

To follow current events and developments within the EU, the following sites are useful.

- EurActiv reports EU current affairs with analysis, and has an easy to navigate system of 'dossiers' which provide an overview of different policy areas (http://www.euractiv.com/en/HomePage); while the
- EUobserver offers coverage of EU current affairs with a very useful email bulletin service (http://euobserver.com/).

Current debates and topics are also addressed in series of think tank websites. Some of the better known include the Centre for European Policy Studies (http://www.ceps.be); the European Policy Centre (http://www.epc.eu); the Centre for European Reform (www.cer.org.uk), and the Trans European Policy Studies Association (www.tepsa.be).

Finally, the Institute for European Politics' (Berlin) website offers an overview of current thinking on EU policies and issues in all the member states (http://www.iep-berlin.de/index.php?id=publikationen&L=1).

 Visit the Online Resource Centre that accompanies this book for additional material: www.oxfordtextbooks.co.uk/orc/bomberg2e/

CHAPTER 2

How Did We Get Here?

Desmond Dinan

Introduction	23	The Emerging European Union	35
Post-War Settlement	24	Economic and Monetary Union	36
Schuman Plan	26	Maastricht and Beyond	36
European Defence Community	27	Post-Cold War Enlargement and	
European Community	28	Constitution Building	38
Consolidating the European		Conclusion	39
Community	31		
Crisis and Compromise	33	DISCUSSION QUESTIONS	40
EC after De Gaulle	33	FURTHER READING	40
Difficult Decade	34	WEB LINKS	41

Chapter Overview

European countries responded to a series of domestic, regional, and global challenges after the Second World War by integrating economically and politically. These challenges ranged from post-war reconstruction, to international financial turmoil, to the consequences of the end of the Cold War. Driven largely by national interests, Franco-German bargains, and American influence, Europeans responded by establishing the European Community and later the European Union. Deeper integration clashed with cherished national concepts of identity, sovereignty, and legitimacy. Successive rounds of enlargement, which saw the EU grow in size from its original six member states, also generated institutional and policy challenges that have shaped the contours of European integration.

Introduction

The history of the European Union presents a fascinating puzzle: why did European states, traditionally jealous of their independence, pool sovereignty in an international organization that increasingly acquired federal attributes? This chapter argues that the answer is as simple as it is paradoxical: because it was in their national interest to do so. Political parties and interest groups did not always agree on what constituted the national interest, and governments themselves were sometimes divided. But at critical junctures in the post-war period, for various strategic and/or economic reasons, national leaders opted for closer integration.

This chapter aims to outline the history of European integration by focusing on national responses to major domestic and international challenges since the end of the Second World War. These responses gave rise to the European Community (EC) and later the European Union (EU). France and Germany played key roles. The EC was a bargain struck (primarily) between them for mutual economic gain. By strengthening post-war Franco-German ties, the EC also had an important political dimension. Indeed, Germany conceded a lot to France in the negotiations that led to the EC in order to deepen Franco-German solidarity, a key step towards binding the Federal Republic to the West. Subsequent milestones in the history of European integration also hinged on Franco-German bargaining.

Ideology—the quest for a united Europe—was not a major motive for European integration (see Box 2.1). The Preamble of the Rome Treaty, the EC's charter, called for an 'ever closer union' among the peoples of Europe. This was a vague assertion of the popular aspiration for European unity, not a guiding principle for the EC. Some

BOX 2.1	Interpreting European integration

Historians have offered different interpretations of how European integration has developed and why. Alan Milward (1984; 2000) is the foremost historian of European integration. He argues that economic interests impelled Western European countries to integrate, but that national governments shared sovereignty only to the extent necessary to resolve problems that would otherwise have undermined their legitimacy and credibility. Paradoxically, European states rescued themselves through limited supranationalism. More recently, Andrew Moravcsik (1998) has complemented Milward's thesis by claiming that national governments, not supranational institutions, controlled the pace and scope of integration. Moravcsik uses historical insights from a series of case studies, from the 1950s to the 1990s, to develop liberal intergovernmentalism as a theory of European integration. Intergovernmentalism generally is in the ascendant in the historiography of European integration, in contrast to the early years of the EC when the arguments of neofunctionalist scholars such as Ernst Haas (1958) and Leon Lindberg (1963) dominated academic discourse on the EC (see Chapter 1).

national and supranational leaders were strongly committed to federalism. But they succeeded in moving Europe in a federal direction only when ideological ambition coincided with national political and economic preferences. The language of European integration, redolent of peace and reconciliation, provided convenient camouflage for the pursuit of national interests based on rational calculations of costs and benefits.

This chapter also argues that the United States (US) has been a major player in the integration process, both positively (as a promoter of integration) and negatively (as an entity against which Europe has integrated). Globalization (see Box 1.5) and its presumed association with Americanization, has driven European integration in recent years. Since the late 1980s, the EU has been in search of strategies to compete globally against the US while retaining a social structure that is relatively egalitarian and distinctly not American.

Post-War Settlement

The most pressing question at the end of the war was what to do about Germany. The question became acute with the onset of the Cold War. As the Soviet Union consolidated its control over the eastern part of the country, the Western Powers—the United Kingdom (UK), France, and the US—facilitated the establishment of democratic and free market institutions in what became the Federal Republic of Germany (FRG). The German question then became how to maximize the economic and military potential of the FRG for the benefit of the West while allaying the understandable concerns of Germany's neighbours, especially France. France accepted a supranational solution to the problem of German economic recovery, but not to the problem of German remilitarization.

The US championed integration as a means of reconciling old enemies, promoting prosperity, and strengthening Western Europe's resistance to communism. The Marshall Plan (see Box 2.2) was the main instrument of American policy. European governments wanted American dollars for post-war reconstruction, but without any strings attached. For their part, the Americans insisted that European recipients co-ordinate their plans for using the aid. That was the extent of European integration in the late 1940s. The UK had no interest in sharing sovereignty. France wanted to keep the old enemy down and keep Germany's coal-rich Ruhr region from becoming a springboard to remilitarization. Few countries were willing to liberalize trade. Winston Churchill's famous call in 1946 for a United States of Europe belied the reality of politicians' unwillingness to change the international status quo.

It was Germany's rapid economic recovery, thanks in part to the Marshall Plan, that made the status quo untenable. The US wanted to accelerate German recovery in order to reduce occupation costs and promote recovery throughout Europe. A weak West Germany, the Americans argued, meant a weak Western Europe. France agreed,

---

BOX 2.2	Key concepts and terms

The **Empty Chair Crisis** was prompted by French President Charles de Gaulle's decision to pull France out of all Council meetings in 1965 thereby leaving one chair empty. De Gaulle was protesting the Commission's plans to extend the EC's powers generally and subject more decisions to **qualified majority voting (QMV)**.

The **Luxembourg Compromise** resolved the empty chair crisis. Reached during a foreign ministers' meeting in 1966, the Compromise was an informal agreement stating that when a decision was subject to QMV, the Council would postpone a decision if any member states felt 'very important interests' were under threat. In effect the compromise meant QMV was used far less often, and unanimity became the norm.

The **Marshall Plan** (1947) was an aid package from the US of $13 billion (a lot of money in 1947, equivalent to 5 per cent of US GNP) to help rebuild West European economies after the war. The aid was given on the condition that European states cooperate and jointly administer these funds.

Qualified Majority Voting (QMV) can be used to reach most decisions in the Council of Ministers. Each member state is granted a number of votes roughly proportional to its population (Germany, UK, France, and Italy have the most; Malta the least). The formula for deciding which country gets how many votes was revised after fierce debate at the Nice Summit in 2000 (see Chapter 3, especially Table 3.2). The Constitutional Treaty radically revised the modalities of QMV, and the 2007 Reform Treaty contained these same provisions.

The **Schengen Agreement** was signed by five member states in 1985 (Belgium, France, Germany, Luxembourg, and the Netherlands) and came into effect ten years later. It removed all border controls among its signatories, which now includes 15 EU member states as well as Norway and Iceland. Ireland and the UK are not signatories, and Denmark has opted out of certain aspects of this agreement.

Subsidiarity is the idea that action should be taken at the level of government which is best able to achieve policy goals, but as close to the citizens as possible.

---

but urged caution. France wanted to modernize its own economy before allowing Germany's economy to rebound. Indeed, France agreed to the establishment of the FRG only on condition that German coal production (a key material for war-making) remained under international control.

German expressions of resentment of French policy fell on receptive American ears. As the Cold War deepened, the US intensified pressure on France to relax its policy toward Germany so that German economic potential could be put at the disposal of the West. Yet the US was not insensitive to French economic and security interests. Instead of imposing a solution, Washington pressed Paris to devise a policy that would allay French concerns about the Ruhr region, without endangering Germany's full recovery.

Given its preference for European integration, the US hoped that France would take a supranational tack.

Originally, the US wanted the UK to lead on the German question. The UK had already taken the initiative on military security in Europe, having pressed the US to negotiate the Washington Treaty (which founded NATO, the North Atlantic Treaty Organization). Yet the UK was reluctant for reasons of history, national sovereignty, and economic policy to go beyond anything but intergovernmental cooperation. The UK's prestige in Europe was then at its height. Continental countries looked to the UK for leadership. Such leadership, however, was absent, and under mounting American pressure, France came up with a novel idea to reconcile Franco-German interests by pooling coal and steel resources under a supranational High Authority.

Schuman Plan

This idea became the Schuman Plan, drafted by Jean Monnet, a senior French civil servant with extensive international experience. Monnet faced intense American pressure to devise a new policy towards Germany but also believed in European unity and saw the Schuman Plan as a first step in that direction. More immediately, it would protect French interests by ensuring continued access to German resources, although on the basis of cooperation rather than coercion. The new plan bore the name of the French Foreign Minister, Robert Schuman, who risked his political life promoting it at a time when most French people deeply distrusted Germany.

Naturally, German Chancellor Konrad Adenauer endorsed the plan, which provided a means of resolving the Ruhr problem and rehabilitating Germany internationally. Schuman and Adenauer trusted each other. They were both Christian Democrats, came from the Franco-German borderlands, and spoke German together. Aware of the UK's attitude towards integration, Schuman did not bother to inform London of the plan. By contrast, the Americans were in on it from the beginning.

The Schuman Plan was a major reversal of French foreign policy. Having tried to keep Germany down since the war, France now sought to turn the inevitability of Germany's economic recovery to its own advantage through the establishment of a common market in coal and steel. The Schuman Declaration of 9 May 1950, announcing the plan, was couched in the language of reconciliation rather than realpolitik. In fact the initiative cleverly combined national and European interests. It represented a dramatic new departure in European as well as in French and German affairs (see Box 2.3).

Participation in the plan was supposedly open to all the countries of Europe. In fact, the list of likely partners was far shorter. The Cold War excluded Central and Eastern Europe from the plan. In Western Europe, the UK and the Scandinavian countries had already rejected supranationalism. Ireland was isolationist; Spain and Portugal, under dictatorial regimes, were international outcasts; and Switzerland was resolutely neutral. That left the Benelux countries (Belgium, the Netherlands, and Luxembourg), which were economically tied to France and Germany, and Italy, which saw integration

BOX 2.3	How it really works

Rhetoric versus reality in the Schuman Plan

Jean Monnet's drafting of the Schuman Plan in 1950 marked a diplomatic breakthrough on the contentious German question. More generally, the plan's proposal for a coal and steel community also advanced the goal of European unity. When outlining the proposal in the Schuman Declaration, a highly publicized initiative, Monnet emphasized the European and idealistic dimension of the proposal. Issued on 9 May, the Schuman Declaration proclaimed that:

World peace can only be safeguarded if constructive efforts are made proportionate to the dangers that threaten it ... France, by advocating for more than twenty years the idea of a united Europe, has always regarded it as an essential objective to serve the purpose of peace ... With this aim in view, the French government proposes to take immediate action on one limited but decisive point. The French government proposes that Franco-German production of coal and steel be placed under a common 'high authority' within an organization open to the participation of the other European nations ... [This] will lay the first concrete foundation for a European federation, which is so indispensable for the preservation of peace.

But Monnet's primary concern was to defend French national interests. He wanted to ensure French access to German raw materials and European markets despite Germany's economic resurgence. In a private note to Schuman some days before the Declaration's unfurling, Monnet explained that France had little choice but to safeguard its interests by taking a new approach. On 1 May Monnet informed Schuman that:

Germany has already asked to be allowed to increase its output [of steel] from 10 to 14 million tons [French output was 9 million tons at the time]. We will refuse but the Americans will insist. Finally, we will make reservations and give way ... There is no need to describe the consequences [of not giving way] in any detail (quoted in Duchêne 1994: 198).

Instead of trying to block Germany's advance, Monnet advocated a European initiative—the Schuman Plan—in defence of French interests.

---

primarily as a means of combating domestic communism and restoring international legitimacy. Consequently the European Coal and Steel Community (ECSC), launched in 1952, included only six countries. The ECSC soon established a common market in coal and steel products, with generous provisions for workers' rights.

European Defence Community

The same six countries ('the Six') signed a treaty to establish a defence community in 1952. The rationale for both communities was the same: supranational institutions provided the best means of managing German recovery. In this case, the outbreak of the Korean War in June 1950, perceived as a possible precursor to a Soviet attack on Western Europe, made German remilitarization imperative. France at first resisted, and then acquiesced on condition that German military units were subsumed into a new European Defence Community (EDC). Like the Schuman Plan, the plan for the EDC sought to make a virtue (European integration) out of necessity (German remilitarization). Although the EDC was a French proposal, most French people fiercely opposed German remilitarization. The EDC became the most divisive issue in the country. In view of the treaty's unpopularity the government delayed ratification for two years. The French parliament ignominiously defeated the treaty in 1954.

Ironically, Germany formed an army anyway, under the auspices of the Western European Union (WEU), an intergovernmental organization comprising the UK and the Six and established in 1954. Germany joined NATO via the WEU in May 1955 and effectively regained full formal sovereignty. Whereas the intergovernmental WEU endured (until it was folded into the EU, beginning in 2000), the European Defence Community was a bridge too far for European integration. At a time when the Six were setting up the ECSC, the launch of a similar supranational initiative in the much more sensitive defence sector was too ambitious. Even if it had come into existence, in all likelihood the EDC would have been unworkable. Resistance to its implementation, especially from the far left and far right, would have been intense. The EDC brought the idea of supranationalism into disrepute. The end of the affair allowed supporters of supranationalism to jettison the baggage of German remilitarization and concentrate on first principles: economic integration.

It is remarkable how quickly the idea of European integration bounced back to life. The ECSC was operating fully, but its political and economic impact was slight. Despite what some observers (and neofunctionalist theorists) predicted, there was little 'spillover' from supranational cooperation in coal and steel to other sectors. Monnet, who became President of the High Authority, was bored in Luxembourg, the ECSC's capital. He left office and returned to Paris in 1955, where he set up a transnational organization, the Action Committee for the United States of Europe, to advocate further integration. His pet scheme was for an Atomic Energy Community (Euratom), along the same lines as the ECSC. The French government was interested, but not for the same reasons as Monnet. Whereas Monnet saw Euratom as a further step towards European unity, the government saw it as a means of bolstering France's nuclear programme for civil and military purposes. Not surprisingly, this idea had little appeal for France's partners.

European Community

The relaunch of European integration after the EDC's collapse was due not to Monnet or support for Euratom, but to changes in international trade relations in the mid-1950s. Thanks largely to liberalization measures in the Organization for

European Economic Cooperation (OEEC) and the General Agreement on Tariffs and Trade (GATT), intra-European trade was on the rise. With it, prosperity increased. European governments wanted more trade, but disagreed on the rate and range of liberalization. The British favoured further liberalization through the OEEC and the GATT, as did influential elements in the German government (notably Ludwig Erhard, the economics minister). The French were instinctively protectionist, although some influential politicians advocated openness. The Dutch, with a small and open economy, wanted full liberalization and were impatient with progress in the OEEC and the GATT, where intergovernmentalism constrained decision-making.

The Dutch had proposed a common market for all industrial sectors in the early 1950s. This would combine a customs union (the phased abolition of tariffs among member states and erection of a common external tariff, see Box 2.4) with the free movement of goods, people, services, and capital, as well as supranational decision-making in areas such as competition policy. They revived the proposal in 1955, arguing that the international economic climate was more propitious than ever for the launch of a common market.

Successful negotiations to establish the European Economic Community (EEC or EC) in 1956, so soon after the collapse of the EDC, owed much to the leadership of politicians such as Paul-Henri Spaak in Belgium, Guy Mollet and Christian Pineau in France, and Konrad Adenauer in Germany. Because of France's political weight in Europe and traditional protectionism, Mollet and Pineau played crucial roles. But their advocacy of the EC came with a price for the other prospective member states. In order to win domestic support they insisted on a special regime for agriculture in the common market, assistance for French overseas territories (France was then in the painful process of decolonization), and the establishment of Euratom.

The negotiations that resulted in the two Rome treaties, one for the EC and the other for Euratom, were arduous. Because the UK opposed supranationalism and the proposed agricultural regime, it did not participate. Germany succeeded in emasculating Euratom and grudgingly accepted the EC's overseas territories provisions. In the meantime, Adenauer resisted Erhard's efforts to jettison the common market in favour of looser free trade arrangements, arguing that the EC was necessary for geopolitical as well as economic reasons. French negotiators fought what they called the 'Battle of Paris', trying to assuage domestic criticism of the proposed common market while simultaneously driving a hard bargain in the negotiations in Brussels.

The ensuing Treaty of Rome establishing the EC was a typical political compromise. Its provisions ranged from the general to the specific, from the mundane to the arcane. Those on the customs union, calling for the phased abolition of tariffs (a tax on trade) between member states and erection of a common external tariff, were the most concrete. The treaty did not outline an agricultural policy, but contained a commitment to negotiate one in the near future. Institutionally, the treaty established a potentially powerful Commission, an Assembly (of appointed, not elected, members) with limited powers, a Council to represent national interests directly in the decision-making process, and a Court of Justice (see Chapter 3).

BOX 2.4   **Compared to what?**

Regional and economic integration

Economic integration in Europe has proceeded through a number of steps or stages. A similar trajectory has occurred in other regions of the world, although nowhere has the level of economic cooperation matched that found in the EU.

In a **free trade area** (FTA) goods travel freely among member states, but these states retain the authority to establish their own external trade policy (tariffs, quotas, and non-tariff barriers) towards third countries. By allowing free access to each other's markets and discriminating favourably towards them, a free trade area stimulates internal trade and can lower consumer costs. But the lack of a common external tariff means complicated rules of origin are required to regulate the import of goods. One example of a FTA outside the EU is the European Free Trade Association (EFTA) which was established under British leadership in 1960 to promote expansion of free trade in non-EC western European countries. The UK left EFTA to join the EC in 1973, but Iceland, Liechtenstein, Norway, and Switzerland are still members. Canada, Mexico, and the US signed the North American Free Trade Agreement (NAFTA) in 1992.

Regional organizations elsewhere have created closer economic ties which may develop into FTAs. For instance the Association of South-east Asian Nations (ASEAN) was established in 1967 to provide economic as well as social cooperation among non-communist countries in the area. A wider forum for regional economic cooperation is found among Pacific Rim countries within APEC (Asia Pacific Economic Cooperation) which includes Australia, China, Indonesia, Japan, Mexico, the Philippines, and the US.

A customs union requires more economic and political cooperation than an FTA. In addition to ensuring free trade among its members, a customs union has a common external tariff and quota system, and a common commercial policy. No member of a customs union may have a separate preferential trading relationship with a third country or group of third countries. A supranational institutional framework is required to ensure its functioning. Customs unions generally create more internal trade and divert more external trade than do free trade areas. The six founding members of the EC agreed to form a customs union, which came into being in 1968, two years ahead of schedule. A customs union also exists in South America. Mercosur (Southern Cone Common Market) was established in 1991 by Argentina, Brazil, Paraguay, and Uruguay.

A common market represents a further step in economic integration by providing for the free movement of services, capital, and labour in addition to the free movement of goods. For various economic and political reasons the Six decided to go beyond a common market (the colloquial name for the EC) by establishing additionally a common competition policy; monetary and fiscal policy coordination; a common agricultural policy (CAP); a common transport policy; and a preferential trade and aid agreement with member states' ex-colonies. Not all these elements were fully implemented. By the 1980s it was clear that the movement of labour and capital was not entirely free, and a host of non-tariff barriers still stymied intra-Community trade in goods and services.

The '1992 project' or single market programme was designed to achieve a true internal market in goods, services, labour, and capital.

An economic and monetary union (EMU) is far more ambitious. It includes a single currency and the unification of monetary and fiscal policy. In the EU, plans to introduce EMU, outlined in the Maastricht Treaty, were successfully implemented in January 1999, with euro notes and coins circulating by January 2002. No other region in modern times has come close to this level of economic cooperation.

The Rome treaties were signed on 25 March 1957, and the EC came into being on 1 January 1958. Most Europeans were unaware of either event. Apart from the EDC, European integration had not impinged much on public opinion. Yet the ECSC and EC were highly significant developments. The Coal and Steel Community represented a revolution in Franco-German relations and international organization; the so-called Common Market had the potential to reorder economic and political relations among its member states.

Consolidating the European Community

The big news in Europe in 1958 was not the launch of the EC but the collapse of the French Fourth Republic and the return to power of General Charles de Gaulle. Events in France had a direct bearing on the EC. De Gaulle helped consolidate the new Community by stabilizing France politically (through the construction of the Fifth Republic) and financially (by devaluing the franc). On the basis of renewed domestic confidence, France participated fully in the phased introduction of the customs union, so much so that it came into existence in 1968, eighteen months ahead of schedule.

De Gaulle also pushed for completion of the Common Agricultural Policy (CAP). With a larger farming sector than any other member state, France had most to gain from establishing a single agricultural market, based on guaranteed prices and export subsidies funded by the Community. France pressed for a generous CAP and had the political weight to prevail. Nevertheless the construction of the CAP, in a series of legendary negotiations in the early 1960s, proved onerous. What emerged was a complicated policy based on protectionist principles, in contrast to the liberalizing ethos of Community policies in most other sectors (see Chapter 6). The contrast represented the competing visions of the EC held by its members, potential members, and the wider international community (see Box 2.5).

Implementation of the customs union and construction of the CAP signalled the Community's initial success, obscuring setbacks in other areas such as the failure to implement a common transport policy. The customs union and the CAP had a major international impact. For instance, as part of its emerging customs union the

> ## BOX 2.5   How it really works
>
> ### British accession and competing visions of Europe
>
> The integration of Europe is sometimes portrayed (not least in the popular press) as an inexorable process following some overarching agreed plan. But in practice integration has proceeded in fits and starts, the result of domestic and international pressures and competing visions of what the EU is or should be. The debates surrounding the UK's first application to join the EC illustrate the very different visions of Europe competing for dominance during the Community's early years.
>
> In a remarkable reversal of policy, the UK applied to join the EC in 1961. The UK wanted unfettered access to EC industrial markets, but also wanted to protect trade preferences for Commonwealth countries (former British colonies) and turn the CAP in a more liberal direction. De Gaulle was unsympathetic to the UK's application. Economically, he wanted a protectionist CAP. Politically, he espoused a 'European Europe', allied to the United States but independent of it. By contrast, the UK acquiesced in America's Grand Design for a more equitable transatlantic relationship built on the twin pillars of the US and a united Europe centred on the EC, a design that arguably disguised America's quest for continued hegemony in NATO. The US supported British membership in the EC as part of its Grand Design. By vetoing the UK's application in January 1963, de Gaulle defended the CAP and thwarted American ambitions in Europe. The episode suggests how international pressure, domestic politics, and competing visions of Europe have shaped the evolution of European integration.

EC developed a common commercial policy, which authorized the Commission to represent the Community in international trade talks, notably the GATT. The CAP tended to distort international trade and irritate the EC's partners. It is no coincidence that the first transatlantic trade dispute was over the CAP (the so-called 'Chicken War' of 1962–3, sparked by higher tariffs on US chicken imports).

The EC's fledgling institutions also began to consolidate during this period. The Commission organized itself in Brussels under the presidency of Walter Hallstein, a former top official in the German foreign ministry and a close colleague of Adenauer's. There were nine Commissioners, two each from the large member states and one each from the small member states (this formula would remain unchanged for nearly fifty years). The Commission's staff came from national civil services and from the ECSC's High Authority, which continued to exist until it merged into the Commission in 1967. In the Council of Ministers, foreign ministers met most often, indicating the EC's growing political as well as economic nature. The Council formed a permanent secretariat in Brussels to assist its work. Member states also established permanent representations of national civil servants in Brussels, whose heads formed the Committee of Permanent Representatives (Coreper), which soon became one of the Community's most powerful bodies. The Assembly, later known as the European Parliament (EP), tried to assert itself from the beginning, demanding for instance that its members be directly elected rather than appointed from national parliaments. But the EP lacked political support from powerful member states. Working quietly in Luxembourg, the Court of Justice began in the 1960s to generate an impressive corpus of case law. In several landmark decisions, the Court developed the essential rules on which the EC legal order rests, including the supremacy of Community law (see Chapter 3).

Crisis and Compromise

De Gaulle's arrival had a negative as well as a positive effect on the consolidation of the nascent EC. De Gaulle openly opposed supranationalism. He and his supporters (Gaullists) had resisted the ECSC and the EDC; they tolerated the EC, but primarily because of its economic potential for France. In de Gaulle's view, the nation-state was supreme. States could and should form alliances and collaborate closely, but only on the basis of intergovernmentalism, not shared sovereignty. Yet de Gaulle thought that the Community could be useful politically as the basis of an intergovernmental organization of European states.

A clash over supranationalism was likely to arise in 1965 as, under the terms of the Rome Treaty, a number of decisions in key policy areas, including agriculture, were due to become subject to qualified majority voting (QMV) (see Box 2.2). Majority voting is a key instrument of supranationalism because member states on the losing side agree to abide by the majority's decision. De Gaulle rejected this idea in principle, seeing QMV as an unacceptable abrogation of national sovereignty. The looming confrontation erupted in June 1965, when de Gaulle triggered the so-called Empty Chair Crisis (see Box 2.2) by withdrawing French representation in the Council ostensibly in protest against Commission proposals to strengthen the EC's budgetary powers, but really in an effort to force other member states to agree not to extend the use of QMV. De Gaulle had a compelling practical reason to resist QMV: he wanted to protect the CAP against a voting coalition of liberal member states.

The crisis ended in January 1966 with the so-called Luxembourg Compromise (see Box 2.2). The Treaty's provisions on QMV would stand, but the Council would not take a vote if a member state insisted that very important interests were at stake. The Luxembourg Compromise tipped the balance toward intergovernmentalism in the Community's decision-making process, with unanimity becoming the norm. This development had a detrimental effect on decision-making until the Single European Act took effect in 1987.

EC after De Gaulle

By 1969, when de Gaulle resigned, the EC was economically strong but politically weak. Supranationalism was in the doldrums. The Commission and Parliament were relatively powerless, and unanimity hobbled effective decision-making in the Council. De Gaulle had twice rebuffed the UK's application for EC membership, in 1963 and in 1967. Following de Gaulle's departure, British membership became inevitable, although accession negotiations were nonetheless difficult. Ireland, Denmark, and Norway negotiated alongside the UK, but a majority of Norwegian voters rejected membership in a referendum in 1972. The UK, Ireland, and Denmark joined the following year.

The EC's first enlargement was a milestone in the organization's history. Unfortunately it coincided with international financial turmoil and a severe economic downturn that slowed the momentum for further integration. Moreover, the UK's early membership was troublesome. A new Labour government insisted on renegotiating the country's accession terms. The renegotiations alienated many of the UK's partners in the EC, especially France and Germany. At the end of the 1970s a new Conservative government, under Margaret Thatcher, demanded a huge budgetary rebate. The UK had a point, but Thatcher's strident manner when pushing her case incensed other member states. The British budgetary question dragged on until 1984, overshadowing a turnaround in the Community's fortunes after a decade of poor economic performance.

Difficult Decade

Because of the UK's early difficulties in the EC and prevailing stagflation in Europe (weak economic growth combined with high inflation and unemployment), the 1970s is generally seen as a dismal decade in the history of integration. Yet a number of important institutional and policy developments occurred at that time. On the policy side, the 1979 launch of the European Monetary System (EMS), the precursor to the single currency, was especially significant. Concerned about America's seeming abdication of international financial leadership, and eager to curb inflation and exchange rate fluctuations in the EC, French and German leaders devised the EMS, with the Exchange Rate Mechanism (ERM) designed to regulate currency fluctuations at its core. The sovereignty-conscious UK declined to participate. By the mid-1980s, the inflation and exchange rates of ERM members began to converge, thus helping to keep their economies stable. The Lomé agreement of 1975, providing preferential trade and development assistance to scores of African, Caribbean, and Pacific countries, was another important achievement for the beleaguered Community, as was the launch of **European Political Cooperation (EPC)**, a mechanism to coordinate member states' foreign policies (see Chapter 10). In terms of closer European integration, the development of EC environmental policy in the 1970s was even more important.

Institutionally, the 1970s saw a gradual improvement in the Commission's political fortunes, especially later in the decade under the presidency of Roy Jenkins. The first direct elections to the EP took place in 1979, raising the institution's political profile and enhancing the EC's formal legitimacy. The inauguration of the European Council (regular meetings of the heads of state and government) in 1975 strengthened intergovernmental cooperation. The European Council soon became the EC's most important agenda-setting body (see Chapter 3), while direct elections laid the basis for the EP's institutional ascension in the 1980s and 1990s. The Court of Justice continued in the 1970s to build an impressive body of case law that maintained the momentum for deeper integration.

By the early 1980s, the EC had weathered the storm of recession and the challenge of British accession. The end of dictatorial regimes in Greece, Portugal, and Spain in the mid-1970s presaged the EC's Mediterranean enlargement (Greece joined in 1981, Portugal and Spain in 1986). By that time the EC was more than a customs union but still less than a full-fledged common market. A plethora of non-tariff barriers (such as divergent technical standards) hobbled intra-Community trade in goods and services, and the movement of people and capital was not entirely free. Intensive foreign competition, especially from the US and Japan, began to focus the attention of political and business leaders on the EC's ability to boost member states' economic growth and international competitiveness. This was the genesis of the **single market** programme, which spearheaded the EC's response to globalization and ushered in the EU.

The Emerging European Union

The single market programme for the free movement of goods, services, capital, and people emerged as a result of collaboration between big business, the Commission, and national leaders in the early 1980s. Several European Councils endorsed the idea. But the initiative only took off when the Commission, under the new presidency of Jacques Delors, unveiled a legislative roadmap (a White Paper on the 'completion' of the **internal market**) in 1985. To ensure the programme's success, the European Council decided to convene an Intergovernmental Conference (IGC) to make the necessary treaty changes. Chief among them was a commitment to use qualified majority voting for most of the White Paper's proposals, thereby ending the legislative gridlock that had hamstrung earlier efforts for full market liberalization.

As well as covering the single market programme, the Single European Act (SEA) of 1986 brought environmental policy into the treaty, strengthened Community policy in research and technological development, and included a section on foreign policy cooperation. It also committed the EC to higher expenditure on regional development (**cohesion policy**), partly as a side payment to the poorer member states, including new entrants Portugal, Spain, and Greece, which were unlikely to benefit as much from market integration as were their richer counterparts. Institutionally, the SEA's most important provisions enhanced the EP's legislative role through the introduction of the **cooperation procedure** (see Box 3.5). This procedure was intended to improve democratic accountability at a time when the EC's remit and visibility were about to increase dramatically.

The single market programme, with a target date of 1992, was a success. Big business responded enthusiastically to the prospect of a fully integrated European marketplace.

'1992' unleashed a wave of Europhoria. The EC was more popular than at any time before or since. Eager to remove barriers to the free movement of people even before implementation of the single market programme, France and Germany agreed in 1984 to press ahead with the abolition of border checks. This led to the Schengen Agreement (see Box 2.2) for the free movement of people, which gradually added other member states and formally became part of the EU under the terms of the 1997 Amsterdam Treaty.

Economic and Monetary Union

The popularity of the single market programme emboldened Commission President Delors to advocate Economic and Monetary Union (EMU). He had the strong support of German Chancellor Helmut Kohl, an avowed 'Euro-federalist'. The Commission publicly justified EMU on economic grounds, as the corollary of the single market programme. But Delors and Kohl saw it primarily as a political undertaking. French President François Mitterrand also supported EMU, for both political and economic reasons. Thatcher opposed EMU vehemently, seeing it as economically unnecessary and politically unwise. Not only did Thatcher fail to turn the tide against EMU; her strident opposition to it contributed to her loss of the leadership of the Conservative Party and thus her prime ministership.

The European Council authorized Delors to set up a committee to explore the road to EMU. The Delors Report of 1989 proposed a three-stage programme, including strict convergence criteria for potential participants and the establishment of a European Central Bank with responsibility primarily for price stability. The report reflected German preferences for EMU. That was understandable, given Germany's economic weight and German obsession with inflation. Even so, opinion in Germany remained sceptical about EMU, with the politically influential German central bank (Bundesbank) opposed to it.

Planning for EMU was well on track by the time the Berlin Wall came down in November 1989. By raising again the spectre of the German question, the end of the Cold War increased the momentum for EMU. Fearful of the prospect, however remote, of a rootless Germany in the post-Cold War world, other Community leaders determined to bind Germany fully into the new Europe, largely through EMU. Kohl was more than happy to oblige and cleverly exploited the concerns of Germany's neighbours to overcome domestic opposition to EMU, especially in the Bundesbank.

Maastricht and Beyond

EC leaders convened two Intergovernmental Conferences in 1990, one on EMU and the other on political union, meaning institutional and non-EMU policy reforms. Both conferences converged in the Maastricht Treaty of 1992, which established the

European Union with its three-pillar structure (see Box 1.2). The first pillar comprised the EC, including EMU; the second comprised the Common Foreign and Security Policy (CFSP), a direct response to the external challenges of the post-Cold War period; the third covered cooperation on justice and home affairs, notably immigration, asylum, and criminal matters. This awkward structure reflected most member states' unwillingness to subject internal security and foreign policy to supranational decision-making. Thus the Commission and the EP were merely associated with Pillar 2 and 3 activities. Within Pillar 1, by contrast, the Maastricht Treaty extended the EP's legislative power by introducing the far-reaching co-decision procedure, which made the Parliament a legally and politically equal legislator to the Council of Ministers (see Chapter 3).

The further extension of the EP's legislative authority, and the introduction of the principle of subsidiarity (whereby decisions should be taken as closely as possible to the people compatible with effective policy delivery; see Box 2.2), demonstrated EU leaders' concerns about the organization's legitimacy. Those concerns were fully vindicated in tough ratification battles in several member states, including the UK, France, and Germany, but especially in Denmark, where a narrow majority rejected the treaty in a referendum in June 1992. Voters approved the treaty, with special concession for Denmark, in a second referendum, in May 1993. Thus the EU came into being six months later.

At issue in Denmark and elsewhere was the so-called democratic deficit: the EU's perceived remoteness and lack of accountability (see Chapter 8). This issue remained a major challenge for the EU into the twenty-first century. The resignation of the Commission under the Presidency of Jacques Santer in March 1999, amid allegations of fraud and mismanagement, increased popular scepticism, although it also demonstrated the Commission's accountability to the EP (the Commission resigned to avoid being sacked by the Parliament). Yet many Europeans saw the EP as part of the problem: few understood exactly the EP's role, and the turnout in subsequent elections declined yet again in 1999 and 2004. For its part, the Commission launched successive rounds of reform, while EU leaders attempted to improve transparency and efficiency in the decision-making process. Nevertheless, as illustrated by the negative results of the first Irish referendum on the Nice Treaty in 2001 and the Dutch and French referenda on the Constitutional Treaty in 2005, public opinion remained highly sceptical of the EU.

Despite considerable public disquiet, the post-Maastricht period saw substantial policy development. The launch of the final stage of EMU in January 1999, in keeping with the Maastricht timetable, was one of the EU's most striking achievements. Euro notes and coins came into circulation in January 2002. The strengthening of the CFSP and the initiation of a European Security and Defence Policy, largely in response to the Balkan wars and uncertainty about US involvement in future European conflicts, was another important policy development. Reform of CFSP was the main outcome of the Amsterdam Treaty, which nevertheless ducked increasingly pressing questions of institutional reform necessitated by impending enlargement.

Post-Cold War Enlargement and Constitution Building

Enlargement was a major challenge for the new EU. As a result of the end of the Cold War, three militarily-neutral European states (Austria, Finland, and Sweden) joined in 1995. (Norway, a non-neutral, again chose not to join in another referendum held in 1994.) The newly independent states of Central and Eastern Europe also applied for EU membership soon after the end of the Cold War (as did Cyprus and Malta). For the Central and Eastern European states the road to membership would be long and difficult, involving major political, economic, and administrative reforms. The slow pace of enlargement disappointed the applicant countries and their supporters in the US, who criticized the EU for being too cautious. The EU countered that enlargement, an inherently complicated process, was even more complex in view of the applicants' history, political culture, and low level of economic development. The EU's approach reflected a widespread lack of enthusiasm for enlargement among politicians and the public in existing member states. Even so, negotiations with the Central and Eastern European applicants eventually began in 1998 (with the five front-runners) and in 2000 (with the five others). Cyprus also began accession negotiations in 1998 and Malta in 2000.

Eight of the Central and Eastern European counties joined in 2004, together with Cyprus and Malta. The other two Eastern European countries, Bulgaria and Romania, joined in 2007. The EU reluctantly acknowledged Turkey as a candidate in December 1999 and, no less reluctantly, opened formal accession negotiations with it in October 2005. However, persistent popular antipathy towards Turkey, as well as specific issues such as the unresolved Cypriot question, bedevilled the country's membership prospects. The EU also began accession negotiations with Croatia in October 2005 and granted candidate status to the Former Yugoslav Republic of Macedonia at the end of the year. Earlier, the EU had acknowledged the 'European perspective' of the Western Balkans, meaning that every country in the region stood a reasonable chance of eventually becoming a member.

As Chapter 9 explains, enlargement has greatly altered the EU. The accession of so many poor, agricultural countries will continue to have a profound effect on the CAP and cohesion policy. The EU reformed both policies as part of its Agenda 2000 initiative, in anticipation of enlargement, but the results were patently inadequate. Further policy reform is inevitable and is bound to trigger bitter budgetary disputes, such as the one that preceded the agreement of December 2005 on the financial perspectives (budget) for the period 2007–13.

The EU's institutions also required reform because of enlargement. Member states avoided the contentious question of institutional reform in the Amsterdam Treaty, agreeing instead to undertake an institutional overhaul in another IGC in 2000. That conference resulted in the Nice Treaty of 2001, which changed the modalities of QMV in anticipation of enlargement, but in a way that complicated rather than clarified legislative decision-making. In other institutional areas the outcome of the 2000 IGC was equally disappointing. The messy compromises that were struck illustrated the growing difficulty of reaching agreement among member states on institutional issues, especially those which tended to drive a wedge between France and Germany, or between the small and large member states.

Appreciating the inadequacies of the Nice Treaty, the European Council decided in December 2001 to hold a convention of national and EU-level politicians to draft a new treaty that would supersede and supposedly simplify the existing treaties. That was the genesis of the Convention on the Future of Europe of 2002–3 and ensuing IGC, which resulted in the Constitutional Treaty of June 2004. Amongst other things, the Constitutional Treaty altered the system of QMV, giving more power to the big member states; incorporated the previously-negotiated Charter of Fundamental Rights into the EU's legal system; called for a standing president of the European Council; and provided for an EU foreign minister. Voters in the Netherlands and France, two of the EU's founding member states, rejected the Constitutional Treaty in spring 2005, for a variety of reasons mostly unrelated to the treaty itself, ranging from domestic political considerations to concerns about the consequences of globalization and fear of further enlargement. The results of the Dutch and French referenda were a severe blow to the image and prestige of the EU but did not derail the process of European integration, to which most European politicians (if not all their publics) remained committed, as was revealed when the 2007 Reform Treaty was agreed. While less ambitious than the Constitutional Treaty (not *much* less ambitious; see Box 1.4), it marked another historically significant step towards closer European integration.

Conclusion

The history of European integration demonstrates the importance of opportunistic political leadership against a backdrop of fluctuating economic and political fortunes. Early post-war Europe threw up a number of challenges to which European leaders responded with an initiative for limited integration, with strong US support. The ECSC was far from the grand design for European integration that the US had envisioned at the time of the Marshall Plan, but it fostered reconciliation in Franco-German relations and laid an economic foundation for further European integration.

The launch of the European Community in 1958 owed more to economic necessity (potential greater trade among the Six) than geopolitical concerns (the German question), and more to European initiative than American prompting. National interests and individual initiatives also played a definitive part. Despite his aversion to supranationalism, de Gaulle appreciated the EC's economic potential and ensured the organization's initial success. De Gaulle's support for the EC, however qualified, reassured Adenauer and strengthened Franco-German relations.

The Single European Act of 1986, which revitalized the EC, and the Maastricht Treaty of 1992, which gave rise to the EU, were also products of Franco-German bargaining.

In both cases France and Germany sought to boost European competitiveness in a globalizing economic system while retaining Europe's distinctive social structure, in contrast to that of the United States. The Commission, under the energetic leadership of Jacques Delors, contributed to these developments, but only in association with France and Germany.

The dynamics of Franco-German relations and leadership in the EU are changing, not least because of enlargement. As recent treaty negotiations have shown, France and Germany are often far apart on institutional issues such as the modalities of QMV, the size and role of the Commission, and the composition of the EP. United Germany is showing signs of greater political assertiveness in the EU. Unsure of its place in the post-Cold War, rapidly-globalizing world, France often seems to lack confidence and direction. Meanwhile, enlargement is shifting the geopolitical balance of the EU eastward, in favour of Germany.

Yet the history of European integration shows how countries can overcome institutional and policy differences for the sake of common economic and political interests. The end of the Cold War changed the context of European integration but not necessarily its substance. With the challenge of globalization greater than ever before, it is in the national interest of all member states to manage the single market and monetary union, and make a success of enlargement. In a sense, they have little choice but to perpetuate European integration.

? DISCUSSION QUESTIONS

1. Are France and Germany bound to lead in Europe?
2. How significant have federalist aspirations been in the history of European integration?
3. Is the United States a 'federator' of Europe?
4. What economic factors impelled European integration during various stages of its history?
5. What impact is the fate of the Reform Treaty likely to have on the process of European integration?

→ FURTHER READING

Dinan (2004) provides a thorough history of the EU. Dinan (2006) examines key developments in EU history and includes a chapter on the historiography of European integration. For a neofunctionalist analysis of the EC's development, see Haas (1958) and Lindberg (1963). Milward (1984, 2000) is the most influential historian of European integration. Moravcsik (1998) blends political science and historical analysis to produce liberal intergovernmentalism, and explain major developments in the history of the EU.

Duchêne (1994) is excellent on Jean Monnet, and Gillingham (1991) provides an authoritative account of the origins of the ECSC. Gillingham (2003) describes the history of European integration as a struggle between economic liberalism and centralization, personified in the 1980s by Delors and Thatcher.

Dinan, D. (2004), *Europe Recast: A History of European Union* (Boulder, CO: Lynne Rienner Publishers and Basingstoke: Palgrave).

_____ (ed.) (2006), *Origins and Evolution of the European Union* (Oxford: Oxford University Press).

Duchêne, F. (1994), *Jean Monnet: The First Statesman of Interdependence* (New York: Norton).

Gillingham, J. (1991), *Coal, Steel and the Rebirth of Europe, 1945–1955* (Cambridge: Cambridge University Press).

_____ (2003), *European Integration, 1950–2003* (Cambridge: Cambridge University Press).

Haas, E. (1958), *The Uniting of Europe: Political, Social, and Economic Forces* (Stanford, CA: Stanford University Press).

Lindberg, L. (1963). *The Political Dynamics of European Economic Integration* (Stanford, CA: Stanford University Press).

Milward, A. (1984), *The Reconstruction of Western Europe, 1945–51* (Berkeley: University of California Press).

_____ (2000), *The European Rescue of the Nation-State,* 2nd edn. (London: Routledge).

Moravcsik, A. (1998), *The Choice for Europe: Social Purpose and State Power from Messina to Maastricht* (Ithaca, NY: Cornell University Press and UCL Press).

 WEB LINKS

The EU's official portal site has its own useful history page:
http://europa.eu/abc/history/index_en.htm

The Florence-based European University Institute (EUI)'s European Integration History Index provides internet resources (in all languages) on post-war European history, with a particular emphasis on the EU:
www.iue.it/LIB/SISSCO/VL/hist-eur-integration/Index.html

Visit the Online Resource Centre that accompanies this book for additional material:
www.oxfordtextbooks.co.uk/orc/bomberg2e/

PART II

Major Actors

CHAPTER 3

The EU's Institutions

Elizabeth Bomberg and Alexander Stubb

Institutions in Treaty and Practice	46	Experimentation and Change	64
European Commission	46	Power-sharing and Consensus	66
Council of Ministers	50	Scope and Capacity	67
European Council (of Heads of State and Government)	57	Conclusion	68
European Parliament	58	DISCUSSION QUESTIONS	69
European Court of Justice	61	FURTHER READING	69
Why Institutions Matter	64	WEB LINKS	70

▌ Chapter Overview

No student of the EU can understand this organization without a basic grasp of its key institutions and how they work. The EU institutions are not just dry organizations (although they are complex); they are dynamic organisms exercising a unique mix of legislative, executive, and judicial power. We begin by introducing the EU's five most important institutions. We outline their structures and formal powers (that is, what the Treaties say they can do), but we also focus on their informal power and procedures—including how they manage to 'squeeze' influence out of sometimes limited Treaty prerogatives. We then explore why these institutions matter in determining EU politics and policy more generally.

Institutions in Treaty and Practice

A big part of what makes the EU unique is its institutions, several of which have no close counterparts at the national or international level. This chapter explores the five institutions that exercise the most power and influence on EU policy and politics: the European Commission, the Council of Ministers, the European Council, the European Parliament (EP), and the European Court of Justice. Table 3.1 summarizes the formal powers conferred on each of these institutions by major Treaty reforms. It does not, however, convey how informal powers have accrued over time, nor the incremental power shifts that may occur between rounds of Treaty reform. The informal institutional politics of European integration are important. A diligent student of the EU would be wise not to ignore them.

European Commission

One of the most important, unique, and controversial institutions of the EU is the European Commission. A hybrid organization, somewhere between an executive and a bureaucracy, the Commission has no obvious counterpart at the national level. The Treaties allocated to the Commission profoundly important tasks: to initiate policies and represent the general interest of the European Union; to act as guardian of the Treaties (to defend both their letter and spirit); to ensure the correct application of EU legislation; and to manage and negotiate international trade and cooperation agreements. In practical terms, the Commission's power is exercised most dramatically in three areas: its right to propose policy, its lead in international trade talks, and its role in competition policy (it has powers to vet and veto mergers—even of companies based outside the EU). Together these powers have afforded the Commission an influence that is both crucial and controversial. Perhaps controversy is unavoidable for an institution that is designed to act independently of the EU's member states, and in the general, supranational interest of the Union as a whole.

The Commission as a term is rather confusingly used to refer to two separate arms of the same body: the College of Commissioners (or executive Commission) and the administrative Commission (the bureaucracy). The College is the powerhouse of the Commission. Headed by a President nominated by national governments and approved by the European Parliament, the College is charged with specific policy tasks but is also expected to provide political direction for the Commission. It is currently made up of 27 Commissioners, with (for now) one appointed by each member state. Most Commissioners hold high office in national politics before being appointed for a five-year term to serve in Brussels.

The Commissioners meet once a week to develop and adopt proposals on new policies and legislation. Once the College takes a decision, if necessary by majority vote but usually by consensus, it becomes the policy of all of the Commission. Each

Commissioner must support it, whatever their own private misgivings, or else (in principle, anyway) they are expected to resign.

Commissioners are each allocated a portfolio, such as agriculture or competition policy, by the President of the Commission. The allocation of portfolios can be politically charged as member states seek to gain control over portfolios that are important to their state's particular interests. For instance, after being chosen as President in 2004, José Manuel Barroso came under pressure from Paris and Berlin to designate the French and German Commissioners as 'super-Commissioners' with especially weighty portfolios. Yet, the Commission President has gradually gained the power—exploited in this case by Barroso—to allocate (or reshuffle) portfolios in an attempt to overcome this type of wrangling. Today the problem is less about wrangling, and more about finding enough serious jobs for an expanding number of commissioners. With the entry in 2007 of two new Commissioners from Bulgaria and Romania, Barroso had to hive off duties from other Commissioners, resulting in some undoubtedly lightweight portfolios (such as multilingualism). In the proposed Reform Treaty the number of Commissioners will be reduced as of 2014 to two-thirds of the number of member states on the basis of equal rotation (so, say, a College of 20 for an EU of 30 member states).

Commissioners each have their own private staff of (around seven) personal advisers called a cabinet. These officials may be drawn from inside or outside the Commission. They perform a very demanding and important role, keeping their Commissioner informed about important developments in their own policy areas as well as wider developments in the Commission bureaucracy and Europe more generally. Like portfolio assignments, the role of cabinets can be highly controversial. Again, according to the Treaties, Commissioners act not in the interest of their national governments but in the general European interest. Yet Commissioners have been notorious for filling their cabinets overwhelmingly with staff of their own nationality. Despite reforms requiring the head or deputy head of the cabinet to hail from a member state different from that of the Commissioner, most cabinets still tend to reflect the national character and priorities of their Commissioner.

Controversy surrounding portfolio assignments and cabinet appointments suggests that the defence of national interests in the Commission can never be entirely removed. Commissioners take an oath of independence when they are appointed. Of course, that does not mean that they totally abandon their national identities once they arrive in Brussels. But too obviously acting as an agent for a member government can backfire on a Commissioner. By the same token, Commissioners can end up being scorned in their home national capital for failing to defend the government that put them there. Most famously, 1980s British Prime Minister Margaret Thatcher despaired at the alleged failure of 'her' Commissioner—Lord Cockfield—to defend the interests of the Thatcher government. Thus Commissioners face a tough balancing act: they must be sensitive to the interests of the member state that (in Brussels-speak) 'they know best', but must not undermine the independence of the Commission.

Each Commissioner is responsible for one or more directorates-general (DGs)— services or departments—which relate to his or her portfolio. These DGs, the Brussels

TABLE 3.1   The institutions: Treaty reform and conferred powers

	Rome (1957)	SEA (1986)	Maastricht (1992)	Amsterdam (1997)	Nice (2001)	Reform Treaty*
European Commission	Right to propose legislation; draft budget; act as guardian of Treaty; negotiate international trade agreements.	Right of initiative expands to new areas related to the completion of the single market.	Powers enhanced in economic and monetary union and in foreign policy; further extension of the right of initiative.	President's role strengthened and right of initiative broadened in line with increase in EU's competences.	President's powers (to reshuffle portfolios) enhanced; size stabilized to one Commissioner per member state up to 27 states; then reduced on basis of equal rotation.	Size capped (as of 2014); a Representative of the Union for Foreign Affairs and Security Policy (shared with Council) established.
Council of Ministers	Power to pass legislation; appoint Commission; agree budget.	Increased use of Qualified Majority Voting (QMV) in areas relating to the single market.	Further extension of QMV; right to propose legislation in justice and foreign affairs pillars together with the Commission.	Further extension of QMV and co-decision with the Parliament.	Continued expansion of QMV; re-weighting of votes between large and small member states.	QMV set at double majority (55% of member states, 65% of population); a Representative of the Union for Foreign Affairs and Security Policy (shared with Commission) established.

European Council	not mentioned in Treaty	Granted legal status.	Assigned responsibility of defining the general political guidelines of the Union.	Confirmed role in EMU and strengthened position in respect of CFSP.	seat moved to Brussels	Becomes an official EU institution; a permanent president replaces rotating presidency.
European Parliament	Right to be consulted on legislation; right to dismiss the Commission.	Extension of legislative authority through the introduction of the cooperation procedure.	Right to pass legislation jointly with Council in limited range of areas (co-decision procedure); greater role in appointing Commission.	Co-decision extended; right to approve appointment of Commission President and Commission as a whole.	Further extension of co-decision procedure; strengthened right to place matters before the Court; legal base established for party funding at European level.	Further extension of co-decision procedure (renamed 'ordinary legislative procedure'); power to elect President of the Commission; maximum number of seats set at 750 plus the President.
European Court of Justice	Guardian of Treaties and EC Law.	Creation of Court of First Instance.	Power to impose fines against member states (but excluded from two inter-governmental pillars).	Increased jurisdiction in third-pillar matters	Further sharing of tasks with Court of First Instance; creation of more specialized Chambers; number of judges limited to one per member state.	Name changed to 'Court of Justice of the European Union'; more specialized courts attached.
						*signed in 2007 but not ratified

equivalents of national ministries, cover the EU's main policy areas such as agriculture, competition, or environment, and are headed by a director-general who reports directly to the relevant Commissioner. There are over twenty such departments or services which together make up the administrative Commission. Although this Brussels bureaucracy is often portrayed in the popular press as an enormous body intent on taking over Europe, it is in fact remarkably small. Fewer than 25,000 civil servants are employed in the administrative Commission, and only around 6,000 of these are in policy-making posts (Nugent 2006: 159). Others are involved in the huge task of translation and interpretation required by the Commission (the Union has 23 official languages; see Box 1.7) or in research and technological development (see Commission 2007a). Put another way, the Commission's entire staff is roughly equal in size to that of a large municipal authority (such as Barcelona) or a medium-sized national government department such as the French Ministry of Culture.

In practice it is difficult to draw a clear line between the administrative Commission and the more political College of Commissioners. While the College is ultimately responsible for any decisions that emanate from this institution, in practice many policy ideas are generated much further down within the administrative structures, or even outside the institution (see Box 3.1). In turn, some Commissioners will be more interventionist than others in seeking to influence the day-to-day functioning of 'their' directorate-general.

A key feature of the Commission bureaucracy is not only its complexity but its limited resources, which must be stretched to cover fundamentally important—and expanding—tasks. How much the member states really want the Commission to embrace an expanding array of tasks has always been a matter of ambiguity. When push comes to shove, many member states can be reluctant to relinquish their control over sensitive or politicized policies. For example, member states have been very cautious about surrendering control over policy areas such as immigration and defence (see Chapters 7 and 10). Traditionally, however, the Commission has proved adept at making the most of the powers given to it, and squeezing additional areas of influence out of them. Thus, in the area of climate change, the Commission has conducted detailed research highlighting the necessity of new initiatives (such as an emissions trading scheme) and a stronger role for the Commission in this area. While, ultimately, member states can curb the powers of the Commission through their control over the Treaties, the Commission has shown again and again that it is far from being simply the servant of the member states.

Council of Ministers

The Council of Ministers (formally, the Council of the European Union) is the EU's primary decision-making body. The Treaties state that the Council shall consist of 'a representative of each member state at ministerial level authorized to commit the government of the member state'. In other words, the Council is there to represent

BOX 3.1   **How it really works**

Who initiates policy?

The formal right to initiate policies is considered one of the Commission's most precious and fundamental powers. Yet in practice many initiatives emanating from the Commission are a response to pressures from other sources. The Commission's 'own initiatives' thus account for only around 10–20 per cent of proposals. Of all the Commission's proposals:

- between 20 and 25 per cent are a follow-up to Council or European Parliament resolutions, European Council initiatives, or requests on the part of the social partners (employers and employees).
- around 30 per cent arise from the EU's international obligations.
- between 10 and 15 per cent have to do with existing obligations under the Treaties or secondary legislation.
- around 20 per cent involve updating existing EU legislation (that is, adapting it to technical or scientific progress).

The Reform Treaty will, if ratified, add a new direct source. Under the Treaty, one million EU citizens can invite the Commission to submit a proposal. The Commission is not legally obliged to act on the initiative, but it would most certainly have to take it into account. The first such initiative arose in Autumn 2006 when over one million Europeans signed a petition calling (unsuccessfully, thus far) for a single seat for the European Parliament (see www.oneseat.eu).

Commission (2001: 6)

the interests of national governments who comprise the EU. It is also responsible for making the major policy decisions of the Union. Alone or with the Parliament, it decides which EU legislation is adopted, and in what form.

The Council is a complex system with multiple levels. The Treaties speak of only one Council, but even at the ministerial level it is made up of different ministers, depending on what policy area is being discussed (agriculture, finance, environment, and so on). Of the nine different configurations the Council with the widest brief is the General Affairs and External Relations Council (GAERC), which brings together foreign ministers. It deals with external political relations, general issues relating to policy initiatives and coordination, or matters that are politically sensitive (see Box 3.2). Other Councils—such as the Agriculture and Fisheries Council or the Competitiveness Council—deal specifically with dedicated subjects or sectors, but ministers can (and do) refer to the GAERC issues that become especially contentious or difficult to resolve.

The Council is aided by a Secretariat (smaller than the Commission but still with around 3000 officials), which plays a powerful role brokering deals and crafting compromises between member states. Even with the help of the Secretariat, the burden

---

BOX 3.2   **Sample Council agenda**

The following provides a glimpse of the full agenda facing foreign ministers in a General Affairs and External Relations Council. Part I deals with external affairs; Part II with general affairs. Note that 'A points' in Part II are items already agreed at Coreper level. They are not discussed unless a minister objects, but such objections are rare. The other issues are game for substantive discussion.

Council of The European Union: Provisional Agenda/General Affairs and External Relations (German Presidency)

Part I: Session on External Relations
2789th meeting of the Council of the European Union
Brussels, Monday 5 and Tuesday 6 March 2007

1. Adoption of the provisional agenda

2. Sudan/Darfur

       —Draft Council conclusions

3. Uzbekistan

       —Draft Council conclusions

4. Western Balkans

       —Draft Council conclusions

5. MEPP [Middle East Peace Process]

6. Iran

       —Draft Council conclusions

7. AOB

Part II: Session on General Affairs
2795th meeting of the Council of the European Union
Luxembourg, Monday 23 April 2007 (10 h 00)

1. Adoption of the provisional agenda

2. Approval of the list of 'A' items

3. Resolutions, opinions, and decisions adopted by the European Parliament at its period of sessions

       —Strasbourg, 12–15 March 2007

       —Brussels, 28/29 March 2007

4. AOB

---

on the GAERC has increased enormously. One upshot is the emergence of consensus on the need for member states to find a way to allow EU foreign ministers to concentrate more directly on foreign policy (see Chapter 10).

The Council meets in some form every few days. The agricultural, foreign, or economic and finance (EcoFin) ministers meet at least once a month, the others from one to six times a year. The ministers' primary job is to agree legislation proposed by the Commission. The Treaties provide them with three basic ways of voting to reach a decision. Unanimity is required when a policy is considered particularly sensitive. It applies mainly to fiscal matters (for example, tax harmonization) or constitutional questions (accession of new members), or new competences. In addition, it is required when the Council wishes to amend a Commission proposal against the Commission's wishes.

Today, majority voting is applied to most decisions. 'Simple majority', with each state wielding one vote, is used primarily for procedural questions. Qualified Majority Voting (QMV) (see Box 2.2) applies to the bulk of decisions, including most legislation related to the single market and proposals designed to implement or clarify existing policies or legislation. Each new treaty has expanded the areas in which QMV can be applied, and the Reform Treaty will increase them yet further. Even without the new Treaty, well over three-quarters of all EU legislation is today agreed by this procedure.

Given the widespread use of majority voting, the question of how a majority is constituted is of critical importance. A qualified or weighted majority means that the more populous member states are given more votes than smaller ones. But how, precisely, weighting should be determined is a sensitive issue (see Chapter 4). The current rules, arduously agreed at the Nice European Council in 2000, are complex. According to the Nice Treaty, decisions require a so-called triple majority: decisions must garner the support of a qualified majority of states, the backing of states representing at least 62 per cent of the EU's population, and the support of at least half the member states, whatever their size or population (see Table 3.2). If ratified, the Reform Treaty will simplify this (as of 2014) to a 'double majority': for a decision to pass it would need the support of a 55 per cent majority of member states representing a 65 per cent majority of the EU's population. During a transitional period ending in 2017 a member state may request a decision to be taken according to the old rules.

In any case, although QMV *can* now be used in a wide variety of areas, it does not mean it is used. In fact, consensus is still widely sought in the Council and votes are seldom forced (see Box 3.3). Whichever decision method is used, these meetings and votes still take place behind closed doors, even if selected debates are now open to the public. A Commission representative attends, but no parliamentarian, or member of the press or public, is present during most of these meetings. Extensive leaks to the press ensure the meetings are not entirely secret, but these leaks reflect the 'spin' of the various national representatives doing the leaking rather than that of an outside observer. This seclusion makes consensus and agreement easier to achieve (and arguably very little would be agreed without it), but it also makes the Council one of the few—if not only—legislative bodies in the democratic world that takes its main decisions behind closed doors.

Coreper

To help brief their ministers, each member state has its own national delegation (or Permanent Representation) in Brussels, which acts as a sort of embassy to the EU.

TABLE 3.2   Voting in the Council of Ministers

Voting in an EU of 27 member states

Member state	Approximate population (millions) in 2007	Number of votes	Number of citizens per vote (millions)
Germany	82.3	29	2.84
France	63.3	29	2.18
UK	60.7	29	2.09
Italy	58.9	29	2.03
Spain	44.5	27	1.65
Poland	38.1	27	1.41
Romania	21.6	14	1.54
Netherlands	16.3	13	1.28
Greece	11.2	12	0.93
Portugal	10.6	12	0.88
Belgium	10.6	12	0.88
Czech Republic	10.3	12	0.86
Hungary	10.1	12	0.84
Sweden	9.1	10	0.91
Austria	8.3	10	0.83
Bulgaria	7.7	10	0.77
Denmark	5.4	7	0.77
Slovakia	5.4	7	0.77
Finland	5.3	7	0.76
Ireland	4.3	7	0.61
Lithuania	3.4	7	0.49
Latvia	2.3	4	0.58
Slovenia	2.0	4	0.50
Estonia	1.3	4	0.33
Cyprus	0.8	4	0.20

TABLE 3.2 (cont.)

Voting in an EU of 27 member states

Member state	Approximate population (millions) in 2007	Number of votes	Number of citizens per vote (millions)
Luxembourg	0.5	4	0.13
Malta	0.4	3	0.13
TOTAL	494.7	345	

Qualified majority under Nice Treaty: 255 votes (around 74 per cent), including a majority of member states, as well as 62 per cent of the EU's population.	*Blocking minority under Nice Treaty:* 91 votes (around 26.5 per cent), or a majority of member states or 38.1 per cent of the EU's population.	*Qualified majority according to the proposed Reform Treaty:* 55 per cent of member states comprising 65 per cent of the EU's population.

Eurostat 2007

National officials who staff these 27 Perm Reps offer the member states representation at the lower levels of the Council system. Much of the substance of EU policy is determined at these levels, particularly by the Committee of Permanent Representatives, known by its French abbreviation Coreper. Led by national ambassadors to the EU, Coreper's job is to prepare the work of the Council and to make decisions delegated to it by the Council. Coreper itself is split (confusingly) into Coreper II, made up of the Permanent ambassadors who deal primarily with the big political, institutional, and budgetary issues; and Coreper I, led by Deputy ambassadors who deal with most other issues. Particularly sensitive areas (such as security, finance, agriculture, and Justice and Home Affairs) have their own special preparatory committees who do their best to lighten the workload of Coreper.

To the uninitiated (and many of the initiated), Coreper's operation is shadowy and complex. National ambassadors and senior civil servants preparing the ground for Council meetings are assisted by numerous working groups and committees of national delegates (many of whom are based in national capitals) who scrutinize Commission proposals, get a feel for what amendments would or would not be acceptable, and hammer out deals in the run-up to the Council sessions. The vast majority of decisions (around 70 per cent) are taken here, before ministers ever become involved (Hayes-Renshaw and Wallace 2006: 14). For some, Coreper's role means it is the real powerhouse, made up of 'the men and women who run Europe'; but for others, and

---

BOX 3.3   **How it really works**

Reaching decisions in the Council

QMV now applies to most areas of decision-making in the Council, and any national representative on the Council can call for its use. Yet in practice, only a small number of decisions that could be agreed under QMV are actually agreed that way (see Hayes-Renshaw and Wallace 2006). Pushing for a formal vote too early or too often could create resentment that disrupts the mood and effectiveness of the Council. Thus, whatever the formal rules stipulate, decision-making in the Council—even one accommodating 27 states—usually proceeds on the understanding that consensus will be sought whenever possible.

How is this consensus achieved? Imagine a contentious item on the Council's agenda (say, dealing with work and safety regulations). Perhaps a majority of states support the initiative but several are opposed or ambivalent. Well before proceeding to a vote, several attempts will be made to achieve some sort of consensus. This bargaining is most intense at the level of Coreper. Phone calls or informal chats between national representatives prepare the ground for subsequent meetings where agreements can be struck. Informal understandings or agreements might also be reached at the meals that are very much a part of both Coreper and Council meetings. Ostensibly a time for break and refreshment, these lunches provide opportunities for a delicate probing of national positions and willingness to deal. Similarly, a good Chairperson can make use of scheduled or requested breaks in the proceedings to explore possibilities for a settlement. These breaks feature off-the-record discussions or 'confessionals' between the Chair and national representatives or amongst representatives themselves. Lubricating these discussions is the familiarity and personal relationships national representatives have built up over time. In the end, the objections of opposing states might be assuaged by a redrafting of certain clauses, a promise of later support for a favoured initiative, or the possibility of a derogation (or postponement) of a policy's implementation for one or more reluctant states. The point is that the day-to-day practice in Coreper and the Council is characterized far more by the search for a consensus than by any straightforward mechanism of strategic voting.

---

for Coreper civil servants themselves, their role is merely that of helping ministers make the best decisions possible. 'If ministers want to let Coreper decide, that is a ministerial decision' in the modest words of one such civil servant (*Economist* 6 Aug 1998).

Council Presidency

Traditionally, the Presidency of the Council of Ministers has been held by a member state for six months on a rotating basis. The country holding the Presidency manages the Council system: it arranges and chairs all meetings of the Council, and has primary responsibility for coordinating the Union's foreign policy (see Chapter 10). More generally, the Presidency's job is to build consensus and move decision-making forward. In an enlarged EU this consensus-building role has become crucial. As one observer of the Presidency post-enlargement noted: '[Negotiation] happens in a much more informal manner outside the meeting room, in bilateral or multilateral contacts ... the bilaterals have, in a way, become more important than the plenary sessions' (Hagemann and De Clerck-Sachsse 2007: 29).

Holding the Presidency does not afford the host country extra formal power, but it can give that country added influence. By arranging the meetings and setting the Council's agenda the Presidency attempts to determine which issues will be given priority and which will not. It also brings the member government holding it a certain amount of prestige and visibility. Of course, holding the Presidency has disadvantages as well. The costs in terms of time required of national officials are daunting if not overwhelming, especially for smaller states such as Slovenia or Luxembourg. Moreover, much can go wrong in six months. EU crises (such as a failed referendum) can tarnish a Presidency whether or not the country holding it was responsible. On the other hand, six months is not usually long enough to accomplish all or even most of that to which the host country aspires. To ease this burden, an informal practice has emerged whereby the Council presidency is effectively shared by a trio of countries over 18 months. The Reform Treaty (if ratified) will formalize this arrangement. An exception to this sharing rule is the establishment of a new 'foreign affairs chief' (formally called High Representative) as a Vice-President of the Commission, who will permanently chair the External Affairs Council.

Given their core function—representing member states' interests in the decision-making process—it would be easy to conclude that the Council of Ministers and Coreper are purely intergovernmental bodies, interested primarily in protecting national sovereignty and halting attempts for further integration. But, as social constructivists would note (see Lewis 2003), regular ministerial meetings, informal contacts, and routine bargaining at the level of Council and Coreper have provided the grounds for continual and close cooperation among executives from different member states. As a result, the Council has constructed a collective identity that is more than an amalgamation of national views, and which has helped push integration forward. In the final analysis, integration has proceeded only with the Council's sanction.

European Council (of Heads of State and Government)

The European Council began in the 1970s as an occasional series of informal fireside chats among the member states' heads of government and heads of state (in the case of member states with elected Presidents such as Finland and France). The European Council now does much more, including settling problems unresolved at lower levels of decision-making and providing political leadership for the entire EU. It is now very much part of the Council system, and might be viewed as its top level. The European Council meetings—usually referred to in the media as Summits—are held four times a year. Traditionally, they were hosted by the country holding the Presidency and were usually known by the name of their host city. After 2001, the Nice Treaty stipulated that official European Council meetings had to be held in Brussels. The location and even meal menus are carefully chosen to create an atmosphere conducive to open discussion, problem resolution, and general bonhomie.

Over the years the European Council has climbed to the top of the EU's decision-making hierarchy and is now a major agenda-setter. Direct elections to the Parliament, monetary union, future enlargement, and the initiative for an EU rapid reaction force have all been launched at the European Council level. Major Treaty reform also is agreed at this level, as occurred when the 2007 German Council Presidency managed to obtain political agreement on the outline of the Reform Treaty to replace the ill-fated Constitutional Treaty. The European Council's far-reaching and dramatic decisions have helped to propel these meetings into the public spotlight where they have become the focal point for media coverage of the EU. Hospitality, including for the press, is lavish. Photo opportunities are abundant and the final press conferences have become elaborately staged events.

The European Council's other broad function, however, is problem resolution, which is less amenable to public display. Issues that cannot be resolved at Coreper or Council levels often can be resolved at this elevated political level, perhaps through informal persuasion, perhaps through the forging of package deals which trade off agreement on one issue (say regional spending) in exchange for concessions on another (say CAP reform). Serious deadlocks on budget agreements often have been resolved only through such deals in late-night meetings.

European Parliament

The European Parliament is the only directly elected EU institution. It is made up of 785 members (MEPs) elected every five years in elections across the 27 member states. (After the 2009 election the number of MEPs will drop to 750.) The Reform Treaty capped the amount of MEPs to 750 plus the President, of which the largest member state may have a maximum of 96 seats and the smallest a minimum of six seats. To its supporters, the Parliament is the voice of the people in European decision-making. To critics, it is little more than an expensive talking shop. Both of these portraits carry elements of truth. Compared to national parliaments the EP appears weak, and its role circumscribed. It does not initiate legislation, and its control of the EU's purse strings is limited. It began life as a consultative assembly, and was only directly elected for the first time in 1979. Its housekeeping arrangements are clumsy. Members must shuttle between Brussels (where committee and other meetings are held) and Strasbourg (where plenary sessions take place), and their home constituency. Yet, every Treaty change from the Single European Act in the mid-1980s up to the 2007 Reform Treaty has strengthened the role of the Parliament in EU decision-making (see Table 3.1). Even in advance of the Reform Treaty's ratification, the Parliament enjoys equal power with the Council in deciding most legislation. Moreover, the EP has proved adept at extracting maximum influence from limited formal powers (see Box 3.4).

BOX 3.4	How the European Parliament 'squeezes' power

The EP has always made the most of its limited powers. Even when it had no power of veto or co-decision as it now has, the Parliament utilized several techniques, such as the threat of delay, to make its influence felt. In budget negotiations the EP's formal power is still limited, but it does have the power to sign off—or not—on the annual budget. It uses this power selectively but often effectively.

Similarly, the EP has stretched fully its specific powers to oversee the Commission. The Parliament does not have the right to hire or fire individual Commissioners, but it has not been shy in using its power of persuasion in the approval process. To illustrate the point: in the parliamentary confirmation hearings of 2004 the EP objected to Italian Commissioner-designate Rocco Buttiglione's statements that homosexuality was 'a sin' and that women 'belonged in the home' (Peterson 2006: 93). These statements were viewed as extreme and inappropriate by many Parliamentarians (especially for a Commissioner with responsibility for civil liberties). The ensuing uproar persuaded Commission President José Manuel Barroso to drop Buttiglione from his team. Note that the Parliament did not have *de jure* power to sack Buttiglione, but *de facto* they did just that. Of course the EP's threats must seem real, and for that to happen it must stay united. Such unity is not easy to come by in such a large and diverse institution with over 700 members from a vast array of parties and backgrounds. Thus, despite its ability to 'squeeze' power, the Parliament does not always get its way.

The Members of the Parliament (MEPs) sit in political groups (not in national blocs), representing over 200 national parties. Most of the Parliament's activities are structured around these groups. The largest groups are comprised of identifiable political families such as the Christian Democrats or Socialists. Other groups are more ad hoc (such as the 'Identity, Tradition, and Sovereignty' Group). They bring together in loose coalitions parties and MEPs seeking to obtain the advantages (such as resources and speaking time) that membership of a group brings. The leaders of the party political groups, along with the Parliament's president, set the EP's agenda. But, like the US Congress, the detailed and most important work of the Parliament is carried out in standing Committees, organized by policy area (such as Transport, Agriculture, or the Environment). Although MEPs usually vote along party lines, national allegiances are never far from the fore. For instance, voting patterns on an important services directive in 2006 revealed clear differences between MEPs from the more protectionist 'old' EU states and the more market liberal newcomers.

The Parliament's powers can be divided under three headings: supervisory (control), legislative, and budgetary. Its power has increased in all three areas, albeit to different degrees. The Parliament exercises supervision or control over the Commission and the Council through its right to question, examine, and debate the large number of reports produced by these two bodies. Its power directly to control the Council is weak but its assent is required before the Council can approve the accession of any new members (see Box 3.5).

BOX 3.5   **Key concepts and terms: legislative procedures**

The EU has several different procedures for agreeing legislation, and the power of the institutions varies across them. The four most important are described below.

The **consultation procedure** was the original device used to decide most legislation. Today it is only used for limited policies relating primarily to agricultural and competition policy as well as issues of police and judicial asylum, visas, or immigration. Under the consultation procedure the Commission submits a proposal to the Council of Ministers. The Council is obliged to seek the opinion of the EP, but not to pay any attention to it.

Under the **cooperation procedure** introduced in the SEA, the Parliament gained more influence. If the Parliament did not like what the Council had done with its proposed amendments it could review the legislation again and ask for further amendments. It could also reject the legislation under this procedure, but the Council could still overrule that objection. Today, cooperation applies only in limited areas of economic and monetary union. The Reform Treaty would abolish this procedure.

The vast majority of legislation (over three quarters) now falls under the **co-decision procedure**. (If ratified, the Reform Treaty would extend this procedure to almost all legislation and rename it the 'ordinary legislative procedure'.) Under co-decision the European Parliament formally shares legal responsibility for legislation jointly with the Council of Ministers. The Parliament and Council must enter into direct negotiations if they cannot agree on a proposal. If these negotiations fail to reach agreement the legislative proposal fails. Essentially, co-decision gives the Parliament the power to veto any legislation that falls under this procedure. Yet its real significance is not the actual veto power it grants the Parliament (it wields this veto rarely). Rather, co-decision has altered the way policy-making players view and interact with the Parliament. Knowing that Parliament matters in ultimately deciding legislation, the Commission, the Council, and skilful lobbyists are keen to listen to, accommodate, and shape the Parliament's views when policies are being formulated.

Finally, the **assent procedure** is used to establish the EP's approval of major decisions concerning international treaties, most EU cohesion funding, and enlargement. The EP cannot add amendments to these proposals. In most cases, the Parliament must agree to assent by an absolute majority. No decision requiring assent can be made without the EP's approval.

The Parliament's increasingly close supervision of the Commission is more noticeable. When a new Commission is appointed by member governments, the EP must approve the Council's nominee for Commission President. It holds hearings with the nominee Commissioners and then appoints (or not) the whole Commission by a vote of confidence (see Box 3.4). More dramatically, the EP has the right to sack the entire Commission through a vote of censure. The Parliament has not yet wielded this 'atom bomb': to do so would require the support of an absolute majority of all MEPs and two-thirds of the votes cast. However, it threatened to do so in 1999 and that threat was real enough to convince the Commission to resign rather than face formal (and almost certain) censure by the Parliament. In other words, the threat of censure—and not just its formal application—is itself a powerful weapon in the Parliament's arsenal of supervisory powers. But it cannot yet remove individual Commissioners, as many Parliamentarians wish it could.

The Parliament's legislative powers also have grown significantly since the Treaty of Rome. Originally Parliament only had the right to give an opinion on a Commission proposal for legislation prior to adoption by the Council. Today, Parliament has the right of co-decision over a wide range of EU legislation (see Box 3.5). Under this procedure no text can be adopted without the formal agreement of both the Council and Parliament. The Council knows it must listen and accommodate the EP, which means many more Parliament amendments now find their way into EU legislation. Yet despite the wide use of co-decision, sensitive areas such as taxation or agricultural prices remain exempt. In these areas Parliament only gives an opinion which can be acted upon or ignored.

When it comes to budgetary matters, the power of the EP is uneven. On one hand, its powers over expenditure are significant. The annual budget only comes into force once the President of the Parliament has signed it. The Parliament has the last word in areas such as spending on the regions, social policy, culture, and education. Its importance is recognized by organized interests who lobby the EP intensely on these issues (see Chapter 5). On the other hand, the Parliament's budgetary role is strictly limited in important respects. It has virtually no say on the revenues side of the budget. Moreover, on issues of agricultural spending (which accounts for nearly half the budget) the Parliament can propose amendments but the Council has the last say.

The European Parliament has seen its powers grow significantly since direct elections were first held in 1979. However, many still question its ability to bring legitimacy to the EU decision-making process. Its claim to represent the peoples of Europe is seriously undermined by low and declining turnouts in European Parliament elections (45 per cent in the 2004 EP elections, and below 30 per cent in five of the new member states). This lack of support, combined with the Parliament's image (accurate or not) as a 'gravy train' might well act as a brake on any further increases in its powers. Ultimately, Parliament's future role is tied up with larger questions of democracy and power in the EU (see Chapter 8).

European Court of Justice

At first glance, the European Court of Justice (ECJ) seems neither a particularly powerful nor controversial institution. It is located in an unremarkable building in Luxembourg, and is comprised of 27 judges plus eight Advocate Generals who draft Opinions for the judges. It is supported in its work by the Court of First Instance, a lower tribunal created in 1989 to ease the growing workload of the Court. (The Court had dealt with nearly 14,000 cases by 2006 and had around 750 cases pending by early 2007.) The role of the ECJ is to ensure that, in the interpretation and application of the Treaties, the law is observed. In practice this function means that the Court is the final arbiter in disputes among EU institutions, and between EU institutions and member states. It is responsible for ensuring that the EU's institutions do not go beyond the powers given to them under the Treaties. It also ensures national compliance with EU Treaties. Since the Maastricht Treaty, the Court can even fine firms or member states that breach EU law.

More generally, the Court has been remarkably innovative in pushing the integration process forward. A series of decisions in the early 1960s widened the Court's jurisdiction and gave real substance to the EU legal system. Two landmark decisions during the 1960s developed the essential rules on which the EU legal order rests. In the 1963 *Van Gend en Loos* case, the Court established the doctrine of direct effect, which mandated that EU citizens had a legal right to expect their governments to adhere to their European obligations. In 1964 (*Costa* v. *ENEL*), the Court established the supremacy of EU law, which means that if a domestic law contradicts an EU obligation, European law prevails.

EU law is thus qualitatively different from international law in that individuals can seek remedy for breaches of it through their domestic courts. The process operates through the preliminary ruling system, which allows national courts to ask the Court for a view on the European aspects of a case before them. Such rulings have shaped national policies as diverse as the right to advertise abortion services, roaming charges for mobile phones, and the age of retirement. These rulings also have contributed to the claim that the Court has, in effect, become a policy-making body in its own right (see Box 3.6).

However, the key contribution of the Court in establishing the direct effect and supremacy of EU law has been to create an important tool other institutions may use in the process of European integration. For instance, in the 1979 landmark *Cassis de Dijon* case the Court established the principle of 'mutual recognition': a product made or sold legally in one member state (in this case a sweet French blackcurrant liqueur) cannot be barred in another member state (in this case, Germany). The principle is fundamental to the single market because it established that national variation in standards could exist as long as trade was not unduly impeded. But the full effect of the ruling was not apparent until the Commission used the principle as a cornerstone of its 1985 proposals to launch the single market (see Chapter 2).

The Court's own exercise of its powers remains contested. While most agree that its policy-making role is inevitable, debate turns on when and to what extent such a role is appropriate (Weiler 1999). In part, perceptions of how activist or otherwise the Court should be depend on the prevailing political climate. In the 1960s and 1970s, a period normally characterized as one of stagnation and 'Euro-sclerosis', the Court played a vital role in pushing the integration process at the very time when political integration seemed paralysed by the use of the national veto. Scholars who take inspiration from neofunctionalist thinking often cite evidence from this period to undermine the intergovernmentalist claim that national interests alone dominate the rhythm of integration. But the Court's power is limited. Above all, it must rely on

BOX 3.6	Compared to what?

The ECJ and the US Supreme Court

The European Court of Justice—like the EU more generally—is in many ways *sui generis*: an international body with no precise counterpart anywhere in Europe or beyond. But interesting parallels, as well as contrasts, can be drawn between the ECJ and the US Supreme Court, both in terms of their power and its limits.

There are some key differences between the two. The US Supreme Court's primary function is to uphold the US constitution, whereas the EU has no such constitution. Yet even here the difference may not be as stark as it first seems. For some legal scholars the cumulative impact of the ECJ's decisions over the years amounts to a 'quiet revolution' in converting the Treaty of Rome into a constitution for Europe (see Chapter 8; Weiler 1999).

A more straightforward difference is jurisdiction, or the power to hear and decide cases. The jurisdiction of the Supreme Court is vast. It includes the constitutionally-conferred right to hear all cases involving legal disputes between the US states. More important is its appellate jurisdiction—the power to hear cases raising constitutional issues invoked by any national treaty, federal law, state law, or act. The ECJ's jurisdiction is far more confined. Its rulings on trade have had a fundamental impact on the single market and the EU more generally. But many matters of national law and most non-trade disputes between states fall outside its remit. Moreover, unlike the US Court the ECJ cannot 'cherry-pick' a few select cases it would like to hear. Finally, recruitment, appointment, and tenure differ, with US Supreme Court justices seated for life following an involved and often highly politicized appointment and confirmation process. Judges on the ECJ, by contrast, are appointed with comparatively little publicity and they remain relatively unknown for their six-year renewable term.

Yet similarities are also telling. In both cases, the interpretations and rulings of these higher courts take precedence over those of lower or national courts. In both cases, these rulings must be enforced by lower courts. Like the US Supreme Court in its early decades, the ECJ's earlier decisions helped consolidate the authority of the Union's central institutions. But perhaps the most interesting similarities involve the debates surrounding these Courts' power and political role. In the case of the US Supreme Court, concerns about the politicization and activism of the Court are well known, especially in its rulings on abortion and racial equality (see Bonneau and Striko 2006). In the EU too, however, concerns about the Court's procedure, its ability to push integration forward, and the possible expansion of its authority have propelled the Court into the heart of political debates about the future of the EU. Thus, whatever their differences, both these Courts have raised fundamental questions about the proper limits of judicial activism and the role of courts in democratic societies more generally.

member states to carry out its rulings. The perception that it has tended to pursue integrationist goals has led member states to grant it only a very limited role in the justice and foreign policy pillars. In short, the precise policy-making powers of the Court—and how they should be wielded—remains a contested issue in EU politics.

The relationship between these main institutional players—Commission, Council, Parliament, and Court—is constantly changing as power swings across and between institutions. This shift is not always reflected in formal treaty changes or reform. For instance, the Council of Ministers' ability to impose its view has declined over the years as the bargaining power of the Parliament has increased, whereas the European Council's accumulation of agenda-setting power has usurped the Commission's traditional and legal right of initiative. Similarly, the emergence of European summits as problem solvers and package dealers has reduced the primacy and manoeuvrability of the Council of Ministers. Finally, the Court has significantly—even fundamentally—shaped integration and policy-making by issuing judgements with significant policy and institutional implications.

Both formal and informal institutional change has contributed to a blurring of powers among the core institutions. This blurring of power does not mean that the formal rules do not matter. Rules and treaty provisions serve as the fundamental base of power from which institutions can and do act. But the formal powers are starting points only: knowing how the institutions exploit, compete for, and ultimately share power is also crucial for grasping how the institutions work (see Box 3.7).

Why Institutions Matter

Examining the institutions and how they work is essential to understand wider themes in EU policy and politics. First, it gives us a starting point from which to examine the Union's policy process. Secondly, it helps us to identify the diversity of actors involved in EU politics, and to understand how they together determine the shape and speed of integration (see Box 3.8). Finally, it reminds us that there are many interesting questions still to be asked about the final destination for European integration. Are we heading towards a European state? How democratic or efficient would it be? Who or what will determine the pace and shape of integration? More particularly, the EU's institutions help illustrate the three central themes of this book: (1) the extent to which the EU is an 'experiment in motion'; (2) the importance of power-sharing and seeking of consensus; and (3) the capacity of the EU structures to cope with the Union's expanding scope.

Experimentation and Change

The EU's system of institutions reveals clearly the extent to which the Union has developed and changed since the establishment of the European Coal and Steel

BOX 3.7	How it really works

Turf wars!

The relationship between the major institutions is both consensual and conflictual. Cooperation is unceasing because of the shared recognition that all institutions must compromise and work together to get a policy through or decision agreed. Even decisions that appear to rest with one institution actually involve extensive institutional cooperation and compromise. For instance, the Treaties say the Council has the 'power to take decisions', but in most cases the Council may only act on the basis of a proposal from the Commission and after consulting, cooperating, or co-deciding with the EP.

Yet inter-institutional rivalry is also fierce as each institution jealously guards its prerogatives (say, to initiate policy or control budgets). New institutionalist scholars such as Armstrong and Bulmer (1998) and Mark Pollack (2004) have underlined the importance of this institutional dynamic. Perceived attempts by one institution to encroach on another's 'turf' often elicit heated responses or fierce demonstrations of institutional loyalty. For example, in 2005 the Commission accused the Council of Ministers (indeed it took the Council to the Court of Justice), claiming the Council's policy to counter the spread of small arms in West Africa clashed with Commission's power over development aid, specifically its regional policy of conflict prevention (*European Voice* 1–8 March 2006). The Commission was not necessarily opposed to the substance of the Council's move (it supported the same), but it did object to Council treading on 'its' turf in the area of development policy.

Community in 1951. As we have seen, the institutions have adapted over time to perform a variety of tasks. Some tasks are formally mandated by the founding Treaties and others have developed in an informal manner. A variety of pressures has combined to encourage a sort of 'task expansion' and the reinventing of the institutions over time. Sometimes institutions such as the Parliament or the Commission have actively sought to expand their influence. On other occasions, very real gaps in the capacity of the EU to respond to events and crises have resulted in an ad hoc expansion of the informal powers of the institutions. For example, the need for common action on the environment meant the informal environmental activities of the EU institutions predated the formal advances introduced by the Treaties. Sometimes member states themselves have felt a need to establish a greater degree of informal cooperation in certain areas, but were not quite ready to be legally bound by formal Treaties. A good example is the gradual expansion of the powers of the EU institutions in the area of Justice and Home Affairs (see Chapter 7). Studying the institutional dynamics of the EU allows us not only to understand the extent to which the EU itself is subject to experimentation and constant change, but also to pose questions about where this process might be headed.

BOX 3.8	Other institutional bodies

Several smaller institutions carry out a variety of representative, oversight, or managerial functions in the EU. By far the most significant of these specialized institutions is the **European Central Bank (ECB)**. Based in Frankfurt and modelled on the fiercely independent German Bundesbank, the ECB is charged with a fundamental task: formulating the EU's monetary policy, including ensuring monetary stability, setting interest rates, and issuing and managing the euro (see Chapter 6). The ECB is steered by an executive board (made up primarily of national central bank governors) and headed by a President who is chosen by member states, but who cannot formally be removed by them. The Bank's independence and power undoubtedly help ensure monetary stability but also have raised concerns about transparency and accountability. Its executive board is appointed by member states, and it must report to the EP several times a year. But its decisions are not made public and it enjoys considerable independence from other institutions or member states themselves. While still a young institution, the Bank is certain to become a more important, but also controversial player in EU politics (see McNamara 2005).

Exercising an oversight function is the **Court of Auditors** whose 27 members are charged with scrutinizing the EU's budget and financial accounts. Acting as the 'financial conscience' of the EU, the Court has increased its stature and visibility in recent years as public concern over fraud and mismanagement has mounted. Its annual and specialized reports consist mainly of dry financial management assessment, but they also have uncovered more spectacular and often serious financial misconduct (see Laffan 2006).

Several smaller institutions carry out a primarily representative function (see Jeffrey 2006). For instance the **Economic and Social Committee (ESC)** represents various employer, trades union, and other social or public interests (such as farmers or consumers) in EU policy-making. Chosen by the national governments, these representatives serve in a part-time function advising the Commission and other institutions on relevant proposals. Their opinions can be well researched but are not usually influential. The **Committee of the Regions and Local Authorities** suffers from a similar lack of influence. Created by the Maastricht Treaty, the Committee must be consulted on proposals affecting regional interests (cohesion funding, urban planning) and can issue its own opinions and reports. However, it is internally divided and its membership debilitatingly diverse (powerful regional leaders from Germany and Belgium sit alongside representatives from English town parishes). It has yet to exert the influence its proponents originally envisioned, but perhaps its real role is as a channel of communication across several layers of governance.

Power-sharing and Consensus

Scholars of European integration have long (and fiercely) debated where power lies in the EU. Do the EU's institutions drive the integration process forward, or do national governments remain in control of the process? The two sides of this debate have been taken up by neofunctionalists and intergovernmentalists respectively. Both sides can cite changes in formal EU rules to buttress their case. For example, as the Parliament has gained powers and the Council of Ministers has accepted more proposals on the basis of QMV rather than unanimous voting, it could be claimed that supranationalism is on the rise. On the other hand, as the European Council has come to dominate high-level agenda setting, or as various countries have formally opted out of certain policies (such as economic and monetary union), it could be said that intergovernmentalism is holding strong.

But depicting integration as a pitched battle between supranational institutions and the member states misses the point. Competition is fierce but so, too, is the search for consensus. Enormous efforts go into forging agreements acceptable to most. The overall trajectory of the integration process is thus a result of toing and froing between a wide variety of actors and external pressures. This image is quite neatly captured in Wallace's (2000) description of EU governance as a pendulum, swinging sometimes towards intergovernmental solutions and sometimes towards supranational solutions but not always in equal measure. In this type of system, institutional power is a product of how well institutions engage with other actors—lobbyists, experts, governments, and other international organizations—at different levels of governance. Focusing on the institutional actors of the EU and how they cooperate or compete with each other and other actors helps us to begin to make sense of the EU's very complex policy-making process.

Scope and Capacity

The study of the EU institutions also helps us to understand the changing scope of the European Union's activity and the extent to which existing structures have the capacity to cope with nearly constant change. With each successive enlargement, and as more and more competences have been formally adopted in the Treaties, the institutions have had to adapt accordingly. Increasingly, scholars have come to ask whether the existing institutional structures, originally conceived for a Community of only six member states, are adequate to cope with the demands of an EU of 27 or more member states (see Box 3.9). This concern was very much in evidence following rejection by French and Dutch voters of the Constitutional Treaty in 2005. Yet by some measures the institutions are functioning surprisingly well even without constitutional reform. In 2006–7, the EU institutions managed to strike a five-year budget settlement (of sorts), passed major legislation deregulating services and another landmark policy regulating chemicals. The predicted decision-making gridlock following enlargement did not occur, although some reform of institutional rules to cope with the recent and future expansion of the Union's membership became widely viewed as both essential and inevitable, and the issue was at least partially addressed in the Reform Treaty.

It is always easy to argue that strengthening European cooperation means further empowering its institutions. Yet, policy cooperation has been extended in a variety of different ways that have expanded the scope of the EU without necessarily expanding the power of its institutions. The careful exclusion of the ECJ from most areas of foreign and security policy is an important example. Similarly, the weak role played by

BOX 3.9	Enlargement's institutional impact

Enlargement brought both opportunities and headaches to the EU's institutions. The impact has varied across institutions, with some adapting more smoothly than others. The European Parliament, despite real linguistic challenges (see Box 1.7), seems to have had the least difficulty absorbing new members. Decisions are based on majority votes and the EP has shown that it is still able to push through difficult legislation even with 785 MEPs. Moreover, the quality of MEPs from new countries is high, with many having held important positions in their own states (including Presidents and Ministers).

In the Commission the new members hold out the prospect of revitalizing and renewing that institution with fresh ideas and reform-minded Europeans. On the other hand, a Commission of 27 has resulted in a less cosy and, arguably, more intergovernmental body as Commissioners find it easier to assert national interests in a larger, less collegial Commission. This dynamic may well change with a reduction in the number of Commissioners after 2014.

In the Council the challenges of enlargement are most keenly felt. Since 2004 the Council has found it increasingly difficult to push through important decisions in areas of foreign policy and police cooperation which require unanimity. National vetoes are not necessarily more common in an EU of 27 (see House of Lords 2006; Hagemann and De Clerck-Sachsse 2007). But Council meetings are certainly more time-consuming and not always as productive. On important questions, all or most member states still want to present their positions and may insist on lengthy interventions. The result is less time for real discussion and compromise-seeking, the essence of what makes the Council function.

All in all, the impact of enlargement on the institutions reflects its wider impact on the EU. It has brought a mix of logistical headaches, challenges, doubts, and crises, but also the promise of fresh impulse and drive and energy for a Union otherwise threatened by stagnation and inertia.

the Commission and EP in most aspects of the Common Foreign and Security Policy reminds us of the potential of the member states to reassert control when required. Finally, if there is one lesson to be learned from the study of the EU institutions, it is their remarkable ability to adapt and change as new requirements are placed upon them. This chapter has tried to show that while the capacity of EU institutions may be limited, their ability to adapt often seems limitless.

Conclusion

The EU's institutions and their interaction is complex, but so, too, is the diverse polity they help to govern. Here, we have attempted to cut through this complexity by focusing on the institutions' powers, and what they do with them. We have stressed, too, the importance of cooperation and rivalry between the institutions. Each institution introduced here has its own agenda, but virtually no important policy area can be agreed without some (and usually, quite a large) measure of consensus spanning the EU's institutions (see Peterson and Shackleton 2006). The institutions are as interdependent as the member states that make up the EU. We have highlighted why these institutions matter, and how they fit into the wider system of EU politics and policy-making. Moreover, we have suggested that institutions do not operate alone. Today the EU's institutions must deal with an ever-broader range of actors, including an increasing number of member states (see Chapters 4 and 9), but also an increasingly active group of organized interests (Chapter 5). Above all, understanding institutions helps us to explore broader questions of how and why the EU works the way it does.

As the EU takes on new tasks, the burden on these institutions will increase. The EU's growing role in areas such as migration, foreign and defence policy, food safety, and global climate change means that other agencies and bodies (including international ones that transcend Europe itself) will join the institutional mix that helps govern EU politics. Further institutional reform is both necessary and inevitable to cope with the increasing size and policy scope of the EU. But given the challenge of obtaining unanimous and public support for major institutional change, we suggest that institutional reform—like so much else in the EU—is likely to be incremental and pragmatic rather than spectacular or far-sighted.

? DISCUSSION QUESTIONS

1. Which EU institution is most 'powerful' in your view and why?
2. Why has the balance of powers between the EU's institutions shifted over time?
3. Which institution could most accurately be described as the 'motor of integration'?
4. Is the relationship between the EU's institutions characterized more by cooperation or conflict?

→ FURTHER READING

For a rich and insightful collection of chapters on all the EU's major institutions, see Peterson and Shackleton (2006). Nugent (2006) provides a thorough and detailed overview of the structure and operation of key institutions. Helpful examinations of individual institutions include: Spence's (2006) analysis of the Commission; Hayes-Renshaw and Wallace's (2006) revised classic study of the Council of Ministers which also includes analysis of the European Council; Corbett *et al.*'s (2007) definitive account of the workings of the Parliament; and Weiler's (1999) provocative and thoughtful essays on the Court and EU's legal identity. Armstrong and Bulmer (1998) use the new institutionalism as a framework to analyse the interaction of these institutions and how they affect EU policy and politics.

Armstrong, K., and Bulmer, S. (1998), *The Governance of the Single European Market* (Manchester and New York: Manchester University Press).

Bulmer, S. (1998), 'New Institutionalism and the Governance of the Single European Market', *Journal of European Public Policy* 5/3: 365–86.

Corbett, R., Jacobs, F., and Shackleton, M. (2007), *The European Parliament*, 7th edn. (London: Cartermill).

Hayes-Renshaw, F., and Wallace, H. (2006), *The Council of Ministers*, 2nd edn. (Basingstoke: Palgrave).

Nugent, N. (2006), *The Government and Politics of the European Union*, 6th edn. (Basingstoke and Durham, NC: Palgrave and Duke University Press).

Peterson, J., and Shackleton, M. (eds.) (2006), *The Institutions of the European Union*, 2nd edn. (Oxford: Oxford University Press).

Spence, D. (ed.) (2006), *The European Commission*, 3rd edn. *(London: John Harper)*.

Weiler, J. H. H. (1999), *The Constitution of Europe* (Cambridge: Cambridge University Press).

WEB LINKS

Most of the EU's institutions have their own website which can be accessed through the EU's official portal site, 'The European Union online' (www.europa.eu). Below are the specific official websites of some of the institutions introduced in this chapter:

- European Commission: http://ec.europa.eu/index_en.htm
- Council of Ministers: http://ue.eu.int/
- European Parliament: http://www.europarl.europa.eu/
- European Court of Justice: http://curia.europa.eu/
- Court of Auditors: www.eca.eu.int.
- Economic and Social Committee: http://eesc.europa.eu/
- Committee of the Regions: http://www.cor.europa.eu/
- European Central Bank: www.ecb.int

Anyone brave enough to consider working as an intern or stagiare in one of the EU's institutions can find out more at http://ec.europa.eu/stages/. For recent updates on institutional developments, especially in relation to treaty reform, see www.euractiv.com. The London-based University Association for Contemporary European Studies (UACES) (www.uaces.org) announces regular workshops and lectures on the EU institutions held in the UK and (occasionally) on the European continent. For information on conferences and lectures held in the US, see the website of the US European Union Studies Association (EUSA) which can be found at www.eustudies.org.

Visit the Online Resource Centre that accompanies this book for additional material: www.oxfordtextbooks.co.uk/orc/bomberg2e/

CHAPTER 4

Member States

Brigid Laffan and Alexander Stubb

Introduction	72	Managing EU Business	86
Six Determining Features	73	Explaining Member States' Engagement	86
Entry Date	73		
Size	76	Conclusion	88
Wealth	78		
State Structure	80	DISCUSSION QUESTIONS	89
Economic Ideology	81	FURTHER READING	89
Integration Preference	81	WEB LINKS	91
Member States in Action	84		

▌ Chapter Overview

This chapter focuses on the European Union's (EU's) most essential component: its member states. It examines six factors that determine how any state engages with the EU: date of entry, size, wealth, state structure, economic ideology, and integration preference. We then explore how member states behave in the Union's institutions and seek to influence the outcome of negotiations in Brussels. We focus throughout on the informal as well as formal activities of the member states. The final section explores the insights offered by theory in analysing the relationship between the EU and its member states.

Introduction

States are the essential building blocks of the EU. Without states there is no EU. All EU treaties are negotiated and ratified by the 'high contracting parties': that is, the governments of the member states. By joining the EU, the traditional nation-state is transformed into a member state. This transformation involves an enduring commitment to participate in political and legal processes that are beyond the state but embrace the state. Membership of the Union has significant effects on national systems of policy-making, on national institutions, and on national identity, sovereignty, and democracy. Put simply, once a state joins the Union, politics may begin at home but they no longer end there. National politics, polities, and policies become 'Europeanized' (see Box 4.1).

Member states shape the EU as much as the EU shapes its member states. The decision to join the Union is a decision to become locked into an additional layer of governance and a distinctive form of 'Euro-politics', which is neither wholly domestic nor international but shares attributes of both. This chapter explores this interactive dynamic. We tackle questions such as: what is the role of the member states in the EU system? What is it about the EU that has led the member states to invest so much

---

BOX 4.1   Key concepts and terms

Acquis communautaire is a French phrase that denotes the rights and obligations derived from the EU treaties, laws, and Court rulings. In principle, new member states joining the EU must accept the entire *acquis*.

Demandeur is the French term often used to refer to those demanding something (say regional or agricultural funds) from the EU.

Europeanization is the process whereby national systems (institutions, policies, governments, and even the polity itself) adapt to EU policies and integration more generally, while also themselves shaping the European Union.

Flexible integration (also called 'reinforced' or 'enhanced cooperation') denotes the possibility for some member states to pursue deeper integration without the participation of others. Examples include EMU and the **Schengen Agreement** in which some member states have decided not to participate fully. The Amsterdam and Nice Treaties institutionalized the concept of flexible integration through their clauses on enhanced cooperation.

Tours de table allow each national delegation in a Council of Ministers meeting to make an intervention on a given subject. In an EU of 27 member states *tours de table* have become less common. If every minister or national official intervened for five minutes on each subject, the Council would not get any business done.

in the collective project? How do member states engage with the EU? What factors determine how any member state behaves as an EU member?

Six Determining Features

The twenty-seven member states bring to the Union their distinctive national histories, state traditions, constitutions, legal principles, political systems, and economic capacity. A variety of languages (there are 23 official working languages in the EU) and an extraordinary diversity of national tastes and cultures accentuate the mosaic-like character of Europe. The continental enlargement of the Union (twelve new states since 2004) has deepened its pre-existing diversity. Managing difference is thus a key challenge to the Union. To understand how the EU really works, we must seek to understand the multinational and multicultural character of the European Union and its institutions.

Classifying the member states—including how and why they joined and how they operate within the EU—is a good first step towards understanding the member states' relationship with the EU. Six factors are extremely important. No one factor determines the relationship between the EU and a member state, but together they provide a guide to understanding member states' engagement with the EU.

Entry Date

It is useful to deploy the metaphor of an onion to characterize the expansion of the Union from its original six states to nine, ten, twelve, fifteen, and finally to 27 or more states in the years ahead (see Figure 4.1). The core of the onion is formed by France, Germany, and the four other founding members. What is now the European Union was originally the creation of six states that were occupied or defeated in the Second World War. It is the creation especially of France, a country that needed to achieve a settlement with its neighbour and historical enemy, Germany. From the outset the key relationship in the European Union was between France and Germany. As explained in Chapter 2, the Franco-German alliance and the Paris–Bonn axis—now Paris–Berlin—have left enduring traces on the fabric of integration. The Elysée Treaty (1963) institutionalized very strong bilateral ties between these two countries. The intensity of interaction should not be taken as evidence of continuous agreement between France and Germany on major European issues. Rather, much of the interaction has worked to iron out conflicts between them.

Close personal relationships between German Chancellor Helmut Schmidt and French President Valery Giscard d'Estaing in the 1970s and Chancellor Helmut Kohl and President François Mitterrand in the 1980s and early 1990s were key to the most ambitious steps forward in European integration, including the creation of the

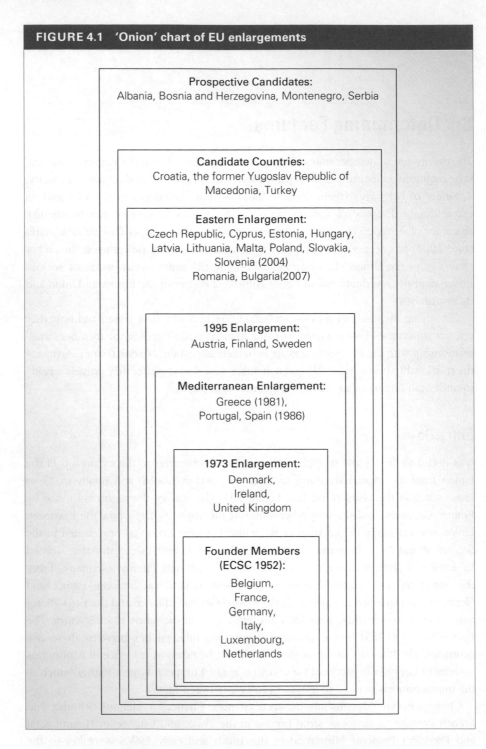

FIGURE 4.1   'Onion' chart of EU enlargements

Prospective Candidates:
Albania, Bosnia and Herzegovina, Montenegro, Serbia

Candidate Countries:
Croatia, the former Yugoslav Republic of
Macedonia, Turkey

Eastern Enlargement:
Czech Republic, Cyprus, Estonia, Hungary,
Latvia, Lithuania, Malta, Poland, Slovakia,
Slovenia (2004)
Romania, Bulgaria(2007)

1995 Enlargement:
Austria, Finland, Sweden

Mediterranean Enlargement:
Greece (1981),
Portugal, Spain (1986)

1973 Enlargement:
Denmark,
Ireland,
United Kingdom

**Founder Members
(ECSC 1952):**
Belgium,
France,
Germany,
Italy,
Luxembourg,
Netherlands

European Monetary System (a precursor to EMU), the single market programme, and the euro. The Franco-German relationship was challenged by geopolitical change in Europe following the collapse of communism. German unification and the opening up of the eastern half of the continent altered the bilateral balance of power, with Germany no longer a junior political partner to France. The change was symbolically captured by the relocation of the German capital to Berlin.

It is premature to talk of the demise of the Franco-German relationship; it remains important. But changing geopolitics and enlargement to the east have profoundly altered the context within which it is played out. To illustrate, France and the UK—not Germany—have been in the forefront of EU defence cooperation. Similarly, in negotiations on the financial framework for 2007–2013, France and the UK often joined forces against Germany, the biggest net contributor of the EU budget. On the other hand, Germany, the UK, and many of the new member states have driven market liberalization against a more protectionist France.

The four other founder member states—Italy, Belgium, Luxembourg, and the Netherlands—see themselves as part of the hard core of the Union. The Benelux countries (Belgium, Luxembourg, and the Netherlands) were traditionally at the centre of developments, often ready to push for deeper integration. They were all deeply committed to the 'Community method' of law-making (institution-led rather than intergovernmental) and supportive of a strong, supranational Union. This dynamic, however, has changed in recent times. Cooperation between the Benelux states began weakening in the 2000 Nice European Council where one of the most bitter disagreements concerned a proposal to give the Netherlands more votes than Belgium in weighted voting on the Council. Since 2005 and Dutch rejection of the Constitutional Treaty, Benelux cooperation has been at best lukewarm, at worst non-existent. In fact, the 2007 EU summit that agreed the text of the new Reform Treaty featured a blazing row between the Belgian and Dutch Prime Ministers, with one attendee commenting: 'we thought they might come to blows' (*Financial Times*, 25 June 2007).

Italy has oscillated between active involvement in EU diplomacy and a passive presence in the system. It has traditionally been enthusiastic about European institution-building, but not consistently so (see Bindi and Cisci 2005). More generally, Italy's relationship with the EU and other member states is hampered not by a lack of enthusiasm but by endemic instability in its governing coalitions.

All states joining the EU after its initial formative period had to accept the Union's existing laws and obligations (or *acquis communautaire*; see Box 4.1), its institutional system, and way of doing business, all of which had been formed without their input. Thus for all latecomers, adjustment and adaptation to the EU was a process that began before their date of accession and continued well after membership. With the expansion of the Union's tasks, the burden of adjustment has grown for each successive wave of accession. As Chapters 6 and 7 demonstrate, the EU has taken on new policy areas over the years ranging from environmental policy to police cooperation. (The *acquis communautaire* has grown to cover over 80,000 pages of legislation.) This expansion has made it even more difficult for outsiders to catch up and adapt to membership (see Chapter 9).

Size

As in all political systems, size matters in the EU. The distinction between large and small states is often evoked in political and media discussions about representation in the EU. At the cumbersome negotiations on the Treaty of Nice, which focused on the re-weighting of votes in the Council and the number of Commissioners each state could appoint, tensions between large and small states escalated. Nice settled little, and battles between large and small states marked negotiations surrounding the 2004 Constitutional Treaty and its replacement in 2007. But battles over voting weights were not only fought between large and small: in 2007, the President of Poland went as far as to argue that his country deserved more votes in the Council to compensate for the number of Poles murdered by the Nazis during the Second World War.

In any event, a more nuanced approach to understanding the impact of size is warranted. The EU really consists of four clusters of states—large, medium, small, and micro-states (see Table 4.1). The first cluster contains six large states: Germany, United Kingdom, France, Italy, Spain, and Poland. Together they make up about 70 per cent of the population of EU-27. (Even here we find dissent: Germany, France, and the UK are certainly seen as the 'big three', with Italy seen as less powerful, and some would dispute Spain's and Poland's categorization as large states.) The next cluster consists of medium-sized states: Romania, the Netherlands, Greece, Belgium, Portugal, the Czech Republic, and Hungary, whose populations range from 10 to 22 million inhabitants. The third cluster is one of small states: Sweden, Austria, Bulgaria, Denmark, Finland, Slovakia, Ireland, Lithuania, Latvia, Slovenia, and Estonia, which all have populations of between 1 and 9 million. The fourth category, micro-states, consists of Cyprus, Luxembourg, and Malta. In recent years there has mostly been an increase of medium, small, and micro-states; Poland is the exception to the rule.

Size has implications for power and presence in the Union's political and economic system. The power of large states is not just expressed in voting power in the Council. It manifests itself in political, economic, and diplomatic influence (see Wallace 2005: 38 ff). Large states can call on far more extensive and specialized administrative and technical resources in the policy process than small states, and their diplomatic presence is far stronger throughout the world. The German Chancellor, regardless of who holds the post, is usually the most powerful politician at European Council meetings. Small states, however, enjoy important advantages in EU negotiations. They tend to have fewer vital interests than larger states, their interests can be aggregated with much greater ease, and the potential for conflict and competing claims among different social groups is reduced. Luxembourg, for example, can concentrate all of its diplomatic energy on protecting its traditional industries, its liberal banking laws, and its presence in EU institutions.

TABLE 4.1 Clusters of member states and candidate countries by size

Current member states

(figure in brackets = approximate population in millions in 2007)

Large	Medium	Small	Micro
Germany (82)	Romania (22)	Sweden (9)	Cyprus (0.8)
France (63)	Netherlands (16)	Austria (8)	Luxembourg (0.5)
UK (61)	Greece (11)	Bulgaria (8)	Malta (0.4)
Italy (59)	Belgium (11)	Denmark (5)	
Spain (44)	Portugal (11)	Finland (5)	
Poland (38)	Czech Republic (10)	Slovakia (5)	
	Hungary (10)	Ireland (4)	
		Lithuania (3)	
		Latvia (2)	
		Slovenia (2)	
		Estonia (1)	

Candidate countries

Large	Medium	Small	Micro
Turkey (73)		Croatia (4)	
		Macedonia (2)	

Eurostat 2007

Although size matters, it has little bearing on national approaches to substantive issues of EU policy that are formed by economic considerations, domestic interests, and the proposed nature of the change. Thus, small states are unlikely to band together against the large states in substantive policy discussions. Their interests, just like those of the larger states, diverge. Coalition patterns in the Council have always consisted of a mix of large and small states in any particular policy domain.

Small states do, however, have a common interest in maintaining the EU's institutional balance, the 'rules of the game', and their level of representation in the system. From the outset, the small EU states have been wary of proposals that privilege a small group of larger states, which could dictate policy for the Union as a whole. Small states are thus keen supporters of procedural and legal orthodoxy in the Union. The key point here is that the multilateral, institutionalized, and legal processes of the Union have created a relatively benign environment for small states.

In the past, the European Union successfully managed to expand its membership to include both large and small states without undermining the balance between them or causing undue tension. This began to change in the 1990s. The 1995 enlargement and the prospect of further enlargement to the east and south heightened the salience of the small-state/large-state divide in the Union. The struggle for power—as reflected in number of Commissioners, votes in the Council, or seats in the European Parliament each member state receives—figured on the EU agenda for over a decade, from 1995 to 2007 and beyond. Negotiating the relative power of member states has not been easy. Many would argue that the institutional debate has been the poisoned chalice of the EU over the past few years.

Wealth

The original European Economic Community had only one serious regional poverty problem: the Italian Mezzogiorno. As such, 'cohesion' (or regional development) was not an important concern. The first enlargement in 1973 to include the UK, Denmark, and Ireland increased the salience of regional disparities in the politics of the Union. The UK had significant regional problems, with declining industrial areas and low levels of economic development in areas such as Northern Scotland, Wales, and Northern Ireland. The Republic of Ireland had per capita incomes that were about 62 per cent of the EU average at the time. The Mediterranean enlargements in the 1980s to include Greece, Spain, and Portugal (all relatively poor states) accentuated the problem of economic divergence.

By the 1980s, the Union as an economic space consisted of a 'golden triangle' which ran from southern England, through France and Germany to northern Italy and southern, western, and northern peripheries. Although committed to harmonious economic development from the outset, the Union did not have to expand its budgetary commitment to poorer Europe until the single market programme in the mid-1980s. At that point, Europe's poorer states successfully linked the economic liberalization of the 1992 programme with an enhanced commitment to greater cohesion in the Union. This commitment manifested itself in a doubling of the financial resources devoted to declining regions, or those with a per capita income less than 75 per cent of the EU average (see Table 4.2). In addition, four member states whose overall gross domestic product (GDP) was low—Spain, Portugal, Greece, and Ireland—were granted extra aid (in the form of a Cohesion Fund) as a prize for agreeing to monetary union. Of the four states, Ireland was the first to lose its cohesion status.

With eastern enlargement in 2004 and 2007, the poverty gap between the member states grew considerably wider. The average income in the new EU-25 was about 10 per cent lower than the EU-15 average. Today GDP per capita in all new member states and candidate countries remains under the EU-27 average (see Table 4.2). Cyprus and Slovenia rank as the richest of the new members, while Romania and Bulgaria—the 2007 entrants—are the poorest.

TABLE 4.2   Member states' gross domestic product in 2005

(1000 € at market prices per inhabitant)

European Union average	22.3		
Luxembourg	64.3	Greece	16.3
Ireland	38.8	Portugal	14.1
Denmark	38.4	Slovenia	13.8
Sweden	31.9	Malta	11.5
Netherlands	31.0	Czech Republic	9.7
Finland	30.0	Hungary	8.8
UK	29.8	Estonia	8.2
Austria	29.8	Slovakia	7.1
Belgium	28.5	Poland	6.4
France	27.3	Lithuania	6.0
Germany	27.2	Latvia	5.7
Italy	24.3	Romania	3.7
Spain	20.9	Bulgaria	2.8
Cyprus	18.0		
Candidate Countries (3)			
Croatia	7.0		
Turkey	4.0		
Macedonia	2.3		

Eurostat 2006

The promotion of economic and social cohesion will continue to resonate in the politics of integration well into the future. During 2007–2013, cohesion policy will account for around 35 per cent of the total EU budget (see Chapter 6). How those funds are distributed between and across member states will be contentious. After eastern enlargement many of the former recipients of cohesion funds (including Spain and Ireland) were no longer eligible for many EU funds which were now funnelled towards the newer and poorer member states.

Economic divergence has a significant impact on how the EU works. First, it influences the pecking order in the Union. The poor countries are perceived as *demandeurs* in the Union, dependent on EU subsidies. Secondly, attitudes towards the size and distribution of the EU budget are influenced by contrasting views between net beneficiaries and net contributors. With the growth of the EU budget, a distinct 'net contributors club' has emerged in the Union, which is led by Germany but joined also by the United Kingdom, the Netherlands, Austria, Sweden, Finland, and Denmark. These states are committed to controlling increases in the EU budget and to limiting the budgetary costs of cohesion. On the other hand, the poor countries as beneficiaries of financial transfers tend to argue for larger budgetary resources and additional instruments.

Thirdly, relative wealth influences attitudes towards EU regulation, notably in relation to environmental and social policy. The richer states have more stringent, developed systems of regulation that impose extra costs on their productive industries. They thus favour the spread of higher standards of regulation to peripheral Europe. By contrast, the poorer states, in their search for economic development, often want to avoid imposing the costs of onerous regulation on their industries. Overall, environmental and social standards have risen in Europe, particularly in peripheral Europe, but not to the extent desired by the wealthier states.

State Structure

The internal constitutional structure of a member state has an impact on how it operates in the EU. The Union of 27 has three federal states—Germany, Austria, and Belgium. Others are unitary states or quasi-unitary. (The line is not always easy to draw. Unitary states can have subnational governments, self-governing regions, and autonomous communities. For example, Spain and the UK can be considered as de facto federations.) The subnational units in all three federal states have played a significant role in the recent constitutional development of the Union. The German Länder, in particular, insisted in the 1990s that they be given an enhanced say in German European policy. They have been advocates of subsidiarity (see Box 2.2) and the creation of the Committee of the Regions. In the 1992 Maastricht Treaty, they won the right to send Länder ministers and officials to represent Germany in the Council of Ministers. Representatives of the German and Austrian Länder, representatives of the Belgian regions and cultural communities, as well as ministers in the Scottish executive now sit at the Council table and can commit their national governments.

In addition to direct representation, there has been an explosion of regional and local offices in Brussels from the mid-1980s onwards. Increasingly, state and regional governments, local authorities, and cities feel the need for direct representation in Brussels. Their offices act as a conduit of information from the EU to the subnational level within the member states. They engage in tracking EU legislation, lobbying for grants, and seeking partners for European projects. Not unexpectedly, there can be tension between national governments and the offices that engage in paradiplomacy in the Brussels arena (see Chapter 5).

Economic Ideology

Much of what the EU does is designed to create the conditions of enhanced economic integration through market-building. The manner in which this economic liberalization has developed has been greatly influenced by the dominant economic and social paradigms of the member states. Different visions of the proper balance between public and private power, or between the state and market have left their traces on how the EU works.

Although all six founding member states might be regarded as adhering to a continental or Christian democratic model of capitalism, there are important differences amongst them. For instance, France traditionally has supported a far more interventionist EU than the German economic model would tolerate. Arguably, the French statist tradition has made little headway in the Union's system of economic governance, at least before 2007 when a new French President, Nicolas Sarkozy, persuaded a German Council Presidency to replace the phrase 'free and undistorted competition' with 'a social market aiming at full employment' as a central goal of the draft EU Reform Treaty.

Differences between France and Germany fade in comparison to differences between continental capitalism and the Anglo-Saxon tradition. The accession of the UK in 1973 and the radical deregulatory policies of successive Conservative governments brought the Anglo-Saxon economic paradigm into the Union. The UK has been a supporter of deregulation and economic liberalization in the Union but not of re-regulation at Union level, particularly in the social and environmental fields. The Anglo-Saxon tradition, however, has been somewhat balanced by the accession of the Nordic states with a social democratic tradition of economic governance and social provision, combined with a strong belief in market liberalization. The Anglo-Saxon economic model gained further ground with the 2004 and 2007 enlargements. The new Eastern states generally favour a more liberal economic agenda. They were instrumental in pushing for a more liberal services directive in 2006. However, as Goetz (2005) argues, the new member states bring a diverse set of interests to EU policy-making and intraregional cooperation between them is weak, making any notion of an 'eastern bloc' more myth than reality.

A battle of ideas continues in the Union, based on competing views about the right balance between state and market, and the role of the EU in social regulation. Competing economic paradigms underpin national preferences and are difficult to change. Generally, the Union has been far more successful in constraining member state action through regulation than in building common policies in contested areas.

Integration Preference

The terms pro- and anti-European, or 'good' European and awkward partner, are frequently bandied about to describe national attitudes towards the EU. The UK, Denmark, Poland, and the Czech Republic are usually portrayed as reluctant Europeans (see Table 4.3). Whilst not entirely false, such categorizations disguise several facts. First, attitudes towards European integration are moulded not just by nationality but

TABLE 4.3 Support for EU membership

Member State	% responding that EU membership is a 'good thing'*
Netherlands	77
Ireland	76
Luxembourg	74
Spain	73
Belgium	70
Poland	67
Romania	67
Denmark	66
Estonia	66
Germany	65
Slovakia	64
Lithuania	63
Slovenia	58
EU AVERAGE	57
Greece	55
Portugal	55
Bulgaria	55
France	52
Italy	51
Malta	51
Sweden	50
Czech Republic	46
Cyprus	44
Finland	42
UK	39
Hungary	37
Latvia	37
Austria	36

*Question: 'Generally speaking, do you think that (YOUR COUNTRY)'s membership of the European Union is a good thing, a bad thing, or good and bad?''
In the figure for Cyprus, only the interviews conducted in the part of the country controlled by the government of the Republic of Cyprus are recorded.
Eurobarometer 2007

(often more powerfully) by factors such as socio-economic class, age, or educational attainment. Secondly, in all states we find a significant split between the attitudes of those who might be called 'the top decision-makers' and the mass public. A very high proportion of elites accept that their state has benefited from EU membership, and that membership is in their state's national interest. These sentiments are not shared by the wider public in many states. Of course, governments must take public opinion into account. When coherent, public opinion sets the broad parameters of what is acceptable policy. But public opinion toward the EU—however reluctant—is only one of several factors shaping a government's position (see Table 4.3).

Some states certainly are more enthusiastic about certain developments (say, enlargement or greater transparency) than are others. But there is often an important difference between rhetoric and reality in EU negotiations. Some member states, including France and Germany, tend to use grandiose language in calling for deeper integration. However, around the negotiating table they are often the ones blocking an increase in qualified majority voting (QMV) on issues such as trade or justice and home affairs. The opposite can be true for states such as the UK. British ministers and officials are inclined to language that makes them seem reluctant about European integration. Yet, in negotiations on, for example, trade liberalization, they are often in the forefront of more or closer cooperation. In short, member states' attitudes towards integration are far more nuanced than is implied by the labels 'pro' or 'anti' Europe.

Different national preferences and attitudes are expressed most vividly during the Intergovernmental Conferences (IGCs) leading to treaty reform. These events traditionally have been managed by the states holding the Council presidency and finalized—amidst much media fanfare—at a European Council by the heads of state and government. An important feature of EU treaty change since the early 1990s has been the greater frequency with which states have been allowed to 'opt out' of certain policy developments. For example, Denmark has opted out of the euro, parts of the Schengen agreement on the free movement of people, and aspects of the Common Foreign and Security Policy.

In each IGC, member states need to decide what is negotiable and what is non-negotiable, or what they could trade in one area in return for concessions in another. The outcome is inevitably a series of complex package deals. Member states will trade off a concession on one issue (such as the size of the Commission) in exchange for the concessions of other member states on a separate issue (such as their voting weight under QMV, see Box 3.2).

Taken together, the six factors introduced in this section tell us a great deal about how the EU works. Styles of economic governance and levels of wealth have a major influence on national approaches to European regulation, and on just how much regulation each state favours at EU level. A hostile or favourable public opinion will help to determine the integration preferences of particular states. How states represent themselves in EU business is partially determined by their state structure and domestic institutions. The point is that EU member states vary across several cross-cutting dimensions, and this mix is part of what makes the EU unique.

BOX 4.2	How it really works

Intergovernmental Conferences

Article 48 of the Treaty on European Union states that 'the Government of any Member State or the Commission may submit to the Council proposals for the amendment of the Treaties on which the Union is founded'. If the Council decides that such a proposal has legs, it then calls for a 'conference of representatives of the governments', or what in EU-speak is called an Intergovernmental Conference (IGC). An IGC is the means by which the EU changes its treaties or enlarges.

An IGC is often a long and tedious process. In most cases, after months of discussions and seemingly endless *tours de table* (which allow the delegations to state and restate their national positions, see Box 4.1), the Council's General Secretariat and Presidency draft a proposed set of treaty amendments. Member states then suggest changes to the draft either in writing or orally in the meeting room. Finally a compromise is hammered out. Some issues can be solved by officials. Others demand the attention of the ministers. The most difficult questions are left to be resolved at the infamous all-night sessions of the European Council.

An IGC is always a cross-sectoral exercise; it affects many different policy areas and has an impact on the entire administrations of member governments. A sound relationship between the national capital and the Permanent Representation in Brussels is crucial for the proper functioning of the system. In many instances the actual IGC negotiators have positions that are closer to each other's than those between ministries at home. During negotiations it is usually not difficult to detect when a negotiator has been unable to coordinate the position at the national level. The code phrase is often: 'we are still studying the question back home'.

Problems of coordination in national capitals can slow progress. The 2000 IGC on the Nice Treaty, for instance, witnessed a total of 370 official negotiating hours and required ten ministerial meetings and three European Councils. To try to achieve a result more quickly but also to widen participation, a new method—a Convention on the Future of Europe (see Chapter 8)—was used to draft the 2004 Constitutional Treaty, which was then approved in a traditional IGC. However, the results of any IGC—an amended treaty—must be ratified in *all* EU member states, either by national parliaments or by referendum. The Constitutional Treaty failed to achieve full ratification, and thus had to be shelved (in favour of the 2007 Reform Treaty).

Member States in Action

Member states are not the only players in town (see Chapters 3 and 5), but national governments retain a privileged position in the EU. What emerge as national interests from domestic systems of preference formation remain central to how the EU works. Member states are not unitary actors. Rather, each consists of a myriad of players who project their preferences in the Brussels arena. National administrations, the wider public service, key interests (notably, business, trades unions, farming organizations, and other societal interests) all seek voice and representation in EU politics. A striking feature of European integration is the extent to which national actors have been drawn out of the domestic arena into the Brussels system of policy-making.

As Chapter 3 highlighted, the national and the European meet in a formal sense in the Council, the EU institution designed to give voice and representation to national preferences. At any given time there are usually around twenty official meeting rooms in use in the Council building (named after the sixteenth-century Belgian philosopher, Justus Lipsius), apart from the month of August when the Brussels system goes on holiday. Formal meetings are supplemented by bilateral meetings on the margins of Council meetings, informal chats over espressos, and by media briefings. Thus the formal system of policy-making is augmented by considerable backroom dealing, arbitrage, and informal politics. In the evenings, national officials (from some member states more than others) frequent the many bars near the Rond Point Schuman, the junction in Brussels where several EU institutions are housed. The evening trains to Zaventem (the Brussels airport) are often full of national officials making their way back to their capitals after a long day in Council working groups. Those within earshot can pick up good anecdotal evidence of how the EU actually works when member states pick over the details of EU proposals.

All member states have built up a cadre of EU specialists in their diplomatic services and domestic administrations who are the 'boundary managers' between the national and the European. Most are at home in the complex institutional and legal processes of the Union, have well-used copies of the EU treaties, read *Agence Europe* (a daily bulletin on European affairs) every morning, know their field and the preferences of their negotiating partners. The EU is a system that privileges those with an intimate knowledge of how the Union's policy process works and how business is conducted in the Council, the EP, and the Commission.

National representatives in Brussels seek to exploit their political, academic, sectoral, and personal networks to the full. With more member states, a widening agenda, and advanced communications technology, there has been a discernible increase in horizontal interaction between the member states at all levels—prime-ministerial, ministerial, senior official, and desk officer. Specialists forge and maintain links with their counterparts in other member states on a continuous basis. Deliberations are no longer left primarily to meetings at working-group level in Brussels. Sophisticated networking is part and parcel of the Brussels game. Officials who have long experience of it build up extensive personal contacts and friendships in the system.

In addition to a cadre of Brussels insiders, many government officials in national capitals find that their work also has a European dimension. For most national officials, however, interaction with the EU is sporadic and driven by developments within a particular sector. A company law specialist may have intense interaction with the EU while a new directive is being negotiated, but may then have little involvement until the same directive is up for renegotiation.

The nature of EU membership demands that all member states must commit resources and personnel to the Union's policy process. Servicing Brussels—by committing time and resources to EU negotiations—has become more onerous with new areas of policy being added, such as justice and home affairs or defence. Once a policy field becomes institutionalized in the EU system, the member states have no choice but to service the relevant committees and Councils. An empty seat at the table undermines the credibility of the state and its commitment to the collective endeavour. Besides, the weakest negotiator is always the one who is absent from the negotiations.

Managing EU Business

All member states engage in internal negotiations and coordination, above all between different national ministries and ministers, in determining what their national position will be in any EU negotiation. The coordination system in most member states is organized hierarchically. National ministers and/or the head of government will usually act as the arbiter of last resort.

In addition, all member states have either a Minister or a State Secretary of European Affairs. The Ministry of Foreign Affairs plays an important role in all member states, and most central EU coordination takes place here. However, there are a number of member states, such as Finland, where the Prime Minister's Office takes the leading role. With the increasing prominence of EU policy in national administrations, more EU business is generally shifting to the offices of Heads of government.

As discussed in Chapter 3, each member state also has a Permanent Representation in Brussels, a kind of EU embassy. In most cases it is the most important and biggest foreign representation the country maintains anywhere in the world. It is, for example, usually much bigger than an embassy in Washington DC or Moscow or a representation to the United Nations. Although the official role or the Permanent Representation of each member state varies, they all participate actively in several stages of the policy-making process. In certain member states they are the key player in the whole process.

Explaining Member States' Engagement

We have looked at the factors that determine the engagement of different states in the EU and at the member states in action. What additional purchase do we get from theory in analysing member states in the Union? The relationship between the EU and its member states has been one of the most enduring puzzles in the literature on European integration. From the outset, the impact of EU membership on statehood and on individual states has been hotly contested. At issue is whether the EU strengthens, transcends, or transforms its member states. Is the Union simply a creature of its member states? Are they still the masters of the Treaties? Or has the EU irrevocably transformed European nation-states? The relationship between the EU and its member states is a live political issue and not simply a point of contention amongst scholars. The theories and approaches introduced in Chapter 1 provide different lenses with which to analyse the member states in the Union.

Liberal intergovernmentalism provides a theoretical framework that enables us to trace the formation of domestic preferences in the member states and then to see how they are bargained in Brussels. It identifies the domestic sources of the underlying preferences and the subsequent process of interstate bargaining. The approach rightly concludes that the EU is an 'institution so firmly grounded in the core interests of national governments that it occupies a permanent position at the heart of the European political landscape' (Moravcsik 1998: 501). This approach is less helpful in tracing the impact of the EU on national preference formation or the cumulative impact of EU membership on its member states. Its focus on one-off bargains provides a snapshot of the Union at any one time rather than a film or 'moving picture' of how membership may generate deep processes of change (see Pierson 1996).

Contemporary theorists who view the EU through the lenses of multilevel (Hooghe and Marks 2003) or supranational governance (Sandholtz and Stone Sweet 1998) emphasize how the national and the European levels of governance have become intertwined, in a way that is fundamental in the EU. These approaches point to the influence of the supranational institutions—notably the Commission, Court, and Parliament—on the EU and its member states. The EU may be grounded in the core interests of the national governments, but the definition of core interest is influenced by membership of the EU and its continuous effects at the national level. Put another way, the EU has evolved into a political system in its own right that is more than the sum of its member states.

The new institutionalism offers at least two crucial insights concerning member states in the EU political system. First, its emphasis on change over time captures the give-and-take nature of EU negotiations and the manner in which norms and procedures are built up over time. Secondly, its concern with path dependency highlights the substantial resources that member states have invested in the Union (Meunier and McNamara 2007). The costs of exit are very high, so high that no state would seriously contemplate it. At best, member states have the choice of opting out of various policy regimes. Even then there are costs associated with having no seat at the table.

A policy network approach captures the fragmented and sectorized nature of the EU. It highlights the fact that the degree and nature of national adaptation differs from one policy area to another, and according to the different mix of players involved. Some policy fields, and the networks that preside over them, have been intensely Europeanized (agriculture) while others have not (transport). This approach helps us to gauge such variation and the varying involvement of different layers of government and public and private actors in different EU policy fields.

Finally, social constructivism helps us to analyse how national participants are socialized into the 'rules of the game' which characterize intergovernmental bargaining (Bulmer and Lequesne 2005a: 15). For constructivists, national interests are not predetermined but are shaped (or 'constructed') by interaction with EU actors and institutions (see Checkel 1999). In fact, the very identities of individual players in EU negotiations are viewed largely as being constructed within those negotiations, and not fixed, leading constructivists to question whether national identities and interests are gradually being replaced by European ones.

Conclusion

It is impossible to understand how the EU works without understanding the member states and their central role in the establishment and operation of the EU. In turn, the

BOX 4.3	How it really works

Decision gridlock?

Taking decisions in a big group is never easy. When the EU almost doubled its membership from 2004 to 2007 many feared that the EU would face permanent gridlock. How did things actually turn out? Studies show that from 2004 to 2006, the amount of legislation decreased compared to the rate prior to the 'big bang' enlargement (Hagemann and DeClerck-Sachsse 2007; Heisenberg 2007). Yet at the same time the EU was able to hammer out compromises at approximately the same pace as before. And the average time from a Commission initiative to an approved legal act remained approximately the same for an EU of 27 as it was for an EU of 15 (Settembri 2007).

Enlargement has, however, changed the political dynamic of the EU institutions and the role of member states within them. All of the main institutions—the Commission, the European Council, the European Parliament, and the Council of Ministers—are less cosy than before. There are simply more players around the table. The dynamic of working groups, committees, and the actual Council meetings has also changed. In Council meetings member states no longer have the ability to express their view on all issues all the time. It would simply take too long. Member states raise issues when they have a serious problem.

Every enlargement is preceded by a debate about the EU's capacity to integrate or 'absorb' new member states. The debate is focused on whether the EU's institutions, budget, and policies can accommodate a larger membership. Those who want to slow down enlargement often argue that the EU is not ready to take on board new member states before it has revised its own institutions and working methods. Previous enlargements, however, seem to indicate that while the EU is never fully prepared to enlarge, it manages just the same.

EU has altered the political, constitutional, economic, and policy framework within which the member state governments govern. Each enlargement is different and each enlargement has changed the dynamics of the EU. Many were afraid that the EU's decision-making would grind to a halt with the latest enlargement. Generally, it seems that these fears were unfounded. As a matter of fact the pace of EU decision-making was not noticeably slower than before, despite (or perhaps because of?) its expansion to 27 member states (see Box 4.3), although it was widely agreed that it needed new rules to streamline decision-making to avoid paralysis in the longer term.

All EU member states, along with some states who aspire to join the EU, are part of a transnational political process that binds them together in a collective endeavour. Their individual engagement with the Union varies enormously depending on their history, location, size, relative wealth, domestic political systems, and attitudes towards the future of the Union. Yet, all member states are actively engaged on a day-to-day basis in Brussels. National ministers, civil servants, and interest groups participate in the Commission's advisory groups, the Council working groups, and meetings of the European Council. All member states engage in bilateral relations with each of their partners, with the Commission's services, and the Council Presidency in their efforts to influence the outcome of EU policy-making. In national capitals, officials and ministers must do their homework in preparation for the continuous cycle of EU meetings. Brussels is thus part and parcel of contemporary governance in Europe. The member states are essential to how the EU works, but in turn being a member of the EU makes a state something rather different from an 'ordinary' nation-state.

? DISCUSSION QUESTIONS

1. What are the most important features determining an EU member state's attitudes towards integration?

2. Which is more powerful: the impact of the EU on its member states, or the impact of the member states on the EU?

3. How useful is theory in explaining the role of the member states in the EU?

4. How different are EU member states from 'ordinary' nation-states?

→ FURTHER READING

The literature on the member states of the Union is very diffuse. There are a large number of country studies (see, for example, George 1998, O'Donnell 2000, Closa and Heywood 2004, and Papadimitriou and Phinnemore 2007), a more limited number of comparative works (including Wessels *et al.* 2003, Bulmer and Lequesne 2005b, and Henderson 2007), and a very extensive body of policy-related work that throws some light on the EU and its member states (see, for example, Falkner 2000 and Baun *et al.*

2006). For discussions of the relationship between statehood and integration, see Hoffmann (1966), Milward (1992), and Moravcsik (1998). On national management of EU business and the impact of the EU on national institutions, see Rometsch and Wessels (1996) and Kassim *et al.* (2001).

Baun, M., Dürr, J., Marek, D., and Šaradín, P. (2006), 'The Europeanization of Czech Politics', *Journal of Common Market Studies*, 44/2: 249–80.

Bulmer, S., and Lequesne, C. (2005a), 'The EU and its Member States: An Overview', in S. Bulmer and C. Lequesne (eds.), *The Member States of the European Union* (Oxford and New York: Oxford University Press): 1–24.

———— (2005b), *The Member States of the European Union* (Oxford and New York: Oxford University Press).

Closa, C., and Heywood, P. S. (2004), *Spain and the European Union* (Basingstoke and New York: Palgrave).

Falkner, G. (2000), 'How Pervasive are Euro-Politics? Effects of EU Membership on a New Member State', *Journal of Common Market Studies* 38/2: 223–50.

George, S. (1998), *An Awkward Partner: Britain in the European Community*, 3rd edn. (Oxford and New York: Oxford University Press).

Goetz, K. H. (2005), 'The New Member States and the EU: Responding to Europe', in S. Bulmer and C. Lequesne (eds.) (2005), *The Member States of the European Union* (Oxford and New York: Oxford University Press): 254–84.

Henderson, K. (2007), *The European Union's New Democracies* (London and New York: Routledge).

Hoffmann, S. (1966), 'Obstinate or Obsolete: The Fate of the Nation-state and the Case of Western Europe', *Daedalus* 95/3: 862–915 (reprinted in S. Hoffmann (1995), *The European Sisyphus: Essays on Europe 1964–1994* (Boulder, CO and Oxford: Westview Press).

Kassim, H., Peters, B. G., and Wright, V. (eds.) (2001), *The National Co-ordination of EU Policy: The European Level* (Oxford and New York: Oxford University Press).

Milward, A. (1992), *The European Rescue of the Nation-state* (London and Berkeley: Routledge and University of California Press).

Moravcsik, A. (1998), *The Choice for Europe: Social Purpose and State Power from Messina to Maastricht* (Ithaca, NY and London: Cornell University Press and UCL Press).

O'Donnell, R. (2000), *Europe: The Irish Experience* (Dublin: Institute of European Affairs).

Papadimitriou, D., and Phinnemore, D. (2007), *Romania and the European Union* (London and New York: Routledge).

Rometsch, D., and Wessels, W. (1996), *The European Union and Member States: Towards Institutional Fusion?* (Manchester: Manchester University Press).

Wessels, W., Maurer, A., and Mittag, J. (eds.) (2003), *Fifteen Into One? The European Union and its Member States* (Manchester and New York: Manchester University Press).

WEB LINKS

The Institute for European Politics' (Berlin) website features an enormously useful 'EU 25–27 watch' which offers a round-up of current thinking on EU policies and issues in all the member states: http://www.iep-berlin.de/index.php?id=publikationen&L=1

The best place to search for websites of the member and candidate states' national administrations is http://www.europa.eu/abc/european_countries/index_en.htm

Other useful links can also be found on the homepage of the European Commission http://ec.europa.eu/index_en.htm

Visit the Online Resource Centre that accompanies this book for additional material: www.oxfordtextbooks.co.uk/orc/bomberg2e/

CHAPTER 5

Organized Interests and Lobbying

Rory Watson and Michael Shackleton

Introduction	93	Lobbying the Commission	101
Types of Actor	94	Lobbying the European Parliament	103
Private Economic Interests	94	Successful Lobbying	105
Public Interest Bodies	95	Conclusion	108
Governmental Actors	96		
The Media in Brussels	98	DISCUSSION QUESTIONS	109
The Rise of Organized Interests	98	FURTHER READING	110
Organized Interests at Work	100	WEB LINKS	110

▌ Chapter Overview

Member states and EU institutions are not the only influential actors in European Union policy-making. A host of other organized interests make their presence felt—usually behind the scenes—in EU policy and politics. They range from pan-European trade associations and regional governments to lawyers, consultants, and multinational companies. Their number has increased as the responsibilities and membership of the Union have expanded. This chapter will examine the nature of these organized interests, and why their influence as lobbyists (see Box 5.1) has increased over time in the EU process. It will also consider how the EU's institutions have responded to lobbying, a phenomenon that was not foreseen when the first Treaties were drafted in the 1950s, but is now an integral part of the EU decision-making process.

BOX 5.1	Key concepts and terms

Civil society refers to the broad collection of associations and groups (including private firms, trade unions, community groups, and non-governmental organizations) active between the level of the individual and state. These groups generally operate independently of direct government control.

Lobbying is an attempt to influence policy-makers to adopt a course of action advantageous, or not detrimental, to a particular group or interest. A lobbyist is a person employed by a group, firm, region, or country to carry out lobbying. Lobbyists in Brussels are often known as consultants or public affairs practitioners when they work on behalf of third parties. These can be governments, companies, or non-profit organizations.

A *rapporteur* is the Member of the European Parliament responsible for preparing a report in one of the Parliament's committees.

'Venue shopping' refers to the activities of an interest group searching or 'shopping' for a decision setting most favourable or receptive to their policy claims.

Introduction

All lobbyists in Brussels try to make their voices heard in the formal, institutional EU decision-making structure. Organized interests provide a wealth of information to EU policy-makers and contribute a diverse range of views to a legislative process that, on paper, features only the formal EU institutions. They also increase substantially the complexity of policy-making and raise questions about whose interests are being served in EU decision-making.

The Treaties provide a first step towards understanding the powers and roles of the different EU institutions. By contrast, there is no easy way to assess the status and influence of the many organized interests that are outside the formal institutions, but very much inside EU policy-making, whether or not they are based in Brussels. One way to start is to categorize this astonishing range of organized interests. We identify three broad and overlapping categories based on their main focus and membership (see Table 5.1):

- private interests, pursuing specific economic goals;
- public interest bodies, pursuing broader non-economic aims;
- governmental actors, representing different levels of government but not forming part of the national administrations of the member states.

As Table 5.1 indicates, these three groups together account for more than 2,500 organizations, which are mainly but not exclusively based in Brussels. They range in size from one or two people, to large offices with scores of staff. As a result,

TABLE 5.1 Overview of organized interests in the EU

Type	Approximate number of organizations	Examples
Private	1375 (plus 270 law firms and consultancies)	European Chemical Industries Council, McDonald's
Public	430 (plus 100 think tanks)	Children are the Future; European Citizen Action Service (ECAS); European Trades Union Confederation (ETUC); Greenpeace
Governmental	475	US Mission to the EU, Land of North Rhine Westphalia, Scottish Executive

Landmarks 2006

and because some lobbyists are not based permanently in Brussels, it is difficult to provide a precise figure for the total number of people working for these different groups. There are often said to be 15,000 lobbyists operating around the institutions at any given time, but the figure for full-time practitioners based in Brussels is much lower, probably between 2,000 and 2,500 (Landmarks 2006). In any case, the overall numbers involved are substantial, especially when compared with the combined personnel of all the EU institutions and specialized agencies, estimated to number only 35,000 permanent and 4,500 temporary staff (*Official Journal* L 78, Vol. 49, 15 March 2006).

Types of Actor

Private Economic Interests

Of the three types of actor we have identified, the largest category, including over 1,500 organizations, consists of private economic and business interests that come together to represent their points of view in pan-European trade federations or associations. They cover a staggering variety of business interests, ranging from the mighty (European Chemical Industry Council) to the tiny (European Lift Components Association); from the broad (Alliance for a Competitive European Industry) to the specific (Association of European Candle Manufacturers). Associations with powerful members such as automobile manufacturers, pharmaceutical companies, or food industries are extremely well resourced.

The economic activity most heavily represented in Brussels is the chemicals industry, which supports 250 organizations. In second place comes the environment sector (230) followed by the food and drink sector (210) and energy and utilities (170) (Landmarks 2006). The main areas of interest are competition policy (particularly in connection with mergers), new regulatory measures, trade defences (against the 'dumping' of foreign goods on the EU's market), product design, and any initiatives that groups see as affecting their competitiveness.

The variety of interests represented is striking. But size, for example, does not necessarily guarantee influence. Major tobacco companies have argued consistently and strongly, but unsuccessfully, against EU policies to restrict cigarette advertising. More important, perhaps, than size is regular access to decision-makers and the opportunity it provides to develop relationships of trust. Among the groups that enjoy the best access are those that represent 'pan-European' interests. In the economic field, these tend to be umbrella associations such as the main confederation of European business (which recently changed its name from the French acronym UNICE to BusinessEurope), the European Trade Union Confederation (ETUC, representing trade unions); and the Committee of Agricultural Organizations in the EU (COPA, representing agricultural interests).

To reinforce their opportunities for exercising influence, it is not unusual for multinational companies or national business organizations to be members of a pan-European or international association, while also maintaining their own representation in Brussels. Major companies, such as McDonald's, Nestlé, and Procter & Gamble, all have offices in Brussels specifically to monitor and influence EU developments that directly concern their activities. But individual firms often find it useful to form alliances with other like-minded companies. Thus, the UK's Confederation of British Industry represents British industry as a whole through its office in Brussels, and is also a collective member of BusinessEurope.

The various private interests can also call on others to assist them. There are over 40 national chambers of commerce, hailing not only from member states such as the UK and France, but also from further afield: the US, Turkey, Brazil, or Vietnam are all concerned to ensure that their own domestic economic interests are not put at risk by EU decisions. In addition, there are 270 or so law firms, political consultancies, and public affairs practitioners specializing in EU issues, all of whom advise clients on how best to present their case to the institutions. Although all EU nationalities are to be found in these various groups, the majority tend to be British or American dominated, which may reflect the greater ease and familiarity of Anglo-Saxon societies with lobbying compared to their continental European neighbours.

Public Interest Bodies

Alongside national or sectoral economic groups has grown up a multitude of European non-profit organizations representing a wide range of public interests. These are now estimated to number well over 400. Many of the smaller ones rely on EU funding for their existence. Among the most active are environmental, public health, human rights, and animal welfare non-governmental organizations (NGOs) such as Greenpeace, the World Wide Fund for Nature (WWF), the European Consumers Organization (BEUC), the European Public Health Alliance, Human Rights Watch, or the International Fund for Animal Welfare. Environmental groups have built up particularly extensive contacts inside the different institutions and, with the help of certain 'greener' governments, have influenced the Commission's sustainable development policies. Others, such as the European Citizen Action Service (ECAS) and the European Youth Forum are specifically concerned with citizens' rights inside the European Union. These types of public interest group often find a welcome reception from Members of the European Parliament (MEPs), who recognize that many of their constituents share the same concerns. MEPs are also aware of the potentially bad publicity if they fail to support 'worthy causes'.

A rather different kind of non-profit interest is represented by the handful of Brussels think tanks, such as the European Policy Centre, the Centre for European Policy Studies, and the leading Brussels-based conference organizer, Forum Europe. In addition to pushing their own ideas for, say, constitutional reform, these bodies bring together officials, academics, interest groups, and the media to analyse topical aspects of EU policy. Landmarks (2006), a Brussels-based information agency, lists over 100 EU-focused think tanks and training institutes. However, their number and resources are modest compared to those in Washington DC as well as, for that matter, those in larger European capitals (see Box 5.2).

Governmental Actors

Our final group category includes governmental organizations and representatives. These comprise the 199 representatives of the different levels of regional government in the EU, the 158 non-EU country embassies accredited to the Union, ranging from Afghanistan to Zimbabwe, and the 119 international organizations monitoring EU developments.

Regional representatives include local authorities, cities, or regional governments. The most influential amongst them are regional governments that have established delegations (they are careful not to call them embassies for fear of angering national capitals) in Brussels. These include the powerful German Länder—some of which, like North Rhine Westphalia, have a larger population and higher gross domestic product than many EU member states—but also many French, Spanish, and British regions.

External embassies and international organizations also maintain close links with all the main institutions. In the Commission, contacts are largely with the appropriate Commissioner or Director-General and, at a lower level, with the desk officers handling their part of the world or the issue that concerns them. In the Parliament, relationships are developed with individual MEPs who have the relevant country expertise, responsibility, or membership in parliamentary delegations. Third countries

BOX 5.2   Compared to what?

Lobbying in Brussels and Washington

At first glance, Brussels and Washington appear to have much in common as political capitals. Both are relatively small cities: Washington ranks as only the twenty-seventh largest city in the US, while Brussels' population is much smaller than those of either London or Paris. Brussels and Washington are federal-style capitals and centres of considerable power. Decisions taken in both affect the lives of millions of citizens far removed from where policy is made. Newcomers to the two cities often express surprise at how much Brussels and Washington feel like 'villages': the number of policy entrepreneurs seems rather small, everybody appears to know everybody, and nothing remains a secret for very long.

However, any lobbyist who approaches lobbying in Brussels in the same way as in Washington is doomed to fail. In Washington successful lobbying campaigns are often highly aggressive and public. They are often more concerned with defeating a bill than achieving some sort of consensus. In contrast, lobbying in Brussels tends to be far more discreet, low-key, consensus-seeking, and informal (Coen 2004). The Scottish Executive's Brussels office, for instance, organizes music and film evenings as a way to break down formal barriers, present itself to different audiences, and extend its network of influence. Successful lobbying in Brussels must be sensitive to over a score of different national (and subnational) cultures, and those who neglect that diversity are unlikely to succeed (see Woll 2006). A big advantage comes from being able to speak multiple languages: English and French as a minimum, but also German (which can also help with new states from Eastern Europe), Spanish, and even Dutch. Since the EU has no elected government (or opposition), political campaign contributions are very rarely used to try to affect EU policy outcomes, in stark contrast to traditional practice in Washington.

Perhaps the biggest difference is in the value attached to reliable expertise and information. The EU's institutions are extremely resource-poor compared to their closest equivalents in Washington. For example, the European Parliament has nothing remotely similar to the respected and well-funded (US) Congressional Research Service. Brussels is home to relatively few think tanks, which generate policy ideas and debates, while Washington boasts a large and diverse collection which is generally much better funded and more closely linked to major political parties (or factions within them). With fewer providers of expertise, and public institutions that are more desperate to acquire it, the power which comes from being able to gather, process, and disseminate reliable information may open more doors in Brussels than in any other major political capital.

---

also nurture direct lines of communication with EU member state governments, often through the member states' permanent representations in Brussels. Most contacts between the EU and third countries focus heavily on commercial questions such as how to boost trade and avoid commercial disputes. Increasingly, however, discussions encompass much broader issues. These include financial matters (linked, say, to the

EU's substantial funding for humanitarian and development aid) or even geostrategic, political, and human rights issues arising from the EU's developing Common Foreign and Security Policy.

The Media in Brussels

Last but not least, the media in Brussels deserve mention, particularly because their role has grown significantly in scale and importance over recent years. With just over 1,200 members, the Brussels-based media is the largest international press corps in the world, ahead of Washington. It contains full-time correspondents, freelance journalists, and (increasingly) online services from around 70 countries, including all 27 EU member states, potential future members such as Croatia and Turkey, as well as countries further afield such as Mexico and Japan. Amongst the most numerous are German and Spanish reporters, reflecting the strongly regionalized press in these countries.

The media shape policy by presenting news in a particular way (for a detailed illustration, see Lefebure and Lagneau 2001). With few exceptions (such as, perhaps, the *Financial Times* or the Brussels-based publications *European Voice*, *Europolitics* and *Agence Europe*), they invariably view EU developments through a national prism. As a social constructivist would remind us (see Table 1.1), these national prisms can lead to the presentation of the same facts in very different ways. Take as examples these different headlines after the June 2006 European summit which considered the future of the EU's Constitutional Treaty. 'New proposals regarding the European Constitution by 2008' (Austria, *Kurier*). 'The constitution has been put on the back burner' (Belgium, *Dernière Heure*). 'No EU-treaty before 2010' (Danish media). 'The 25 want to renegotiate the Constitution' (France, *Le Monde*). 'EU Constitution must survive' (Germany, *Frankfurter Allgemeine Zeitung*). 'Constitution a corpse' (UK, *Times*).

Lobbyists inevitably cultivate contacts with the media, looking to use them to present their case to a wider audience. It is not uncommon for a particular proposal or idea to be leaked to a favoured newspaper before details are officially in the public domain. The tactic is used both by supporters of a proposal, in an attempt to influence the debate by presenting details in the most sympathetic light, and by critics looking to build up a groundswell of opposition. Hence, the media do not only report, analyse, and comment. In the EU as elsewhere, the distinction between commenting on events and trying to influence them is blurred.

The Rise of Organized Interests

The precise number of economic, public, and governmental groups involved in EU affairs has increased massively since the inception of the European Community in the 1950s. This astounding growth reflects not just the expanding scope of EU policies, but also its enlarged size; lobbyists from 27 member countries (and plenty from outside it) now converge on Brussels. Even since the 1970s the number of organized interests has grown six-fold from the mere 400 or so such bodies that existed at that time (Wessels 1997; Woll 2006). How can we explain this increase? Essentially, it has occurred as a result of, and in parallel with, the deepening and widening of the European Union itself. More legislative responsibilities have been transferred to the EU through successive treaty revisions. As a result, national organizations have gradually realized that they need to argue their case in the corridors of Brussels and Strasbourg. Similarly, as the Union's budget has increased, particularly for overseas expenditure, so, too, has the attention of international NGOs, firms, and third countries.

Hence, different types of interest have congregated in Brussels in a series of waves. In the 1960s, the most dominant actors tended to be specific sets of commercial interests; and their importance and dominance continue. For instance, one of the largest single categories of trade associations remains the food and beverages industries. Its high profile is undoubtedly due to the existence of the Common Agricultural Policy—the first truly pan-European policy after coal and steel.

While trade union, employer, and public sector organizations were well represented from the early days of the Union, broader public interest organizations, notably Europe's consumer (BEUC) and environment (European Environmental Bureau) organizations, did not mobilize in Brussels until the 1970s and the advent of increased legislation in these areas. Concerns for the rights of European citizens were subsequently consolidated with the formation in 1990 of the European Citizen Action Service (ECAS). Originally made up of a dozen or so different European NGOs, by 2007 it had over 60 members. With the recent enlargements of the Union, ECAS now finds its focus is moving away from Brussels to the new member states as it increasingly helps non-governmental organizations in those countries to develop civil society (see Box 5.1) and access EU structural funding and decision-makers.

Preparation for the single market programme in the late 1980s proved to be a still more important catalyst for interest mobilization. Numerous trade associations and individual companies (including American firms) scrambled to Brussels to ensure that their views were fed into plans to encourage the free movement of goods. The late 1980s also saw an increase in the presence of regional governments in Brussels. The initial incentive for these representations was undoubtedly the attraction of EU funding for regional and social projects. Political decentralization across Europe, combined with a massive increase in the EU's budget for research, regional and social spending, sparked the creation of a plethora of regional offices, as local authorities realized the advantages of direct representation in Brussels and the funding it could bring (see Chapter 6; Laffan 1989). Today, economic development remains a high priority, but interests are far wider, extending to environmental quality, social inclusion, support for business, and cultural and tourism activities.

This regional presence is not always easy to develop. For instance, British regions operate under the aegis—if not watchful eye—of the UK's Permanent Representation, since it is central government that formally represents the country inside the European

Union. In this regard, few British regions enjoy the powers of their counterparts in (say) Belgium, where regional ministers occasionally represent the federal state in the Council of Ministers, or in Germany, where the regions have their own permanent observer in the Council.

Whatever their restrictions, the growing activities of British regions—like sub-national authorities across the EU—suggest that formal channels of representation such as the Economic and Social Committee (ESC) or Committee of Regions (CoR) are deemed insufficient. These bodies have neither the legislative clout nor institutional weight of the European Parliament or the Council of Ministers, nor the Commission's power to initiate legislation. The CoR was specifically created in 1993 to raise the profile and input of regions in the Union (see Box 3.8). Yet, its limited power and lack of unified purpose have encouraged a far more informal system of networking and lobbying through which representatives can put their case directly to the relevant policy-makers, particularly those in the Commission and EP (see Jeffrey 2006). One cannot therefore understand how the EU really works as a lobbying system merely by studying its formal institutions and their reputed purposes.

Organized Interests at Work

Whatever their type, non-institutional actors seek to shape EU decision-making through lobbying. In simple terms, lobbyists are policy framers: 'they spend much of their time attempting to convince others that their issue should be seen in a particular light' (Baumgartner 2007: 485). Virtually all groups include in their strategies a focused effort to influence key EU institutions. Although the Council of Ministers is generally considered the most powerful institution, it is not usually the primary target of interest groups. It remains extremely difficult for lobbyists to obtain access to the Council, so attempts to influence EU governments tend to be concentrated at the national level or in individual member states' permanent representations in Brussels.

Ease of access alone does not determine where lobbyists flock. For instance, most spend little time targeting their efforts at the Economic and Social Committee or the Committee of the Regions. Again, the vast bulk of lobbying is directed towards the Commission and Parliament.

Recognition of the need to concentrate on these two institutions does not reduce the complexity of the task, particularly since the enlargements of 2004 and 2007. This complexity is due not so much to the arrival of extra organized interests, although there have been some, but to the changing dynamics of EU decision-making. The presence of 27 national delegations in the Council, the arrival of additional members of the Parliament and more Commissioners, and the increased number of possible alliances make it harder to predict the outcome of ministerial negotiations, parliamentary votes, and decisions taken in Council working groups. One practitioner explains:

There is more competition on issues and more people who can put a spanner in the works. You cannot count on something being adopted. As a lobbyist, you have to think far more carefully about what you used to take for granted (interview, July 2006).

Lobbying the Commission

Most lobbyists worth their salt will seek to nurture relations with the Commission. It is, after all, the institution that initiates policy and drafts proposals. The Commission's basic approach is to maintain as open and wide a dialogue as possible with all interested parties, believing that this is beneficial both to itself (it needs the specialized knowledge, contacts, and goodwill of the affected parties) and to the groups. The Commission insists that all groups should be treated equally and claims to make no distinction in its handling of these relationships between private and public interests. However, it displays a distinct preference for dealing with pan-European associations or groups which have already reached a common position among their members, rather than with national or individual organizations. Moreover, the more political and economic clout an organization has, the easier it is to gain access to policy-makers and put across a case (Eising 2007).

The contacts can either be formalized in the shape of advisory committees or groups of experts, or conducted on an ad hoc basis. The Commission also actively solicits input from outside interests on policy initiatives being considered by the institution. Although it already consults nearly 700 ad hoc bodies on a wide range of policies, the Commission has committed itself to extending that dialogue even further. In 2005, as part of the drive for an improvement in the quality of EU legislation (often referred to as 'Better Regulation' initiatives) the Commission made 'consultation with stakeholders' an essential element of its policy preparation.

Commission officials are relatively open to lobbyists' courting, but their time and patience is limited. Noted one Commission official: 'Sometimes people want to see the new text [of a proposal] every time a comma is changed in a draft directive. That is unrealistic . . . You need to balance efficiency with respect for democratic values' (interview, 26 June 2001, Brussels).

The Commission recognizes that for consultation to be efficient, it is not sufficient simply to post a proposal on a website. Guidelines are required on how the information fed back should be properly processed and slotted into the legislative machinery. Another delicate issue is the exact moment when civil society or corporate interests should be consulted: before or after the European Parliament? If before, then this practice could be seen as usurping the role of democratically elected MEPs. If afterwards, then there might not be sufficient opportunity to take account of contrasting outside views.

A particularly complex set of relationships exists between NGOs and the Commission. The point is well illustrated by the small organizations that rely largely on EU finance for their existence. Several hundred NGOs receive funding for projects from the Commission. The annual sums add up to over €1 billion. The major part is allocated to external projects (such as development or democracy programmes and humanitarian aid), but internal EU social, educational, and environmental programmes and their NGO sponsors also benefit. Moreover, several NGOs sit on Commission consultative committees and a number act as its agents in the implementation of policy (in, for instance, the delivery of humanitarian aid). While such assistance undoubtedly helps these organizations and the Commission, critics argue that the close relationship lessens the independence of NGOs and makes them less willing to undertake forceful advocacy work or be critical of the institution. Striking the right balance in the relationship can be difficult.

Wider questions of ethics and propriety always surround lobbying. The Commission has specific institutional rules to ensure clarity and probity in the activities of its own officials, and in contacts between outside interests and its own officials. These rules cover the receipt of gifts, engagement in outside activities, and employment after leaving the service of the institution. But the Commission traditionally has had no formal rules—such as accreditation, registration, or codes of conduct—specifically regulating outside interest groups. Instead, it has consistently encouraged organized interests to draw up their own codes of conduct on the basis of minimum criteria proposed by the Commission.

In response to these demands for transparency, a new European Public Affairs Consultancies Association (EPACA) was founded in January 2005 to formalize a long-standing code of conduct for the lobbying profession and to establish self-regulatory structures to enforce it. EPACA consists of close to 40 consultancies with over 600 employees representing around two-thirds of the total professional European public affairs consultancy market in Brussels. Its most recent code is reproduced in Box 5.3. In March 2007 the Commission introduced a public register and asked all interest-group representatives to sign it and provide details of their clients, funding, and objectives. The register recognizes the legitimacy of lobbying, but also the need for clarity about who lobbyists represent. While the register is voluntary the Commission has provided incentives: it has pledged to consult signatories on all policy initiatives that might impact on their interests.

Of course transparency is not restricted to rules governing the behaviour of lobbyists and the institutions. Other information—financial and political—can help to shed light on the impact of outside interests. The Commission already publishes details of those benefiting from the 20 per cent of the annual budget it manages centrally. From 2008, it will extend this transparency to cover recipients of regional and social funding. More ambitiously, individual payments under the Common Agricultural Policy will also be made public from 2009. In addition to these formal mechanisms, lobbyists are subject to informal scrutiny by non-governmental organizations. Some NGOs—Friends of the Earth Europe, Corporate Europe Observatory, LobbyControl, and Spinwatch—join forces to give the annual 'Worst EU Lobby Awards'. In 2006, the recipient was ExxonMobil. We see here how lobbyists can exercise control of each other.

Lobbying the European Parliament

The Parliament's growing power over the last decade has prompted a dramatic change in its relationship with lobbyists. This development was neatly summed up by one long-serving MEP who said, only partly in jest: 'In 1979, we were begging people to come and see us. Now we are trying to keep them away' (interview, June 2001). Many of his colleagues share that view.

The rules, too, have changed. Until 1994, a lobbyist needed the support of an MEP to obtain a pass giving access to the Parliament's premises. The institution has since adopted a more open and practical approach to regulate its relationship with outside interests. Anyone seeking a regular visitor's pass need only fill out a form and submit a supporting letter of justification. In most cases, the request is approved. The information is contained in a register, which holds around 3,400 names and may be consulted on the Parliament's website. With the annual pass, lobbyists can enter the Parliament's buildings. But neither they, nor the media nor occasional visitors, have carte blanche to roam at will. Certain areas of the institution's premises in Brussels, Strasbourg, and Luxembourg are declared out of bounds to outsiders unless they are specifically invited by an MEP.

Parliament has approved a code of conduct that holders of passes must respect. The code contains provisions broadly similar to those adopted by lobbyists themselves (see above). However, it also states that any assistance that outside actors might give to MEPs, such as the provision of staff or office equipment, should be declared in a special register. To reinforce this principle, parallel rules have been introduced requiring MEPs to detail any outside financial support in their own register, which is also accessible via the Parliament website. The aim is to dispel the image of the Parliament as a 'gravy train', while keeping the policy process accessible to a variety of interests.

In general, the activities of outside actors in relation to the Parliament are far more visible—and often more colourful—than those directed at the Commission. For example, during the lengthy debates in 2005 on a software patenting directive, supporters of the introduction of such patents hired a launch boat that was moored in front of the Parliament's building in Strasbourg urging MEPs to say yes to patents. Not to be outdone, opponents launched a series of small kayaks that weaved their way around the launch trying to draw attention to their support for open access.

Intergroups in the EP—cross-party bodies of MEPs who share some kind of interest in a particular issue or theme—are another vehicle for injecting outside opinions into the formal EU process. These intergroups engage with topics ranging from animal welfare, anti-racism, and the cinema, to friends of football and minority languages. The group's secretariat is usually provided by an outside body, either an NGO or a consultancy. Helping to administer these groups allows outside interests to focus the attention of MEPs from different parliamentary committees and political groups on a specific subject. The enthusiastic sponsorship of intergroups by organized interests suggests that as the EP's power grows, the attention of individual MEPs becomes increasingly valued by interests keen to shape policy.

BOX 5.3	EPACA code of conduct

Below is an excerpt from the EPACA code:

'This code of conduct applies to public affairs practitioners dealing with EU institutions.

Our work as public affairs practitioners contributes to a healthy democratic process, acting as a link between the world of business and civil society and European policy-makers. The signatories to this code are all committed to abide by it, acting in an honest, responsible and courteous manner at all times and seeking to apply the highest professional standards.

In their dealings with the EU institutions public affairs practitioners shall:

- identify themselves by name and by company;
- declare the interest represented;
- neither intentionally misrepresent their status nor the nature of inquiries to officials of the EU institutions nor create any false impression in relation thereto;
- neither directly nor indirectly misrepresent links with the EU institutions;
- honour confidential information given to them;
- not disseminate false or misleading information knowingly or recklessly and shall exercise proper care to avoid doing so inadvertently;
- not sell for profit to third parties copies of documents obtained from EU institutions;
- not obtain information from EU institutions by dishonest means;
- avoid any professional conflicts of interest;
- neither directly nor indirectly offer nor give any financial inducement to
    - any EU official, nor
    - Member of the European Parliament, nor
    - their staff;
- neither propose nor undertake any action which would constitute an improper influence on them;
- only employ EU personnel subject to the rules and confidentiality requirements of the EU institutions.

'All signatories agree that they and all employees of their company will adhere to the above Code, and be subject to the disciplinary rules of EPACA ... in case of breach of the Code. The signatories will meet annually to review this code.'

Available at: http://www.epaca.org/code_of_conduct.php

Successful Lobbying

Information and Alliances

The art of lobbying has come a long way in the EU. Skilful lobbyists know that the information they provide is crucial to making the policy-making system work. Still, it must be tailored appropriately. The European Commission attaches special attention to accurate, unbiased information that will provide officials with the necessary technical expertise in drafting legislation. MEPs need information from their constituents as well as specific interests. Successful lobbyists will target their expertise accordingly.

Another skill common to successful lobbyists is an ability to build alliances or networks across nationalities, institutions, and groups in a common cause. As explained in Chapter 1, policy networks that link together stakeholders in specific policy sectors can play a crucial role in shaping EU policies. Coalitions of like-minded actors, which sometimes bring together some unlikely partners, can 'load' the policy process in favour of certain outcomes. In 1995, for instance, the EU's proposed biotechnology patenting directive was soundly rejected in the European Parliament as MEPs expressed their concerns about the 'patenting of life'. By 1998, when a second draft directive was put to the Parliament for its final approval, it won the support of a vast majority of members. The turnaround was achieved through lobbying by a carefully constructed network made up of the pharmaceutical industry in alliance with patient groups, many of whose members hoped that the new technology would deliver new cures for disease.

A quite different sort of coalition-building was evident in recent chemicals legislation, known as REACH, which has probably seen the heaviest lobbying campaign of any legislation inside the EU so far (see Box 5.4). The wider point is that relationships between organized interests and their national and institutional allies are not fixed; skilful lobbyists are those that can build alliances across a wide range of member states, institutions, and interests.

New Technology, Old Techniques

More than in most political capitals, new technology has made its presence felt in Brussels. In particular, electronic means of communication help organized interests to put their message across swiftly and efficiently. Emails are a convenient way for lobbyists to maintain a dialogue with Commission staff, national officials, parliamentarians, and their assistants (although an increasing number of MEPs now complain that they are being deluged with unsolicited messages). More generally, email remains an enormously handy and time-saving device for widely disseminating draft amendments and a useful instrument for quickly gathering together a coalition of interests.

These advantages are particularly valuable to pan-European trade associations that have huge logistical problems trying to secure the agreement of each of their national member organizations for a coordinated position. With the click of a mouse, they can engage sympathetic MEPs and other like-minded groups to construct a broad coalition behind their cause quickly and pass the information to journalists. Websites are proving

BOX 5.4 **How it really works**

Lobbying and the REACH Regulation on Chemicals

The REACH Regulation on Chemicals (Registration, Evaluation, Authorization, and Restriction of Chemicals) took over three years to be approved. The Commission introduced its proposal in 2003 and it was adopted by Parliament and Council in December 2006. This unusually long period reflected bitter divisions between those for and against the legislation, and allowed organized interests to make full use of their various lobbying techniques.

The legislation was subject to considerable controversy even before the Commission presented its proposal. Drafting had started two years earlier in 2001 and had immediately provoked a powerful reaction from both sides of the debate. Those in favour of the restrictions on the use of chemicals required by the legislation pointed to a significant reduction of occupational cancer cases per year, and savings in health benefits of €50 billion over 30 years. In contrast, the chemical industry forecast a cost of many billions due to lost revenue, an undermining of its international competitiveness, and major job losses.

Given the controversy surrounding the measure, the Commission took the unusual step of organizing an Internet consultation between May and July 2003. The response was dramatic, with many third country governments, notably the US, China, and Japan, making their concerns known. Although environmental groups from inside and outside the EU argued in favour of the proposal, the version that emerged in the autumn of 2003 was significantly weaker than the original. It was then a matter for the Council and Parliament to discuss, as the proposal was covered by the co-decision procedure, involving both branches of the legislative authority.

Co-decision rules allow the European Parliament to give its view first and it decided to wait until after the European elections of 2004 to resume discussion of the proposal. The pause gave organized interests further time to prepare their arguments. At that point, the Commission took another unusual step: it set up a high-level group composed of two Commissioners, three MEPs, the Council Presidency, plus representatives of industry and environmental groups. The group met from September 2004 until June 2005 and produced three business case studies to try to assess the impact of the proposal. These case studies suggested that the proposals were workable but that there would be significant costs for small and medium-sized enterprises (SMEs) and for the new accession countries.

During this phase it became apparent that the opponents of the proposals were not of one mind. The level of opposition varied across different parts of the chemical sector. A more flexible approach from the French, British, and Italian industries was accompanied by a much harder line from German companies. This tough stance was reflected in the position of most German MEPs who favoured, for example, setting a high threshold beyond which a chemical would need to be tested. The higher threshold would reduce the cost of testing imposed on industry.

MEPs and others working for the Parliament sought to bring together opposing interests. After a vote in the Environment Committee in October 2005 and before the vote in the plenary in November, a technical working group met not just with MEPs but also with lobbyists and experts from industry, the scientific community, and representatives from the Commission. This group offered a key opportunity for interests to put forward their point of view.

The effort paid off. A compromise was reached on parts of the proposal and the Parliament was able to complete its first reading in November 2005 and return the proposal to the Council. Here organized interests had yet another chance to influence ministers' views. After further negotiations the Council presented its position to the Parliament in summer 2006 and eventually—at the very end of the four months allowed under the co-decision procedure—the Parliament and Council were able to negotiate an agreement that was acceptable to a majority. The resulting final legislation adopted in December 2006 proved weaker than the Commission's original proposal, but rather stronger than many in the chemical industry would have liked at the outset. In other words, REACH was a compromise, reflecting effective lobbying on both sides of the issue.

to be another useful lobbying tool. Both EU institutions and other organizations use sites to publicize background information and allow easy access to it.

But these technological developments are no substitute for old-fashioned face-to-face contact, particularly at the outset of a lobbying relationship. Personal contacts over a drink or meal or in a private meeting are still seen as essential ingredients needed to insert outside views into the formal EU decision-making process. Consultants, lobbyists, and pressure groups inevitably try to break into the busy agendas of European and national officials and parliamentarians in Brussels and Strasbourg. Despite the time required to travel to Strasbourg from Brussels (a five-hour journey by train), it remains an especially popular venue for lobbying because virtually everyone who travels there for EP plenaries is away from home and has their evenings free. The particular rhythm of business there—to say nothing of the fine wine and food—means that it is generally easier for MEPs and officials to find time for external visitors. Thus, whatever the cost and other disadvantages of the MEPs' 'travelling circus' from Brussels to Strasbourg and back again, it does allow the prime opportunities for an impromptu word on the train, in hotel lobbies, and in airport lounges.

Timing

A successful lobbyist is also sensitive to the timing and stages of EU decision-making. At the outset, when legislation is being mooted, as with the REACH regulation, lobbyists tend to focus on the European Commission where the proposed text is being drafted. Lobbyists are aware that it is far harder to change something once it is put down in writing than when an official is faced with a blank screen. Once the proposal has been formally adopted by the Commission, attention usually shifts to national governments and the European Parliament, particularly if the measures under consideration are subject to co-decision, as is the case with around 75 per cent of EU legislation. Organizations interested in the contents of the draft legislation, especially those keen to amend it, will try to put their views across to individual MEPs. They will pay particular attention to the parliamentary *rapporteur* (the MEP responsible for the text; see Box 5.1), and the members of the relevant parliamentary committee that will examine the proposal. At this committee stage, it is a fairly common practice for interested outside parties even to draft amendments for sympathetic MEPs in the hope that these will be tabled and win wider support. Indeed, one estimate suggests that up to 75–80 per cent of amendments tabled in the most active parliamentary committees emanate from outside Parliament (Judge and Earnshaw 2002). Most of this lobbying occurs well before the proposal is submitted to a plenary session for the institution's formal opinion.

Conclusion

What impact do organized interests have on the EU and how it works? The question is central to debates about the EU's democratic deficit (see Chapter 8). Opinions certainly differ. On the one hand, it is widely recognized that well-resourced organizations with a clear mission can lobby very effectively, whereas smaller or less well-funded bodies generally do not have the same level of access and find it harder to put their message across. Very broad coalitions of pan-European interests—such as BusinessEurope or the ETUC—often find it more difficult to agree internally on a clear, common position than do individual private firms or mission-oriented NGOs. The EU may be less technocratic and more open to lobbying than it once was—and arguably more open than are many member states—but resources are by no means distributed evenly (see Eising 2007). This imbalance concerns those who argue that EU policy is determined by a few well-financed interest groups at the expense of other public interests that are less well resourced.

Others have found that the EU provides an alternative arena where groups that are not gaining access at the national level (say environmental or women's groups) have a second chance to be heard. The EU's complex and multilevel character can make access difficult (see Aspinwall and Greenwood 1998) but it can also provide groups with opportunities for venue shopping—that is, pushing issues toward the level, institution, or venue with the greatest receptivity to their own point of view (see Box 5.1; Baumgartner 2007: 484).

A related question concerns the overall effect of the growth in the number and range of such interests. Has it generally been a positive phenomenon? Or does it represent a danger for democracy and efficiency in the EU? On the positive side, the range of subjects now covered by the EU is so wide that virtually any actor can find opportunities to further their cause or defend their interests. NGOs and public interest groups have helped ensure that many issues of public concern—sustainable development, employment, social inclusion, and public health—are now discussed at the very highest levels of EU decision-making, including the European Council. The growing involvement of these groups, as well as regional and local authorities, in EU affairs can also encourage governments and the Union's institutions to involve individual citizens more closely in Europe's development. They thus can divert the criticism that decisions are taken by an inner elite, detached from the concerns of ordinary citizens.

The upsurge in the number and range of interests also has a downside. The most obvious is that of overcrowding and the imbalances it may cause. Outside groups are now so numerous that hard-pressed officials within the institutions have less and less time to listen to individual concerns, thereby potentially reducing consultation to a formality without real substance. Enlargement has exacerbated this problem. The number of staff in the institutions has not grown substantially. There is an ever-wider set of outside interests chasing after the 'eartime' of relatively few and ever more harassed officials.

In short, not everyone believes that the arrival of civil society in Brussels has been a positive development. For some, it represents a move towards a political process where outcomes depend on the relative strength of determined lobbyists and backroom deal-making. What is needed is a more open policy debate in which more voices are heard by EU decision-makers.

Yet it seems highly improbable that we will return to the situation that prevailed before the arrival of these groups. Demands for transparency and pressures for outside interests to see, and seek to influence, what is happening inside the institutions are powerful and gaining in strength. Perhaps the key issue is to make explicit the terms under which such activity takes place so that all can be aware of the role played by those outside and the links they enjoy with those inside. If these terms are perceived to be fair and transparent, it is reasonable to argue that the developments described in this chapter could be part of the solution to the democratic deficit in the European Union, rather than part of its cause.

?   **DISCUSSION QUESTIONS**

1. Does the increasing involvement of outside interests in the EU's decision-making process make for better policy?

2. Is democracy strengthened or undermined by the presence of non-elected interest groups in the EU decision-making process?

3. Should subnational layers of government be given a stronger formal role in the EU's decision-making process? If so, how could this be achieved?

4. What are the arguments against giving 'civil society' a more powerful role in EU decision-making?

→ **FURTHER READING**

The very wide literature on lobbying in the European Union can be divided into general texts, specific case studies or analyses, and practical guides and reference works. The most recent general text is Coen and Richardson (2007), but Greenwood (2003) also provides a useful, detailed examination of different interest groups. A special issue of the *Journal of European Public Policy* (2007) is devoted specifically to lobbying. Goergen (2006) offers a very comprehensive practical guide to lobbying, and the regularly updated publication of Landmarks (2006) offers an overview of the wide range of actors involved. On the European Parliament, including its intergroups, see Corbett *et al.* (2007, Chapter 10) and Judge and Earnshaw (2002).

Coen, D., and Richardson, J. (2007), *Lobbying in the European Union: Institutions, Actors and Issues* (Oxford and New York: Oxford University Press)

Corbett, R., Jacobs, F., and Shackleton, M. (2007), *The European Parliament*, 7th edn. (London: Cartermill).

Goergen, P. (2006), *Lobbying in Brussels: A Practical Guide to the European Union for Cities, Regions, Networks and Enterprises* (Brussels, D&P Services).

Greenwood, J. (2003), *Interest Representation in the EU* (Basingstoke: Palgrave).

Journal of European Public Policy (2007), Special issue on 'Empirical and Theoretical Studies in EU Lobbying', 14/3.

Judge, D., and Earnshaw, D. (2002), 'No Simple Dichotomies: Lobbyists and the European Parliament', in *Journal of Legislative Studies* 8/4: 61–79.

Landmarks (2006), *The European Public Affairs Directory* (Brussels: Landmarks sa/nv).

⊕ **WEB LINKS**

The Commission has established a directory of non-profit pan-European organizations. This electronic database, known as 'Consultation, the European Commission and Civil Society' (Coneccs), now holds details of nearly 1,000 European bodies grouped by category—for instance trade unions, professional federations, and religious interests. The site provides basic data on each organization and lists representatives with which the Commission has formal and structured consultations. It can be found at: www.europa.eu.int/comm/civil_society/coneccs/.

The websites of the major umbrella organizations mentioned in this chapter (BusinessEurope, ETUC, COPA) can also all be accessed via the Coneccs site.

For the public register of expert groups advising the Commission, see www.europa.eu.int/comm/secretariat_general/regexp/; for details of recipients of EU grants, see www.ec.europa.eu/grants/beneficiaries_en.htm and for beneficiaries of EU public contracts, see www.ec.europa.eu./public_contracts/beneficiaries_en.htm

This 'world newspapers' site provides links to newspapers from all over the world, including pan-European newspapers and links:

http://www.world-newspapers.com/europe.html

Some of the organized interests discussed in this chapter are also represented through formal institutions. See the websites of the Committee of the Regions (www.cor.europa.eu) and the Economic and Social Committee (www.eesc.europa.eu/index_en.asp/).

Finally, the websites of several think tanks mentioned include the Centre for European Policy Studies (www.ceps.be); the European Policy Centre (www.theepc.be/); the Centre for European Reform (www.cer.org.uk); and the Trans European Policy Studies Association (www.tepsa.be).

 Visit the Online Resource Centre that accompanies this book for additional material: www.oxfordtextbooks.co.uk/orc/bomberg2e/

PART III

Policies and Policy-making

CHAPTER 6

Key Policies

Alberta Sbragia and Francesco Stolfi

Introduction   116
Key Features of EU Policies   118
  Differences between National and EU
  Policies   118
  The Primacy of Economic Integration 123
Market-building Policies   124
  Competition Policy   125
  Commercial (Trade) Policy   126
  Economic and Monetary Union (EMU)   126
Market-correcting and -cushioning
Policies   128

Common Agricultural Policy (CAP)   128
Cohesion Policy   128
  Environmental and Social Regulation 132
Comparing EU Policy Types   133
Conclusion   134

DISCUSSION QUESTIONS   135
FURTHER READING   136
WEB LINKS   136

▮ Chapter Overview

European Union policies affect the lives of millions of people in Europe and beyond. Because of the variety of actors involved, the wide range of policy types, and their constant evolution, policy-making in the EU is a challenging but fascinating area of study. This chapter describes some of the most important areas of policy-making in the European Union, focusing primarily on economic and related policies. We begin by explaining how EU policy-making differs from national policy-making, and then describe the most important policies for building the internal market and limiting its potentially negative impact on individuals, society, and the environment. We show how these policies are made and also how they matter.

Introduction

The European Union sets policies in so many areas that it is difficult to think about national policy-making in Europe in isolation from Brussels. While the euro—the common currency used by fifteen of the EU's twenty-seven member states—is perhaps the most visible manifestation of European integration, a diverse set of public policies (see Box 6.1) affecting the everyday lives of Europeans are shaped by decisions taken at the EU level. Agriculture, environmental protection, international trade, and the movement of goods, services, labour, and capital across borders are all affected in important ways by policies made in Brussels.

Yet the role of the EU should not be over-estimated. It is not a 'superstate' exercising control over all areas of policy. The Union should be thought of as a selective policy-maker whose power varies significantly across policy areas. Most of the policies for which it is responsible are related to markets (see Box 6.1): some policies build markets, some protect producers from market forces, some try to cushion the impact of market forces.

The differentiated role of the EU across policy areas is not unusual if we compare it to federal systems where power is shared between the national and subnational level (see Box 6.1). In such systems the national level may not be allowed to legislate in certain areas and policy discretion is left to the constituent units. Canadians, Australians, and Americans, for example, take for granted that many decisions affecting their lives will be taken at the state or provincial level rather than at the national level. In the European Union, citizens are becoming accustomed to such a system of differentiated policy responsibilities. Just as Washington lets each state decide whether to allow the death penalty within its borders, the EU does not legislate on Ireland's abortion policy, Spain's policy on bullfighting, or Sweden's alcohol control policy (although the European Court of Justice (ECJ) repeatedly has ruled on the latter's compatibility with the single market). Citizens of a federal polity accept that at least some unequal treatment comes with living in a federation. In a similar vein, it matters a great deal—and will continue to matter—where one lives within the European Union.

However, the impact of the European Union is such that its member states are, in many ways, much more alike now than they were fifty years ago. In certain policy areas, especially those related to economic activity, member state governments as well as private firms either have had to engage in new activities (such as environmental protection) or alternatively change their traditional practices. The introduction of the euro has not only changed the landscape of monetary affairs but also made the average citizen aware of that changed landscape literally on a daily, even hourly, basis.

The world of money and business has been changed by EU policies in fundamental ways, but so have many related areas. Environmental protection, gender equality in the workplace, and occupational health and safety have all moved the EU towards a system in which many of the negative consequences of market activity are addressed in

BOX 6.1	Key concepts and terms

Benchmarking is the use of comparisons with other states or organizations (for instance on issues such as pension reform and employment practices) with the aim of improving performance by learning from the experience of others.

A **directive** is the most common form of EU legislation. It stipulates the ends to be achieved (say, limiting the emissions of a harmful pollutant) but allows each member state to choose the form and method for achieving that end. It can be contrasted with a regulation, which is binding in its entirety on all member states.

The **Eurozone** refers to the countries that are part of the Economic and Monetary Union (EMU). EMU was launched in 1999 (with notes and coins entering into circulation in 2002) with eleven members (Austria, Belgium, France, Germany, Finland, Ireland, Italy, Luxembourg, the Netherlands, Portugal, and Spain); Greece joined in 2001, Slovenia in 2007, and Cyprus and Malta in 2008. All remaining new EU member states are expected to join once their economies are ready. The UK, Sweden, and Denmark have thus far chosen not to join.

Federalism is a constitutional arrangement in which the power to make decisions and execute policy is divided between national and subnational levels of government. In a federal system both national and subnational units wield a measure of final authority in their own spheres and neither level can alter or abolish the other.

A **market** is a system of exchange bringing together buyers and sellers of goods and services. In most markets, money is used as means of exchange. Markets are regulated by price fluctuations that reflect the balance of supply and demand. To function properly, markets require the existence of law, regulation, and property rights. Virtually all markets are subject to some sort of regulation.

Non-tariff barriers refer to regulations, such as national standards or requirements (for instance health requirements) that increase the cost of imports and thus have the equivalent effect of tariffs. Often these regulations do not only serve bona fide social purposes (such as the protection of the environment or of consumer health), but also protect national producers from foreign competition.

Public policy is a course of action (decisions, actions, rules, laws, and so on) or inaction taken by government in regard to some public problem or issue.

Brussels rather than in national capitals. This expansion in the EU's remit is the result not of some well-orchestrated plan but rather the product of constant problem-solving, bargaining, and experimentation (see Chapter 1).

This chapter introduces some of the key policies of the European Union. Since economic integration is at the core of what the EU does, we focus primarily on economic and related policies. The inclusiveness of these policies—how open they are to a large number of actors—varies, but a constant across policies is the preference for consensus-building rather than conflict. Furthermore, the chapter shows how the

EU's remit has dramatically increased over time, but also how in many policy areas its capacity has remained limited when compared to that of a 'traditional' nation-state.

Key Features of EU Policies

Differences between National and EU Policies

Policies in the European Union differ in important ways from policies decided at the national level by member state governments. At their most basic level, policies are different because the European Union and its member states are structured and financed very differently. These varying financial structures lead to three wider differences between national and EU policies:

- with a few exceptions, EU policies typically involve the spending of very little money, whereas many national policies involve spending a good deal of it;
- the distance between those who formulate policy and those who actually execute it in practice is far greater in the EU than in most of its member states;
- the EU is active in a narrower range of policies than are national governments.

Thus, knowing about national policies is not a particularly good template for understanding EU policies. Let us examine each of these differences in more detail.

Money

One way to understand the European Union's relative poverty in terms of public finance is to compare its budget with those of central governments in its member states. As Table 6.1 illustrates, even though the central governments of France, Germany, and the UK are each responsible for only a fraction of the EU's total population, each of those central governments spends a great deal more than does Brussels. Another useful comparison is with the federal government's budget in the US. The EU has a considerably larger population than does the US, but the budget of the US federal government is roughly thirty times as large as the Union's budget.

The Union relies on the power of law (as embodied in legislation and court decisions) rather than money to carry out most of its policies. That dynamic shapes what the content of its policies can be. The Union has only a small number of policy areas which cost a great deal, whereas national systems typically have a large number of expensive policy areas, including those that fall under the rubric of the welfare state. Given its current fiscal structure, the EU could not, for example, finance health care or provide pensions or finance systems of public education. Overwhelmingly, the EU regulates economic activity; that is, it subjects it to rules and standards. However, in spite of the relatively small size of the EU budget, the process of agreeing the revenues and expenditures of the European Union can become highly contentious (see Box 6.2).

TABLE 6.1   Compared to what? EU and national budgets compared

EU Budget (2006)	Germany Federal Budget (2004)	France Central Budget (2004)	UK Central Budget (2004)	US Federal Budget (2004)
€122 billion	€1038 billion	€881 billion	€509 billion	€3398 billion*

*US dollars converted to euros at average exchange rate for 2004.
For the EU, Commission 2006d. For the national budgets, OECD 2005.

BOX 6.2   How it really works

Budget bargaining

Unlike national governments, the EU cannot run a deficit; its revenues limit the amounts it can spend. Various economic formulae are used to help determine the EU's overall budget *revenue* (derived primarily from custom duties, value added tax, and national contributions) and budget *allocation* (who gets what?). On the expenditure side, two documents are important: the yearly budget, which sets the overall expenditure level and how it is to be divided between the various policy areas, and the multiyear 'financial perspective' which sets broad spending patterns for seven-year periods.

Formulae aside, the EU's budget is a result of politics as much as mathematics. Reaching a decision over the financial perspective can be a highly contentious and decidedly intergovernmental affair. Although the absolute amounts involved are not large—the overall EU budget equals only around 1 per cent of the member states' GDP—no government wants to appear weak in the eyes of its voters during the negotiations with other member states. Moreover, and especially in the case of the CAP, the amounts involved can mean a great deal to strong domestic constituencies.

It is thus not surprising that the intergovernmental negotiations for the last financial perspective in December 2005 almost collapsed. UK Prime Minister Tony Blair tried to hold on to the rebate that Margaret Thatcher had negotiated for Britain's contributions in the 1980s, while French President Jacques Chirac defended the CAP, some of whose main beneficiaries were French farmers. A late-night agreement was finally reached only when Blair agreed to give up part of the rebate, and Chirac accepted a (postponed) review of the CAP, starting in 2008.

Legislation versus Execution

In most national systems, the national government makes policy decisions and then has numerous ways of ensuring that those policies are actually executed 'on the ground'. Although that link is far from perfect in practice, it is far tighter in most national systems than it is when EU policy is involved. Policy decided in Brussels faces several unique hurdles before it can be successfully executed on the ground.

The first step is known as transposition. That is, laws (known as directives, see Box 6.1) adopted by the Council of Ministers need to be 'transposed' into national legal codes before they can be executed by the member state's public administration or formally shape the behaviour of private actors in significant ways. Although transposition has become increasingly timely (as of 2006 the average rate of directive implementation across the then twenty-five EU members was 99.16 per cent; see Commission 2006e), differences still exist among the member states. Interestingly, the new member states do better at implementation than the older ones. Of the countries that have performed below the EU average, only one—Malta—is a new member state, while all the others—Spain, France, Italy, Portugal, Greece, and Luxembourg—are longtime members (Commission 2006e).

Moreover, when transposition occurs, the Commission may still feel (and argue to the ECJ) that the transposition does not adequately reflect the intent of the EU's legislation. National transposition may be overzealous (see Box 6.5) or it may be too lax. If the ECJ upholds the Commission's position, the national government will need to transpose the EU's legislation in a different way. Thus, Union policies do not become 'policy' at the national level uniformly across the EU's member states. For example, a directive transposed in Finland shortly after its adoption in Brussels may not be transposed in France or Greece until several years after the Finnish action.

These differences suggest that Brussels formulates and adopts policy but, as discussed in Chapter 4, actual policy impact will be shaped by national systems of governance. National governments play a central role in the EU's policy process because they hold a monopoly of power in the actual execution of most policies adopted in Brussels. The EU has no administrative presence within the member states. The Commission, for example, has few field offices (and only in national capitals) from which it can monitor the execution of EU law. It must instead rely on complaints from citizens, firms, and non-governmental organizations. Even then, it can only try to persuade national governments to improve execution.

The difficulties surrounding execution and monitoring mean that policies affecting a dispersed set of actors are less likely to be executed uniformly than are those policies which affect a few. For example, environmental policy, which attempts to shape the behaviour of huge numbers of both public and private actors, is executed with a tremendous degree of variability within the Union. By contrast, the Commission's decisions about mergers and acquisitions are implemented uniformly. The number of firms affected by any single Commission decision is very small and a non-complying firm would be very visible.

Jurisdiction

A third difference between EU and national policies concerns policy competencies (see Box 6.3). While certainly broader than other international organizations, the EU's policy remit is narrower than that of national governments. Consider how many areas are not subject to EU legislation because it has not been given competence

---

BOX 6.3 **The policy competencies of the EU**

Policy competence refers to the primary legal authority to act in particular policy areas. EU competencies, which are based on the Treaties, are traditionally divided into three categories: *exclusive* competencies, *shared* competencies between the EU and its member states, and competencies belonging mostly to the *member states*.

1. The EU has *exclusive* competence in few, but important, policy areas: external trade in goods and some services, monetary policy (for the Eurozone), customs, and fisheries.

2. The majority of policy competencies are *shared* between the EU and its member states. Shared competencies include, for example, environmental policy, consumer protection, mergers and acquisitions, development aid, transport policy, visas, asylum, and immigration.

3. Finally, there are policy areas where the *member states* are the main players, even if the EU is involved in some general coordination or is engaged in a few specific projects. Education, culture, employment, public health, research, social and urban policy, and most foreign and security policies fall into this domain.

In some policy areas it is difficult to place policies in one of these categories because the line between shared competencies and member-state competencies is blurred. In foreign and security policies, for instance, it is often unclear how much weight the EU has because the member states in the final analysis must allocate the resources necessary to execute the EU's foreign and security policy (see Chapter 10).

---

by its member states: health care, urban regeneration, family assistance, pensions, public health, industrial relations, child care, poverty alleviation, abortion, prison administration, and education, for example. Other areas remain under national control because of the decision-making rules which apply to that area. In taxation and energy, for example, the decision-making rule is one of unanimity (although pressures for a common EU energy policy are increasingly powerful). Since the member states have been unable to agree on any single policy, those policy areas effectively remain under national control.

Recently, various 'soft' measures (involving no EU enforcement powers) such as benchmarking (see Box 6.1) or the 'open method of coordination' (OMC) of national policies have been used to encourage national governments to address issues such as their pension burden (see Box 6.4). But in general the welfare state and the direct provision of social services are primarily under national control. The notable exception, of course, is welfare related to agriculture (see below).

Policies that have a moral or cultural dimension also remain under national control. Abortion, for example, is not permitted in Ireland, and the EU does not have the power to tell the Irish either to change their abortion law or to keep it. The Swedish and Finnish alcohol control system has been under strain due to the ability of individual

BOX 6.4	The policy process: three modes

Policy varies enormously in the EU, and so too does the policy-making process. But broadly speaking, we can identify three main policy-making modes in the EU: the Community method, the intergovernmental method, and the newer 'open method of coordination' (OMC). Member states' and institutions' power vary across these three modes.

1. The *Community method* is the most **supranational** mode and is used in the oldest areas of European integration, such as the internal market, the CAP, and competition policy. Its key features are:

   - the central roles played by the EU's main institutions including the Commission, the Council of Ministers, the European Court of Justice, and the European Parliament (the latter, however, traditionally has been excluded from the CAP);
   - the Commission's clear right of initiative and important role as agenda setter and overseer of policy implementation;
   - the ECJ's strong power to intervene to set the boundaries between the authority of the EU and the authority of the member states.

   This traditional method of policy-making in the EU seems to have lost some of its attractiveness in recent years, and has not been adopted in new areas where the EU has extended its competence (such as monetary policy).

2. The *intergovernmental method* is used in the areas, such as fiscal policy, where member states have an interest in cooperation but are still jealous of their sovereignty. Some of the main features of this method are:

   - the central role of the European Council in defining policy direction;
   - a strong role for the Council of Ministers in managing the policy;
   - the marginal role of the Commission;
   - the exclusion of the European Parliament and the ECJ.

   An example of the intergovernmental method is the revision of the Stability and Growth Pact mentioned in the text. The risk of this method, as that episode exemplified, is that the interests of the largest states may trump those of the smaller states or of the European Union as a whole.

3. The *Open Method of Coordination* (OMC) refers to the development and diffusion of best practices among the members of the EU. It is used for policy areas where the EU has few or no formal powers, such as employment policies or welfare state reform. Some of the features of the OMC are:

   - the EU institutions serve primarily as fora where new approaches can be discussed and compared among the member states;
   - the Commission's brokerage role—it focuses attention on specific problems and ways to solve them, and encourages coalitions of state and non-state actors to achieve its favoured solution;
   - the central role of transnational networks of policy experts.

OMC relies not on directives or 'hard law' but rather on 'soft' policy instruments such as benchmarking, 'naming and shaming', and policy learning. Because the OMC does not include any instrument to enforce compliance, the results are often patchy. For instance, one of the most high-profile uses of this method has been the Lisbon Strategy decided at the 2000 European Council in Lisbon. By stimulating employment-creating policies in the member states, the strategy aimed to make the EU 'the most competitive and dynamic knowledge-based economy in the world' by 2010. Despite improvements in the European economy, the EU remained far from achieving this goal with only a few years to go before the deadline.

revellers to bring liquor home from other EU countries, but alcohol control policy in both Sweden and Finland is under national control (Kurzer 2001).

However, and in spite of the circumscribed jurisdiction of the EU, it is important to note that the EU can and often does have important indirect effects beyond the immediate scope of its competencies. For instance, the EU's commitment to the Kyoto Protocol on climate change stimulated the creation of a European market where industrial producers can trade carbon emissions permits, with the purpose of limiting overall emissions. To take another example, education at both pre-university and university levels is under national control, but the EU has been a prime mover in encouraging university students to study in another member state. These Commission programmes for student mobility within the Union have led to major changes in universities' administrative structures and have encouraged university officials to work towards much greater cross-national standardization in degree programmes (such as the length of time required to receive a first degree). The lack of formal competence at the EU level does not mean that Brussels lacks influence in shaping the terms of debate within a policy area. The programmes that Brussels adopts, while not legally binding in the way that legislation is, are very important in providing incentives to national and subnational governments to carry out certain activities.

The Primacy of Economic Integration

The EU's unique history and development has privileged some areas as important for the Union while leaving others aside. As Chapter 2 explained, in the 1950s European states chose to defend each other within a transatlantic rather than a European organization (NATO includes Canada and the US). Policy areas concerning defence as well as foreign policy and security, therefore, were not central to the integration process and have become salient only recently.

By contrast, policies related to economic integration came to form the core of what the EU does. Economic cooperation was viewed as a politically acceptable way of increasing integration while laying the groundwork for political cooperation at a future date. Consequently, policy areas related to economics have been privileged from the very beginning. The 1957 Treaty of Rome, by calling for a customs union and a common market (now referred to as a single or internal market), steered the process of European integration towards the liberalization of cross-border trade, a unitary trade policy vis-à-vis non-members, and the free movement of capital, goods, services, and labour. The centrality of that effort to European integration symbolizes the importance that economic integration has within the European Union.

Market-building Policies

The focus on liberalization and creation of a single market highlights the EU's concern with 'market building' and what is sometimes termed negative integration. Building markets involves both removing barriers to trade and carrying out regulatory reform. So negative integration includes the elimination of various tariff and non-tariff barriers (see Box 6.1) to trade, reform of economic regulation, and the encouragement of competition between firms. The goal is to facilitate cross-border economic transactions with the expectation that the resulting greater efficiency will lead to higher levels of prosperity for the citizens of Europe. This same aim is pursued globally within the World Trade Organization (WTO).

The political economy of the member states has been profoundly affected by the privileging of economic policies at the EU level (Sbragia 2001). In this arena, policies adopted in Brussels usually pre-empt national policies and the EU is said to have 'exclusive competence'. Monetary policy falls under this category, although it only applies to the members of the Eurozone (see Box 6.1).

In general, the kind of negative integration that characterizes the EU is far more penetrating than that found at the global (WTO) level or in other regional arrangements such as the North American Free Trade Agreement (NAFTA). The EU's market-building ambitions are very serious and their scope very wide. The very foundation of the single market involves the four freedoms—free movement of capital, goods, services, and labour. However, a single market such as that envisaged by the founders of the Community does not occur simply by removing obstacles to trade. A whole host of interventions must be put into place to ensure that the hoped-for market will operate smoothly and efficiently. The construction of the European market has led to such widespread regulation from Brussels that Giandomenico Majone (1999) has termed the EU a 'regulatory state'. Whereas a welfare state engages in redistribution and spends a great deal of money in providing social welfare (such as social security), a regulatory state exercises its influence primarily by passing legislation that regulates the behaviour of actors in the economy. The development of a far-reaching regulatory regime in Brussels has also led to frequent complaints from those affected by such regulation—who typically blame 'Eurocrats' even when the blame should be placed elsewhere (see Booker 1996).

BOX 6.5   How it really works

'Goldplating' and EU Policy

Sometimes the member states implement EU legislation in a far more stringent manner than was ever intended. In the UK the sometimes overzealous interpretation of EU legislation on the part of the bureaucracy has attracted much popular attention, even receiving its own moniker: 'goldplating'. The extent to which seemingly anodyne EU directives can be transformed into nightmare regulations is illustrated below with some examples from the UK.

Mountaineers: look out for heights!

In 2001 the EU adopted a work safety directive (2001/45/EC) designed to protect people who work at heights, such as window cleaners and construction workers. But as interpreted by the UK's Health and Safety Commission the bill became the bane of British mountaineers. The British regulation went well beyond the original directive, extending to climbers and other outdoor enthusiasts' safety requirements such as the use of double ropes, limitations of operations in adverse weather conditions, and signs to climbers when they are approaching snowy and icy surfaces (House of Lords 2004).

Civil servants working overtime

Another illustration of British civil servants 'over-defining' EU directives is found in amendments to the Working Time Directive (2003/88/EC). Transposition of that directive into Swedish law took just two sheets of paper; for England and Wales, the same piece of legislation was published in a booklet with more than 60 pages of often rigidly defined rules and regulations (see *Financial Times*, 3/4 January 2004: 3).

Competition Policy

One of the most important market-building powers given to the EU—the Commission specifically—is that of competition policy. The Commission operates as an independent institution in this policy area, and the Council of Ministers is not usually involved in these policy decisions. In essence, competition policy—known as anti-trust policy in the United States—is about encouraging competition among firms and battling monopolistic or oligopolistic practices or those which privilege national producers over those in other EU member states. The requirements can be tough for any member state, but competition policy poses particular challenges for the new member states from Central and Eastern Europe. Moving from an economy that was largely under public control to one in which the market is dominant is difficult. The rigour of the EU's competition policy makes that transition, in some respects, even more onerous.

The Commission has the authority to rule on many mergers and acquisitions, fight cartels, and judge the appropriateness of many forms of state aid given by national or regional authorities to firms. In this policy area, the Commission is an international actor as well as an EU actor. Given the level of foreign direct investment in Europe by American firms, the Commission has the power to sanction the strategies of American firms with extensive operations in Europe even if they have been approved by American anti-trust authorities. Just to mention a few high-profile cases: the Commission vetoed the proposed merger between General Electric and Honeywell in 2001, and fined Microsoft a total of €780 million for anti-competitive behaviour between 2004 and 2006 (*Financial Times*, 13 July 2006).

Trade associations and firms as well as member-state authorities and ministers (and at times prime ministers and presidents) lobby, especially informally, on specific competition cases. However, the Commission needs to engage in far less negotiation than is required in other policy domains, and sometimes turns a deaf ear to lobbying even by leading national politicians. In this area, the Directorate-General for Competition and the Commissioner for Competition are the central actors.

Commercial (Trade) Policy

The key goal of the Treaty of Rome was to create a common market across national borders. The objective required liberalizing many national markets (that is, allowing imports to compete with domestically-produced goods) that had been heavily protected for many decades. Over time, the national economies of the member states have become far more interdependent. In 2005 trade within the EU-25 accounted for 66 per cent of the overall exports of the member states and 62 per cent of their imports (IMF 2006). However, trade with countries outside the EU is still very important for many member states.

The application of a single external tariff (which is applied to non-EU producers) in the late 1960s led to the decision that the European Economic Community (as the EU was then known) would speak with one voice in negotiations involving international trade policy. The Treaty of Rome gave the EEC competence in international trade negotiations involving trade in goods. The Commission was granted the power to act as sole negotiator for the Community in, for example, world trade talks. That power was strengthened in the Treaty of Nice, which gave the Commission the right to negotiate (with certain exceptions) trade in services. However, the competence to decide the EU's position in international trade negotiations was given to 'the member states operating through the European institutions', not to the Commission acting on its own. Therefore, although the Commission is the negotiator, the member states play a key role in shaping the negotiating mandate that the Commission pursues.

Economic and Monetary Union (EMU)

At Maastricht the members of the EU decided to create an Economic and Monetary Union (EMU), with a common currency and centralized responsibility for monetary policy. For the first time since the Roman Empire, Western Europe was to have a common currency. It was thought that a common currency would help keep a unified Germany tied to the project of European integration, would help increase economic efficiency in the EU and thereby raise the standard of living, and would help develop a sense of 'European' identity. A common currency requires a single central bank in charge of monetary policy, and the European Central Bank (ECB) (see Box 3.9) was created to run monetary policy with the goal of price stability (anti-inflation) as its top priority.

Part of the bargain that underpinned the decision to move to a single currency by 1999 was an agreement that states wishing to adopt the euro had to meet certain requirements (informally known as the Maastricht criteria) with regard to the level of inflation and of interest rates, and the size of the government deficit and debt. The decision was taken by the heads of state and government, but the preparation of the decision was carried out by finance ministers and a relatively small group of national civil servants and central bank staff. Private businesses such as banks were not intimately involved, and the policy process was relatively closed.

The decision to move towards a single currency had profound implications for the member states, as the budget deficit requirements forced the restructuring of public finances in several states adopting the Euro (the so-called Eurozone countries). In the Italian case, the restructuring was so profound that the country's ministerial organization and budgetary process had to be radically transformed. In some cases, the desire to join the EMU was so strong that countries—Greece for instance—resorted to questionable budgetary tricks in order to qualify.

Even after the creation of the EMU, the stringent fiscal requirements remained, as the EMU members agreed to respect a Stability and Growth Pact (SGP), which included provisions for financial penalties for the countries that violate it. Following the adoption of the euro in 1999 (notes and coins became available on 1 January 2002), several member states found their macro-economic policies under scrutiny as they struggled to meet the budget deficit requirements of EMU membership. By 2003, four countries, including the three largest economies of the Eurozone (Germany, France, and Italy), were in breach of the fiscal requirements set by the SGP. When the Commission recommended the application of the penalties mandated by the SGP, the Ecofin Council (of finance ministers) elected to disregard the recommendation. In 2005 the SGP was modified to make it less stringent.

More generally, membership of the euro means these countries no longer have an independent monetary policy. The European Central Bank, headquartered in Frankfurt, makes decisions about monetary policy that apply to all member states using the euro. National governments therefore can no longer control the level of interest rates, a control that previously gave national governments some leverage over the direction of the economy. The European Central Bank is mandated to privilege price stability and thereby avoid inflation but it has been criticized by some (including some Eurozone governments, such as France's) who would prefer it to adopt lower interest rates so as to stimulate the Eurozone economy and hopefully create more employment. The Bank, however, has argued that job creation requires the adoption of a more flexible labour market and greater liberalization of markets in general. It has not tailored its interest rate policy to the wishes of the member states, nor to societal actors. The ECB has become an important, and very independent, actor in the field of economic policy-making.

Market-correcting and -cushioning Policies

Although market-building policies have been a central feature of EU policy activity, the Union has also been very active in developing policies that might be viewed as 'market correcting' and 'market cushioning'. Market-correcting policies, such as the Common Agricultural Policy (CAP) and cohesion policy, attempt to limit inequalities or compensate for the cost to particular groups imposed by the building of markets. Market-cushioning policies, such as environmental and social regulation, attempt to limit the potentially harmful effects of the market on human beings and the environment.

Common Agricultural Policy (CAP)

Perhaps the best-known policy designed to offset market forces is the CAP—for which the European Union has almost exclusive competence. Although welfare state policies have been peripheral to the EU's policy agenda, the CAP, with its system of agricultural support and subsidies, is an exception to that rule. As Rieger (2005: 182) argues: 'The key to understanding this policy domain is to see the CAP as an integral part of the west European welfare state'. The CAP is also unique in the amount of money it receives from the EU budget (see Figure 6.1), and the amount of contestation it causes. Although the CAP created a market for agricultural goods within the EU, its market-correcting properties have been the most controversial outside the EU because third parties have found their agricultural goods subject to high tariffs when exported to the EU. In July 2006 the Doha Round of WTO negotiations stalled mostly over a dispute on agricultural tariffs between the US and the EU.

The CAP stirs up plenty of internal debate as well. The benefits of the CAP are distributed very unequally across member states. Although new member states depend much more on agriculture than do older members, the largest recipients are still all older members (see Table 6.2). However, some redistribution of agricultural funds from the older to the new member states has already occurred: from 2007 the funds for farmers in the old member states began to decline in order to make room for greater allocations for the farmers in the new member states.

More generally, pressure from enlargement has spurred some CAP reform including a shift from supporting production, which in the past had often led to overproduction and waste, to supporting rural development and environmental protection. However, the radical, fundamental reforms arguably needed to address CAP's failures have not yet been agreed, not least because any important decision on reform would require unanimity amongst all member states.

Cohesion Policy

Cohesion policy was introduced to reduce inequality between regions and to compensate governments of poor countries for the costs of economic integration. To

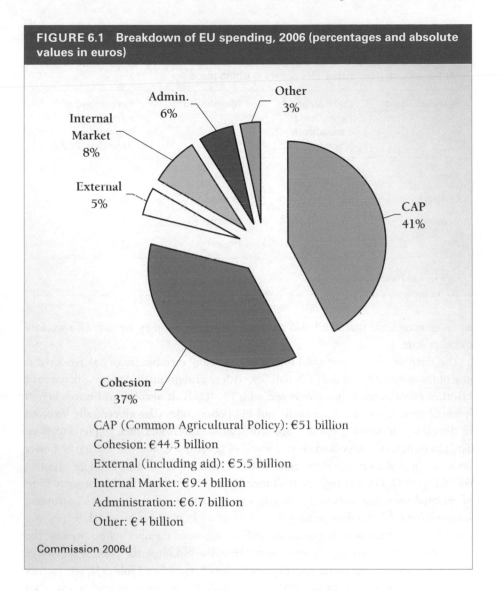

FIGURE 6.1   Breakdown of EU spending, 2006 (percentages and absolute values in euros)

Admin. 6%

Other 3%

Internal Market 8%

External 5%

CAP 41%

Cohesion 37%

CAP (Common Agricultural Policy): €51 billion

Cohesion: €44.5 billion

External (including aid): €5.5 billion

Internal Market: €9.4 billion

Administration: €6.7 billion

Other: €4 billion

Commission 2006d

help offset some of the costs faced by member states in adjusting their economies to EU standards, cohesion policy was introduced after the first enlargement (UK, Denmark, and Ireland). Cohesion policy has increased in importance over time, and now represents one of the most important areas for public expenditure (see Figure 6.1).

The budget for cohesion policy represents approximately 37 per cent of the EU's budget (the CAP accounts for roughly 41 per cent). Every member state receives some cohesion policy monies which makes this policy politically acceptable to all. However, most of the funding is spent in the neediest regions, where per capita GDP is below 75 per cent of the EU average (see Table 6.3). Regions with specific problems (such

TABLE 6.2 CAP spending breakdown

This table shows France is the big winner from CAP spending, while Poland, the largest of the new member states, only comes in eighth place.

Member State	Percentage of agricultural expenditure (rounded, 2005)	Member State	Percentage of agricultural expenditure (rounded, 2005)
France	20	UK	9
Germany	13	Greece	6
Spain	13	Ireland	4
Italy	9	Poland	3

Commission 2006c; 2006a

as a declining industrial base) also receive funding even if they are part of a wealthy member state.

The distribution of structural funding across many member states has rendered it one of the most visible of the EU's policies, with road signs often signifying that a road or other public work is being financed with EU funds. It also features actors across levels of governance: local, national, and EU policy-makers are all centrally involved in decisions surrounding the allocation of regional funds and their implementation. The interaction of actors from several levels of governance, and the sharing of power between them gives rise to the notion of the EU as a system of **multilevel governance** (see Chapter 1). Because regions in all member states have benefited from some form of regional spending, cohesion policy has escaped some of the intense controversy surrounding CAP. However, enlargement has made it more controversial, pitting net contributors against new recipients, or 'old' versus 'new' member states. Because the new member states are significantly poorer than the old ones, the poorest regions of Europe are now all concentrated in the new member states (see Table 6.3), and further changes are anticipated. In the 2007–13 period, for instance, Poland is expected to overtake Spain as the largest recipient of cohesion funds (*Financial Times*, 14 July 2006).

TABLE 6.3 Poor regions

The tables on the next page show how the concentration of the EU poorest regions has changed with the inclusion of the new member states. Table 6.3a shows the ten poorest regions of the EU-15 in 1999. Table 6.3b shows the ten poorest regions of the EU-25 in 2003 (before accession).

TABLE 6.3a   Regional per capita GDP in the ten poorest regions of the EU in 1999

(in purchasing power parities, EU-15 = 100)

Rank	Region and country	PPP
1	Réunion (France)	51
2	Ipeiros (Greece)	51
3	Guyane (France)	51
4	Extremadura (Spain)	52
5	Azores (Portugal)	53
6	Dytiki Ellada (Greece)	53
7	Peloponnisos (Greece)	55
8	Anatoliki Makedonia, Thraki (Greece)	56
9	Guadeloupe (France)	56
10	Centro (Portugal)	57

Eurostat 2002

TABLE 6.3b   Regional per capita GDP in the ten poorest regions of the EU in 2003

(in purchasing power parities, EU-25 = 100)

Rank	Region and country	PPP
1	Lubelskie (Poland)	33
2	Podkarpackie (Poland)	33
3	Podlaskie (Poland)	36
4	Świętokrzyskie (Poland)	37
5	Warmińsko-Mazurskie (Poland)	37
6	Opolskie (Poland)	37
7	Észak Magyarország (Hungary)	38
8	Východné Slovensko (Slovakia)	39
9	Eszag-Alföld (Hungary)	39
10	Dél-Alföld (Hungary)	40

Eurostat 2006

Environmental and Social Regulation

Although the CAP and cohesion policy are probably the best-known of the EU's policies outside of the single market, other policies began life as relatively marginal and then became far more important over time. Such policies may be grouped together under the rubric of 'social regulation' since they are designed to cushion the impact of the market on society. Occupational health and safety legislation is one area where the EU acted quite early on. Another important type of social regulation is concerned with the protection of the environment. In environmental policy (especially in the area of pollution control) the EU became active after a customs union had been created, but before many of its member states had become environmentally conscious. Environmental policy was initially put on the agenda both because of its international salience and because it would affect trade in goods such as automobiles. Over time, the focus has widened to include areas that are not market-related, such as the protection of environmentally sensitive habitats.

In many areas of environmental policy (primarily those outside of pollution control), national governments are free to supplement EU legislation. Some do. In general, the Scandinavian member states, Austria, the Netherlands, and Germany are the most active in supplementing EU legislation with their own. But most member states choose not to act unilaterally, thereby making the EU the de facto primary actor in this area. One of the EU's most recent initiatives in this policy area is the so-called REACH directive for the 'Registration, Evaluation, and Authorization of Chemicals' which covers about 30,000 chemical products (see Box 5.4).

Another area of 'social regulation' is consumer protection. A series of food scares and concern over genetically modified organisms (GMOs) have propelled this issue up the EU's agenda and resulted in the establishment of a European Food Safety Authority. It has also caused conflict with the US, which is the largest producer of GMOs, and accuses the EU of using unscientific concerns as a way to shield European agriculture from foreign competition. Social regulatory policies that are related directly to the single market (such as regulations on product safety) pre-empt national policies, whereas in other areas (such as hygiene standards) the EU stipulates minimum standards which national governments can exceed if they so wish.

The EU has also been active in the area of gender equality. National pension systems have had to be restructured to treat men and women equally. More generally, the EU has been a significant actor in the move toward equal pay (both in terms of income and benefits) in the workplace (Caporaso 2001). Most recently, the EU passed laws against sexual harassment. While some member states already had tough laws, Spain, Portugal, Greece, and Italy had no laws that held employers responsible for harassment within the workplace, and Germany defined sexual harassment more narrowly than did the EU legislation. Member states can adopt stricter definitions of harassment, but now EU legislation provides a 'floor' for any national legislative activity in that area.

Comparing EU Policy Types

How can we make sense of all these policies? To start, note that each category of policy has certain characteristics that distinguish it from others. While the categories are not watertight, policies that fit within them do differ in significant ways along a number of dimensions (see Table 6.4). First, *market-building* policies stimulate market forces and encourage regulatory reform. Because of their emphasis on competition, such policies tend in practice to favour (although not require) privatization and the withdrawal of the state from those areas in which it has protected national producers. Many of the policies in this category are regulatory. In general, they also tend to be made by the Community method (see Box 6.4) in which the EU's supranational institutions are normally most active, the Union's competence tends to be most comprehensive, and national policy activity is largely pre-empted.

The creation of markets is also marked by a variety of political dynamics and a range of political actors. The different theoretical approaches introduced in Chapter 1 shed light on these different dynamics. A few policy areas, such as energy and pharmaceuticals, feature what Peterson and Bomberg (1999: 81) describe as 'a relatively stable and cohesive policy network'. That is, policies are shaped by a tight and insular group of actors. Similarly, monetary policy is quite insulated from actors outside the central banking community. But most other areas related to trade do not exhibit such single-mindedness among the key actors who interact in what are often fragmented and internally divided networks.

Market-correcting policies differ from market-building ones in that they tend to protect producers from market forces. Most are redistributive—from consumers to farmers, and from rich regions to poor regions. Because they are so overtly redistributive rather than regulatory, they tend to be very difficult to change as the impact of any change is quite transparent. For this reason, market-correcting policies tend to be dominated by intergovernmental bargaining rather than by the EU institutions. Liberal intergovernmentalists show how major decisions in these areas are dominated by national governments. These governments are responding to strong societal actors (such as agricultural lobbies), but national ministers ultimately decide when other considerations will trump the demands of those lobbies.

Market-cushioning policies try to minimize the harm economic activities impose on nature and humans. These policies tend to be regulatory in nature, impose demands on private actors, and fall under the shared competence of the EU because both Brussels and national capitals typically 'co-govern' in these areas. The active role of EU institutions in developing these areas at the Union level, often with strong support from a variety of representatives of civil society (see Chapter 5), provides fertile ground for the new institutionalist claim that 'institutions matter'.

TABLE 6.4 Policy types in the EU				
Type	Level of EU competence	Key features	Primary actors	Examples
Market-building	Nearly exclusive; covering an extensive range of economic policies	Emphasis on liberalization and increasing economic efficiency; strong role for supranational institutions	Business actors; EU institutions; national finance officials; central bankers	Internal market policies (such as telecommunications or air transport); EMU
Market-correcting	Often exclusive but only in limited areas	Controversial; with redistributive implications; effective exclusion of EP	Farm lobbies, national officials; Commission	CAP; cohesion policy; fisheries
Market-cushioning	Shared with member states	Significant implementation problems	Supranational institutions; sectoral ministers; public interest groups	Environmental protection; occupational health and safety; gender equality in the workplace

Conclusion

If institutions and member states are the skeleton of the EU, policies are its flesh. It is through its policies that the EU affects people's lives, within and beyond its own borders. The Italian retailer who can sell non-durum wheat pasta in face of the opposition of the Italian authorities, or the British holidaymaker who may pay less for his mobile phone calls when holidaying in Spain, both feel the influence of the European Union in their daily lives. So does the American shareholder who sees the price of her Microsoft stocks affected by the competition policy decisions of the European Commission, or the Indian farmer adversely affected by the high tariffs the EU imposes on agricultural products.

What makes studying EU policies enormously challenging—as well as fascinating—is that each policy has its own features and trajectory, as this chapter has illustrated. But amidst all that variation, common themes also emerge. In particular, policies and policy-making in the EU reflect the three major themes of this volume:

experimentation as a driving force of European integration; the astonishing array of actors and power-sharing and consensus-building amongst them; and the gap between the scope and the capacity of the EU.

The creation of EMU was in part the result of dramatic experimentation. One of the main reasons for moving to a common currency was that the old status quo, with exchange rate agreements that were prone to collapse, was no longer tenable. Yet monetary union as the way forward was an untested course. As the former chief economist of the ECB has argued, European governments met the challenge by consciously choosing to take a risk and take 'the big leap into monetary union' (quoted in the *Financial Times*, 27 October 2006).

Different policy areas also show different levels of inclusiveness and power-sharing. In some areas, such as competition policy and monetary policy, power is highly concentrated. In many others, however, a larger set of actors is involved. Both environmental and cohesion policy involve a large number of actors at different levels of governance—including EU institutions, national governments, and private stakeholders—and reveal a strong preference for consensus-building. But consensus-building in Brussels comes at a price: decisions made by the EU, even if well thought-out, seem to many Europeans to be made in a system that they cannot control. Citizen input is still largely exercised through the democratic process in each member state rather than through citizen participation in European decision-making (see Chapter 8).

Finally, we have seen how the pressure of economic integration has led to the continuing expansion of the scope of the EU's policy remit, from policies directly related to market-building, to market-correcting and then market-cushioning policies. At the same time, however, the policy capacity of the EU falls well short of any nation-state, relying as it does on a very limited budget and on the national implementation of EU legislation. As the EU's policy remit expands further, into areas not just of economic growth but of internal and external security, this scope–capacity gap becomes ever wider.

?   **DISCUSSION QUESTIONS**

   1. Why has the EU privileged economic policies over social welfare policies?

   2. Why is the EU budget so much smaller than that of its major member states?

   3. What obstacles to the execution of EU policies exist that do not exist at the national level?

   4. How is enlargement expected to affect the EU's economic policies?

→ FURTHER READING

For an in-depth analysis of the EU's major policy areas, including those discussed in this chapter, see Wallace *et al.* (2005). Another excellent review of EU policy-making is Nugent (2006). Egan (2001) analyses the construction of the European internal market in a particularly comprehensive and insightful fashion. Zito (2000) presents a sophisticated explanation of the evolution of EU environmental policy. Comprehensive overviews of environmental policy include Jordan (2005) and Lenschow (2002). A detailed account of how individual member states contributed to the creation of the EMU is Dyson and Featherstone (1999). Multi-country studies of the impact of the EMU are provided by Martin and Ross (2004) and Dyson (2002). A very clear explanation of the economics of the EMU is De Grauwe (2002).

De Grauwe, P. (2002), *Economics of Monetary Union*, 5th edn. (Oxford: Oxford University Press).

Dyson, K. (ed.) (2002), *European States and the Euro: Europeanization, Variation, and Convergence* (Oxford: Oxford University Press).

_____ and Featherstone, K. (1999), *The Road to Maastricht: Negotiating Economic and Monetary Union* (Oxford: Oxford University Press).

Egan, M. (2001), *Constructing a European Market: Standards, Regulation, and Governance* (Oxford: Oxford University Press).

Jordan, A. (ed.) (2005), *Environmental Policy in the European Union*, 2nd edn. (London and Sterling, VA: Earthscan Publications).

Lenschow, A. (ed.) (2002), *Environmental Policy Integration: Greening Sectoral Policies in Europe* (London and Sterling, VA: Earthscan Publications).

Martin, A., and Ross, G. (eds.) (2004), *Euros and Europeans: Monetary Integration and the European Model of Society* (Cambridge: Cambridge University Press).

Nugent, N. (2006), *The Government and Politics of the European Union*, 6th edn. (Basingstoke and Durham, NC: Palgrave and Duke University Press).

Wallace, H., Wallace W., and Pollack M. (eds.) (2005), *Policy-making in the European Union*, 5th edn. (Oxford and New York: Oxford University Press).

Zito, A. (2000), *Creating Environmental Policy in the European Union* (Basingstoke and New York: Palgrave).

⊕ WEB LINKS

To locate EU publications covering policy, try the EU portal EUR-Lex at www.europa.eu.int/eur-lex/. It is bibliographical in nature, but contains links to many full-text documents. For a record of EU legislation, search this site from the European Parliament: www.europarl.eu.int/guide/search/docsearch_en.htm.

For full-text, non-EU documents see the websites 'European Integration Online Papers' at www.eiop.or.at/eiop/ and 'European Research Papers Archive' at http://eiop.or.at/erpa/

 Visit the Online Resource Centre that accompanies this book for additional material: www.oxfordtextbooks.co.uk/orc/bomberg2e/

CHAPTER 7

A Secure Europe? Internal Security Policies

John D. Occhipinti

Introduction	139	Visa Policy	152
Development of the Third Pillar	140	Illegal Immigration	152
Early Years	140	Asylum and Refugee Policy	155
The Amsterdam Era	142	Conclusion	156
Crime-Fighting and Counter-Terrorism	145		
Institutions	146	DISCUSSION QUESTIONS	157
Criminal Law and Counter-Terrorism	148	FURTHER READING	158
Border Management	151	WEB LINKS	158
Immigration and Schengen	151		

▌ Chapter Overview

The expansion of EU Justice and Home Affairs (JHA) policy has been rapid and re-markable. This chapter examines the origins, development, and key features of JHA policy, focusing on crime-fighting, counter-terrorism, and border management issues, as well as associated institutional changes. EU policy has sparked significant changes to national laws designed to help fight cross-border crime and terrorism, and manage external borders. Competing, and not always compatible concerns for sovereignty, internal security, civil liberties, and human rights have shaped institutional devel-opments, the harmonization of national laws, and relations with non-EU countries. Cooperation on JHA, especially since 2001, has been driven by crises related to terror-ism and illegal immigration, yet the implementation of EU legislation at the national level has been uneven and contentious.

Introduction

EU policy-making on Justice and Home Affairs (JHA) is aimed primarily at facilitating international cooperation on border management, migration, crime-fighting, counter-terrorism, and other issues linked to internal security. It also extends to the promotion of judicial cooperation on civil law, or the body of law dealing with the rights of citizens, such as family law. The goal of the 'four freedoms' (free movement for people, goods, services, and money) is as old as the EU itself and has always posed challenges to internal security and cross-border justice. Yet, it was not until the creation of the so-called third pillar in 1993 by the Maastricht Treaty that JHA became a formal policy area of the EU. Progress on JHA was slow until 1999, when the Amsterdam Treaty took effect, thus empowering the Commission to initiate legislation. Member states agreed to prioritize internal security goals the same year.

In some ways, Europe's most fundamental security challenges have changed little over time. Land, sea, and air borders have always required protection from cross-border crime and illegal immigrants, while the needs of refugees continue to challenge notions of human rights and the limits of national resources. Likewise, organized crime and drug trafficking have been pressing concerns for decades. Yet, JHA policy has expanded rapidly in response to the demise of the Soviet bloc (which, if nothing else, offered managed borders), post-Cold War military conflict (in ex-Yugoslavia, Somalia, Afghanistan, and so on), and extreme poverty, particularly in Africa. The threat of terrorism has endured over time as well, although extreme left- and right-wing organizations have been overshadowed by cells orchestrated or motivated by Al Qaeda.

In a context of both continuity and change, JHA is now a major growth area for EU policy-making. Beginning in the mid-1990s but especially since 2001, a series of crises has prompted a significant extension of cooperation in JHA. Numerous institutions, instruments, and databases have been developed to help national authorities coordinate their efforts and share information and best practices. Cooperation has been facilitated by EU legislation harmonizing national visa and asylum policy (see Box 7.1), as well as some aspects of criminal law. By 2006, 17 per cent of all the legislative proposals made by the Commission were in the area of JHA (*European Report*, 29 June 2006), making it the most prolific area of EU law-making in recent times. Moreover, the EU planned to spend about twice as much on JHA between 2007 and 2013 as it did during the previous budgetary period (*European Report*, 18 February 2006).

The key dynamic in the evolution of JHA has been the EU's response to internal security challenges that arise from the embrace of the four freedoms. A negative side effect of these freedoms has been greater mobility for organized crime groups and their contraband. The extension of free movement to new and future member states, especially the planned widening of the passport-free 'Schengen zone' (see Box 2.2), has provided further impetus for legislation at the EU level. Borders both within the Schengen area and at its external frontiers are quite porous, meaning that organized crime and terrorism are frequently transnational in nature, thus necessitating

> **BOX 7.1** **Key concepts and terms**
>
> **Asylum** is protection under the terms of the Geneva Convention that is provided by a government to a foreigner who is unable to stay in his/her country of citizenship/residence for fear of persecution due to political views, race, religion, nationality, or membership of a particular social group. Asylum is not afforded to 'economic refugees'.
>
> **Biometric technology** allows measurements of unique physical characteristics, such as fingerprints, eye retinas, and facial features, to be taken and stored digitally in passports, visas, or databases. Biometric measurements of travellers at border checkpoints can be used to authenticate biometric travel documents or search computer records.
>
> **Framework Decisions (FDs)** are legislative 'blueprints' used to harmonize national criminal law. They specify how national laws must be changed but leave the specifics of this 'transposition' to each EU country.
>
> **Human trafficking** is the criminal enterprise of transporting people (mainly women and children), who are often enslaved for profitable exploitation, such as forced prostitution or labour. Human trafficking is linked to human smuggling; in these cases would-be immigrants voluntarily pay criminal organizations for illegal passage into a country but may unwittingly become victims of human trafficking.
>
> **Transposition** is the act of changing national law to meet the specifications of EU directives or framework decisions. JHA legislation typically includes deadlines for transposition and a legal measure is not considered to be implemented until it has been 'transposed', although the gap between legal transposition and substantive implementation is sometimes wide.

a multinational approach. However, progress at the EU level has been inhibited by member states' concerns for their sovereignty in this sensitive area. Moreover, JHA policy has been shaped by the competing imperatives of national security, civil liberties, and human rights.

This chapter begins by explaining the origins and development of JHA as a key area of EU policy. It then examines crime-fighting and counter-terrorism policies. Finally, it turns to conflicts and cooperation surrounding issues of border management, including immigration, visas, and asylum.

Development of the Third Pillar

Early Years

As with the birth of the EU's second (foreign policy) pillar, events in the 1970s helped foster the political pressures and policy demands to make JHA an official EU policy area. The earliest steps in this direction were instigated by the terrorist attack at the 1972 Olympic Games in Munich and the burgeoning problem of domestic terrorism in Europe. Interior and justice ministers of the then nine EC members initiated a series of meetings in 1976 designed to facilitate information sharing and coordination on terrorism. The 'Trevi Group', as it became known, created intergovernmental working groups on several internal security topics, but lacked a developed treaty base or institutional infrastructure.

By the 1980s it was evident that eliminating internal borders among EU members would create criminal justice challenges that necessitated going beyond the weak and loosely organized Trevi Group. The Single European Act of 1986 sought to eliminate barriers to the free movement of goods, services, and capital, and was aspirational (rather than substantive) on the removal of barriers to the free movement of persons. However, plans for the removal of physical barriers at borders were set in motion by the Schengen Agreement of 1985, which was agreed entirely outside any EU context by five states: France, Germany, and the Benelux states. Schengen's founders agreed a trade-off: no systematic border controls (as opposed to checks or internal controls over persons) between signatories but strengthened external borders vis-à-vis non-Schengen countries. The enactment of Schengen was obviously problematic for the rest of the EU and neighbouring countries. Meanwhile, within the Schengen zone, law-abiding citizens, but also illegal immigrants, organized crime groups, and terrorists could enjoy free movement across national borders. At the same time, cooperation between member states' criminal justice and border management authorities was impeded by jurisdictional limitations and competing legal structures. In short, the need for policy cooperation was clear, but the EU's institutional capacity was lacking.

This mismatch between scope and capacity (see Chapter 1) encouraged European leaders to agree that JHA should be established as one of the three pillars of the new EU as established by the Maastricht Treaty. As explained in Chapter 1 (see Box 1.2), almost all decision-making in the new third JHA pillar was originally intergovernmental because member states were reluctant to share much sovereignty in this area. The Maastricht Treaty provisions for this pillar dictated that proposals could be made only by member states, not the Commission, and decision-making in the Council was by unanimity. The Commission, but also the European Parliament and the European Court of Justice were largely shut out. Under these arrangements, the third pillar produced only modest achievements.

This situation began to change in the mid-1990s once the EU began to feel the effects of the Cold War's end. The conflict in the Balkans led to a European refugee crisis and the need for international cooperation to deal with it. Meanwhile, doubts about the quality of border controls maintained by central and eastern European countries and the growth of organized crime in southeastern Europe created new source- and transit-states for a variety of illicit trafficking enterprises targeting the EU. The impact of these problems was soon magnified by the implementation of the passport-free Schengen zone in 1995. By this time it was also evident that many central and east European states would someday become EU members and participate in that passport-free zone.

This realization contributed to a growing sense of urgency amongst existing member states. The result was agreement on the need to speed up progress on JHA at the EU level and to pressure the applicant states to institute reforms in line with the EU's evolving body of legislation in this area (see, for example, Henderson 2005).

The Amsterdam Era

The development of JHA policy was a major topic at the 1996–7 intergovernmental conference that produced the Amsterdam Treaty. The Treaty established the goal of an 'Area of Freedom, Security and Justice' and empowered the Commission to share in the right to initiate legislative proposals. In October 1999, a special European Council held at Tampere, Finland established a list of general 'milestones' and specific objectives that served as the EU's JHA agenda until 2004.

The Amsterdam Treaty also changed the nature of JHA policy-making by shifting the legal basis of cooperation on civil law, immigration, and asylum from the third to the first pillar. Doing so meant employing the Community method of decision-making for these policies, with the Commission as main initiator, unanimity not required, and the EP and ECJ given a bigger role. The shift to the Community method was meant to address a perceived democratic deficit on JHA by giving more power to elected Members of the European Parliament (MEPs; see Chapter 8). The introduction of qualified majority voting (QMV) was designed to mitigate the gridlock that some feared would follow enlargement.

Although the Amsterdam Treaty included several provisions designed to streamline decision-making, not all of them were implemented, or were implemented only after significant delay. For instance, the agreement to subject some JHA matters to the Community method did not happen on schedule, as some member states were unwilling to relinquish their veto power until work on sensitive legislation on border issues was completed. Similarly, a new so-called *passarelle* (literally, in French, 'footbridge') clause allowed for the transfer of certain JHA measures into the first pillar on the basis of unanimous votes, but it was never used. With the entry into force of the Nice Treaty in 2003, the Community method was applied to some civil law, but the other changes foreseen in the Treaty only came much later. Not until 2005 did the Council decide to apply the Community method to some aspects of border management, such as burden sharing for refugees. Even then, other areas (such as asylum policy) were still handled by the intergovernmental method into 2006. The result is that today JHA policy-making consists of a complicated mix of different rules across pillars and policies (see Box 7.2).

Another noteworthy development since enactment of the Amsterdam Treaty has been the EU's increasing attention to the external dimensions of its internal security. Hoping to deal with a broad range of security problems closer to their source, and in response to the shifting of its own borders, the EU has forged new partnerships with a variety of non-EU countries, especially those covered by the European Neighbourhood

BOX 7.2	How it really works

Policy-making in JHA

In many respects, JHA policy is characterized by anomalous rules and dynamics. For those JHA policies based in the first pillar, such as civil law and many aspects of border management, the Community method of decision-making is used. However, on third-pillar matters the EP and ECJ are largely sidelined and the Commission must share its right of initiative with member states themselves. JHAs are especially hard to track because of the combination of opt-out/in provisions in both the Amsterdam Treaty and 2007 Reform Treaty. The so-called *passerelle* (bridging) provisions mean that the management of specific JHA matters moves over time between procedures and pillars. Moreover, the membership of individual JHA regimes changes over time as states are admitted to Schengen or accede to the Prüm Convention (see p. 145).

The legislative outputs of the third pillar have not been the traditional directives that make up the bulk of EU legislation in economic and related affairs (as discussed in Chapter 6). Rather, they have taken the form of either 'decisions' (such as the decision to establish a new agency), and Framework Decisions (FDs), as defined in Box 7.1. Framework decisions are reached not by the Community method but by the Council working intergovernmentally.

The preparation of JHA legislation is also anomalous. The JHA Council's work is largely prepared not by Coreper, but by one of two bodies of national specialists. Third-pillar matters have been considered by the Article 36 Committee (named after a paragraph of the Maastricht Treaty and commonly known as 'CATS'), while border management issues are handled by the Strategic Committee on Immigration, Frontiers, and Asylum (SCIFA). The EP's standing committee on Civil Liberties, Justice and Home Affairs prepares Parliament's opinions on JHA proposals and often raises concerns linked to civil liberties.

QMV is permitted for an increasing number of first-pillar JHA issues, but the need for unanimity in the Council has endured in the third pillar. The Parliament has the power of co-decision on most first-pillar JHA items that are covered by QMV, but the Council can largely ignore the Parliament's opinion on third-pillar matters. Indeed it has often reached its informal decisions before receiving Parliament's suggested amendments.

The ECJ's role is much weaker than in most other policy areas, but it is growing. On first-pillar JHA issues, the Treaties state that the ECJ is barred from hearing cases 'relating to the maintenance of law and order and the safeguarding of internal security'. For the third-pillar issues, the Court's power is even more limited. Member states must declare their willingness to allow the ECJ to make preliminary rulings. By 2006, only fourteen governments had done so. However, in its landmark preliminary ruling of 2005 in the Pupino case, the ECJ specified that governments had to apply national laws in close accord with FDs. This ruling implied that FDs enjoyed a kind of direct effect—similar to directives under the first pillar. Thus, while policy-making rules have differed significantly between pillars 1 and 3, they have become more similar over time. The Reform Treaty (like the Constitutional Treaty) proposed to scrap the pillar system but did not implement a uniform decision-making process for all JHA matters.

Policy (ENP; see Chapter 9 and Occhipinti 2007). The EU has also concluded a number of key security agreements with the US following the terrorist attacks of 9/11 (see Box 7.3; Occhipinti 2005).

Currently, the EU's policy agenda for JHA is specified in the so-called Hague Programme (see Box 7.4), which was developed during the Dutch EU Presidency of

---

BOX 7.3   Transatlantic cooperation

Despite the appearance of a souring of transatlantic relations, the post-9/11 era can actually be viewed as a period of greater, not lesser, EU–US cooperation on JHA. In fact, a regular process of consultation begun in 2004 has helped improve relations in the following areas:

- **Europol**: agreements reached with the US in 2001–2 allow the exchange of liaison officers and the sharing of criminal intelligence. To date, however, this link has not been used much.

- Mutual Legal Assistance: a 2003 agreement modernizes member states' bilateral arrangements with the US on joint investigation teams, banking secrecy, and the sharing of evidence for prosecution.

- Extradition: a 2003 agreement obliges the US not to impose the death penalty on suspects transferred from the EU, while American extradition requests to an EU member state will not necessarily be trumped by a European Arrest Warrant (EAW) issued by another EU country.

- Shipping Security: America's Container Security Initiative obliges foreign ports to establish terminals dedicated to US-bound shipping; these are to be staffed by American customs inspectors. The Initiative requires further that shipping manifests (listing what is to be shipped) be provided to US officials 24 hours before a container is loaded onto a freighter. By 2007, 23 ports in ten EU countries were participating.

- Airline Security: a 2004 agreement specified that European carriers must meet the US requirement to share passenger name record (PNR) data with American authorities prior to take-off. The EP argued that this agreement violated EU data protection rules. In May 2006, the ECJ annulled the pact, though on technical rather than substantive grounds. The ECJ's decision necessitated new negotiations, with compromises made by both sides. Overall, however, American authorities used the new negotiations in 2006–7 to press for terms more favourable to the US. At issue was how and which European PNR data could be accessed, stored, and shared.

- Travel Documents: the Bush administration won a series of extensions for Europeans when the US Congress threatened that EU citizens carrying newly issued non-biometric passports would no longer qualify for the US Visa Waiver Program (VWP). Eventually, all the affected EU member states agreed to issue the new **biometric** passports. However, the EU continued to protest at America's delay in including most of the newer EU member states in the VWP. The matter was to be reconsidered by the US Congress in 2008.

BOX 7.4	Hague Programme

Approved by the European Council in late 2004, the Hague Programme identifies several specific goals under the headings 'Strengthening Freedom', 'Strengthening Security', and 'Strengthening Justice'. The agenda also calls for attention to fundamental rights, constrained financial resources, and the external dimensions of JHA. In May 2005, the Commission transformed the Hague Programme into an action plan of specific tasks. One key priority identified in the Hague Programme is the creation of a common asylum area, with the goal of implementing a common application procedure and a uniform status for refugees throughout the EU by 2010. These aims are ambitious, but they need not be decided by unanimity; much of the legislation for the new asylum system will be subject to the Community method.

2004 as the successor to the Tampere agenda. This plan will guide the EU on JHA until 2010. It entails a mix of new initiatives and attention to the implementation and effectiveness of existing measures. However, a number of its goals are likely to prove difficult to realize, at least until the proposed 2007 Reform Treaty is fully implemented. Of the 40 new areas to which the Treaty extended QMV, most related to police and judicial cooperation.

Crime-Fighting and Counter-Terrorism

Progress on JHA is often (justly) criticized for slow decision-making at the EU level and delayed implementation in the member states. Developments in the area of crime-fighting and counter-terrorism, however, are remarkable when viewed in the context of the relatively short history of the third pillar. A network of criminal justice bodies now exists at the EU level to promote the sharing of criminal intelligence, evidence for prosecution, and best practices for training. These initiatives are supported by a variety of databases and funding programmes. Similarly ambitious is the 2005 Prüm Convention on criminal justice cooperation, which (again) began life as a non-EU agreement (built on a bilateral arrangement between Luxembourg and Germany), but which snowballed to include seven signatories. It allows the automatic sharing of national fingerprint and DNA data and 'mixed' patrols of police officers operating on foreign soil. By 2007, sixteen states had indicated their desire to sign on to the treaty, and some of its provisions were in the process of being folded into EU law. In addition, through the approximation (harmonization) of national substantive and procedural criminal law, a legal infrastructure of crime-fighting was being developed to facilitate greater cooperation and coordination among the member states and prevent criminals from escaping justice simply by moving from one state to another.

Institutions

From the beginning, the European Police Office—Europol (see Box 7.5)—has been at the centre of the EU's institutional infrastructure for crime-fighting. Its primary role is to maintain a network of liaison officers and a database of criminal intelligence that are available to support and coordinate the investigations of national criminal police authorities. The 1992 Maastricht Treaty provided the legal basis for Europol, but its creation was delayed by subsequent disputes in and among member states. Europol finally became operational in July 1999 (see Occhipinti 2003).

Since 2002, Europol has been paired in The Hague with Eurojust, which provides a network for criminal prosecutors and judges to share information and evidence concerning investigations and trials. With a permanent staff of around 70, Eurojust also provides legal analysis for prosecutions and serves as the conduit for making requests for extradition, or the delivery of a person, suspected or convicted of a crime, from the state where they have taken refuge to the state that claims jurisdiction. As with Europol, Eurojust may use its analyses to request that a member state launch a criminal investigation, but it has no way of compelling national authorities to do so.

In recent years, national authorities have made greater use of Europol and Eurojust in their criminal investigations. Both bodies have experienced significant increases in their caseloads and the volume of information shared through their channels. The directors of Europol and Eurojust continue to bemoan the lack of cooperation across member states and have implored national authorities to share more and better-quality criminal intelligence with and through their respective organizations. But there is no doubt that both of these EU-level institutions are far more active and engaged than ever before.

Along with facilitating cooperation, the EU's evolving institutional infrastructure of crime-fighting promotes the sharing of best practices and police training. At the forefront, in some respects, is the European Police College, known as CEPOL, which is the EU's 'virtual' police academy for high-level police officials. Created in 2000, CEPOL aims to develop a distinctive European approach to crime-fighting by helping to fund and coordinate training programmes hosted by the member states. For example, CEPOL has developed common training curricula for national police academies to 'train the trainers' who serve there. However, CEPOL is not without problems, including difficulties in recruiting staff to its UK headquarters in Bramshill (about 70 miles from London on an inferior train-line).

Yet another institution for crime-fighting is the Police Chiefs Task Force (PCTF), launched in 2000. It meets once per EU presidency, bringing together high-ranking police officers to share best practices and consult on strategic planning. While the PCTF, along with other recently-minted JHA institutions, is not central to operational matters, its launch illustrates the EU's rapidly developing and expanding cooperation in the area of JHA.

BOX 7.5   Compared to what?

Europol and the Federal Bureau of Investigation (FBI)

Europol remains a far a cry from a European FBI, yet it has grown steadily since its inception. Created as the Europol Drugs Unit in 1994 and operating out of a portable trailer in Strasbourg, Europol's crime-fight remit has been gradually expanded to cover all forms of serious transnational organized crime. After years of delay, Europol's computerized database became fully operational, allowing 24-hour access to criminal intelligence in any official EU language. Europol also maintains liaison relationships with Interpol (an international crime-fighting network) and several non-EU states, such as those in the Schengen zone, the US, and Canada. Europol's effectiveness in actual police operations has been questioned, but it is being increasingly used by member states. In 2006, Europol published its first annual Organized Crime Threat Assessment, intended to guide strategic planning on crime-fighting in the EU.

As the table illustrates, the FBI dwarfs Europol in nearly every regard, although it should be noted that numerous EU states invest significant national resources in FBI-type activites. The key question for European states concerns what resources to pool, and thus Europol's history has been radically different from that of the FBI. However, the FBI, too, grew out of humble beginnings. The forerunner of the FBI was a small corps of agents founded by the US Attorney General in 1908 to replace private detectives and officers borrowed from other agencies. It was not until 1934 that FBI agents were empowered to carry guns and make arrests. As with Europol, the FBI's growth was initially inhibited by a lack of federal criminal statutes and scepticism about impinging on state and local authorities. Counter-terrorism became the FBI's primary mission after 11 September amid reform of its information technology and the assignment to it of a new role in the restructured US intelligence community (see Box 7.6). In sum, despite important differences between them, both Europol and FBI started small and grew incrementally into important crime-fighting bodies.

	EUROPOL	FBI
Budget	€67.9 million (2007)	$6 billion (2007)
Personnel	590 (including 90 liaison officers)	31,000 (including 12,500 special agents)
Locations	Headquarters in The Hague with contact points to national authorities through its liaison officers	Headquarters in Washington, DC and 56 field offices
Powers	May not conduct independent investigations or make arrests	Full policing powers

FBI website: www.fbi.gov/quickfacts.htm
Europol website: www.europol.europa.eu/index.asp?page=facts

Criminal Law and Counter-Terrorism

Cooperation on criminal law, the body of law that deals with crimes and their punishments, has advanced rapidly in recent years. Criminal law includes both substantive and procedural components. Substantive criminal law defines crimes and related sanctions, while procedural criminal law governs the execution of law enforcement and defendants' rights. Compared to the very limited operational powers given to the EU's new crime-fighting bodies, the approximation of substantive and procedural criminal law goes to the very heart of national sovereignty.

The harmonization of criminal law has occurred primarily through framework decisions (FDs) (see Box 7.1): legislative blueprints specifying how and when national laws must be changed, but leaving the specifics of that change to each member state. The Council has approved several framework decisions on substantive criminal law, specifying definitions and ranges of criminal sanctions for crimes such as counterfeiting the euro, human trafficking, child sexual exploitation, environmental crime, cyber crime, drug trafficking, and terrorism.

The passage of the framework decision on terrorism illustrates how JHA cooperation is often driven by crises. Within two weeks of 11 September 2001, the Commission pushed the terrorism framework decision from the drawing board of the Tampere programme to consideration by the Council. This legislation established common definitions for particular terrorist offences and minimum thresholds for criminal sanctions associated with these crimes. At the time, only Germany, Spain, France, Italy, Portugal, and the UK had specific anti-terrorism laws in their penal codes.

By October 2001, a few member states, notably Italy and Ireland, had expressed opposition to the framework decision's definition of terrorism. They echoed fears expressed by some MEPs and civil liberties groups that the framework decision would permit member states to suppress legitimate forms of public protest. Given these concerns and the overall sensitivity of the issue, it is likely that the debate on the decision could have lasted months, if not years. Yet the political push of 9/11 helped the Belgian Presidency, aided by the Commission, to forge an agreement in the Council by December 2001.

Agreement is one thing, implementation another. Several EU members missed the FD's original deadline of December 2002 for transposing the decision into national law, and the same was true for the updated target of June 2004, even after the terrorist attacks in Madrid earlier that year. By 2007, transposition (see Box 7.1) of the FD was still incomplete in a few member states, though finished in most. Moreover, legal transposition is the 'easy part' and it by no means guarantees effective implementation or enforcement. In sum, terrorist attacks have certainly provided impetus for change in the EU on counter-terrorism, but these reforms continue to fall short in important respects (see Box 7.6).

In contrast to the rapid agreements on counter-terrorism, the drug-trafficking FD illustrates how progress can be slow without a crisis to provide momentum. The framework decision is designed to combat and prevent illegal drug-trafficking. An

BOX 7.6	Compared to what?

Counter-terrorism: the EU and US

Counter-terrorism efforts in both the EU and US have focused on legal and institutional reforms designed to promote greater coordination among key actors and the sharing of intelligence among them. However, institutional change has been more dramatic in the US, which began from a standing start and without much prior experience of domestic terrorism (unlike the UK, Germany, Italy, Spain, and France). A total of 28 federal agencies were merged to create the US Department of Homeland Security. The intelligence community was overhauled and put under the authority of a new Director of National Intelligence. The USA Patriot Act, rapidly approved after 9/11, eliminated the so-called 'wall' between the FBI and Central Intelligence Agency (CIA). It allowed the two agencies to share intelligence through bodies such as the Joint Terrorism Task Forces composed of law enforcement officers from all levels of government. As the immediate memory of 9/11 faded, civil liberties concerns complicated the Bush administration's efforts to make permanent the more controversial aspects of the Patriot Act.

In the EU, the 9/11 attacks hastened a variety of measures, including the creation of a counter-terrorism task force in Europol, a framework decision on terrorism, the European Arrest Warrant, and initiatives to fight the financing of terrorism. The 2004 terrorist attacks in Madrid restored a sense of urgency in fighting terrorism, and the EU responded by creating the post of counter-terrorism coordinator, a post held until March 2007 by Gijs de Vries of the Netherlands. Lacking the operational or budgetary authority of his American counterpart, the European Union's coordinator (or 'Mr Terror' as he was dubbed) was charged with pressuring governments to implement EU-level counter-terrorism initiatives and encouraging better international intelligence sharing. To promote this goal, national officials from *domestic* intelligence services have been allowed to join their counterparts from *foreign* intelligence services at the EU's Situation Center (SitCen), housed in the Council Secretariat.

Progress here, as elsewhere, has been crisis-driven. Following the London bombings of July 2005, the UK successfully pressed for the adoption of a data-retention directive requiring telecoms firms to make customers' communications records available for counter-terrorism purposes. In the absence of crisis, however, action on counter-terrorism tends to stall. In 2007, the naming of a new counter-terrorism coordinator was delayed as the EU reconsidered the power and influence of this post, highlighting the tension between the member states' desire for more effective counter-terrorism measures and their reluctance to grant EU-level actors greater operational authority in this area.

initial version of the measure, proposed by the Commission in May 2001, was first amended to meet several states' concerns on various issues. However, further progress was held up by the Dutch, who feared the earlier amendments would criminalize the possession of small amounts of drugs for personal use and thus force the closure of their popular drug 'coffee houses'. After months of delay, the other member states finally dropped the amendments opposed by the Dutch and the measure passed in October 2004. Drug trafficking is a serious problem in the EU and is linked to other forms of trafficking, such as tobacco or human trafficking. However, in the absence of a serious crisis that might induce consensus, the concerns of individual states have proven hard to overcome.

Political crises have also spurred EU legislation on criminal procedure. By far the most significant achievement in this field has been the framework decision establishing the European Arrest Warrant (EAW). The warrant is aimed at simplifying and hastening extradition of suspected criminals. As with the terrorism framework decision, the EAW was proposed by the Commission and rapidly approved by the Council just weeks after 9/11, overcoming disputes among the member states on several issues that would otherwise have delayed its passage (see Kaunert 2007).

The EAW has changed extradition from an often politicized judicial process to a simplified administrative transfer. By implementing the principle of 'mutual recognition' for a list of 32 crimes, the arrest warrant eliminated a traditional rationale for refusing an extradition request, namely the principle of double-criminality, according to which an offender cannot be transferred across borders unless the offence is a crime in both the transferring and receiving countries. It also lifted the traditional ban in some member states on extraditing one's own nationals. However, soon after Italy became the last EU member state to implement (belatedly) the EAW in April 2005, legal questions arose in Cyprus, Poland, Germany, and Belgium, mostly concerning its compatibility with national constitutions in these countries (see Box 8.4). In 2005 the domestic federal constitutional court voided Germany's original legislation implementing the warrant because it violated Germany's constitutional protection of its own nationals regarding extradition and trials abroad. Nevertheless, the EAW is already being widely used by the states that have implemented it, and has reduced the average time for handing over suspects from nine months to just 43 days. In the summer of 2005, for example, the UK used the EAW to win the return of one of the unsuccessful London bombers less than two months after his arrest in Italy.

Constitutional concerns raised by the EAW extended beyond this particular decision. For instance, the fundamental legal issues arising from the arrest warrant contributed to delays to a second procedural measure, the European Evidence Warrant (EEW), which was first proposed by the Commission in November 2003. Covering the same list of 32 crimes noted in the arrest warrant, the evidence warrant is designed to limit delays in a member state's reaction to requests to exercise search warrants on its territory. However, several governments became concerned that the EU had acted too hastily on the arrest warrant and were determined not to repeat the mistake. In particular, the Dutch threatened to veto the evidence warrant until they could ensure that they would not be overrun with requests related to drug-trafficking cases. Meanwhile, the Germans, mindful of their constitutional court's negative ruling on the arrest warrant, wanted to opt out of obligations under the evidence warrant for six crimes which they argued were poorly defined. Not until June 2006 was a deal reached that addressed the Dutch and German concerns. Collectively, these illustrations show that crises can help promote the passage of controversial framework decisions on matters of criminal law, but they will not guarantee their timely transposition or help them resist subsequent legal challenges.

Border Management

Border management in the EU involves visa policy, the fight against illegal immigration, and policies on refugees and asylum. In addressing these issues, the EU has attempted to balance several competing concerns. First is the principle of 'free movement', including movement of persons, which numerous member states have hesitated to extend to non-EU or new EU members, leading to fears of an emergent 'fortress Europe'. Secondly, border management is viewed as a crime control matter, entailing the fight against a variety of transnational criminal activity, but especially human trafficking and human smuggling (see Box 7.1). Thirdly, policies related to border management must be attentive to human rights, including the legitimate needs of refugees escaping wars and natural disasters, asylum seekers fearing persecution, and the victims of trafficking fleeing their captors. Finally, EU border management has been shaped by concerns for financial burden-sharing regarding the costs associated with refugees, asylum applicants, illegal immigrants, and the need to patrol long coastlines and land borders.

Immigration and Schengen

As with its crime-fighting initiatives, most of the EU's progress on border management has occurred since the Amsterdam Treaty. One of its key innovations was bringing the Schengen agreement and its established acquis into the EU's treaty framework. Yet this development has led to the anomalous situation whereby not all EU members participate in the free travel Schengen area, but some non-EU countries do. For instance, the UK and Ireland have their own free-travel zone and do not belong to the Schengen area. However, they do participate in the sharing of criminal data facilitated by the Schengen Information System (SIS), which helps manage comings and goings into the passport-free zone and can flag wanted criminals. Moreover, the UK, Ireland, and Denmark have opt-outs from some EU border management issues through protocols attached to the Amsterdam Treaty. On the other hand, Norway and Iceland do not belong to the EU, but participate in the Schengen area because of their pre-existing free-travel agreement with the Nordic members of the EU. Similarly, non-EU member Switzerland signed the Schengen agreement in 2004 but is unlikely to implement passport-free travel until 2009.

Since their accession, the EU's new member states have been legally committed to joining the Schengen zone. However, a specific date was not specified until after the EU could determine that their external land, sea, and air borders were sufficiently secure. Originally, the expansion of the Schengen zone was not to occur until the implementation of an updated computer system (SIS II). But when this system was delayed, a deal was brokered to allow passport-free land travel by the start of 2008 and air travel by March 2009.

Schengen's anomalies co-exist with, and perhaps encourage, pragmatic flexibility. Schengen rules allow participating states to reinstate border controls temporarily for security reasons, as France did following the London bombings on July 2005. Several states have done the same for major international sporting events in an effort to prevent terrorist attacks or limit the influx of football (soccer) hooligans.

Visa Policy

Unlike other JHA policies, the legal basis of visa policy has always been located in the first pillar ever since the Maastricht Treaty was agreed. The approximation of national visa policies has been a goal of the EU since then, but the establishment of the Schengen zone made this step a necessity rather than mere aspiration. Consequently, the JHA Council has established and periodically updated a common 'white list' of countries whose citizens do not need visas to visit the EU for less than three months. Other states are on the much longer 'black list', which means their citizens need an appropriate visa (see Box 7.7). Since 1996 the JHA Council's amendments to the white and black visa lists have been decided using QMV, although not via co-decision with the European Parliament. These lists do not apply to the UK and Ireland, which exercise their opt-outs in these areas. Denmark, as a member of the Schengen zone, does apply them.

As well as inhibiting the free movement of organized criminals or the victims of human trafficking, the EU's black list is intended to prevent citizens of 'at-risk' countries from gaining entry to the EU on tourist visas when it is likely that their actual intention is to work or reside illegally in a member state. In 2006, the JHA Council finalized legislation for the Visa Information System (VIS), which will allow national consular officials to collect and share biometric data on visa applicants (see Box 7.1). The intention of VIS is to prevent forgeries of travel documents and inhibit those denied a Schengen visa by one member state from applying again through another (a process known as 'visa shopping').

Illegal Immigration

EU member states will be challenged by illegal immigration as long as they restrict legal immigration (and most are becoming more, not less, restrictive) and remain bastions of political freedom and economic prosperity relative to the developing world (see, for example, Guiraudon and Jileva 2006). In general, those who attempt to enter the EU illegally do so because they cannot afford the cost of a visa, have had their application

BOX 7.7	White and black visa lists

The JHA Council decides which third countries' citizens require special visas to enter the EU. The original white list of exempted countries (not requiring special visas) was agreed upon by member states in 2001 and included 43 states, as well as holders of passports issued by the administrative districts of Hong Kong and Macao. The only substantive change to this list came in 2003, when Ecuador was moved to the black list after it was determined that too many of its citizens were staying illegally in the EU after entering legally. The first white list also contained Switzerland until its free movement agreement with the EU took effect in 2002, which allowed it to be removed from all lists.

The white list includes:

- Europe: the twelve newest EU members plus Croatia, Andorra, Monaco, San Marino, and the Holy See (Vatican City)

- Central America: all countries except Belize

- South America: all countries aside from Guyana, Suriname, French Guiana, and Ecuador

- Middle East: only Israel

- Asia: only Brunei, Japan, Malaysia, Singapore, and South Korea

- Others: US, Canada, Australia, and New Zealand

The black list includes:

- Africa: all countries

- Middle East: all countries leaving aside Brunei and Israel

- Central Asia: all countries

- Asia: all countries except those noted above

- Former Soviet Union: all countries besides the Baltic (EU) states

- Caribbean: all countries

- Former Yugoslavia: all countries aside from Slovenia and Croatia

- Turkey

denied, or expect denial if they were to apply. Smugglers sell illegal immigrants forged travel documents, passage on ships bound for the EU, or hiding places in shipping containers. Routes are adjusted frequently to stay one step ahead of border officials. In 2004, the flashpoint for illegal immigration was Italy's southernmost island of Lampedusa, but by late 2005, the hotspots were Malta and the Spanish enclaves of Ceuta and Melilla in Morocco. In 2006, shiploads of African illegal immigrants created unprecedented crises in Spain's Canary Islands.

The gradually widening Schengen zone means that one country's inability to prevent illegal immigration can become a problem for another. This spillover provides the main rationale for a common EU approach. Initially, the EU's response was limited to the efforts of Europol, framework decisions on human trafficking and human smuggling, and co-financing for training and cooperation on border management. Responding to a series of illegal immigration crises, the Seville European Council of June 2002 provided a much-needed boost to several initiatives that had languished after being introduced in the Tampere programme years earlier. European leaders could not agree in Seville on bold plans for an EU border patrol, but they did endorse the creation of a unit composed of the heads of the national border services to promote coordination and a common curriculum for training border guards. Within a year, the Commission proposed moving beyond this informal coordination by creating an EU border management agency. Following Council approval, the new agency, known as Frontex (*Frontières extérieures*) and sited in Warsaw, became operational in April 2005.

With a small staff of about 50, the Frontex agency promotes operational cooperation by developing common standards and procedures among the member states and supporting them with training, risk-analyses, and technical assistance. Frontex has helped to coordinate member states' joint sea and air patrols of trouble spots, as it did in summer 2006 when it was called upon to organize the EU's aerial and marine support to Spain, Malta, and Italy to help them address their illegal immigration crises. In this context, the Commission also proposed the creation of standing, rapid-reaction teams of border guards drawn from the member states that could be used to respond to future incidents. Frontex would play the lead role in selecting and training personnel for these units and oversee their operations when deployed. However, it was not until 2007 that member states started to deliver on commitments to endow Frontex with adequate resources, including ships and helicopters. Even then, after international patrols coordinated by Frontex enjoyed some success in intercepting boat-loads of illegal immigrants in EU waters, the member states could not agree who was responsible for receiving and deporting them.

In addition to creating Frontex, the EU has also intensified cooperation with non-EU countries in its fight against illegal immigration. Readmission (deportation) agreements are an important part of this effort, hastening the return of illegal immigrants or unsuccessful asylum applicants to the state from which they came, no matter what their nationality. States that agree to deportation agreements typically want something in return, such as a simplified or less expensive means for their citizens to obtain a Schengen visa. By 2006, the EU had achieved readmission agreements with Russia, Hong Kong, Macau, Sri Lanka, Albania, and Ukraine. Talks with Morocco had stalled on the issue of returning illegal immigrants who transit through that country but are not its citizens, thus reflecting the increasing tendency of north African and eastern Mediterranean countries to be transit countries for illegal immigration, rather than sources.

Readmission agreements are also prominent goals of the EU's European Neighbour-hood Policy (ENP) (see Chapter 9). In December 2005, with illegal immigration crises flaring in Malta and the Canaries, the European Council announced that the EU would allocate 3 per cent of its future ENP funding to third countries to support joint patrols and other improved interdiction methods, especially in the priority countries of Morocco, Algeria, and Libya. In an attempt to address the problem at its source, the heads of governments also agreed to contribute EU funds towards economic development in sub-Saharan Africa.

Asylum and Refugee Policy

All EU members offer asylum under the terms of the Geneva Convention of 1951 and the 1967 protocol on the status of refugees. The overarching goal of EU asylum policy is to eliminate discrepancies between member states in the implementation of these accords. For example, an asylum seeker may find it much easier to obtain refugee status in Sweden as compared to Greece. One specific objective is to guarantee a minimum level of protection for refugees. Another is to ensure an equitable sharing of the burden of providing asylum among EU members. A common asylum policy would help to achieve this goal by reducing incentives for 'asylum shopping', which occurs when a would-be refugee applies for asylum in several states simultaneously, looking for the most favourable conditions.

Asylum policy has been in the EU's purview since the Maastricht Treaty, but there was little progress until the Tampere programme. In the wake of the 1990s Balkans' refugee crises, most European countries developed national schemes to provide 'temporary protection' for sudden, mass influxes of people displaced by wars and natural disasters when time or resources were insufficient for the normal asylum process. In 2001, the JHA Council passed a directive specifying minimum standards for temporary protection; these standards were designed to reduce disparities in reception conditions among EU countries and consequently promote burden-sharing. Financial 'solidarity' for sudden influxes of refugees is also provided to member states by the European Refugee Fund (ERF), which has been in place since 2000.

Meanwhile, the EU has continued its attempt to limit asylum shopping through the implementation of the Eurodac database. In operation since 2003, Eurodac is a centralized system for collecting, storing, and sharing biometric data (mainly digital fingerprint images) on asylum applicants. Its initial years of operation confirmed what border management officials had long suspected, namely that thousands of refugees shuttle throughout the EU to lodge multiple asylum applications. Eurodac enables authorities to reject these applications and return applicants to their original country of application. Ultimately, the EU hopes that refugees will realize that asylum shopping is no longer worthwhile, although the experiences of ex-Yugoslavia, Afghanistan, and Iraq all suggest that local conditions, far more than EU policy, determine the flow of refugees.

In contrast to its progress on Eurodac, the JHA Council for many years was unable to agree on how to harmonize asylum policy. Momentum was provided in 2002 by a series of immigration-related crises that prompted EU leaders to rededicate themselves to immigration reform. At the 2002 Seville summit leaders agreed and eventually approved a package of measures establishing minimum rules and standards on asylum.

These measures are important in themselves, but their cumulative effect was to pave the way for the harmonization of asylum policy as outlined in the Hague Programme (see Box 7.4)

Conclusion

The constant change and experimentation endemic to the EU generally (see Chapter 1) is nowhere more apparent than in the area of JHA. Since 2001 JHA policy has experienced a remarkable period of development. Many changes have come in the form of new agencies and shared resources such as databases, as well as legislation aimed at harmonizing member states' laws on crime-fighting, counter-terrorism, and border management. In addition, a variety of liaison networks and training initiatives have been created.

How can the development of JHA policy be best understood and examined? Different theoretical paradigms of European integration can help. For example, neo-functional analysis focuses our attention on how agreements on free movement of goods 'spilled over' into cooperation on free movement of people and issues arising from that phenomenon. Historical institutionalism's emphasis on 'path dependence' can explain how informal cooperation (such as the Trevi Group) put the EU on a path leading to JHA cooperation later on. What began as the informal exchange of ideas cultivated shared norms and practices that made possible more formal treaty changes. Studies of Europeanization (see Chapter 4) also help us examine how incremental or informal small steps—the harmonization of border management standards or EU-level training initiatives—can lead to normative or policy-related changes in the member states. Meanwhile, liberal intergovernmentalism draws our attention to the tenacious endurance of national interests, the clashing interests of asymmetrically powerful states, and the resulting bargains struck at IGCs. The development of JHA is resistant to simple or singular theoretical explanations because it is driven by competing phenomena: the need for European states to upgrade their national capacities in response to events such as the wars in ex-Yugoslvia or 9/11, the imperative to cooperate to deal with quintessentially cross-border problems, and the need to address sovereignty and civil liberty concerns.

What now? Looking ahead, the EU faces two key challenges on JHA. The first is how to make progress on new third-pillar initiatives in the face of national vetoes in the Council. While some member states insist that significant progress has been made on numerous matters even with unanimity, others complain about decision-making delays or the need to water down legislation to achieve unanimity. The second task is to improve the nature and pace of transposition of agreements into national law. When (and if) implemented, the Reform Treaty is likely to help on both fronts because it retains most of the substantive changes on JHA envisioned in the original Constitutional Treaty. For instance, the Reform Treaty will apply the Community method to decision-making on the structure and powers of Europol and Eurojust, eliminating national vetoes and giving the EP the influence over these bodies that it has long sought.

More dramatically, the Reform Treaty will encourage the transposition of JHA legislation into national law by allowing the ECJ to rule on infringement cases (which seek to oblige member states to fulfil their legal obligations as EU members). Under existing treaties, the ECJ enjoyed this power on first-pillar JHA policies (such as many asylum matters), but not on third-pillar policies. The Court's (and Commission's) weaker enforcement role helps to explain why the EU's implementation record on JHA has been the worst of any policy domain.

Although the new treaty will empower the ECJ in some areas of JHA decision-making, it will not replace the existing patchwork of JHA decision-making methods with a single approach. For example, EU decisions on family law will still be made intergovernmentally, and the extension of the Community method to this area of civil law will now be subject to approval of national parliaments. The Reform Treaty will apply the Community method to most remaining aspects of border management, but measures concerning passports and other immigration documents will be handled intergovernmentally. The sensitive area of legal immigration quotas will be left in the hands of the individual member states (as now). Despite the Reform Treaty's promise to eliminate the pillar system, one could interpret the survival of multiple decision-making mechanisms (even with their single legal basis) as effectively the survival of the pillars. Moreover, the UK's opt-out on the new Treaty's JHA provisions only adds to the complexity of this policy area.

The handling of JHA in the Reform Treaty reveals that consensus is unlikely to emerge soon regarding how, and how fast, to develop EU policies and powers in this area. Progress in an EU of 27 may rely on smaller groups of states taking the lead and bringing other countries along later. One variation of this approach is provided by the so-called 'G-6', which periodically brings together the largest EU members to discuss ways of promoting cooperation on issues such as JHA. In addition, the Schengen zone, Prüm Convention, and related EU legislation together have established a precedent for cooperation to begin with just a few member states and to involve others after it has proven its value.

In sum, making JHA policies work has always been and will continue to be a major challenge for the EU. The benefits of closer cooperation are clear and widely acknowledged. But so too are the concerns raised by this remarkable area of EU policy, which touches directly on fundamental issues of national sovereignty, security, and civil liberties.

?   **DISCUSSION QUESTIONS**

1. How has the Schengen zone influenced the development of JHA?

2. Which EU institution is most important for JHA?

3. In what ways has JHA become important in the EU's relations with non-EU members?

4. In which areas of JHA should the EU pursue closer integration in the future?

→ FURTHER READING

JHA remains an under-researched area of the EU but scholarship is expanding and improving. Monar's (2006) work remains essential reading and Geddes (2006) offers a helpful overview. Henderson's useful volume (2005) focuses on the new member states. Occhipinti (2007) examines the interface between JHA and European Neighbourhood Policy. Sasse and Thielemann (2005) compile the work of leading experts on EU border management issues. Rees (2006) makes a timely and valuable general contribution; Peers has updated his seminal work on JHA law (2006).

Geddes, A. (2006), 'The Politics of European Union Domestic Order', in K. E. Jørgensen, M. A. Pollack, and B. Rosamond (eds.), *Handbook of European Union Politics* (London and Thousand Oaks: Sage): 449–12.

Henderson, K. (ed.) (2005), *The Area of Freedom, Security, and Justice in the Enlarged Europe* (New York and Basingstoke: Palgrave Macmillan).

Monar, J. (2006), 'Justice and Home Affairs', *Journal of Common Market Studies*, 44/1: 101–18.

Occhipinti, J. (2007), 'Justice and Home Affairs: Immigration and Policing', in M. Smith, K. Weber, and M. Baun (eds.), *Governing Europe's Neighbourhood: Partners or Periphery?* (Manchester and New York: University of Manchester Press).

Peers, S. (2006), *EU Justice and Home Affairs Law*, 2nd edn. (Oxford: Oxford University Press).

Rees, W. (2006), *Transatlantic Counter-terrorism Cooperation: The New Imperative* (London and New York: Routledge).

Sasse, G, and Thielemann E. (eds.) (2005), 'Migrants and Minorities in Europe', Special Issue of *Journal of Common Market Studies*, 43/4.

⊕ WEB LINKS

The Commission DG Justice, Freedom and Security maintains a nice website on all aspects of JHA at ec.europa.eu/justice_home/index_en.htm. Europol's various publications on organized crime can be found at www.europol.europa.eu/. The website of the Eurojust network of criminal prosecutors and judges can be found at: http://eurojust.europa.eu/

For critical perspective on JHA, see the publications of Statewatch, a civil liberties NGO: www.statewatch.org/.

Visit the Online Resource Centre that accompanies this book for additional material: www.oxfordtextbooks.co.uk/orc/bomberg2e/

CHAPTER 8

Constitutionalism and Democracy in the EU

Neil MacCormick

Introduction: Constitutionalism and Democracy	160	Supranational Democracy in the Community Pillar	169
Constitutionalism without a Constitution?	161	Intergovernmentalism and the Council	171
The EU's Constitutional Charter	163	European Democracy: Competing Views	173
Rights	164	Conclusion	174
Separation of Powers, Checks, and Balances	166	DISCUSSION QUESTIONS	175
Constitutionalism in the EU	167	FURTHER READING	175
Is Democracy Possible in the EU?	169	WEB LINKS	176

▌ Chapter Overview

Democracy flourishes in politics that have a constitution and a sense of common citizenship that leads citizens to respect it. But the European Union has so far failed to adopt a formal constitution. Is the EU undemocratic, then? Constitutions may be functional (as in the United Kingdom) or explicit texts (as in most European countries), and the EU has a kind of functional constitution. Moreover, the EU is a Union of democratic states. The question is: are these enough to characterize the EU as democratic by extension? Or does the Union require direct democratic credentials? Does this multistate, multilingual union have a sufficient sense of common citizenship to make genuine democracy possible? This chapter examines the nature of constitutionalism and democracy in the EU and how they work.

Introduction: Constitutionalism and Democracy

Constitutionalism concerns respect for the rules and values in a constitution. It means ensuring that the constitution is faithfully implemented, the powers it confers are not abused or exceeded, and checks and balances among different political institutions are successfully maintained. Constitutionalism thus involves imposing limits on government power, adhering to the rule of law, and protecting fundamental rights (Rosenfeld 1994: 3).

Over fifty years, the European Union has developed what is in functional terms a constitutional framework (sometimes called a constitutional charter, see Box 8.1). It exists in the Treaties establishing the Union and enabling its enlargement (Weiler 1999). This functional constitution and a more general set of constitutional values are respected in the working life of the Union and its institutions. However, the Union does not have a formal constitution: an attempt to move to an explicit constitution, with a core text proposed by a Convention on the Future of Europe (see Box 8.2), caused political turmoil and the text was never ratified.

Whether this state of affairs ensures a form of *democratic* constitutionalism is questionable. That there is a democratic deficit (see Box 8.1) in the EU is a frequently heard complaint. It is a complaint about the character of decision-making of the Union's institutions, especially those concerned with making rules that are binding on the member states and citizens of the Union. In all EU member states, the conditions for successful democracy exist, but there are grounds to doubt whether these conditions can exist in the Union as a whole. European constitutional debate is likely to focus on whether a full-fledged European democracy is possible, and, if so, in what form.

Constitutionalism and democracy are thus closely related. Democratic government requires some constitutional framework that allocates the various powers essential to the effective governance of a state (or other polity or organization) to the appropriate institutions, and lays down the conditions concerning their proper exercise. In a democratic constitution, there must also be provisions enabling citizens to participate on equal terms in elections or other forms of popular vote. Such provisions ensure the popular accountability of those who exercise power within the institutions set up by the constitution. Democracy in its fullest sense requires maximum popular accountability of both legislative and executive institutions established in a constitution. (One can even argue that it requires popular adoption of the constitution itself, through a referendum in which all citizens participate, though this question remains open.)

In any case, without adequate accountability and checks and balances, even the most ostensibly democratic constitution will become a sham because the possibility of effectively holding office-holders to account before the people would be severely diminished or even negated. So, democracy presupposes having a constitution *and* respecting its provisions (including accountability). But is the EU's functional constitution enough to anchor the Union in an effectively democratic framework, especially

---

BOX 8.1	Key concepts

The Charter of Fundamental Rights of the European Union seeks to strengthen and promote fundamental human rights for all persons in the EU by setting out a series of rights such as freedom of speech and fair working conditions. It was adopted as a non-binding political declaration in 2000 at Nice, and then incorporated into the draft Constitutional Treaty in 2004.

Constitutional charter is the name the European Court of Justice has given to the Treaties' constitutional elements that amount to an informal constitution enshrined in custom, law, and treaties. It is also sometimes referred to as a 'functional constitution'.

Constitutionalism concerns respect for the rules and values in a constitution, including the protection of fundamental rights. It is a value ensuring that the constitution is faithfully implemented, that the powers it confers are not abused or exceeded, and that checks and balances among the different institutions are successfully maintained.

Democratic deficit refers broadly to the belief that the EU lacks sufficient democratic control. Neither the Commission, which proposes legislation, nor the Council, which enacts it, is directly accountable to the public or to national parliaments.

Separation of powers is the constitutional principle according to which different governmental functions (executive, legislative, and judicial) should be exercised by different institutions. The idea behind the principle is to ensure that power is not concentrated in one single authority such as a president.

---

given allegations of a democratic deficit? We explore this question by examining the unique nature of constitutionalism in the EU.

Constitutionalism without a Constitution?

The EU has tried, but apparently failed, to adopt a formal constitution. The European Council met at Laeken in Belgium in 2001 and set up the Convention on the Future of Europe to try to bring the European institutions closer to the citizens. Its remit included considering whether a proper constitution of the European Union was a possibility, and, if so, how to achieve it (see Box 8.2).

The Convention did succeed in drafting a 'Treaty Establishing a Constitution for Europe', which it submitted to the Council. In 2004, European leaders unanimously agreed to adopt a new treaty based on the Convention's work with relatively insignificant amendments. This Constitutional Treaty was then sent to the member states for ratification according to their own constitutional processes. But two referenda, one in France and another in the Netherlands in May/June 2005, both decisively rejected the Constitutional Treaty. By mid-2007, eighteen member states had ratified the text, two

BOX 8.2	How it really work(ed)

The European 'Constitutional Convention'

The Constitutional Treaty may appear to be a dry document drawn up by select bureaucrats. But this exhibit portrays a bustling, open, somewhat hectic Convention which prepared an important part of the draft Treaty.

The Convention on the Future of Europe, chaired by former French President Valéry Giscard d'Estaing, began its work in February 2002, and finished in July 2003. It comprised a wide range of actors:

- governmental representatives of all member states, acceding states, and candidate states—28 in all;
- representatives from the national parliaments—56 in all;
- sixteen MEPs elected by the European Parliament on a party-proportional basis;
- two representatives from the European Commission, Michel Barnier and Antonio Vitorino;
- observers including the European Ombudsman, and representatives from the Economic and Social Committee (ESC) and the Committee of the Regions;
- a Secretary-General, Sir John Kerr, former head of the UK Foreign Office, assisted by an extremely able and industrious secretariat drawn from the civil services of the Council, the Parliament, and the Commission.

Given the number of (full and alternate) members, the Convention sessions could include over 200 people in the room actively engaged in the debate, with a further thirteen observers entitled to speak. Then there were assistants, advisers to ministers, diplomats, press persons, and Convention staff. When the Convention was sitting a considerable buzz of activity floated in and around the large Committee Room in the European Parliament building, and in the adjacent public space and Hemicycle Bar.

Openness of deliberation was fostered by the Convention's website which published all its official documents, all contributions by members, all amendments proposed by them, and the verbatim record of proceedings. This site connected also to the Forum website, where citizens at large and non-governmental organizations (NGOs) could state and explain their opinions (see http://european-convention.europa.eu).

The Convention's work was divided into phases. The first was a listening phase, with wide-ranging consultations across Europe. Then came an analysis phase, with a dozen working groups examining issues such as subsidiarity, the Charter of Fundamental Rights, the EU's legal personality, how to simplify the Treaties, the role of national parliaments, defence and external affairs, and so on. Reports of the working groups were debated in plenary sittings of the Convention in 2002–3.

Last was the writing phase. The publication of a preliminary draft in late 2002 was followed by the serious job of fleshing out the skeleton table of constitutional contents with draft Articles. This phase was overseen by the Praesidium, which comprised the President and Vice-Presidents, two European parliamentarians, two national parliamentarians, two Commissioners, two national government representatives, and a delegate to watch out for the interests and concerns of acceding states. By this stage Convention members had agreed that they were discussing the Articles of a draft constitution, not just a revised treaty.

As the draft Articles were delivered, a torrent of amendments flowed in from the pens of the members and alternate members of the Convention. In May and June, the Praesidium responded to amendments and debates about the Articles by redrafting and redrafting again. The end-game in summer 2003 was exceedingly hectic. The final text was hammered out by such consensus as could be achieved in each of the subsets of the whole Convention, and in the political groups that participated in it. The President presented the Convention's final conclusions to the member states' governments at the European Council in Thessaloniki on 20 June 2003. Within a month, after final adjustments, the final text was delivered to the European Council to be discussed, and ultimately agreed, by government leaders.

(Spain and Luxembourg) by processes involving a referendum of all citizens. At this point, attention shifted to proposals to produce a revised text—which turned out to be the 2007 Reform Treaty—that would carry forward much of the substance of the Constitutional Treaty, but without ever using the term 'constitution'.

The Union thus could have had a formal constitution, but (so far, at least) it has failed to adopt the only one on offer. Can there then be no European constitutionalism? Is it impossible for the EU to constitute itself as a properly democratic union of European states?

The EU's Constitutional Charter

In thinking about these questions, we should note that a political entity can have a kind of constitution even without adopting a text formally entitled 'The Constitution' that compendiously defines and empowers all the principal institutions of government. The UK is a conspicuous example of a state with a long-standing democratic tradition which nevertheless has no written constitution. Yet governments and parliaments and law-courts exist in the UK, elections take place, laws are enacted, and generally the rule of law prevails. Functionally, the UK has a constitution enshrined in custom, common law, statutes, and treaties, even though it has never chosen to adopt a formal written text codifying these constitutional rules into a single text. This functional constitution seems over the decades and even centuries to have been as good a basis for a robust constitutionalism as anything found in countries that have adopted a formal constitution.

Is there some possible analogy between this example and the European Union? Yes, to the extent that the Union also functions in a constitutionalist way within the framework of the treaties that establish it. But the analogy is an imperfect one. For the UK is a state, while the EU is a treaty-based union of many states and is considered by many to be a novel kind of political entity. It is one of its own kind (*sui generis*).

On the basis of this imperfect analogy, one can argue as follows: the Union, and, as one pillar within it, the European Community (EC), were deliberately set up by the member states, starting from the original six states that agreed the Treaty of Paris (1950) and the Treaties of Rome (1957) establishing the original European Communities. The whole, cumulative set of treaties—from Paris and Rome through to Nice in 2000 and various Accession Treaties—have been considered as comprising a constitutional charter for the EU (see Box 8.1).

The phrase 'constitutional charter' comes from a decision by the European Court of Justice (ECJ). A series of fundamentally important ECJ decisions established the idea that EC law was a special new body of law 'of its own kind' (again, *sui generis*), neither national law nor public international law, but something in between. Out of these decisions emerged the doctrine of the supremacy (sometimes called 'primacy') of Community law over that of each member state in any case of conflict (see Chapter 3). Under the sister doctrine of 'direct effect', Community law directly establishes rights and duties for individuals and corporations and other persons residing in the member states, as well as conferring rights and duties on the states themselves.

This line of decisions effectively gave the Community (later the Union) and its institutions a distinctive legal order of their own, within which they interact with the member states rather than being subordinate to them. Their effect was to 'constitution-alize' the Treaties. Put another way, the treaties contain a body of fundamental rules and principles that amount to a functional, albeit not a formal constitution.

Rights

To be democratic a constitution (formal or functional) must uphold fundamental rights. One grave difficulty that arose out of the EU's 'supremacy' doctrine was the implication it had for states that enshrine fundamental human rights in their own national consti-tutions. The test case was (then) West Germany, where democracy was being rebuilt around the idea of 'constitutional patriotism'. The experiences of the years 1933–45 led to an insistence that a new basic law must protect human rights in absolute terms, as inviolable. This is a ground-floor element of West Germany's 1949 constitutional 'Basic Law'. If Community law could override German law, what about these fundamental rights? Had they ceased to be inviolable? If so, the ECJ's interpretations of primacy and direct effect were unacceptable. The German Federal Constitutional Court so decided, and similar tribunals in other states could well have followed suit.

The ECJ responded, in a series of judgments beginning in 1970, by holding that human rights were already implicitly present in the EU's existing treaties. Otherwise, supremacy would indeed be unacceptable. The judges' reasoning was that the Treaty regime must be interpreted as requiring full respect for the constitutional traditions of the member states. This principle applies in particular to the fundamental rights they guarantee. Also, since all EU member states subscribe to the European Convention on Human Rights (ECHR; see Box 8.3), these fundamental human rights must also be acknowledged as imposing strict limits on the law-making power of the Community's institutions.

> **BOX 8.3**   **Compared to what?**
>
> ## Two kinds of 'convention'
>
> The word 'convention' is ambiguous in the present context. In one sense, a convention is a body of people gathered together to deliberate about some public question and come to decisions or recommendations about it. In another sense, it is a treaty or agreement among several states. It is the output of a 'coming together' of states to achieve common agreement about standards that should prevail amongst them.
>
> The **Convention on the Future of Europe** (Box 8.2) was a convention in the first sense—a body of people gathered together to discuss a policy issue and reach decisions or recommendations. It was not the first such convention. It was preceded in 2000 by a similar representative convention chaired by former German President Roman Herzog, whose task was to produce a concise and coherent statement of the rights that EU citizens enjoy in their capacity as such. These included rights, such as the 'four freedoms' (free movement of goods, persons, services, and capital) directly conferred by the EU's existing treaties; rights recognized through the European Convention on Human Rights (ECHR), and rights emerging from common constitutional principles. The Herzog Convention produced a Charter of Fundamental Rights of the European Union which was adopted by the European Council at the 2000 Nice summit. However, at the insistence of the UK, the Charter of Rights was adopted only as a legally non-binding 'political declaration', which meant that the ECJ was denied any effective jurisdiction to enforce the Charter. Nevertheless, the Commission and the Parliament have declared their firm intention to act as though the Charter were fully binding on them.
>
> Conventions in the other sense (multilateral international treaties) are also relevant to human rights in the EU. A striking example is the **European Convention for the Protection of Human Rights and Fundamental Freedoms** (sometimes abbreviated to 'European Convention on Human Rights' or just ECHR). The ECHR was agreed originally in 1950 and has remained in force with occasional amendments ever since. Based partly on the Universal Declaration of Human Rights agreed by the UN in 1947, it lays down basic standards for the protection of human rights. It is designed to stamp out the kinds of inhuman conduct that characterized so much of Europe's history in the middle part of the twentieth century. The Convention is not limited to the EU; it was agreed in the framework of the Council of Europe, which is quite distinct from (and broader than) the EU. It is enforced by the Court of Human Rights based in Strasbourg. Although the ECHR is not one of the EU treaties, observance of the rights contained in this Convention is obligatory also for (nearly all) member states of the EU.

In due course these implicit constraints were made explicit in the process of treaty revision. Since 1992, Article 6 of the (Maastricht) Treaty on European Union acknowledges the binding character of the principles common to the constitutional traditions of the member states, and of the rights guaranteed in the European Human Rights Convention. Under the 2001 Treaty of Nice, a Charter of Fundamental Rights of the European Union (see Box 8.1) has been adopted in the form of a political declaration that stipulates all the rights that EU citizens (and other residents) enjoy by virtue of their citizenship.

Separation of Powers, Checks, and Balances

Separation of powers (see Box 8.1) is the political-cum-constitutional principle according to which different governmental functions should be exercised by different agencies. Executive decision-making concerns the pursuit of policies and their development through decision-making in individual cases, with possibly some delegated rule-making functions. Ministers in the executive branch of government are the proper executive decision-makers. Executive powers should be distinguished from those of general law-making, which belong to a more broadly based and representative legislature, usually a Parliament, in which all parts of the polity, all shades of opinion, and all classes and kinds of people can be represented.

The third great public power exercised within states is that of adjudication. Once the rules have been made, someone has to decide how they properly apply in particular cases, whether in cases of disputes between government and citizen or between citizen and citizen. The separation of powers doctrine demands that there be a system of courts staffed by competent and conscientious judges who are independent of the executive and the legislature, and who determine such disputes solely on the basis of the established law according to what they consider its most appropriate interpretation. Without courts to 'hold the ring', legislative power is apt to collapse into the hands of the executive.

The independence of the judiciary is of the greatest importance. Without it, the citizen has no real protection against corrupt or oppressive governmental action. But it is an open question how far this means that judges should be able to go in checking or overruling executive decisions or acts of the legislature. Different constitutions take very different lines on what is known as 'judicial review' of the acts of the other arms of government (see Box 3.7).

Whether and how far executive power must be strictly separated from legislative power is a more controversial matter, and different constitutional traditions handle this question in different ways. For example, the French, German, and American constitutions differ significantly in the ways in which they handle the separation of powers. The British system differs from all three. In the UK, ministers belonging to the executive branch of government also sit as members of one or other House of Parliament, and fully participate in its legislative activities. Indeed, the government, by virtue of its control of the majority party in the House of Commons, can normally secure the passage of legislation in a form that has effectively been decided by the cabinet or some committee or subcommittee of it.

Despite all these variations, and whether or not there is ever a perfect separation of powers and functions between different institutions of government, constitutionalism requires that government powers be 'checked'. That is, power must be distributed among institutions and agencies that can effectively check the propriety of each other's actions, and hold them within the limits of power conferred. When this is achieved, the rule of law may be said to apply. Government is conducted under, and shows respect for, laws and the fundamental rights of human beings. The rule of law is the political value that is realized when constitutionalism prevails.

The distribution of functions among the institutions of the Union allows for some mutual checking and balancing. For instance, the Commission is answerable to the Parliament for the way it exercises its powers, but it is also subject to guidance from the European Council. Under the co-decision procedure, neither the Council of Ministers nor the Parliament can enact binding laws without the agreement of the other. The Court of Justice is the final arbiter of the legality of conduct, whether by the other institutions or by states or corporations or citizens.

A final check comes from the people themselves. The democratic character of a constitution depends upon the accountability of law-makers and executive ministers to the people who are bound by the laws, and by executive decisions that implement the laws. Election by universal suffrage to the principal chamber of the legislature (such as the House of Commons in the UK or the *Assemblée Nationale* in France) is essential to accountability. The chief executive is in some states directly elected (as is the President of the French Republic), in other cases indirectly (such as the UK Prime Minister).

Constitutionalism in the EU

We are now in a position to ask whether the EU does not merely have a functional constitution, but whether in that light it achieves the virtues of constitutionalism. Is there an actually functioning separation of powers among the institutions of the Union? Does the rule of law prevail within the Union? Are the affairs of the Union conducted in ways that sufficiently respect the constitutional rules, rights, and principles expressed and implied in the constitutional elements of the treaties? One useful way to approach these questions is to explore how the EU makes policy in different areas, and the power of the different actors in this process.

We can begin with the method by which the majority of policy is made, the so-called Community method (see Box 6.4) employed to decide policy emerging in the Union's first pillar. Here, where the majority of single market and related policies are made, we can reasonably and confidently answer the above questions in the affirmative, while acknowledging that there may be many minor irregularities here and there. As 'guardian of the treaties' the Commission must ensure that the Community law is upheld both by the Commission and its officials and by the member states, against which it can take action before the ECJ in the event of a failure to settle a point of complaint consensually. To the Commission also belongs the task of ensuring that the single market is kept in proper working order, including by the proposal of new legislation.

In areas governed by co-decision, the Commission's proposals go before the European Parliament (EP) and Council of Ministers for consideration. Parliament may amend the Commission's proposal at both of two different stages of scrutiny (first and second 'readings'), and in response the Council adopts a 'common position' that either endorses or not the Parliament's amendments. At any point the Commission may withdraw a draft if it finds unacceptable the amendments insisted on by the EP or Council. Finally, in the event of continuing disagreement, a conciliation committee (representative equally of Parliament and Council) is set up to try to achieve by compromise a final text, which then goes back for a third reading by Parliament and for final consideration by the Council (for an illustration, see Box 5.4). Only by the final resolution of both Parliament and Council (not necessarily a foregone conclusion even at this stage) does the legislation come into force as law.

In terms of rigorous scrutiny and ensuring that the executive cannot make laws without full parliamentary debate and endorsement, the co-decision process generally works well. Indeed, the EP functions with far greater independence from the executive (the Commission, in this case) than is typical of contemporary national parliaments. Similarly, the Parliament fulfils other requirements of constitutionalism, such as ensuring real answerability for any executive misdoing.

A clear illustration is found in the fate of the Santer Commission (Peterson 2006: 86–7). In 1999, President Jacques Santer and the whole of his Commission resigned en bloc in the face of near-certainty that the EP was about to carry a vote of no confidence. The Parliament had found evidence of wrong-doing by two Commissioners in a report by a Committee of Independent Experts (that the EP itself had appointed), and an absence of effective acceptance of common responsibility by the Commission.

Finally, in the first pillar the European Court of Justice (ECJ) has exercised its functions with full independence of judgment, and has ensured the lawfulness of the acts of the Commission, the Parliament, the Council, and the member states. At least once, in the case of the Directive on Tobacco Advertising in 2000, it has struck down Community legislation on the grounds that it lacked an adequate legal base in the Treaties. The rule of law in the EU is secured through an interaction of the ECJ and the Courts of the member states, seemingly to good effect in the great majority of cases, although often with a painful slowness in reaching final results. As far as citizens and corporations are concerned, most of the occasions when EC law is enforced on their behalf or against them, the effective decision that binds them is one by their own national court. As in all human institutions, there are blemishes here and there, some graver than others. But it could not be seriously contended that there is any deep failure in constitutionalism in the EU's first or 'community' pillar.

The EU's other two pillars (covering, respectively, Common Foreign and Security Policy (CFSP), and Justice and Home Affairs (JHA)) were established under the Maastricht Treaty with the deliberate intention that they should function on an intergovernmental basis and avoid the Community method. Decision-making for these pillars was designed to lie outside the 'constitutional charter' and to work in a different way. Not surprisingly, constitutionalism is a less salient feature of these pillars.

Is Democracy Possible in the EU?

Democracy, as we have suggested, depends on the accountability of law-makers and executive ministers to the people they govern. This accountability requires election by universal suffrage to the principal chamber of the legislature, and either direct or indirect election of those who exercise executive power. At the level of EU member states this requirement applies reasonably clearly and not very controversially. While it applies less clearly to the European Union as a whole, it is most visible in the 'supranational' form of governance exhibited in the first or Community pillar.

Supranational Democracy in the Community Pillar

Throughout the Community pillar, to the extent that co-decision between Parliament and Council prevails, decision-making is substantially democratic in character (although often quite different from decision-making at national level). We can explore the extent of and limits to this 'supranational democracy' by focusing on the powers and accountability of key institutions.

Legislative Initiative

The right of legislative initiative is vested mainly in the Commission. Although they may call for new legislation on certain matters, the Parliament and Council can normally act only on a proposal put forward by the Commission. In response to the Commission's proposal a kind of two-chamber legislative process kicks in, with the directly elected Parliament representing the Union's citizens as such, while the Council operates as a chamber of the states. The consent of both is required before any legislation can be adopted. Parliamentary amendments to Commission proposals are extensive. It seems clear that the European Parliament actually has a *more* proactive role in law-making than most, perhaps all, member-state parliaments. At the national level the government of the day usually has a fairly powerful degree of control or at least influence over members' voting through party whips and other inducements.

Nevertheless, it is clear that the EP is not yet the primary chamber of the legislature. On many sensitive topics—such as taxation and the Common Agricultural Policy (CAP)—the Council remains the primary legislator and the directly elected Parliament is often only consulted. In the case of enlargement (an executive decision rather than a matter of 'legislation') the EP is called upon only to assent or dissent. But on other topics—a growing list of them—co-decision prevails, and the Parliament exercises the full powers normally associated with the lower house of a state's legislature. The Parliament has also acquired similar budget-setting powers on certain elements of the spending power of the Union. But that budgetary power does not extend to the huge expenditure on the CAP, or to any matter of taxation.

Electing the Executive

We have established that where co-decision does prevail, the Parliament has somewhat greater practical power over legislation than is normally found in a national parliament. Yet this democratic 'surplus' arises directly from what some consider a serious deficit in the Union's striving towards democracy: the unelected nature of the executive (in this case, the Commission). The Commission is not directly elected, and the element of indirect election—Commissioners are nominated by elected national governments—is weaker than in any of the member states (although broadly similar to the system for selecting the Swiss executive).

The Parliament's role in choosing a President is growing, but still limited. After each EP election, it falls to the Council to nominate a new Commission President. Since the 1999 Amsterdam Treaty, this nominee has had to be approved by Parliament, so the Council must be sensitive to the outcome of the EP election and must nominate someone who will receive at least majority support in the Parliament. But there is no party leader of a victorious party who can lay claim to the presidency in the way a British Prime Minister or German Chancellor can claim office by virtue of his or her party's winning an election, or taking the role of senior partner in a coalition.

Next, the Council in consultation with the new Commission President puts forward a list of nominees for the remaining seats in the Commission, and this list is sent to the Parliament. The Parliament holds hearings of all the nominee commissioners, and at the end Parliament votes to confirm or reject the new Commission as a whole. In the hearings of autumn 2004, Parliament made clear that it would refuse to confirm the Commission under José Manuel Barroso's presidency unless the Italian nominee, Rocco Buttiglione, was withdrawn from nomination (Peterson 2006: 93; see also Chapter 3). It used to be thought that Parliament's powers in relation to the Commission were too much of a 'doomsday weapon' ever to be effectively invoked, but it is no longer so. The real answerability of the executive to the Parliament is now an established fact, and the Parliament can even in practice use its power of en-bloc approval or rejection to exclude a particular nominee.

Institutional Accountability

The unelected nature of the Commission also affects its accountability. On one hand, the Commission is much more closely subject to democratic accountability than is usually acknowledged. Its composition does have to be approved by the democratically elected Parliament, which can also throw the College of the Commission out of office on a vote of no confidence. Yet nominees to the College still come forward from the member states, not the EP, and are vetted first by the Council. Arguably, this process falls a long way short of the way in which an election determines the formation of a government in Spain, Sweden, or Slovenia. The Commission has a genuine degree of democratic legitimacy, but it is not comparable to that of an elected government in the member states of the Union.

Conversely, the Commission lacks the tight grip on Parliament that a dominant and successful Prime Minister and Cabinet can have on, for example, the British Parliament. The Council also lacks such a grip. Although ministers from each member state will find in Parliament representatives of their own national party, and may use normal inducements to try and secure their support for the national government's line, they have no similar influence over other members of the same political group from other member states. Thus, although the EP remains ultimately accountable to voters, it is not subject to the same sort of party or executive control found in most member states.

Party control of MEPs is further weakened by the way in which the EP exercises its functions through specialist committees, dealing with such domains as legal affairs, the single market, human rights, industry and research, and so on. Members working in these committees can acquire very substantial expertise and the style of deliberation is often rather non-partisan, with the weight of a member's argument counting for as much as her or his party affiliation. The report which emerges from the committee under the care of a *rapporteur* (see Box 5.1) decisively shapes the debate and voting in the plenary session at which the whole Parliament comes to its conclusion about the matter at issue. This process contributes to a more discursive, deliberative, and less fiercely adversarial approach to decision-making than may prevail in many national parliaments. Expertise sometimes trumps party doctrine in the legislative process, especially under co-decision. While this consensual, committee-based approach makes agreement possible in a Parliament of over 700, it also weakens control of national parties over 'their' MEPs.

Our discussion suggests that the democratic element in the European legislative process in some ways falls short of that which prevails in most or perhaps all member states. The absence of direct elections of the executive or strong party control weakens accountability of the EU's key institutions. But other distinctive elements of the EU system—such as its incentives for consensus or the autonomous and growing role of the elected Parliament—suggest the contrasts are not all to the disadvantage of the Community model.

Intergovernmentalism and the Council

More problematic for accountability are the domains in which the Community model and co-decision do not apply, chiefly in relation to agriculture and fisheries within the single market, and the pillars for JHA and the CFSP. An instance of intergovernmentalism at work is the European Arrest Warrant (see Box 8.4). Its adoption illustrates how the Council of Ministers operates as the legislative powerhouse of the EU when not constrained by co-decision with Parliament.

The Council has partly a diplomatic, deal-making character. Deals made behind closed doors in the Council can ease the path to common agreements. It also has partly a democratic, law-making character in that ministers are publicly accountable through domestic parliaments for the line they take and the votes they cast at Council

---

BOX 8.4	How it really works

The European Arrest Warrant (EAW)

An EU-wide arrest warrant was agreed by government leaders in 2006. This is how it works: if you were a suspect under this agreement a warrant could be issued for your arrest in any member state and then taken to the courts of the member state where you are currently resident. Subject to minimal scrutiny, these courts (or the specific court authorized for this purpose) must then 'execute' the warrant by having you arrested and delivered to stand trial in that other country according to *its* rules and procedures.

This may be an excellent idea, well geared to preventing or deterring or punishing cross-border criminal activity in the Union. But the basic rules that established this system were made intergovernmentally in the form of a framework decision of the EU's Council of Ministers (see Chapter 7). The EP had to be consulted about the terms of this framework decision, and did suggest amendments to the original idea for the European Warrant. But the Council was under no obligation to act on the Parliament's comments. It could be argued that law-making by the Council alone on issues that concern the rights of the individual, which are in the area of what one would expect to be within the basic constitutional parameters of a democratic system, is open to strong challenge.

Moreover, once a framework decision came into force, it was binding on the national parliaments of the member states. Each of them had to put it into effect as part of their own law. They did have some choice as to the legal instrument used to bring the Arrest Warrant into operation, whether to couple it (for example) with a more general revision of the law about extradition to other countries of persons accused of crimes there, and how to involve their national parliaments (such as via pre-legislative scrutiny). But national parliaments had no opportunity to reject the very idea of the EAW after it was agreed, even in countries (such as Germany and Poland) where there were questions about its compatibility with national constitutions.

Is this somewhat alarming? Here is an issue that affects the liberty of every citizen. It is an issue that affects a citizen's right to the protection of the familiar rules and procedures of the courts in her/his own state, such as conducting all their decision-making in the citizen's own language. Yet, no Parliament had any real say about the rules adopted in the framework decision—not the EP, which was only consulted, and not the national parliaments, which did not even have to be consulted. The principle that a citizen's liberty should be limitable only under laws agreed by his or her elected representatives had gone out of the window. It could be argued that the EAW illustrates clearly a democratic deficit in the context of the intergovernmental pillar of JHA. It also suggests that the constant tension between security and liberty faced by national governments is also present at the EU level.

---

meetings. But since much of the work of the Council goes forward in private, under wraps of secrecy, this form of accountability is very weak.

It may be said, of course, that national governments are also elected. The ministers who attend the Council are members of the elected government in each state, so why is this not democratic? The reply must be that not all democratically elected or accountable officials ought to have powers of general law-making. Indeed, the democratic understandings built into the constitutions of essentially all the member states insist in one way or another on a separation of powers. Elected national presidents in France or Finland, for instance, are not allowed to usurp the law-making powers of their national parliaments or assemblies. How does it then become acceptable at the European level?

For this reason, the strict intergovernmentalism that applies to the JHA domain is viewed with deep concern by those who accuse the EU of a democratic deficit (see, for example, the citizens group Statewatch.org). Yet it was the deliberate strategy of EU leaders at the 1992 Maastricht EU summit to keep these matters for decision on an intergovernmental basis, most commonly with a requirement of unanimity, and to keep the Commission, Court, and Parliament at arm's length. The UK and certain other states insisted on this condition in the intergovernmental conference (IGC) leading up to Maastricht. They feared for the integrity of the domestic system of justice if the Community institutions were to acquire power to override domestic law under the principle of supremacy. They feared further that as a consequence the ECJ would be enabled to second-guess domestic courts and overrule them on issues of interpretation of new European laws—for example, on matters such as the European Arrest Warrant (EAW). Over time, however, concerns about both the lack of democratic legitimacy of JHA policy, *and* the inability to take decisions by unanimity in an enlarged Council, led to moves at successive, subsequent IGCs to subject it to the Community method and, eventually, to eliminate the pillars system altogether.

European Democracy: Competing Views

It is on those very grounds of democracy that those who uphold intergovernmentalism do so. They see it as vital to preserving democracy in Europe. They claim that the necessary preconditions for democracy obtain fully in the member states, but only weakly if at all at EU level (see Allott 2002; Siedentop 2000). The more supranational Community method, and the EP's key role in it, are phoney democracy because democracy demands genuine and widespread citizen involvement in government, particularly via participation in democratic elections on a scale that Europe will never achieve. Member states have real citizenship: not just a constitutional formality but a real sense of social solidarity and common 'peoplehood'. Etymologically, democracy signifies rule by the demos; the demos means the people, so where no 'people' exists, no real democracy is possible. Europe is a union of peoples, not a polity with a single people. Citizenship of the EU exists, but only as something that is additional and even extraneous to the citizenship that gives most Europeans their sense of identity, namely that of their own member state. It is in the member states that democracy can flourish.

According to this reasoning, the European Union's licence to act should be kept strictly in the intergovernmental mode. Governments have the care of democracy in their own countries, and the people, the press, and the parliaments watch jealously over what governments do. A transfer of authority over to European institutions deciding by co-decision and with QMV in Council cheats on democracy. Such a transfer does not represent a new flowering of greater democracy on an all-Europe level, for that level does not satisfy the conditions for a working democracy. There is no sense of common peoplehood. There is no vibrant European political class that shares an agenda of concern and debate. There are no common media of communication to focus a shared public attention on current European issues. Even EP elections are contested more as mid-term votes on national politics, for or against governments, rather than expressing citizens' judgments about the proper future course of European governance and law-making. Finally, this intergovernmentalist view of EU democracy suggests that only bureaucrats in Brussels, and some in member states, are expert in European affairs. So, instead of controlling the bureaucrats, the European Parliament and its elected members are effectively co-opted into the great 'bureaucratic quagmire' of Brussels.

There is some force in this critique, but it also rests on questionable assumptions (see Moravcsik 2001; MacCormick 2005a). First we must beware of a mystification that comes through personifying the 'demos'. National identity is a contested issue in many member states, and nearly all contain some minorities, often sizable ones with their own strong sense of nationhood, as, for example, in Wales or Catalonia. An attractive feature of the EU is that even large national groups are minorities there—everyone belongs to a minority though some are larger than others. To the extent that there is a common constitution (or, for now, constitutional charter), there is a basis for a common civic citizenship, a shared 'constitutional patriotism'. The very fact of common political institutions, above all a single representative parliament, creates the conditions for the progressive emergence of a relatively unified European political class.

Moreover, it could be argued that the power of the Council is as much a threat to member state democracy as a bulwark of it (see Box 8.4). At the domestic level, legislative and executive powers can check each other. At the EU level, intergovernmentalism violates the separation of powers within the member states. The Council (only indirectly elected) participates in law-making activity whose output binds the national legislature. This is the central conundrum of European constitutionalism and European democracy.

Conclusion

The intergovernmentalist conception of democracy that we have considered urges Europeans to cherish their states and to ensure that democracy flourishes within them, both centrally and at regional and local levels. Democratic self-government is realizable among citizens in these contexts. Citizenship of the EU is too thin a kind of citizenship to bear the weight of true continent-wide democracy. Intergovernmental cooperation should thus remain the main basis of operation at the all-Europe level, even if it does to some extent weaken democratic accountability for law made through EU institutions.

A rival supranational conception of democracy says that there is already a serious form of democratic accountability and democratic decision-making at the European level, chiefly through the European Parliament. What is needed is to extend and strengthen the Community method to areas where it makes sense, and to bring the two other pillars progressively into alignment with that method (with exceptions for certain areas, such as foreign affairs). This is what could have been achieved by adoption of the Constitutional Treaty. It acknowledged that democracy at the national, regional, and local levels remains vital to all citizens, and called for respect for the principle of subsidiarity (Box 2.2) to ensure continuing vitality of democratic self-government at these levels.

Both arguments are powerful ones. Both need to be considered seriously. Current and future debates about Europe's constitutional settlement—even if the word 'constitution' is now effectively banned—and about the direction and style of European integration will in the end determine which argument prevails.

? DISCUSSION QUESTIONS

1. In what, if any, sense does the EU have a constitution?
2. To what extent is the Union democratic in its way of working?
3. Is democracy possible at a level above that of the member states?
4. Assess intergovernmental and supranational conceptions of democracy in the EU.

→ FURTHER READING

For clarification of the character of current EU constitutional law and the constitutionalization of the treaties, see Douglas-Scott (2002), especially Chapters 1 and 15. See also Weiler (1999), whose Chapters 6–8 are relevant also to the issue of democracy at the European level. Allott (2002) and Siedentop (2000) both cast grave doubt on the possibility of EU-level democracy, at any rate in present conditions. For critiques of these positions, see Moravcsik (2001) and MacCormick (2005a). MacCormick (2005b) and Norman (2003) give accounts, Norman's much more detailed, of the working of the European Convention. MacCormick (2005b) also gives a short and readable summary of the draft Constitution, and the reasons for believing its adoption might have improved the quality of European democracy and diminished the democratic deficit.

Allott, P. (2002), *The Health of Nations: Society and Law Beyond the State* (Cambridge and New York: Cambridge University Press).

Douglas-Scott, S. (2002), *The Constitutional Law of the European Union* (Harlow: Longman/Pearson Educational).

MacCormick, N. (2005a), 'The Health of Nations and the Health of Europe', in *The Cambridge Yearbook of European Legal Studies* 7: 1–16.

_____ (2005b), *Who's Afraid of a European Constitution?* (Exeter: Imprint Academic).

Moravcsik, A. (2001), 'Despotism in Brussels? Misreading the European Union', *Foreign Affairs* 80:3: 114–22.

Norman, P. (2003), *The Accidental Constitution* (Brussels: Euro Comment).

Siedentop, L. (2000), *Democracy in Europe* (Harmondsworth Allen Lane/Penguin Press).

Weiler, J. H. H. (1999), *The Constitution of Europe* (Cambridge and New York: Cambridge University Press).

WEB LINKS

Several official EU websites provide further information on the issues raised in this chapter. The first listed here is that of the Convention on the Future of Europe, the second the Commission's information page concerning current and recent constitutional developments, the third an historical account of the development of constitutional law in the EU.

- http://european-convention.europa.eu/
- http://europa.eu/constitution/index_en.htm
- http://europa.eu/roadtoconstitution/index_en.htm

Euractive http://www.euractive.com is a commercial website discussing European developments relevant to democracy and constitutionalism.

The following two websites give illustrations of academic discussion of issues covered in the present chapter.

- http://www.jeanmonnetprogram.org/papers
- http://erg.politics.ox.ac.uk/projects/index.asp (then click on national identity project)

Visit the Online Resource Centre that accompanies this book for additional material: www.oxfordtextbooks.co.uk/orc/bomberg2e/

PART IV

The EU and the Wider World

CHAPTER 9

EU Expansion and Wider Europe

Graham Avery

Introduction   180
  Widening Versus Deepening   180
  The Transformative Power of
  Enlargement   182
  An Institutional Paradox   182
How the EU has Expanded   184
  Why Countries Want to Join   187
  Recent Enlargements   187
Countries on the Way to EU
Membership   189
  Balkan Countries   189
  Turkey   192

The Forgotten Enlargement   193
Wider Europe   194
  European Neighbourhood Policy   194
What Limits for the EU?   195
  What Frontiers?   195
  What is Europe?   196
Conclusion   199

DISCUSSION QUESTIONS   199
FURTHER READING   199
WEB LINKS   200

▌ Chapter Overview

The European Union (EU) has expanded to include many European countries, and its widening continues. Enlargement demonstrates the success of the European model of integration, but poses fundamental questions. It has implications both for how the EU works (its structure and institutions) and for what it does (its policies). The recent expansion to include countries of Central and Eastern Europe has shown how the EU's transformative power can promote stability, prosperity, and security. The EU has opened the prospect of membership to countries of the Balkans and Turkey. It has also developed a 'neighbourhood' policy towards other countries, some of whom aim at future membership. The EU now operates on a continental scale: where will its final frontiers lie?

Introduction

Why is the EU's process of expansion so interesting for students of European affairs? Enlargement goes to the heart of important questions about the nature and functioning of the EU. Who decides the shape and size of the EU? How should the EU interact with its neighbours? Where is the EU headed? Enlargement is also ongoing: the EU is committed to further expansion, so past experience can help to guide future policy.

It is often said that enlargement is the EU's most successful foreign policy. Certainly the extraordinary success of the EU in extending prosperity, stability, and good governance to neighbouring countries by means of its membership criteria gives enlargement a special place among the EU's external instruments and policies. But enlargement is much more than foreign policy: enlargement is the process whereby the *external* becomes *internal*. It is about how non-member countries become members, and shape the development of the EU itself. In accepting new partners, and deciding the conditions under which they join, existing members define the EU's future composition and collective identity. In that sense, enlargement could better be described as 'existential' policy: the EU determines its own nature whenever it chooses to (or not to) enlarge its membership.

Widening Versus Deepening

For applicant countries, the prospect of accession (see Box 9.1) to the EU is interrogative: they have to analyse how it will affect them. What will membership

---

BOX 9.1	Key concepts and terms

Absorption capacity refers to the EU's ability to integrate new members into its system.

Accession is the process whereby a country joins the EU and becomes a member state.

Candidate refers to a country whose application is confirmed by the EU but is not yet a member.

Conditionality means (in the context of enlargement) that accession is conditional on fulfilling the criteria for membership.

European Economic Area (EEA) is a free trade area linking the EU with non-EU West European states including Norway, Iceland, and Liechtenstein.

Screening occurs at the start of negotiations when the applicant and the Commission examine the **acquis** to see if there are particular problems to be resolved.

Transitional period refers to a period after accession when application of some of the rules may be phased in or delayed.

of the EU mean in political and economic terms? What will be the costs and benefits? What should be the country's long-term aims as a member? This kind of reflection raises questions of national strategy and even identity.

Enlargement also poses fundamental questions for existing members. A recurrent theme in the development of the EU has been the tension between 'widening' its membership and 'deepening' cooperation between its existing members, such as by expanding the Union's remit or the role of EU institutions. Each time the EU contemplates a further expansion, its members are compelled to ask fundamental questions about its organization and future direction, questions which do not present themselves to policy-makers in the normal course of events.

When considering *who* should be new members, the EU has to reflect on *what* it should do with them (what set of common policies?) and *how* to do it (what institutional set-up?). Debates on the future of European integration regularly accompany the enlargement process, although for countries trying to join the EU it can be surprising to observe that existing members suddenly discover such fundamental questions. To outsiders, the 'widening versus deepening' debate can seem introspective, and even a tactic for delaying enlargement.

But the impact of enlargement on the Union's capacity to act and take decisions raises serious questions about how the EU works. Non-members apply to join the EU because it is attractive, and one of the reasons why it is attractive is that it is effective in taking decisions and developing policies. To expand without ensuring effectiveness would be an error. As France's President François Mitterrand remarked, the risk of enlargement is that just as the last candidate country takes its seat at the table, the system may collapse under the strain of expansion. Enlargement policy is thus linked with the wider debate on European integration; in fact, the accession of new members often provides an occasion for institutional and constitutional change.

Have successive enlargements weakened the EU? While it is true that the arrival of new members requires a period of 'settling-in', it is often followed by the development of new policies and the strengthening of the institutional framework. For example, the EU's structural funds and a more ambitious cohesion policy resulted from the accession of Greece, Portugal, and Spain, poorer countries needing financial aid. The signature of the Single European Act—an important act of deepening of the EU—took place soon after their arrival, and only because the new Mediterranean states accepted a programme of market liberalization in exchange for an increase in regional development spending. Later it was feared that the accession of Austria, Sweden, and Finland, countries which had pursued neutrality or military non-alliance, would put a stop to the development of the EU's Common Foreign and Security Policy (CFSP). But in practice they have viewed its progress more favourably than some of the older members.

From time to time 'old members' (those already in the EU) complain that it was easier to take decisions when the EU was smaller. That may be true (though crises were a regular feature of the EU even in its early days), but successive increases in size have without doubt allowed the EU to develop more substantial and effective policies, internally and externally, than would have been possible with a smaller group. The process of widening has often accompanied or reinforced deepening: *more* has not necessarily led to *less*.

The Transformative Power of Enlargement

The success of recent enlargements in helping to drive political and economic change in Central and East European countries offers a clear illustration of the EU's 'soft power' (Grabbe 2006), or its power to persuade others to do what the Union wants them to do. External pressures—the 'demands of Brussels' during the pre-accession period—were a powerful factor for these countries. The conditionality (see Box 9.1) or leverage of prospective membership encouraged policy-makers to pursue basic reforms that were necessary for EU membership, and desirable even without it.

Conditionality was not employed in earlier enlargements. When the Commission proposed in 1975 that Greece's membership should be preceded by a period of preparation, the idea was rejected by the EU's leaders. Later, Austria, Sweden, and Finland were able to join within two or three years of applying for membership.

Why was the principle of conditionality developed in the 1990s for the countries of Central and Eastern Europe? First, they were in transition from political and economic structures of the Communist period to western models, a process requiring external assistance and encouragement over a period of time. Moreover, the existing members were apprehensive that taking in so many new countries without adequate preparation could impair the EU. It was enlightened self-interest, rather than altruism, that led the EU in 1993 to facilitate and define the membership criteria for the countries of Central and Eastern Europe.

These membership requirements (referred to as the Copenhagen criteria, see Box 9.2) have become the template for enlargement, and have had a remarkable impact. They require a wide-ranging assessment of a country's political, economic, and administrative standards, going further than any examination made by the EU of its existing members. This has led to the complaint that the Union demands higher standards of new members than it does of itself. Moreover, the leverage is effective only in the pre-accession period; after joining, an applicant country becomes a member like others, and the EU cannot apply the accession criteria to its existing members.

An Institutional Paradox

For the functioning of the EU's institutions, the enlargement process is of special interest. The modes of decision-making for enlargement and the organization of negotiations with applicant countries are essentially intergovernmental in character. The EU's positions are adopted by the Council by unanimity; they are presented to the applicant countries by the member state holding the Presidency. Accession negotiations take place in an intergovernmental conference organized between the

BOX 9.2	Criteria for membership

Treaty Provisions

The Amsterdam Treaty (1997) confirms the following:

- Article 49 *Any European state which respects the principles set out in Article 6 (1) may apply to become a member of the Union.*

- Article 6 (1) *The Union is founded on the principles of liberty, democracy, respect for human rights and fundamental freedoms, and the rule of law, principles which are common to the member states.*

Copenhagen Criteria

The Conclusions of the European Council at Copenhagen (1993) stated that:

Membership requires:

1. *that the candidate country has achieved stability of institutions guaranteeing democracy, the rule of law, human rights and respect for and protection of minorities*

2. *the existence of a functioning market economy as well as the capacity to cope with competitive pressure and market forces within the Union*

3. *the presupposition of the candidate's ability to take on the obligations of membership including adherence to the aims of political, economic and monetary union*

The Council Conclusions added that

The Union's capacity to absorb new members, while maintaining the momentum of European integration, is also an important consideration in the general interest of both the Union and the candidate countries.

member states and the applicant state. The result is an Accession Treaty, signed and ratified between sovereign member states. Unanimity is thus the rule. Although proposals are periodically made to extend the scope of majority voting in many areas of EU decision making, no one has ever suggested extending it to enlargement.

In the process of enlargement, as in other intergovernmental activities, the role of the European Parliament is limited. Although the Single European Act in 1986 gave it the right to approve enlargement by assent (see Box 3.5), this occurs at the end of the process, when Parliament votes on an Accession Treaty on a yes/no basis, without being able to modify the text. During the accession negotiations, Parliament is informed regularly, but has no seat at the table.

The Commission's status in accession negotiations is not the same as in external negotiations where it acts as spokesperson on matters of 'Community competence' (such as trade, see Chapter 10). In intergovernmental accession conferences it is the Council Presidency that officially presents EU positions, even on Community matters.

Formally the Commission is not the EU's negotiator, although it may be mandated by the Council to 'seek solutions' with applicants.

In practice the Commission plays an extremely influential role in the process of enlargement. Its position provides a good illustration of the new institutionalist notion that influence can be exercised even in the absence of formal power. The Commission is better equipped technically than member states to monitor the progress of applicant countries in respect of the criteria for EU membership; its regular reports on each country provide the benchmarks for decisions on the conduct of enlargement. In matters of Community competence, it has the sole right to present proposals to the Council for 'common positions' to be taken by the EU side in the negotiations. It is thus in a privileged position to act as interlocutor and intermediary with the applicant countries, and it can (and should) make proposals that reflect the views of the future members as well as existing members. Paradoxically, although enlargement is an intergovernmental process, the Commission plays a key role: it exercises more influence over applicant countries than subsequently when they are members.

How the EU has Expanded

The first applications for membership were made by Britain, Denmark, and Ireland in 1961, soon after the European Communities (ECs) came into existence. Although that first attempt was stopped when France's President Charles de Gaulle said 'no', the three tried again and joined in 1973. This first enlargement was followed by others (see Box 9.3) and more are in prospect. Over time the number of EU member states has quadrupled, its population has tripled, and its official languages have increased from four to 23. In fact there have been few periods in the life of the EU when it was not engaged in discussions with prospective members—a remarkable tribute to its magnetism.

But for countries wishing to join, the path to membership is not easy. Negotiations for accession are arduous (see Box 9.4): there is no guarantee that they will end in agreement by a certain date, and the bargaining is one-sided with the EU often presenting its positions on a take-it-or-leave-it basis. In particular, the EU insists that applicant countries accept all its rules (known as the *acquis*) on accession, and allows delays of application (transitional periods, see Box 9.1) only in exceptional cases.

Meanwhile, as the EU's policies have expanded over the years, prospective members, like athletes, face a 'bar' set at an ever higher level. Getting over it is tough for applicant countries. But after all, they applied to join the EU, not vice versa. The EU has never invited others to join its club—in fact, it has tended to discourage them. In this sense, the EU's strategy for enlargement has been reactive rather than pro-active: it has grown mostly under pressure from its neighbours, not as a result of imperialist ambition.

BOX 9.3	**Chronology of enlargement**

Country	Application for membership	Opening of negotiations	Accession
UK	1967	1970	1973
Denmark	1967	1970	1973
Ireland	1967	1970	1973
Greece	1975	1976	1981
Portugal	1977	1978	1986
Spain	1977	1979	1986
Austria	1989	1993	1995
Sweden	1991	1993	1995
Finland	1992	1993	1995
Hungary	1994	1998	2004
Poland	1994	1998	2004
Slovakia	1995	2000	2004
Latvia	1995	2000	2004
Estonia	1995	1998	2004
Lithuania	1995	2000	2004
Czech Republic	1996	1998	2004
Slovenia	1996	1998	2004
Cyprus	1990	1998	2004
Malta	1990	2000	2004
Romania	1995	2000	2007
Bulgaria	1995	2000	2007
Turkey	1987	2005	
Croatia	2003	2005	
Macedonia (FYROM)	2004		

Notes

- The UK, Denmark, and Ireland first applied in 1961, but negotiations ended in 1963 after France vetoed their admission.

- Norway applied twice (1967, 1992) and completed negotiations (begun in 1970, 1993), but Norwegians twice said 'no' in referenda (1972, 1994).

- Switzerland made an application in 1992 but withdrew it in the same year after the 'no' vote in a referendum on the EEA.

- A 'silent' enlargement took place in 1990 when the German Democratic Republic reunited with the German Federal Republic.

BOX 9.4	The path to membership

Finish. The Treaty of Accession comes into force, and the applicant becomes a member state.

12. The signatory state(s) ratify the Treaty according to national procedures (which may require referenda).

11. The member states and the applicant(s) sign the Treaty.

10. The European Parliament gives its assent to the Treaty.

9. The Commission issues its Opinion on the Treaty.

8. When all chapters are closed, the EU and the applicant agree on a draft Treaty of Accession (which may cover other applicants).

7. After agreement is reached on a chapter, the EU decides whether to close it.

6. For each chapter in the negotiations the EU decides to open, the applicant presents a position; the Commission proposes a 'common position'; the Council approves it for presentation to the applicant.

5. The Commission screens (see Box 9.1) the different chapters of the *acquis* with the applicant.

4. Negotiations commence in an intergovernmental conference between the EU member states and each applicant individually.

3. The Council decides to open accession negotiations.

2. The Commission delivers its Opinion to the Council.

1. The Council confirms the applicant country's candidate status and asks the Commission for an Opinion.

Start. A country submits an application for membership to the European Union's Council of Ministers.

Why Countries Want to Join

Countries apply to join the EU because they think membership is in their political and economic interest. While opinions have differed, according to the country, on whether economics or politics were the most important factor, both have always counted. In the case of the United Kingdom (UK), its application was motivated by the prospective benefits of the common market for its trade and economic growth. But its leaders also understood that the European Economic Community Six were on the way to creating a European system from which the UK could not afford to be excluded politically. With their tradition of agricultural exports to the UK and the Six, it was natural for Ireland and Denmark to follow.

The applications from Greece, Portugal, and Spain were made in different circumstances. After getting rid of totalitarian regimes, these countries wanted membership as a confirmation (and guarantee) of their return to democracy. The sense of being accepted back into the European family was as important for them as the prospect of access to the European market and the European budget. Austria, Sweden, and Finland applied for membership despite having full access to the common market through the EEA (see Box 9.1). In their eyes, the EEA's economic benefits were compromised by the obligation to accept rules from Brussels without having a say in deciding them. These countries also realized that the collapse of the Soviet bloc was leading to a new political situation in Europe in which their traditional neutrality could become less appropriate.

For the ten countries of Central and Eastern Europe, the EU was an aspiration already during the time of communism and Soviet domination. As soon as they made the change of regime, they turned to the EU not only for economic help but for membership. Like Greece, Spain, and Portugal, they wanted to rejoin the European family, and to consolidate their return to democracy. But there were other reasons. For their transition from central planning to market economy, the EU's system and standards offered a convenient 'template'. Uncertain of Russia's future role, they wanted EU membership for national security and as a back-up to NATO membership, which they pursued at the same time (see Box 9.5). For the Central and East European countries, German reunification was another factor. If the former German Democratic Republic—a bastion of communism—could enter the EU by the 'back door', surely others could join the club?

Recent Enlargements

The collapse of the Soviet bloc in 1989 was a seismic shock, creating risks of instability in Europe. Civil war broke out in ex-Yugoslavia, and could have happened elsewhere if events had unfolded differently. But the countries of Central and Eastern Europe succeeded in charting a route to democracy, stability, and prosperity by making far-reaching economic, social, and political reforms. The prospect of EU membership served to guide them in a peaceful 'regime change' in which the process of

---

BOX 9.5	Compared to what?

EU and NATO—a double race to membership

After the end of the Cold War, most of the countries of Central and Eastern Europe wanted to join the North Atlantic Treaty Organization (NATO) as well as the EU. NATO is a transatlantic alliance created in 1949 in face of the perceived threat from the Soviet Union. Under Article 5 of the Washington Treaty, signatories commit themselves to mutual assistance: 'an armed attack against one or more of them in Europe or North America shall be considered an attack against them all'.
NATO now has 26 members:

- Two from North America (US and Canada);
- 24 from Europe:
  - 21 EU states (EU-27 minus Austria, Cyprus, Finland, Ireland, Malta, and Sweden); plus
  - Norway, Iceland, Turkey.

Most other European states, including Russia, have an association with NATO but are not full members.

For the countries of Central and Eastern Europe, concerned about Russia's future intentions, NATO offered *hard security* in the military sense, including the US's nuclear 'umbrella'. The EU offered *soft security* through its political union (see Chapter 10). Even without a mutual defence clause this soft security was important, but the Central and East European countries considered the EU's nascent security and defence policy insufficient to guarantee their territorial integrity. Their accession to NATO in 1999 and 2004 preceded their joining the EU in 2004 and 2007. It was easier for these countries to join NATO for two reasons. First, NATO has simpler tasks and requirements than the EU. Its membership conditions mainly concern the organization and equipment of troops, while the EU has a wide range of political, economic, and administrative requirements. Secondly, NATO's leading member, the US, decided to push for its enlargement, much to the irritation of Russia.

The result of the double enlargement is that the membership of the two organizations now largely overlaps, which makes it easier for them to work together. But the NATO/EU relationship is not simple, and there remains a basic asymmetry. NATO, unlike the EU, includes the US. Moreover, NATO's role is now less focused on territorial defence and more on intervention in other regions. In these regions NATO still has the best military tools to deal with the *results* of insecurity, for example in Afghanistan. But the EU has the best civilian tools to deal with its *causes*, by promoting economic integration, prosperity, and good governance.

Europeanization (adapting domestic politics to the EU's rules, norms, and policies) played a key role (see Chapter 4 and Grabbe 2006).

Faced with many new aspirants for membership by the early 1990s, the EU's first response was cautious (see Box 9.6). In its Europe Agreements (covering aid, trade, and political links with these countries) the EU refused to include the promise of membership. But at the Copenhagen summit in 1993 the EU accepted that the countries of Central and Eastern Europe could join when they fulfilled certain criteria for membership. These Copenhagen criteria (Box 9.2) were defined for the first time at the summit.

In the accession negotiations, which opened with six applicant countries in 1998 and six more in 2000, the main problems (see Avery 2004) were:

- free movement of labour: the EU allowed old members to maintain restrictions on workers from new member states for up to seven years;
- agricultural policy: the EU insisted on a period of twelve years for introducing direct payments to farmers in the new member states; and
- money: the level of payments to new members from the EU budget.

But the negotiations were less important than the preparation for membership in the applicant countries themselves: the 'conditionality' of the process required them to make political and economic reforms and prepare for the correct application of EU policies by strengthening administrative and judicial capacity. The resulting expansion to include ten countries in 2004 and two more in 2007 was an extraordinary episode in the history of European integration. According to the European Commission (2006b) the enlargement fulfilled favourable economic expectations, and created conditions for the European economy to face increased global competition. Moreover, as Kok (2003) observes, it was different from other expansions because it shifted the EU's scale of activity to a continental level. Previous enlargements took place in a Europe divided between East and West. These enlargements helped to unite it.

Countries on the Way to EU Membership

We now consider the countries which the EU officially considers as prospective members: the Balkan countries and Turkey. Although the Treaty says any European country may apply to become a member (see Box 9.2), other countries are at present discouraged from applying.

Balkan Countries

In South-east Europe the following states, with a total population of about 25 million, remain outside the EU:

- Albania: population of 3.6 million
- Bosnia-Herzegovina: 4.5 million

BOX 9.6	How it really works

Joining the EU singly or together

The EU says it treats all applicant countries on their merits: the path to membership depends on individual progress in meeting the criteria, with no linkage between applicants. This is the principle of 'differentiation'—there is no predetermined grouping of countries for accession. Various metaphors are used to describe the process, such as the 'regatta model' which suggests that applicant countries, like boats, can overtake each other.

Accession negotiations are conducted by the EU with each applicant separately. This confirms the principle of differentiation, but gives the EU the possibility to play them off against each other ('divide and rule'). Moreover, the EU prefers an organized process, with intervals between enlargements. So, although each accession negotiation is separate, there have always been groups or waves of accession. Most have been in threes: only Greece joined singly in 1979, and that was really part of a southern enlargement with Spain and Portugal joining in 1986. A 'big bang' enlargement brought in ten countries in 2004. Applicants hoping to improve their chances in the race may be tempted to apply for membership prematurely in the hope of joining a good 'convoy'. For example, Macedonia applied soon after Croatia, but it did not succeed in having its accession negotiations opened at the same time.

The EU brings the market into the enlargement process by creating competition between applicant countries in their domestic preparation and in the accession negotiations. This 'group dynamic' (the wish to emulate others, and the fear of being left behind) helped to push the Central and East European countries forward to membership together. Applicants often demand a target date for membership, but the EU refuses to concede it until towards the end of negotiations. It considers that the promise of a date weakens the conditionality of the process. In accession negotiations the EU is undoubtedly in the stronger bargaining position.

- Croatia: 4.5 million
- Former Yugoslav Republic of Macedonia (FYROM): 2.1 million
- Montenegro: 0.7 million
- Serbia (including Kosovo): 10.2 million.

A glance at the map (Figure 9.1) shows that these countries—sometimes known as the Western Balkans—are surrounded by the EU. They have received a promise of EU membership, and are trying to make the political and economic reforms necessary to join. But these countries have a difficult legacy to overcome. Over the centuries, the region has experienced many political, social, and religious vicissitudes. At one time it was united in the federation of Yugoslavia, but when that state disintegrated in the 1990s, ethnic and religious conflict led to civil war and the intervention of the UN and NATO.

FIGURE 9.1 European Neighbourhood Policy

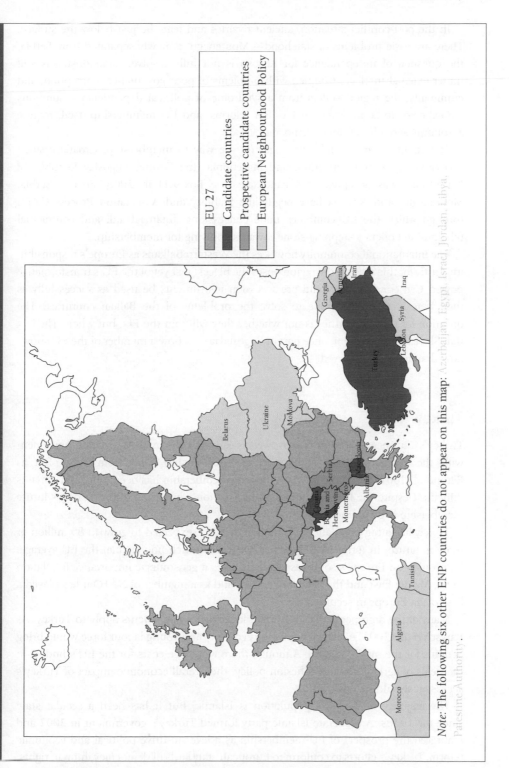

EU 27

Candidate countries

Prospective candidate countries

European Neighbourhood Policy

Note: The following six other ENP countries do not appear on this map: Azerbaijan, Egypt, Israel, Jordan, Libya, Palestine Authority.

In the post-conflict situation, ancient rivalries and fears lie just below the surface. There are basic problems of statehood—Montenegro is newly separated from Serbia, the question of independence for Kosovo is not fully resolved, and Bosnia is still under external tutelage. Coupled with problems of poor governance, corruption, and criminality, the region suffers from a syndrome of political dependency—solutions are expected to come from outside. But reforms, and EU membership itself, require autonomy and a functioning democracy.

The countries are at different stages on the way to membership. Croatia opened accession negotiations in 2005, and Macedonia (the Former Yugoslav Republic of Macedonia) was accepted as a candidate (see Box 9.1) in 2006. Bosnia, Serbia, Montenegro, and Albania have begun the Stability and Association Process (SAP), through which the EU combines trade concessions, financial aid, and contractual relations and offers a stepping-stone towards applying for membership.

The international community now sees the Western Balkans as Europe's responsibility. Partly for this reason, the region poses the biggest test yet of the EU's transformative power. Can conditionality and pre-accession instruments be used as successfully as they were in Central Europe to solve the problems of the Balkan countries? The question for those countries is not whether they will join the EU, but when. The fact that Slovenia—like them, once part of Yugoslavia—is now a member of the EU shows how that might be achieved.

Turkey

Turkey's 'European vocation' was avowed as early as 1964 in its Association Agreement with the Community. Its application for membership dates from 1987. But as Redmond (2007) recounts, the path towards membership has been long, and remains difficult. Despite the fact that accession negotiations opened in 2005, Turkey's future membership is by no means assured.

Turkey has a big population: 72 million in 2007, expected to grow to 85 million or more in future. In terms of income per head, it is much poorer than the EU average. Its position on Europe's southeastern flank gives it geostrategic importance in relation to the Middle East and the Black Sea region, and as a member of NATO it has played a key role in European security.

Many of the arguments that were valid for earlier enlargements apply to Turkey. As Barysch et al. (2005) explain, its growing economy and young labour force would bring benefits for the single market. Although there would be costs for the EU's budget in the fields of agriculture and cohesion policy, the overall economic impact of Turkey's accession should be positive.

The majority of Turkey's population is Islamic, but it has been a secular state since the 1930s. A moderate Islamic party formed Turkey's government in 2002 and embraced the prospect of EU membership as a lever to drive political and economic reform. Turkey's efforts to conform to European standards of democracy, human rights, and rule of law are monitored closely by the EU. Progress has been made towards meeting the Copenhagen criteria, but more still needs to be done. Amongst the main problems are Turkey's treatment of its Kurdish minority, its restrictions on freedom of expression, and the political role of its military.

In foreign policy, Turkey's membership would be positive for the EU in many ways. For example, Turkey has more soldiers than any other European member of NATO. But it would also bring new problems and risks. With Turkey's accession, the EU's external frontiers would extend to Azerbaijan, Armenia, Iran, Iraq, and Syria. The EU would share a border and be in direct contact with regions of instability.

Many argue that by admitting Turkey, the EU would give a powerful signal to other countries that it accepts Islam. To refuse Turkey would show that Europe is culturally prejudiced, and might lead to a reversal of Turkey's reforms, or even turn it against the West. Others reject this argument: just as religion is not a reason to say 'no' to Turkey, it is not a reason to say 'yes'. Although Turkey's population is Islamic, it is not an Arab country, and it has a historic legacy of difficult relations with neighbours such as Armenia.

Public opinion in the EU is influenced by fear of an influx of Turkish migrant workers, and the idea that Turkey is different—that it is not part of Europe in geographical or cultural terms. Objections to Turkish membership are expressed by politicians particularly in France, Germany, and Austria, where Turkey's accession tends to be opposed not only for populist reasons but also on the grounds that the EU could not function effectively with Turkey as a member.

Cyprus is a further thorn of contention. Since Turkey intervened militarily in 1974, the Turkish Republic of Northern Cyprus—not recognized by the rest of the international community—has been separated from the south by a UN peacekeeping force. Hopes of reuniting the two parts of the island were dashed by referenda in 2003 when the Greek Cypriots in the south said 'no' to a UN plan that was accepted by the north. As a result, the EU's enlargement of 2004 brought in a divided island. All these problems put a question-mark over Turkey's bid for EU membership. Some argue that, even if it does not finally become a member, Turkey has an interest in continued modernization in line with European criteria. But with an uncertain prospect of membership, the leverage for change is less effective.

The Forgotten Enlargement

It is sometimes forgotten that membership applications have been made by Norway and Switzerland (see Box 9.3). Oil-rich Norway negotiated and signed two Accession Treaties, but did not join after its people said 'no' twice in referenda. This divisive experience has made its politicians reluctant to reopen the question of EU membership. As a member of the EEA, it has access to the common market and participates in other EU policies. In fact, the EEA (which also includes Iceland and Liechtenstein) is the closest form of relationship that the EU has made with non-member countries.

Generally, Norway finds it frustrating not to have a full voice in EU decisions which directly affect it, so one day it may apply again to become a member. In that case, Iceland would probably follow. The EU's common fisheries policy would be the main problem for these countries.

Switzerland's application for EU membership was withdrawn when its people said 'no' in a referendum on the EEA; since then it has pursued its interests through bilateral agreements with the EU. While the French-speaking part of the population is broadly in favour of the EU, a majority of German-speakers are opposed. Switzerland's neutrality and use of referenda could pose problems of membership. Small, rich countries such as these are ideal candidates for the EU: if they decided to apply again, they would rapidly be accepted.

Wider Europe

European Neighbourhood Policy

With expansion to include Central and Eastern Europe, the EU encountered a series of new neighbours to the east. It already had a Euro-Mediterranean Partnership with countries to the south, and now it was obliged to rethink relations with the countries of Eastern Europe that were formerly in the Soviet Union. New EU members such as Poland and Hungary did not want to see their accession lead to the erection of new barriers to countries with which they have cultural, social, and economic links.

The result was the development of the European Neighbourhood Policy (ENP) covering sixteen countries: Morocco, Algeria, Tunisia, Libya, Egypt, Israel, Jordan, Palestine Authority, Lebanon, Syria, Armenia, Azerbaijan, Georgia, Moldova, Ukraine, and Belarus (see Figure 9.1). Its aim is to extend stability, prosperity, and security, and create a 'ring of friends' by developing political links and economic integration with the EU. Its main instrument is a series of Action Plans negotiated with each partner country and backed by financial and technical assistance. These plans cover political dialogue, economic and social reform, trade, cooperation in justice and security affairs, transport, energy, environment, education, and so on. They require the neighbours to take on European regulation and a large part of the *acquis*: the system is modelled, in fact, on the EU's Accession Partnerships with future members.

But the ENP lacks the big incentive of the enlargement process—the 'golden carrot' of accession. Its message is 'be like us' not 'be one of us'. For the East European neighbours such as Ukraine, the fact that the policy is 'accession-neutral' is a disappointment. Although it offers long-term benefits, it demands reforms that are difficult and costly, and does not fully satisfy participants' wishes in fields such as trade in agriculture, or visas for travel to the Union. But ENP does provide increased financial aid and a closer political relationship, and it can be developed further.

The ENP is sometimes criticized as a 'one size fits all' formula for two groups of countries with different interests and problems—neighbours *of* Europe in the south, and neighbours *in* Europe in the east. But in practice Action Plans are tailored to fit the individual needs of the countries, and grouping the countries together strikes a necessary balance between the different geographical and political priorities of EU members such as Germany and Poland on the one hand, and Italy, France, and Spain on the other.

The EU's offer of Neighbourhood Policy to Russia was rejected. Russia has preferred to see itself as a 'strategic partner', and remains suspicious of the EU's links with countries that it considers historically as part of its 'near-abroad'. Belarus is also still outside the ENP because of its undemocratic regime. But the EU decided to include Libya when it improved relations with the West.

The ENP is an innovative approach that uses techniques derived from the EU's enlargement process to promote good governance and European values in neighbouring countries. Its potential to deal with problems of transnational crime, security of energy supplies, and migratory pressures from those countries offers benefits to the EU. But it remains to be seen whether it can satisfy the needs and demands of the neighbours, particularly those who hope for EU membership.

What Limits for the EU?

The EU has used the prospect of membership very successfully to extend stability and prosperity to neighbouring countries. But is it realistic to continue without predetermined limits? Logically, the EU cannot expand indefinitely: it was not designed to be a world system of government, but an 'ever-closer union' of European peoples. How far can the European Union's expansion continue? Where should its final frontiers lie? This debate on limits is welcomed by those who oppose further expansion, while those in favour of enlargement tend to avoid it.

What Frontiers?

Does the EU really need fixed borders? With globalization, frontiers are less significant, and when they divide peoples with historic links they can cause social and economic problems. To alleviate this problem, could the EU not function with 'fuzzy borders'? The answer seems to be no. As Wallace (2002) argues, states need boundaries to function, because they define where laws apply. Although the EU is not a state, it is based on laws, and needs a territorial definition for the operation of its policies.

But the EU can have different frontiers for different policies. This is already the case for the euro and Schengen (see Chapter 7). In this sense, the EU is already a multi-frontier system. But problems arise when its multi-tier potential is perceived as leading to a 'core-group', with some states having more rights than others. All members want to have full rights in decision-making. From an institutional point of view, a territorial distinction between membership and non-membership is necessary.

What is Europe?

The Treaty of Rome in 1957 said 'any European state may apply to become a member'. The Treaty of Amsterdam in 1997 added a reference to values (see Box 9.2). It is sometimes suggested that the EU is based on shared values rather than geography. But if this argument were correct we would expect like-minded states in distant parts of the world—such as New Zealand—to be considered as future members. In fact geographic contiguity or proximity is a precondition for membership. The exception which proves the rule is France's overseas departments (such as Guadeloupe or Martinique) which are in the EU because they are part of French territory.

What are the geographical limits of the European continent? To the North, West, and South, it is defined by seas and oceans, but to the East there is no clear boundary. Although the Ural Mountains and the Caspian Sea are often invoked as natural frontiers, some geographers consider Europe as the western peninsula of the Asian landmass—a subcontinent rather than a continent.

In any case, different geographical, political, and cultural concepts of Europe have prevailed at different times. Asia Minor and Northern Africa were included in the political and economic area of the Roman Empire, but much of today's EU was outside it. Other historical periods are cited as characterizing Europe in cultural terms, such as the experience of the Renaissance and the Enlightenment. For some, the Christian religion is a defining factor. Such examples show how difficult it is to arrive at an agreed definition. The European Commission (1992) has taken the view that:

The term 'European' has not been officially defined. It combines geographical, historical and cultural elements which all contribute to the European identity. The shared experience of proximity, ideas, values and historical interaction cannot be condensed into a simple formula, and is subject to review by each succeeding generation. It is neither possible nor opportune to establish now the frontiers of the European Union, whose contours will be shaped over many years to come.

Other European intergovernmental organizations such as the Council of Europe and the Organization for Security and Cooperation in Europe (OSCE) have a wider membership than the EU (see Box 9.7). These organizations include the following European states which are not yet members of the EU:

• Albania, Bosnia-Herzegovina, Croatia, Macedonia, Montenegro, Serbia
• Turkey
• Iceland, Norway, Switzerland

BOX 9.7	Other Europeans

Not all European states are in the EU. Here are the other main European organizations and their membership.

The Council of Europe founded in 1949 is mainly concerned with human rights, social and legal affairs, and culture. It has 47 members:

- EU countries (27)
- Albania, Bosnia-Herzegovina, Croatia, Macedonia (FYROM), Montenegro, Serbia
- Turkey
- Iceland, Norway, Switzerland
- Armenia, Azerbaijan, Georgia, Moldova, Russian Federation, Ukraine
- Andorra, Liechtenstein, Monaco, San Marino

The Organization for Security and Cooperation in Europe (OSCE) has been concerned since 1975 with early warning, crisis prevention and management, and post-conflict rehabilitation. It has 56 members:

- Council of Europe countries (47)
- Belarus, Kazakhstan, Kyrgyzstan, Tajikistan, Turkmenistan, Uzbekistan
- Canada, US
- Holy See (Vatican City)

Looking at these organizations in relation to membership of the EU, we should leave aside

- mini-states which have no interest in joining the EU (Andorra, Liechtenstein, Monaco, San Marino, the Holy See)
- the 'Central Asian' members of OSCE (Kazakhstan, Kyrgyzstan, Tajikistan, Turkmenistan, Uzbekistan)
- the transatlantic members of OSCE (US, Canada)

That leaves seventeen states recognized as European that are not (yet) in the EU.

- Armenia, Azerbaijan, Georgia, Moldova, Belarus, Ukraine
- Russia.

Of these seventeen states, the first seven are considered by the EU as potential members. Could it eventually embrace all the others? Will the final limits of the EU be set at 44 countries?

An attempt by the EU institutions to decide its future limits—a decision requiring unanimity—would not give a clear answer. Member states have differing views on future membership. Those sharing borders with non-members often wish to include them in the EU, for reasons of stability and security. Poland, for example, wants its neighbour Ukraine to be a member of the EU in the long term. But other states such as France have a more restrictive position, even on the inclusion of Turkey. In fact, a discussion of the 'limits of Europe' can easily become a debate on 'should Turkey join?'

What are the prospects for countries such as Ukraine, which are presently in the framework of the EU's European Neighbourhood Policy? They are so far from meeting the Copenhagen criteria that EU membership is impossible for many years. So why try to decide 'yes or no' prematurely, particularly when 'no' could have undesirable consequences for both sides? Anyhow, the long-term alternative to membership of the EU is not yet clear: would it be their present status under the Neighbourhood Policy, or an enhanced relationship?

Russians consider their country to be European as well as Asian, and the idea of its membership of the EU has been mentioned by leaders on both sides. But could Russia, with its self-identity as a great power, accept the EU's *acquis*? Its geographic expanse and population of 140 million mean that Russia's joining the EU would be more like the EU joining Russia. But with its population declining towards 100 million by mid-century, and facing 1.4 billion Chinese, maybe Russia will one day look with more interest to the EU.

In this situation, prudence argues for keeping open the prospect of EU enlargement. Aspirant countries may be willing to modify their behaviour significantly in the hope of obtaining membership. To define the EU's ultimate borders now would demotivate those excluded, and diminish the leverage for those included. Thus a diplomatic policy of 'constructive ambiguity' seems likely to prevail.

Finally, the pace of further enlargement will depend also on the attitude of publics and politicians in the EU (see House of Lords 2006). After its expansion to 27 the EU experienced 'enlargement fatigue', and the question of absorption capacity (see Box 9.1) became an element in debate. This latter notion, introduced at Copenhagen in 1993 (see Box 9.2), refers to the need to 'maintain the momentum of European integration'. It thus explicitly links future enlargement to the development of the EU's institutions, policies, and budget.

In the years following 1993, when reforms were in the pipeline in successive Treaties, this criterion was not problematic, and the 2004 enlargement went in parallel with the preparation of the Constitutional Treaty. But after the Constitution was rejected by French and Dutch voters in 2005, institutional reform of some kind has been considered to be a precondition for further expansion.

The increase from 15 to 27 has not paralysed the EU's decision-making. It seems to work as well, or as badly, as it did in the past (see Chapter 3). However, the EU already made the commitment at Nice that, before going beyond 27 members, it would reform the composition of the European Commission so that it has a smaller number of Commissioners than member states. That commitment is fleshed out in the 2007 Reform Treaty, which more broadly seems finally to deliver on the aspiration to reform the EU's institutional system to accommodate enlargement, as the 2001 Treaty of Nice sought to do with very limited success. Still, enlargement may thus encounter more problems on the EU side than in the past, particularly if enlargement is subject to referenda in member states. The EU will be rigorous in applying conditions for potential members, and cautious in making promises to others.

Conclusion

The expansion of the EU has been remarkable in its pace and impact. But after increasing its membership from twelve to 27 states and its population by a third in the period from 1995 to 2007, the EU will expand more slowly in future. In the medium term, it will limit its expansion to the countries of the Balkans plus Turkey, whose accession is uncertain and in any case will not take place for many years. Norway, Iceland, and Switzerland—if they applied for membership—could join more rapidly. In the longer term the EU may eventually accept other East European countries such as Ukraine, but in the meantime they remain in the framework of its Neighbourhood Policy. Thus the final limits of the European Union are likely to result from the course of events and successive political decisions, rather than from a strategic choice made in advance.

?   **DISCUSSION QUESTIONS**

1. Has the EU's enlargement to 27 members weakened its capacity for effective action? Has the 'widening' stopped the 'deepening'?

2. Turkey's application for membership dates from 1987: why is it so difficult for the EU to handle, and will it ever succeed in joining?

3. Although the Treaty says 'any European state may apply for membership' the EU distinguishes between 'potential members' and other European countries. Explain why.

4. The EU's Neighbourhood Policy aims at making a 'ring of friendly countries': can it be a substitute for joining the EU?

→   **FURTHER READING**

The enlargements of 2004 and 2007 are the subject of a voluminous literature, particularly on transition and reform in Central and Eastern Europe. Nugent (2004) offers a good overview. The early stages of the process are covered in Mayhew (1998), Torreblanca (2001), and Ziclonka (2002), while the accession negotiations are described in Avery (2004). Analyses of the theoretical aspects of enlargement can be found in Schimmelfennig and Sedelmeier (2005), and a treatment of 'Europeanization' (with bibliography) in Grabbe (2006). On previous rounds of enlargement, see Preston (1997).

On neighbourhood policy, see Dannreuther (2004), Emerson (2005), Wissels (2006), and EPIC (2007).

Avery, G. (2004), 'The Enlargement Negotiations', in F. Cameron (ed.), *The Future of Europe, Integration and Enlargement* (London: Routledge): 35–62.

Dannreuther, R. (ed.), (2004), *European Union Foreign and Security Policy: Towards a Neighbourhood Strategy* (London and New York: Routledge).

Emerson, M. (ed.) (2005), *Democratisation in the European Neighbourhood* (Brussels: Centre for European Policy Studies).

EPIC (2007), 'European Neighbourhood Policy', Special Issue of *European Political Economy Review*, 7 (summer), available online at: http://www.lse.ac.uk/collections/EPER.

Grabbe, H. (2006), *The EU's Transformative Power: Europeanization through Conditionality in Central and Eastern Europe* (Basingstoke: Palgrave Macmillan).

Mayhew, A. (1998), *Recreating Europe: The European Union's Policy towards Central and Eastern Europe* (Cambridge: Cambridge University Press).

Nugent, N. (ed.), (2004), *European Union Enlargement* (Basingstoke and New York: Palgrave).

Preston, C. (1997), *Enlargement and Integration in the European Union* (London: Routledge).

Schimmelfennig, F., and Sedelmeier, U. (eds.) (2005), *The Politics of European Union Enlargement: Theoretical Approaches* (London: Routledge).

Torreblanca, J. I. (2001), *The Reuniting of Europe: Promises, Negotiations and Compromises* (Aldershot: Ashgate).

Wissels, R. (2006), 'The Development of the European Neighbourhood Policy', in *Foreign Policy in Dialogue* 7/19 (Trier: University of Trier). Available online at http://www.deutsche-aussenpolitik.de/newsletter/issue19.pdf

Ziclonka, T. (ed.), (2002), *Europe Unbound: Enlarging and Reshaping the Boundaries of the European Union* (London and New York: Routledge).

⊕ WEB LINKS

The European Commission's websites provide information, official documents, and speeches on Enlargement at http://ec.europa.eu/enlargement and on Neighbourhood Policy at http://ec.europa.eu/world/enp (including a bibliography of academic research). A useful interactive map including the EU 27 and ENP participants is available at: http://ec.europa.eu/world/enp/partners/index_en.htm

For regular analyses and updates on developments in both areas see the newsletter www.euractiv.com and publications of the Centre for European Policy Studies http://www.ceps.be (especially its newsletter 'European Neighbourhood Watch'), the European Policy Centre http://www.epc.eu/ and the Centre for European Reform http://www.cer.org.uk

 Visit the Online Resource Centre that accompanies this book for additional material: www.oxfordtextbooks.co.uk/orc/bomberg2e/

CHAPTER 10

The EU as a Global Actor

John Peterson

Introducing European Foreign Policy 202

Development 203

The Basics 204

A National 'System' of Foreign Policies 206

The Community System 208

Commercial (Trade) Policy 208

Aid and Development 208

Externalizing 'Internal' Policies 211

The EU System 213

The Common Foreign and Security Policy 213

A European Security and Defence Policy? 215

Theorizing the EU as a Global Actor 216

Conclusion 218

DISCUSSION QUESTIONS 219
FURTHER READING 219
WEB LINKS 220

▌ Chapter Overview

The European Union's ambitions to be a global power are a surprising by-product of European integration. Students of 'European foreign policy' focus on EU trade, aid, and the Common Foreign and Security Policy (CFSP), but cannot neglect the extensive national foreign policy activities of its member states. On most economic issues, the EU is able to speak with a genuinely single voice through the Commission. It has more difficulty showing solidarity on aid policy, but is powerful when it does. The Union's foreign policy aspirations now extend to traditional foreign and security policy, including defence. But distinctly national policies persist and the EU suffers from weak or fragmented leadership. Debates about European foreign policy tend to be about whether the glass is half-full—with the EU more active globally than ever before—or half-empty, and mainly about disappointed expectations.

Introducing European Foreign Policy

One of the founding fathers of what is now the European Union (EU), Jean Monnet, once described European integration as a 'key step towards the organization of tomorrow's world' (quoted in Jørgensen 2006: 521). Nevertheless, Monnet and the other founders of the original European Economic Community (EEC) had little ambition to create a new kind of international power. In fact, the EEC was given no external powers outside of the ability to conduct international trade negotiations, since a common market could not, by definition, exist without a common trade policy.

The European Union now aspires to be a global power: that is, a major international actor that can, like the United States (US) or China, influence developments anywhere in the world, and draw on a full range of economic, political, and security instruments in pursuit of its foreign policy goals. It can be argued that 'foreign policy has been one of the areas in which European integration has made the most dynamic advances' (Tonra and Christiansen 2004: 545). Still, the EU is a strange and often ineffective global actor. Distinctive *national* foreign policies endure in Europe and show few signs of disappearing. Thus, the notion of 'European foreign policy', comprising all of what the EU and its member states do in world politics, collectively or not, has gained prominence (see Hill and Smith 2005; Carlsnaes 2006).

Debates about European foreign policy tend to be about whether the glass is half-full or half-empty. On one hand, the EU has used enlargement as a tool of foreign policy and dramatically transformed the regions to its east and south (see Chapter 9). The Union is an economic superpower. It is gradually developing a military capability for crisis management or humanitarian intervention.

On the other hand, the EU suffers from chronic problems of disunity, incoherence, and weak leadership. European foreign policy can be undermined by all manner of rivalries: between its member governments, between EU institutions, and between them and national foreign ministries. The EU was entirely sidelined during the 2003 war in Iraq because it could not come even remotely close to a common policy (see Peterson and Pollack 2003). Some argue that the Union provided 'far too little leadership far too late' to the aborted 2005 effort to reform the United Nations (UN) (Laatikainen and Smith 2006: 21–2).

Often, the same international event or issue can be used to defend either the half-full or half-empty thesis. Consider the call by the head of the leading non-governmental organization, Human Rights Watch, for the EU to 'fill the leadership void' on human rights post-Iraq, after the US was widely viewed as flaunting them. Here, we might see the Union as a beacon of hope for a more progressive, humane international order. Or, we might share the despair of the issuer of the plea at how the EU continues to 'punch well beneath its weight' on human rights (Roth 2007). The EU consistently fails to meet expectations while never ceasing to develop new and bolder ambitions.

Development

The EU's international ambitions have their origins in the 1960s. French rejection of the proposed European Defence Community in 1950 effectively guaranteed the ascendancy of NATO in defence matters (see Chapter 2). However, American disregard for European preferences in Vietnam and the Middle East presented the Community with incentives to defend its interests collectively, and thus more effectively, in foreign policy. According to a logic known as the 'politics of scale', the whole—the EU speaking and acting as one—is more powerful than the sum of it parts, or member states acting individually (Ginsberg 2001).

By 1970, a loose intergovernmental framework, European Political Cooperation (EPC), was created to try to coordinate national foreign policies. Linked to the Community, but independent of it, EPC was very much dominated by national foreign ministers and ministries. Member governments identified where their national interests overlapped, without any pretension to a 'common' foreign policy. The European Commission was little more than an invited guest, and the European Parliament was entirely excluded.

Nonetheless, EPC fostered consensus on difficult issues in the 1970s and 80s, including the Arab–Israeli conflict and relations with the Soviet bloc (through what became the Organization for Security and Cooperation in Europe, or OSCE). EPC also helped the Community burnish its reputation as a defender of human rights by becoming the vehicle for its condemnation of South Africa's apartheid system. Europe was mostly limited to saying things—issuing diplomatic démarches—as opposed to doing things via EPC. But increasingly it backed up EPC positions with European Community actions using economic aid or sanctions (which were applied to Argentina during the Falklands War).

The perceived successes of EPC led to claims that Europe could become a 'civilian power' (see Galtung 1973). That is, the EC could uphold multilateralism, liberalism, and human rights as values, and be a powerful advocate for peaceful conflict resolution. EPC was given treaty status and formally linked to the activities of the Community in the 1986 Single European Act.

Yet, the geopolitical earthquakes that shook Europe beginning in 1989 exposed EPC as wholly inadequate. The idea of strengthening foreign policy cooperation in a new 'political union' was given impetus by the dramatic transitions in Central and Eastern Europe, the Gulf War, the attempted coup against Mikhail Gorbachev (and subsequent collapse of the Soviet Union), and war in Yugoslavia. Thus, the 1992 Maastricht Treaty grafted a new CFSP (along with a new Justice and Home Affairs (JHA) policy) onto the existing Treaty of Rome, resulting in the European Union's three-pillar structure. There is no question that the EU became far more active internationally in the years that followed. There is considerable debate about whether it also became more effective.

The Basics

The EU aspires to international power for two basic reasons. First, even the Union's largest states are medium-sized powers compared to, say, the US or China. All European states, especially—but not only—smaller ones, seek to use the EU as a 'multiplier' of their power and influence. There is controversy about whether the Union is a truly global (as opposed to a regional) power. However, its largest member states—France, Germany, Italy, and the UK—give the Union a 'pull towards the global perspective which many of the 2[7] simply do not have as part of their foreign policy traditions' (Hill 2006: 67). New EU military and civilian missions in Africa and Afghanistan, as well as the Balkans and Middle East, illustrate the point.

Secondly, the Union's international weight increases each time it enlarges or expands its policy competence. The twelve countries that joined after 2004 were all (besides Poland) small and (mostly) pro-American states with limited foreign policy ambitions. But EU membership allowed them to distance or defend themselves from the US on issues such as climate change or trade policy, while making the Union a potentially more powerful player on these and other international issues. Meanwhile, the EU has accumulated new foreign policy tools, beginning with aid programmes for Africa in 1963 and most recently a European Security and Defence Policy (ESDP; see below). The EU is powerful internationally above all because it presides over a market of nearly 500 million consumers, or around 40 per cent more than the US.

Whatever its accomplishments, European foreign policy is hindered by three basic gaps. One is between task expansion, which has been considerable, and the integration of authority, which has been limited. The total number of European diplomatic staff worldwide (EU plus national officials) is more than 40,000 diplomats in 1,500 missions. Yet, no minister or government can give orders to this huge collection of officials; in fact, no single EU official can direct even the Union's own staff because of fragmented institutional structures in Brussels. No one claims that the US—with around 15,000 staff in 300 missions—is weaker because it is so outnumbered (Everts 2002: 26).

The gap between the EU's economic power and political weakness is a related but separate problem. Europe manages to defend its interests on matters of 'low politics'—economic, trade, and (less often) monetary issues—with a more or less single voice. External trade policy is made via the Community method of decision-making (see Box 6.4), which delegates considerable power to the Union's institutions. The EU also has considerable authority in aid and development policy, and has emerged as a major power in international environmental diplomacy. In contrast, the Union often fails to speak as one on matters of traditional diplomacy, or 'high politics', which touch most directly on national sovereignty, prestige, or vital interests. The CFSP created by the Maastricht Treaty was meant to cover 'all aspects of foreign and security policy'. However, there is no *single* EU foreign policy in the sense of one that replaces or eliminates national policies. In contrast to (say) EU trade policy, the CFSP relies overwhelmingly on intergovernmental consensus. It remains difficult to envisage member states ever delegating power to decide life and death questions, such as whether to use military force, to the Union's institutions. In short, the gap between the EU's economic power and political weight endures largely because the Community system remains more efficient, decisive, and (on the whole) politically acceptable to the member states than the CFSP system.

A final gap is between the world's expectations of the EU and its capacity to meet them (Hill 1998). In the early days of the post-Cold War period, European foreign policy-makers often oversold the Union's ability to act quickly or decisively in international affairs. Nearly two decades later, the rhetoric had muted but the EU still struggled to be a truly global, as opposed to a regional power in its European neighbourhood. Chris Patten (2005: 176), a former Commissioner for External Relations, was frank:

America is a superpower, partly because it is the only country whose will and intentions matter everywhere, and are everywhere decisive to the settlement of the world's problems. Europe can help to solve these problems, but there are only some parts of the world—like the Balkans—where our role (while not necessarily crucial) is as important as, or more important than, that of China in the case of North Korea.

These three gaps—between task expansion and integration, economic unity and political division, and capabilities and expectations—all contribute to a more general mismatch between aspirations and accomplishments. To understand its persistence, we need to unpack European foreign policy and consider it as the product of three distinct but interdependent systems of decision-making (White 2001):

- a national system of foreign policies;
- a Community system focused on economic policy (and based within the first pillar in the EU's tri-pillar structure); and
- an EU system centred on the CFSP (or second pillar).

These systems remain distinct even if there is considerable overlap between them (see Table 10.1). Europe is the world's largest foreign aid donor, but only when the disparate and largely uncoordinated contributions of the Union and its member states are added together. EU environmental policy is made via the Community method but it is often unclear who speaks for Europe in international environmental diplomacy. Leadership of the EU system sometimes falls to sub-groups of member states, as illustrated by the 'EU-3', with France, Germany, and the UK taking the lead on nuclear diplomacy towards Iran.

Overlaps between these systems reflect how high and low politics often blur together in the twenty-first century. Disputes arising from Europe's dependence on Russia for energy, or the tendency of Chinese exporters to flood European markets, can touch upon vital national interests and preoccupy diplomats and governments at the highest political levels. Meanwhile, the EU has begun work on a security and defence policy: the ultimate expression of high politics. Blurred boundaries between both policy realms and systems for decision-making make European foreign policy an elusive subject that

TABLE 10.1 European foreign policy: three systems

System	Key characteristic	Pillar (or Treaty base)	Primary actors	Policy example
National	Loose (or no) coordination	Outside EU's structures	National ministers and ministries	War in Iraq
Overlap	Some coordination of national and EU efforts	Pillar 1 with nuances (i.e. in annexes to Treaty; no funds from Community budget)	National ministers and ministries, Commission	Cotonou agreement
Community	EU usually speaks with single voice	Pillar 1*	Commission and Council	Commercial (trade) policy
Overlap	Turf battles	Pillars 1 and 2	Council and Commission	Economic sanctions policy
EU	'Common, not single' policy	Pillar 2*	High Representative; national ministers and ministries (especially of large states)	Nuclear diplomacy towards Iran

*It should be noted that the 2007 Reform Treaty proposed essentially to eliminate the EU system of pillars.

is far more difficult to 'source' or study than (say) American, Chinese, or South African foreign policy.

A National 'System' of Foreign Policies

Distinctive national foreign policies have not disappeared from Europe, even if the EU has become a more important reference point. France uses the EU to try to enhance its own foreign policy leadership of a Europe that is autonomous from the US. Germany has wrapped its post-war foreign policy in a European cloak in order to rehabilitate itself as an international power. The UK views the EU as useful for organizing pragmatic cooperation on a case-by-case basis. Small states have considerably 'Europeanized' their foreign policies (Tonra 2001) and rely on the EU to have a voice in debates dominated by large states. But all EU member states conduct their own, individual, *national* foreign policy.

Whether or not national foreign policies in Europe form a true 'system', they are notable for:

- their endurance;
- their continued centrality to European foreign policy; and
- their frequent resistance to coordination.

The last observation points to what makes foreign policy different from other EU policies: the logic of foreign policy coordination differs markedly from the logic of market integration. Integrating markets mostly involves negative integration: sweeping away old barriers to trade. Separate national policies can be tolerated as long as they do not impede free movement of goods, services, and people. Market integration typically has clear goals, such as zero tariffs or common standards. Progress can usually be measured and pursued according to timetables.

In contrast, it is plausible to think that a common foreign policy (analogous, for example, to the Common Agricultural Policy (CAP)) requires positive integration: new EU institutions and structures to replace national ones. Foreign policy often has a black or white quality: if all states do not toe the line when the EU condemns a human rights violation or imposes an arms embargo, then the Union cannot be said to have a policy at all. Foreign policy coordination is often difficult to tie to specific goals or timetables. Compare the two main policy projects of the Maastricht Treaty (see Smith 1997). Monetary union had a clear goal—the euro—a timetable for achieving it, and criteria for measuring progress. The CFSP as a general concept was given no clear goal, nor any timetable or criteria for achieving it.

Defenders of Europe's system of foreign policy coordination, such as Chris Patten (2001), concede that Europe lacks a *single* foreign policy. However, they insist that the EU usually has a *common* foreign policy through which its member states and institutions act collectively. Each plays to its strengths and contributes policy resources to a (more or less) common cause. Increasingly, all member states tend to respect common EU policies and procedures.

Critics counter-claim that the war in Iraq showed how the EU is easily marginalized on matters of high politics. Decisions on whether to support the war were almost entirely made in national EU capitals, not Brussels. Nation-states have long been primary sources of European foreign policy. They are likely to remain so.

The Community System

The Community system for foreign policy-making consists of three main elements: external trade policy; aid and development policy; and actions to 'externalize' the internal market.

Commercial (Trade) Policy

The European Union is a major trading power. It is the world's largest exporter and second largest importer. It accounts for more than one-fifth of all global trade, and claims a higher share than the US. The EU is sometimes portrayed as a purveyor of neoliberalism (which emphasizes the benefits of the free market and limited government interference; see Cafruny and Ryner 2003). Yet, all trading blocs discriminate against outsiders and more than half of all EU trade is internal trade, crossing European borders within a market that is meant to be borderless. EU member states are sometimes accused of acting like a protectionist club in which each agrees to take in the others' 'high cost washing', or products that are lower in quality or higher in price than goods produced outside Europe, ostensibly to protect European jobs.

In practice, the EU is a schizophrenic trading power, not least because it blends very different national traditions of political economy. Generally, its southern member states are far less imbued with free-market values than those in the north or east. One consequence is that it is sometimes more difficult for the EU to agree internally than for it to agree deals with its trading partners. The power of the Commission in external trade policy is easy to overestimate (see Box 10.1). However, the EU does a remarkably good job of reconciling Europe's differences on trade. When the EU can agree, international negotiations become far more efficient. There is capacity in the Community system for shaming reluctant states into accepting trade agreements that serve general EU foreign policy interests. For example, in 2001 the Union agreed to offer the world's poorest countries duty-free access to the EU's markets for 'everything but arms', which France opposed but essentially was forced to accept. The deal was criticized for not doing enough to promote third-world development. But the EU generally claims that it offers the world's poorest countries a better deal than do most industrialized countries.

Aid and Development

Together with its member states, the EU is the world's leading donor of development aid, accounting for over half of the global total. Aid and access to the Union's huge market are frequently combined, along with other policy instruments, as in the cases of the EU's free trade agreements with Mexico and South Africa. Market access or aid also may be part of political cooperation agreements designed to promote democracy

BOX 10.1	How it really works

Commercial (trade) policy

Trade policy is the most integrated of all EU external policies. Case law and the Treaty establishing the European Community (not the separate 'Treaty on European Union') state that the Commission negotiates for the EU as a whole in most cases. There is no specific Council of Trade Ministers, and effective oversight by member states (through the so-called Article 133 Committee, made up of national trade officials) is limited. The EP has only the right to be consulted, although its assent is required for any agreement that establishes international institutions or has important budgetary implications, such as the EU's customs union with Turkey. The Commission's position thus seems indomitable.

In practice, power is considerably diffused. Member governments defend their own economic interests robustly at all stages: when defining the Commission's mandate for negotiations, during the negotiations themselves, and when the Council ratifies draft deals. At the last stage, the Treaty says that the Council can decide by qualified majority. In practice, important external trade measures almost never pass without unanimity. Thus, tensions between intergovernmentalism and supranationalism exist at the heart of the Community system even though the EU has a solid record of achievement in trade policy.

or human rights. The EU's relations with its most important neighbours — such as Turkey, Ukraine, or Russia (see Box 10.2)—are usually conducted through complex package deals involving trade, aid, and political dialogue.

Increasingly, the EU seeks region-to-region agreements such as the EuroMed partnership with the countries of the Mediterranean, and the Cotonou agreement, a trade and aid accord between the EU and 77 African, Caribbean, and Pacific (ACP) states. Such package deals require links between different systems for making European foreign policy. For example, most aid to the ACP states is distributed via the European Development Fund (EDF), which member states finance directly and which is not part of the EU's general budget.

The EU's aid policy has faced serious challenges in recent years. Evidence that EU aid programmes are not very effectively managed has contributed to 'donor fatigue'. The new wisdom—reflected in World Trade Organization (WTO) rules—is that poorer countries need trade more than aid. Trade is seen as helping poorer countries to grow from within in a sustainable way, while aid is often wasted, especially through corruption. The labelling of the twenty-first century's first global trading round as the Doha development agenda both reflected the new wisdom and focused global attention on the EU (and US) for their reluctance to open (especially) their agricultural markets to developing countries.

The world's poorest countries continue to insist that they need large injections of aid, and remain wary of the EU's new preference (driven by WTO rules as well as political choices) for creating free-trade areas. Large transfers of EU aid continue to flow

---

BOX 10.2   **How it really works**

The EU and Russia

The EU's relationship with Russia is a classic glass half-empty or half-full story. A pessimist would make much of the EU's dependence on Russia for energy, particularly since price disputes between Moscow and former Soviet republics in 2005–6 led to interruptions (or threats of them) in flows of Russian natural gas. The EU's concern for its energy security is often viewed as making it the weaker partner in its relationship with Moscow. One upshot, according to this view, is that it is reluctant to speak truth of power about the erosion of Russian democracy, the suppression of human rights in Chechnya, or even the 2007 cyber-war waged (apparently) by Russia on Estonia, an EU member state.

   In practice, the EU and Russia are mutually and heavily interdependent. The EU relies on Russia to supply more than a quarter of both its oil and natural gas. But sales of raw materials to the EU account for most of Russia's hard currency earnings and fund nearly 40 per cent of Russia's federal budget. Around 60 per cent of Russia's export earnings come from energy, most of it in the form of sales to the EU. One former EU diplomat puts it bluntly: 'Europe should clearly work for a comprehensive partnership with Russia, but at the moment it is nonsense to suggest that this will be based on shared values' (Patten 2005: 178). The point was illustrated at the 2006 Lahti summit held under a Finnish EU Council Presidency. Vladimir Putin was invited to participate, a first for a Russian President. By all accounts, the meeting was fraught and Putin bristled at any criticism of his government. When the President of the EP, Josep Borrell (a Spaniard), told Putin that the EU could not trade oil for human rights, Putin reportedly replied that corruption was rife in Spain. Putin also noted that mafia was an Italian word, not a Russian one. The French President, Jacques Chirac, enraged other EU delegations by arguing that morality should not be mixed with business in the EU's dealings with Russia.

   Still, the Finnish Presidency could plausibly claim that the European foreign policy glass was half-full. The (then) EU of 25—including former Soviet republics (such as Estonia) or satellites—delivered a more-or-less common message to Russia for the first time. The German Chancellor, Angela Merkel, insisted that she would continue to push Putin on human rights in Russia. And Lahti was one of Chirac's last EU summits, with one diplomat commenting: 'Chirac is a tired old man ... with a tad of hysteria in his voice' (*European Voice*, 26 October 2006).

---

to the Cotonou countries, most of which are in Africa. In fact, if all EU aid programmes, including those for North Africa and the Middle East, were added together, the total flow to Africa in 2004 alone was nearly €13 billion (and was projected to rise to more than €18 billion by 2010).

The Mediterranean (around €5.4 billion for 2000–6) and the Balkans (€4.6 billion for the same period) are also priority areas for Community spending. 'Foreign' aid to Central and Eastern Europe (€6.7 billion for 1995–9) has fallen as recipient

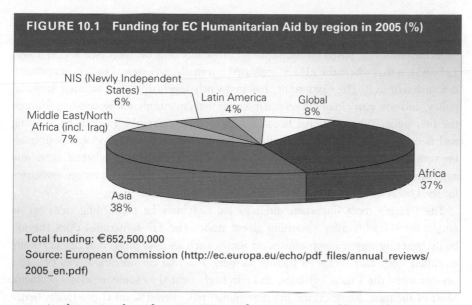

FIGURE 10.1   Funding for EC Humanitarian Aid by region in 2005 (%)

NIS (Newly Independent States) 6%

Latin America 4%

Global 8%

Middle East/North Africa (incl. Iraq) 7%

Africa 37%

Asia 38%

Total funding: €652,500,000

Source: European Commission (http://ec.europa.eu/echo/pdf_files/annual_reviews/2005_en.pdf)

states in the region have become EU members. In a sign of how enlargement has slid down its list of policy priorities, the Union budgeted less than €11.5 million for 2007–13 for 'pre-accession' aid to candidate countries.

The Union has also become the world's largest donor of humanitarian aid through the European Community Humanitarian Office (ECHO), located within the Commission. It announced the largest contribution of any donor to humanitarian aid in Afghanistan within days of the start of the 2001 war. ECHO also contributed more relief than any other donor to areas affected by the 2004 Asian Tsunami, while still maintaining levels of assistance to victims of what it called 'forgotten' (but protracted) humanitarian crises in Africa (see Figure 10.1).

The EU's good deeds are often marred by bad 'plumbing'. ECHO was slammed for its lax spending controls by the Committee of Independent Experts whose 1999 report sparked the mass resignation of the Santer Commission. Commissioner Patten made reform of the EU's development programmes a personal crusade, and EU aid delivery certainly became more efficient. But the Commission still has some distance to go before it escapes the memorable charge (made by a UK Minister for Development) that it is the 'worst development agency in the world' (Short 2000).

Externalizing 'Internal' Policies

In a sense, the European Union has no truly internal policies: its market is so huge that every major decision it makes to regulate it (or not) has international effects. When the Union negotiates internal agreements on fishing rights or agricultural subsidies, the implications for fishermen in Iceland or farmers in California can be immediate and direct. The ultimate act of externalizing internal policies occurs when the EU enlarges its membership, as it did to impressive effect in the dozen years beginning in 1995 when it more than doubled in size from twelve to 27 member states.

A rule of thumb, based on a landmark European Court decision (see Weiler 1999: 171–83), is that where the EU has legislated internally, an external policy competence is transferred to it. The Community has frequently taken this route in environmental policy, and now participates in several international environmental agreements through the first pillar. Where internal lines of authority are clear, the EU can be a strong and decisive negotiator. The Commission has become a powerful, global policeman for vetting mergers between large firms. When the Union seeks bilateral economic agreements, whether with Canada, Cameroon, or China, the Commission negotiates for the Union as a whole.

The Union's most important international task may be reconciling rules on its single market with rules governing global trade. The EU sometimes does the job badly, agreeing messy compromises on issues such as data protection or genetically modified foods that enrage its trading partners. External considerations can be a low priority when the Union legislates, and effectively treated as someone else's problem. Most of the time, however, the internal market has offered non-EU producers better or similar terms of access than they were offered before the internal market existed (Young 2002).

An increasingly important international task for the EU is reconciling its internal policies in Justice and Home Affairs (JHA) with its external obligations. What are often called 'soft' security issues, such as migration and transnational crime, have risen to the top of the policy agenda, especially since the terrorist attacks in the US, Madrid, and London of 2001–5. To the surprise of many, the EU managed rapidly to reach ambitious agreements on a common definition of terrorism and a European arrest warrant in the immediate aftermath of 11 September 2001 (9.11). However, JHA decision-making soon reverted to its previously uneven pace (see Chapter 7).

In contrast, EU enlargement has arguably been the most effective tool of European *foreign* policy in terms of exporting security and prosperity (Nugent 2004; Smith 2005). It has also produced enlargement fatigue and the European Neighbourhood Policy, a framework for cooperation with states on or near EU borders such as Ukraine or Russia which, in the Brussels jargon, do not have the 'perspective' of membership anytime soon (Dannreuther 2004). It is difficult to see how the powerful lure of actual membership could ever come close to being replicated by a policy that forecloses that possibility. Member states continue to tussle over how far the neighbourhood policy is a direct alternative, rather than a potential stepping stone to, EU membership. As suggested in Chapter 9, the EU's neighbourhood policy is another area where the EU struggles to meet expectations.

The EU System

The gap between the Union's growing economic power and its limited political clout was a source of increasing frustration in the early 1990s. Thus, a distinct EU system of making foreign policy was created, with the second pillar and the CFSP at its centre. This new system overlapped with but did not replace the Community system. Over time, it incorporated a nascent European Security and Defence Policy (ESDP). Confusingly, the CFSP and ESDP are mainly labels for 'institutions that *make* [policies] but *are* not proper policies' in themselves (Jørgensen 2006: 509).

The Common Foreign and Security Policy

The CFSP unveiled in the Maastricht Treaty marked a considerable advance on the European Political Cooperation mechanism but still disappointed proponents of closer foreign policy cooperation. It gave the Commission the right—shared with member governments—to initiate proposals. The CFSP even allowed for limited qualified majority voting, although it was always clear that most second-pillar actions would require unanimity. Compliance mechanisms in the CFSP were not as strong as those in the first pillar, with the European Court of Justice mostly excluded. The Common Foreign and Security Policy (like JHA policy) remained largely intergovernmental, even if links to the Community system were gradually strengthened (see Box 10.3).

Established habits of exchange between foreign ministries meant that member governments were able to agree a considerable number of common positions and joint actions in its early years (see Nuttall 2000: 184–8). Some measures, such as the 1993 Stability Pacts to stabilize borders in Central and Eastern Europe, or support for democratic elections in Bosnia (in 1995 and 1997) went well beyond the usual EPC declarations. Nevertheless, critics scorned the CFSP's inability to deal with more complex or urgent security issues, above all the wars in ex-Yugoslavia.

The CFSP was thus ripe for reform when the Treaty of Amsterdam was negotiated in 1997. This time, controversy over majority voting was mostly avoided by creating a new doctrine of 'flexibility', also known as constructive abstention or enhanced cooperation (see Stubb 2002). Under any name, it allows member states to opt out of certain CFSP actions (particularly those involving defence) as an alternative to vetoing them.

The Amsterdam Treaty's main second-pillar innovation was the creation of a new High Representative for the CFSP (who also served as Secretary-General of the Council; see Chapter 3). The High Representative was meant to help give the EU a single voice and the CFSP a single face. After his appointment to the post in 1999, former NATO Secretary General Javier Solana at times proved a skilful coordinator of different actions and instruments, whether sourced in Brussels or national capitals. He fronted the Union's diplomatic efforts, in cooperation with NATO, to head off civil war in Macedonia in 2001, and has had a leading role in nuclear dialogue with Tehran.

> ### BOX 10.3   How it really works
>
> **Making foreign policy decisions**
>
> Provisions in the Maastricht Treaty for Qualified Majority Voting (QMV) on foreign policy seemed to mark a major change from European Political Cooperation. However, QMV has rarely been used in the second (or third) pillar. The glass remains (at least) half-empty: rules on when QMV may be used are far more complex than in the first pillar, and nearly all important CFSP decisions require a consensus. Because it could not agree a unanimous position on Iraq (far from it), the EU was completely sidelined during the drift to war in 2003. It is difficult to identify any major foreign policy decision of the George W. Bush administration that was influenced by any CFSP decision, except perhaps a relative softening in tactics for dealing with the Iran nuclear dossier. The CFSP's annual budget is in the range of a paltry €150 million. Looking to the future, foreign policy by unanimity seems impractical, even impossible, in an EU of 27 plus. Procedurally, it is clear how the CFSP works. Substantively, there is controversy about whether it works at all.
>
> But there is a case for viewing the glass as half-full. Each time the EU is faced with an international crisis, it tends to act more quickly, coherently, and decisively than it did in response to the *last* crisis. Following the terrorist attacks of 9/11, the EU agreed a raft of statements or decisions within days. Subsequently, the EU moved decisively—sometimes controversially so—and gave its consent to counter-terrorist agreements with the US on issues such as airline passenger records and container security (see Box 7.3; Rees 2006). The EU's diplomacy (through the 'EU-3') on Iran, its participation in the Middle East Quartet (on an equal footing with the US, Russia, and the UN), and a range of CFSP actions in central Africa and the Balkans suggest a steady integration of European foreign policy.

However, the EU continued to be represented externally by its *troika*, with Solana joined by the Foreign Ministers of the state holding the Council Presidency and the country next in line, and the European Commissioner for External Affairs. In some cases, such as the Group of Eight summits, special formulae for representation involved a confusing mix of Commission and national officials.

There has thus never been a clear answer to the legendary (and apparently apocryphal) question asked by the US Secretary of State, Henry Kissinger, in the 1970s: 'What number do I call when I want to speak to "Europe"?' The 2004 Constitutional Treaty proposed to assign that single number to a new EU Minister for Foreign Affairs (MFA). The MFA would combine the roles of the High Representative and the Commissioner for External Affairs, with its holder serving as Vice-President of the Commission and chairing EU Councils of Foreign Ministers, in perhaps the most audacious attempt ever to combine the supranational with the intergovernmental in one position. The Constitutional Treaty also contained provisions for a new EU External Action Service, working under the authority of the MFA and bringing under one roof EU and national diplomats. An intended effect was to make the EU's missions in foreign capitals more like real embassies, with clout and resources. But no clear consensus was reached over whether all EU officials working on external issues (such as those responsible for development or trade policy) would fall under the MFA's authority.

The rejection of the Constitutional Treaty in the French and Dutch referenda in 2005 left these reforms in limbo. However, the 2007 Reform Treaty rescued nearly all of them, even though fresh (primarily British) objections to the title 'Minister of Foreign Affairs' meant that the title 'High Representative' was retained for this post (with nearly all of the same duties as assigned to the MFA in the Constitutional Treaty). Many EU diplomats agree that 'one day in the future we will have a better framework for the conduct of European foreign affairs ... The logic of history, of international politics, of diplomacy, even of public finance, all point in that direction' (Avery 2005). When that day comes, it will have been a long time in coming, even if foreign policy remains one of the youngest of all EU policies.

A European Security and Defence Policy?

Given the CFSP's mixed record, as well as Europe's claims to be a 'civilian power', it might seem paradoxical to extend the EU system into the realm of defence. Most EU states have long accepted the supremacy of NATO on defence matters. Yet, the EU has taken small but decisive steps in recent years towards creating an ESDP. The 1999 crisis in Kosovo marked a turning point. Again, the EU appeared timid and weak as it had earlier in Bosnia. NATO took the lead in pushing both crises towards resolution, and the US military contributions dwarfed those of Europe. Thus, the EU made firmer Treaty commitments to security cooperation, first in Amsterdam but especially at Nice. In particular, the so-called Petersberg tasks—humanitarian and rescue missions, peacekeeping, and crisis management, including 'peacemaking'—were marked out as basic EU foreign policy goals. A new Political and Security Committee of senior national officials was created and designated the linchpin linking ESDP to the CFSP. Plans were agreed to enable deployment of a EU Rapid Reaction Force of up to 60,000 troops.

Sceptics argued that the real problem lay not with Treaty language or institutions but with Europe's weak and under-funded militaries. Military spending in most EU states declined sharply after the Cold War, leaving the US to extend its lead in the application of new technologies to military hardware. The target date for declaring the EU Rapid Reaction Force concept operational was delayed and then fudged. The American administration under George W. Bush initially refused European offers to contribute troops to the war in Afghanistan in 2001, in large part because there was almost nothing that US forces could not do more effectively on their own.

The ESDP has thus been restricted to modest missions, and is central to no EU member state's national defence policy (Cooper 2004b: 189). Its supporters insist that it has produced tangible achievements. The French-led 2002 intervention in Bunia (Congo) came in response to a UN request and was designed to keep a humanitarian disaster from escalating, although its scope was very limited and its benefits questioned. Similarly, the EU claimed success in taking over from NATO command of a large peacekeeping force in Bosnia in 2004, but was criticized for perpetuating a culture of 'dependency, helplessness, and disillusionment' and failing to 'coordinate complex civil and military matters' (see Manners 2006: 190–1). More recently the EU has launched small civilian missions (for policing and training) in Aceh, Gaza, and Afghanistan.

What is clear is that the ESDP has become a framework for combining European military assets at the 'hard' end of capabilities in specialized areas such as jungle or desert fighting or coping with a chemical weapons attack through the so-called European battle groups (Smith *et al.* 2006: 263). Meanwhile, the European Defence Agency has sought to coax sorely needed cooperation between defence ministries and arms makers, quietly but gradually, since its launch in 2004. ESDP remains an area with a large gap between ambitions and achievements, but it is also a continuing growth area for European integration.

Theorizing the EU as a Global Actor

The expansion of the EU's foreign policy role confounds many international relations (IR) theorists, particularly those in the realist tradition. Most realists make two assumptions. First, power in international politics is a zero-sum commodity. Secondly, all alliances between states are temporary (see Mearsheimer 2001; Waltz 2002). On one hand, realists claim to be able to explain why the EU is often weak or divided on matters of high politics, such as Iraq or North Korea. On the other hand, realists find it difficult to explain the EU's international ambitions and activities, or even why it does not collapse altogether. More generally, twenty-first century works of IR theory often barely mention the EU, or ignore it altogether (see Sullivan 2001; Elman and Elman 2003; Burchill *et al.* 2005).

One consequence is that research on European foreign policy 'has come to resemble an archipelago' (Jørgensen 2006: 507), which is only barely connected to the study of IR more generally. Consider intergovernmentalist approaches to European integration, which are themselves derived from liberal theories of international politics (see Moravcsik 1998). Intergovernmentalists assume that governments respond to powerful, domestic economic pressures. When governments agree economic policy deals that benefit national economic interests, they try to lock in those gains by giving EU institutions strong powers of enforcement. In contrast, governments face far weaker incentives to delegate foreign or defence policy powers to EU institutions, which explains why the EU's trade policy is far more integrated than the CFSP. Beyond that insight, however, intergovernmentalists have shown little interest in the EU's global ambitions. As such, what has been described as 'the most suitable theoretical tradition'

BOX 10.4   Compared to what?

The European Security Strategy

Equipping the EU with a military capability made it possible also to give the Union a *security strategy*: a set of principles that could guide foreign policy action and specify how ESDP might be deployed together with other EU policy instruments. The 2003 European Security Strategy (ESS) was agreed at a tumultuous time after the Union's sharp and bitter divisions over Iraq. It was possible to view the ESS as a step forward for the Union as a global actor (see Biscop 2005), but also impossible not to view it as partly, at least, a response to the 2002 US National Security Strategy (NSS; see Dannreuther and Peterson 2006).

The NSS was unveiled, with powerful symbolism, one year and one day after the terrorist attacks of 9/11. Many US allies were shocked by the strength of its endorsement of three principles: the need for shifting coalitions in a war on terrorism, the sanctity of unchallenged US military strength, and the inevitability of having to 'pre-empt' threats to American security unilaterally. Other US agencies were consulted, but the NSS was primarily written in the back rooms of the National Security Council by White House advisors. The NSS was full of dark warnings about the nature of the terrorist threat and how the US would respond to it.

In contrast, the tone of the ESS was largely celebratory: extolling the achievements of European integration, while urging that European habits of cooperation and multilateralism needed to be exported. The ESS was penned by officials in the Council General Secretariat working under Javier Solana, but was reviewed and redrafted in a series of workshops with academics and experts in different European venues. The ESS ended up being a much shorter document than the Bush administration's NSS. In places, it reads more like a set of ambitions than a genuine strategy (Heisbourg 2004). On balance, there was just enough that was common to the two strategies—especially about the need for strong, proactive policies to counter terrorism—to make it possible to think that the transatlantic alliance might be more durable than it sometimes appeared around the time of the Iraq war (see Baylis and Roper 2006).

for explaining European integration also seems to be 'currently running out of steam and relevance' to European foreign policy (Jørgensen 2006: 519).

In contrast, the oldest theory of European integration—neofunctionalism—may still have mileage, at least by proxy. Institutionalism, a theoretical 'cousin' of neofunctionalism (see Haas 2001), focuses on how the EU produces habits that eventually mature into institutionalized rules of behaviour. For example, habits established through twenty years of foreign policy exchanges within EPC led to the CFSP. The EU often creates new roles or organizations—such as the High Representative or the Political and Security Committee—which develop their own interests, missions, and escape close intergovernmental control. Institutionalism has established itself as the leading theory of EU politics (Cowles and Curtis 2004), and has shed interesting light on European foreign policy (M. E. Smith 2003; 2004).

Yet, the leading theory of European foreign policy clearly has become constructivism (see Tonra and Christiansen 2004; Bretherton and Vogler 2006). As discussed in Chapter 1, constructivists depart from realists and liberals in insisting that the interests and identities of EU member states are not fixed before they bargain with each other. Rather, they are 'constructed' through bargaining, which is a highly social process. Constructivists, in contrast to institutionalists, insist that ideas matter as much as (or more than) institutions in IR. Alexander Wendt (1992; 1999) portrays the EU as more than a temporary alliance because its member states assume a measure of common identity through shared ideas, including ones about the desirability of multilateralism, environmental protection, and so on. Many constructivists do not shy from questions about what the EU *should* do in foreign policy, insisting on the importance of a 'normative power Europe' that stands up for its values and principles (Manners 2002).

Conclusion

When the former British Prime Minister, Tony Blair, urged that the EU should become a 'superpower but not a superstate' in 2000, he provoked little controversy outside of his own country. The idea that the EU should take a lead in expressing European power internationally has become almost a mainstream view (see Morgan 2005; Smith *et al.* 2006). The EU has come a long way from humble origins in foreign policy. But it remains an odd global power, which has difficulty living up to its ambitions. It has increased its potential international power each time it has enlarged. Yet, EU foreign policy is only as good as the quality of the consensus amongst its members, and it is often of poor quality in an enlarged EU of 27+ member states.

One reason why assessments of European foreign policy vary so widely is because it is unclear how the EU's success as a global actor should be measured. There is no question that the Union is far more active internationally than its founders ever imagined it could be. In several policy areas, especially economic ones, it is a global power. No other international organization in history has even tried, let alone claimed, to have a 'common' foreign policy.

There were signs post-Iraq that foreign policy was being reclaimed by European national capitals, or groups of states acting together, even if none appeared to be giving up on the EU system altogether (see Hill 2004). The Reform Treaty's institutional reforms might move the EU closer to a truly common foreign policy. Or, its effect might be, yet again, to raise expectations that cannot be met. How, for example, would coherence emerge from the constellation of a new EU President, a new Foreign Minister (still called the 'High Representative') and a continued Commission President and (probably) Commissioners for development and trade policy? Consider the (cryptic? confused?) comments of the US Secretary of State, Condoleezza Rice, on a post-Iraq fence-mending visit to Brussels:

As Europe unifies further and has a common foreign policy—I understand what is going to happen with the Constitution and that there will be unification, in effect, under a foreign minister—I think that also will be a very good development (quoted in *Financial Times*, 11 February 2005: 1).

The future of European foreign policy will be determined largely by two factors: the EU's relationship with the US and its ability to wield its 'soft power', or its power to persuade rather than coerce (Nye Jr. 2004). Whether the George W. Bush era marked a glitch or a watershed in transatlantic relations is an open question. The failure of hard (mostly) American military power to achieve US policy goals in Afghanistan or Iraq, let alone Iran or North Korea or the Middle East, rekindles questions about whether Europe's soft power might make it an alternative source of leadership in the twenty-first century (Rifkin 2004; Leonard 2005). Alternatively, Europe's declining population and military weakness might foreclose such questions. One of the EU's top diplomats argues that Europe will never maximize its soft power until it invests far more in hard power (Cooper 2004a).

It is easy to see why debates about Europe as a global actor are so lively. The EU is likely to remain an often uncertain and hesitant global power but one that never stops trying to be more coherent and effective. It will no doubt continue to frustrate its partners, but sometimes show surprising unity, and fascinate—probably as much as it confounds—future students of international politics.

? DISCUSSION QUESTIONS

1. Define 'European foreign policy'. Explain why this term has assumed wide usage amongst those who study the EU's international role.

2. Why has cooperation in foreign policy been so much more difficult to organize at the EU level than economic cooperation?

3. Why is the most effective way for the EU to promote development in the less-developed world increasingly seen as 'trade not aid'?

4. Can the EU remain a 'civilian power' if it also becomes a military power?

→ FURTHER READING

The best single source text on Europe as a global actor is Hill and Smith (2005). Useful overviews include K. E. Smith (2003) and Bretherton and Vogler (2006). Good historical treatments are available, told both from the points of view of a practitioner (Nuttall 2000) and an academic institutionalist (M. E. Smith 2003). The EU's neighbourhood policy is scrutinized in Dannreuther (2004) and its Security Strategy is the focus for Biscop (2005) as well as Dannreuther and Peterson (2006), who compare it to its US counterpart. The Union's contribution to the United Nations, as well as multilateralism more generally, is scrutinized by Laatikainen and Smith (2006). On the idea of the EU as a 'civilian power', see Sjursen (2006). A good review of recent debates about ESDP is Howorth (2007).

Biscop, S. (2005), *The European Security Strategy: A Global Agenda for Positive Power* (Aldershot and Burlington, VT: Ashgate).

Bretherton, C., and Vogler, J. (2006), *The European Union as a Global Actor*, 2nd edn. (London and New York: Routledge).

Dannreuther, R. (ed.) (2004), *European Union Foreign and Security Policy: Towards a Neighbourhood Strategy* (London and New York: Routledge).

Dannreuther, R., and Peterson, J. (eds.) (2006), *Security Strategy and Transatlantic Relations* (London and New York: Routledge).

Ginsberg, R. (2001), *The European Union in International Politics: Baptism by Fire* (Boulder, CO and Oxford: Rowman & Littlefield).

Hill, C., and Smith, M. (eds.) (2005), *International Relations and the European Union* (Oxford and New York: Oxford University Press).

Howorth, J. (2007), *Security and Defence Policy in the European Union* (Basingstoke and New York: Palgrave).

Laatikainen, K. V., and Smith, K. E. (eds.) (2006), *The European Union at the United Nations: Intersecting Multilateralisms* (Basingstoke and New York: Palgrave Macmillan).

Nuttall, S. (2000), *European Foreign Policy* (Oxford and New York: Oxford University Press).

Sjursen, H. (ed.) (2006), 'What Kind of Europe? European Foreign Policy in Perspective', Special Issue of *Journal of European Public Policy* 13/2.

Smith, K. E. (2003), *European Union Foreign Policy in a Changing World* (Oxford and Malden MA: Polity).

Smith, M. E. (2003), *Europe's Foreign and Security Policy* (Cambridge and New York: Cambridge University Press).

WEB LINKS

A good place to start researching the EU's external policy role is the website of the Paris-based Institute for Security Studies (www.iss.europa.eu), which formally became an autonomous European Union agency in 2002. Other specific areas of EU policy have their own, dedicated websites:

- European Defence Agency: http://www.eda.europa.eu/
- External relations (general): www.europa.eu/pol/ext/index_en.htm
- Foreign and security policy: www.europa.eu/pol/cfsp/index_en.htm
- Humanitarian aid: www.europa.eu.int/pol/hum/index_en.htm
- Justice/home affairs: www.europa.eu.int/pol/justice/index_en.htm
- Trade: www.europa.eu.int/pol/comm/index_en.htm
- Development: www.europa.eu.int/po/index_en.htm

The Commission's site (www.europa.eu.int/comm/index_en.htm) has general information about EU foreign policy, but the websites of national foreign ministries often reveal more. On the EU's relationship with the US, see www.eurunion.org and www.useu.be. Weblinks on the EU's other important relationships include ones devoted to the Cotonou convention (www.acpsec.org), EU–Canadian relations (www.canada-europe.org), and the Union's relationship with Latin America (http://aei.pitt.edu/view/subjects/D002022.html).

 Visit the Online Resource Centre that accompanies this book for additional material: www.oxfordtextbooks.co.uk/orc/bomberg2e/

CHAPTER 11

Conclusion

John Peterson, Elizabeth Bomberg, and Alexander Stubb

Introduction	223	A Comparative Politics Approach	227
Three Themes	223	A Public Policy Approach	228
Experimentation and Change	223	A Sociological/Cultural Approach	229
Sharing Power and Seeking Consensus	224	Where do we go from Here?	229
Scope and Capacity	225	Debating the Future of Europe	230
Explaining the EU	226	How *Will* it Work?	231
International Relations Approaches	226	Conclusion	233

▮ Chapter Overview

The European Union (EU) is exceptional, complex, and, in important respects, unique. This concluding chapter revisits three key themes that guide understanding of the EU, before returning to the question: how can we best *explain* the EU and how it works? We review leading theoretical approaches, and identify what each approach claims is most important to explain about the EU, and why. Finally we confront the question: 'where do we go from here'? Does knowing how the EU works give us clues about how it might work in the future?

Introduction

This book has offered a basic introduction to how the European Union works. A vast body of work has emerged in recent years to satisfy those who wish to know more. Much that has been written about the EU may seem confusing or obfuscatory to the curious non-expert. We—together with our authors—have tried to do better and be clearer. For example, we have emphasized throughout how the EU works in practice, not just in theory. We have also tried to show that the EU is not so exceptional that it resists all comparisons.

Yet, it does not take much study of the EU before one is struck (or becomes frustrated) by how complex and ever-shifting it seems to be. Most of our 'compared to what' exercises have ended up drawing contrasts—some quite sharp—between politics and policy-making in Brussels and these same processes elsewhere. There are very few analytical 'bottom lines' about how the EU works, except that it works quite differently from any other system for deciding who gets what, when, and how.

Three Themes

We have offered (Chapter 1) three general themes as guides to understanding how the EU works. The first is experimentation and change. The European Union refuses to stand still: about the only thing that can be safely predicted about its future is that it is unlikely to remain static for long. Secondly, EU governance is an exercise in sharing power between states and institutions, and seeking consensus across different levels of governance. Getting to 'yes' in a system with so many diverse stakeholders often requires resort to informal methods of reaching agreement, about which the EU's Treaties and official publications are silent. Thirdly and finally, the gap between the EU's policy scope and its capacity—between what it *tries* to do and what it is *equipped* to do—has widened. The EU has been a remarkable success in many respects, but its future success is by no means assured. We briefly revisit each of these themes below.

Experimentation and Change

Every chapter in this book, each from a different angle, has painted a picture of constant evolution and change. Few would deny that the European Union has developed into more than an 'ordinary' international organization. However, its development has not been guided by any master plan. Rather, it has evolved through messy compromises struck after complex political bargaining between member states (Chapters 2 and 4), institutions (Chapter 3), and organized interests (Chapter 5).

One consequence is that when the EU changes, it usually changes incrementally. Radical reform proposals naturally tend to be scaled back in the direction of modesty in a system with so many different kinds of interest to satisfy. The unsuccessful attempt to establish a Constitutional Treaty for the EU proves the point. For many, the constitution with its fundamental rights, legal personality, catalogue of competences, president, foreign minister, and security guarantees, simply went too far. As a consequence, it was deemed necessary to scale back the constitutional symbolism of the treaty—everything from the name 'Constitution' to a European anthem—as well as to offer recalcitrant states (including Poland, the UK, and France) a variety of concessions in order to agree on a 'Reform Treaty' that had a chance of being ratified in all EU countries.

However, apparently unexceptional acts of fine-tuning, such as slightly increasing the EP's power or sending an encouraging political signal to an applicant state, can sometimes gather momentum like a snowball rolling down a hill. Moreover, the EU's potential for wrenching and fundamental change, as illustrated by the launch of the single currency or dramatic decisions by the European Court of Justice (ECJ), cannot be denied. Perhaps because the EU is such a young political system, it is sometimes surprisingly easy to change its structure or remit.

The more general point is that the EU is a fundamentally experimental union (Laffan *et al.* 2000). Nobody argues that it always works like a smooth, well-oiled machine. It has become far more difficult to shift it in any particular direction as its membership has more than doubled in the space of around a decade. Equally, almost no one denies that it is remarkably successful in coaxing cooperative, collective action out of sovereign states that regularly, almost routinely, went to war with each other a few generations ago. Increasingly, the Union is seen as a model or laboratory worthy, in some respects, of mimicry by other regional organizations in other parts of the world (Farrell 2007; see also Box 2.4).

Sharing Power and Seeking Consensus

A second theme that cannot be avoided in studying the EU is that power is distributed widely—between states, institutions, and organized interests. At the same time, consensus and compromise are highly valued. Enormous efforts are often required to strike agreements that are acceptable to all who have a slice of power to determine outcomes. Just being able to agree is often viewed as an achievement in itself. Once sealed, EU agreements are almost always portrayed as positive sum—that is, bringing greater good to a greater number of citizens than did the previous policy. Of course, nearly every policy creates losers as well as winners. But the perceived need to preserve support for the Brussels system means that heroic attempts are usually made to avoid creating *clear* losers.

It follows that coming to grips with how the EU works does not (just) mean mastering the Treaties. The formal powers of institutions and member states, and formal rules of policy-making, are not unimportant. But they do not come close to telling the whole story, since informal understandings and norms are crucial in determining outcomes. Most of our investigations of 'how it really works' have accentuated the importance of unwritten rules that have emerged over time and through practice, almost organically—as opposed to being mandated in formal or legal terms. These rules and norms have then been learned and internalized by EU policy-makers. For example, it is widely accepted in Brussels that formal votes in the Council should be avoided whenever possible. The idea that consensus should be the ultimate aim, and that long negotiations and manifold compromises are an acceptable price to pay for it, is powerfully engrained. These norms often matter far more than what the Treaties say about which state has how many votes, what constitutes a qualified majority, or where QMV applies and where it does not. The latest enlargements in 2004 and 2007 suggested that representatives of new states learn the rules of the game rather quickly. They were, for instance, able to lend their weight to a broad alliance supporting further liberalization of the services sector—not by threatening a blocking minority, but by constructively arguing their case.

Moreover, the EU is a uniquely multilevel system of governance. Even the most decentralized, federal nation-states—such as Germany or the US or Switzerland—have a government and an opposition. The European Union has neither. As such, it often suffers (not least in foreign policy) from a lack of leadership. Rarely does one institution or member state, or alliance thereof, offer consistent or decisive political direction. Instead, grand bargains to agree quasi-constitutional change, as well as many more mundane agreements, result from a unique kind of power-sharing across levels of governance, as well as between EU institutions and member states. It is this diversity and mix of actors—regional, national and supranational, public and private—the wide dispersal of power between them, and the need always to try to increase the number of 'winners' that render the European Union absolutely unique.

Scope and Capacity

Thirdly and finally, we have suggested that the EU's scope—both in terms of policy remit and constituent states—has grown much faster than its capacity to manage its affairs. Chapters 6 and 7 outlined the uneven yet unmistakable expansion of EU policy responsibilities. Chapter 9 focused on why, and with what consequences, the EU has continued to enlarge its membership and has tried to improve its relations to countries in its near abroad. Chapter 10 showed how the EU has evolved, almost by stealth, into a global power. With no agreed-upon 'end goal', the EU has taken on new tasks and members, but without a concomitant increase in capacity, or tools and resources to perform its designated tasks. For instance, Chapter 3 highlighted the institutional limits of the EU. Can the Commission, equivalent in size to the administration of a medium-sized European city, manage an ever larger and more ambitious Union? Perhaps its emphasis under the Presidency of José Manuel Barroso on a 'Europe of results' reflects, in part, acceptance of Majone's (2005) argument that EU policies need to solve actual problems, as opposed to serving the political purpose of furthering political integration, which often seemed to be their primary goal in the past.

The Commission is far from alone in confronting a gap between scope and capacity. Can one Parliament adequately represent nearly 500 million citizens? Can 27 or more ministers sit around the Council table and have a meaningful negotiation?

Crucially, the EU's political and geographic scope has increased without explicit support from its citizens. This gap between scope and capacity (institutional and political) raises broader questions about the EU's future. It seems risky to assume that the European Union can continue to take on ever more tasks and member states, while retaining its status as the most successful experiment in international cooperation in modern history.

Explaining the EU

While seeking above all to describe how the EU works, this book has also introduced—and tried to demystify—debates about what are the most important forces driving EU politics. Just as there is no consensus on the desirability of European integration, there is no consensus about what is most important about it. Social scientists disagree about what it is about the EU that is most important to *explain*. The position they take on this question usually reflects their own approach to understanding the EU: as an international organization (IO)? A polity in its own right? A source of constructed identity? Or as a source of public policies?

We have seen how theory can help us frame interesting questions, and help us determine what evidence is needed to answer them. If it is accepted that the European Union is exceptionally complex, then it stands to reason that there can be no one 'best' theory of EU politics. What the Commission President, Jacques Delors, once called an 'unidentified political object' is a little bit like other IOs such as NATO or the United Nations (UN), a little bit like federal states including Germany and Canada, and a little bit like the other leading system for generating legally binding international rules, the World Trade Organization (WTO). But it closely resembles none of them. It makes sense in the circumstances to approach the EU with a well-stocked toolkit of theoretical approaches, and to be clear about what each singles out as most important in determining how it really works.

International Relations Approaches

International relations (IR) scholars bring important insights to the study of the EU. They can always be relied upon to ask hard, stimulating questions about the nature of power in international politics, and the extent to which cooperation is possible or durable in the absence of any international government. In seeking answers to these questions, students of IR add value—in two principal ways—to debates about the nature and significance of European integration.

First, approaching the EU as a system within a system—a regional alliance in the wider scheme of global politics—encourages us to ask why European states have chosen to pool a large share of their sovereignty. For neofunctionalists, the answer lies in the way that the choices open to states become narrower after they decide to free trade and thus to increase their economic interdependence (Börzel 2005). EU institutions, in alliance with interest groups, guide and encourage 'spill-over' of cooperation in one sphere (the internal market) to new spheres (environmental policy). States remain powerful but they must share power with EU institutions and non-institutional actors in Brussels, as well as those in national and regional political capitals. For neofunctionalists, what is most important to explain about EU politics is how and why European integration moves inexorably forward. There are crucial differences between EU member states and ordinary nation-states in international politics, to the extent that European integration is largely irreversible.

For intergovernmentalists member states remain free to choose how the EU should work (Moravcsik 1998). The Union is built on a series of bargains between its member states, which are self-interested and rational in pursuing EU outcomes that serve their economic interests. Of course, conflict may arise in bargaining between states, whose preferences are never identical. But, ultimately, the status quo changes only when acceptable compromises are struck between national interests, especially those of its largest states. The EU's institutions are relatively weak in the face of the power of its member states, which can determine precisely how much authority they wish to delegate to the Commission, Parliament, and Court to enforce and police intergovernmental bargains. For intergovernmentalists, what is most important to explain about the EU is how national interests are reconciled in intergovernmental bargains. European states are 'ordinary' states, whose national interests happen to be compatible often enough to produce unusually institutionalized cooperation. The EU 'occupies a permanent position at the heart of the European landscape' (Moravcsik 1998: 501) but only because member governments want it that way. Much about European integration remains reversible, and always will be.

A Comparative Politics Approach

As the European Union's policy remit has expanded, many comparativists have found themselves unable to understand their subjects—at least in Europe—without knowing how the EU works. In particular, new institutionalists, whose work has become deeply influential in the study of comparative politics as well as across the social sciences, have developed insightful analyses of how the EU works. Institutionalists view the EU as a system where cooperation is now normal and accepted. Policy-makers in Brussels have become used to working in a system where power is shared, in particular between its major institutions. Bargaining in the making of day-to-day, 'ordinary' EU policy is as much between institutions as it is between governments, in contrast to bargaining—primarily intergovernmental—in episodic rounds of Treaty reform. A key determinant of actual policy outcomes is the extent to which path dependency has become institutionalized and radical policy change is precluded.

Institutionalists share important assumptions with neofunctionalists, particularly about the need to view European integration as a continuous process (see Pierson 1996). But institutionalists tend to study the Union as a political system in itself, analogous to national systems, as opposed to a system of international relations. For them, what is crucial to explain about EU politics is how its institutions develop their own agendas and priorities, and thus load the EU system in favour of certain outcomes over others (Meunier and McNamara 2007). The European Union is extraordinary, above all because it has such extraordinary institutions.

A Public Policy Approach

Studying EU politics without studying what it produces—actual policies—is like studying a factory but ignoring the product it manufactures. We have seen (especially in Chapter 6) that most EU policies are regulatory policies, many of them highly technical. We have also seen how resource-poor the EU's institutions are, and how reliant they are on expertise and resources held beyond Brussels and/or by non-public actors. Advocates of policy network analysis insist that EU policy outcomes are shaped in important ways by informal bargaining, much of which takes place outside formal institutions or policy process (Peterson 2004). By the time that ministers vote in the Council or MEPs vote in plenary, legislative proposals usually have been picked over and scrutinized line-by-line by a huge range of officials and, usually, lobbyists. Often, the proposal bears little or no relationship to what it looked like in its first draft. Policy network analysis assumes that policy details are agreed in a world far removed from the political world of ministers and MEPs.

Moreover, the EU is distinctive in its lack of hierarchy: it has no government to impose a policy agenda, so policy stakeholders bargain over what the agenda should be. No one actor is in charge, so they must work together and exchange resources—legitimacy, money, expertise—to realize their goals. For policy network analysts, what is most important to explain about the EU is its policies and who determines them. Making sense of policy outputs means investigating how sectoral networks are structured: are their memberships stable or volatile, are they tightly or loosely integrated, and how are resources distributed within them? The EU is, in effect, a series of different and diverse subsystems for making different kinds of policy. What is common across the full range of EU activities is interdependence between actors: even those with the most formidable formal powers—the member states and EU institutions—are highly dependent on one another, and indeed on actors that have no formal power at all.

A Sociological/Cultural Approach

What is the most important feature of the EU that requires explanation? For constructivists, it is how interests and identities are constructed. EU decision-makers are the same as anyone else: they are fundamentally social beings. But they are also different from most other political actors in that they interact intensively and extensively with actors whose national identity, language, and culture are different from their own. Brussels (along with Luxembourg and Strasbourg) is a truly multinational crossroads and there is no other political capital in the world that features a more diverse cultural mix. In a sense, Brussels is unlike the rest of Europe and one effect is to encourage a sort of disconnect between the EU and its citizens. But the European identity which often seems barely to register amongst a majority of citizens in Europe's heartlands is very much in evidence amongst those who are closely involved in EU politics and policy.

Again, it is worth reiterating that constructivism is not a substantive theory of regional integration comparable to intergovernmentalism or institutionalism (see Risse 2004). It is a philosophical, even 'metaphysical' position that insists that our social reality is constructed by human beings and reproduced in day-to-day practice. The main upshot is that we cannot explain how the EU works simply by calculating what is in the material interest of each member state, EU institution, or lobbyist and then assuming that Brussels is a vacuum in which those interests are unchanging, unaffected by the informal rules of the game that have arisen to govern EU bargaining, or untouched by how those at the centre of the EU system view themselves as part of a major collective, political endeavour. Of course, EU decision-makers are self-interested and egoistic. There is much about the EU that does not work very well. But it produces far more collective action than any system ever invented, or 'constructed', for the reconciliation of multinational interests. The insights of constructivism are inescapable and essential to explaining why.

There is no one approach with a monopoly of wisdom on EU politics. All shed important light on key features of how the EU works. All downplay, even ignore, factors that others argue are important—or can be in the right circumstances—in determining who gets what from the EU. A first step in making sense of the EU is deciding what it is about this unidentified political object that is most important to explain.

Where do we go from Here?

When we ponder where the European Union may be headed, we have to remember where it has been. For over two decades, the Union has been either preparing, negotiating, or ratifying a new treaty. In the fifteen years after 1985, the EU modified its basic treaties five times. The next treaty change is already in the pipeline (albeit severely slowed down after the Dutch and French rejections of the Constitutional Treaty in 2005). No western nation-state has ever made five major changes to its constitution, including hundreds of amendments, within the span of twenty years. By way of comparison, the US Constitution has been subject to fewer than thirty amendments over 200 years.

Agreeing to reform the EU's institutions, disagreeing on the details, and then agreeing to try to agree again in a future intergovernmental conference (IGC) has become routine. Meanwhile, the EU's policy remit has expanded, as has its membership (see Chapters 6 and 9). The Treaty of Nice (2001) marked an attempt to reform the EU's institutions to prepare the Union for enlargement. Its success in doing so was, to be charitable, limited (see Chapter 2). The institutional reforms mandated in the so-called Reform Treaty—a slimmed-down text containing most of the institutional reforms proposed in the Constitutional Treaty—may be more successful. Still, it will be many years before these reforms take full effect. Even given that prospect, it is difficult to argue that institutional development has kept pace with changes in the EU's policy remit and membership. So, where do we go from here?

Debating the Future of Europe

Sometimes it seems as if a debate on the future of the EU is simply 'more of the same'. The debates of the 1950s dealt with many of the same challenges that the EU faces today. Institutional reform, enlargement, policy remit, money, and foreign policy have always been on the EU agenda. The changes over the past 50 years might seem incremental in the short term. However, measured over time, the EU has actually experienced a radical metamorphosis from an institutionally weak small club with a limited policy arsenal, separate currencies, and no foreign policy, to an institutional powerhouse of 27 members, a plethora of policies, a single currency, and a central role in world politics.

The first decade of the new millennium brought with it new themes to the European agenda. Peace, prosperity, and security remain the cornerstones of integration, but the agenda has shifted markedly towards economic reform, climate change, and energy. On one hand, the economic reform agenda resists simple solutions because an EU of 27 is far more economically diverse than ever before. On the other hand, there were signs of fresh life in the EU's economy as the first decade of the 2000s approached its end, with measures such as the liberalization of services important in the policy mix. The Union managed to take the global lead on climate change by pledging to cut greenhouse emissions by 20 per cent by the year 2020 and encouraging the rest of the industrialized world to follow its lead. The Union remained far from a common energy policy but at least encouraged European citizens to see connections between energy security and environmental protection.

After French and Dutch voters rejected the Constitutional Treaty, the EU went into a state of institutional hibernation. After a reflection period of two years the impasse was broken by a German Council Presidency in 2007. The member states—now numbering 27, twelve more than when the Treaty of Nice was agreed—were able to agree on the trimmed-down Reform Treaty. The substance of the Treaty did not change radically, but all symbolic references to the constitution were dropped. The EU's most fervent supporters lamented what they viewed as a missed opportunity to give the EU a secure constitutional foundation. A more optimistic view was that the EU was now ready to tackle other pressing issues, including economics, energy, and the environment but also accession negotiations with Turkey, the financial system of the EU, Europe's relationships between Russia, China, and India, and the Union's ever expanding foreign policy agenda more generally.

How *Will* it Work?

We conclude with a few thoughts—we will not call them 'predictions'—about the changes ahead in 2008 and beyond. We have seen that there is no shortage of controversy concerning what is most important in determining how the EU really works. Be that as it may, it is useful to resort to models or visions of how the EU *should* work to stimulate thinking about different potential futures. These models are by no means mutually exclusive. On the contrary, the EU has always been a hybrid of the:

(1) *Intergovernmental*;

(2) *Federal*; and

(3) *Functional*.

An *intergovernmental* outcome to the 2007 IGC would have meant a repatriation of competences, a weakening of the institutional triangle between the Commission, the Council, and the European Parliament, and a return to unanimous decision-making—with many decisions taken outside the current institutional framework. In some ways, the outcome of the IGC was likely to be the opposite. In a detailed political agreement that preceded the IGC, QMV was extended to some 30 new areas of policy. The pillar structure was collapsed. The EU was given a legal personality and all of its key institutions were strengthened (see Chapters 6 and 8). All member states realized that if the EU wanted to be a serious player on the international scene, strict intergovernmentalism was not an option. The experience of the Nice negotiations and the need for efficiency in an enlarged Union produced a new appreciation of methods of power-sharing that had worked in the past.

A more *federal* Europe post-2007 would have meant the adoption of something closer in form and substance to the Constitutional Treaty. Crucially, in symbolic terms, it would have been called a Constitution and have included constitutional symbols such as the European anthem and flag, a president, and a foreign minister. But a truly federal EU, at least for ardent enthusiasts of the idea, would mean going beyond the Constitutional Treaty and giving the Union an elected government and a bicameral parliament. Arguably, a federal structure could be more transparent and democratic.

Power-sharing in most federal regimes is governed by the subsidiarity principle (see Box 2.2), with powers formally divided in a way that brings government as close to the citizen as possible.

Put simply, member governments and their publics remain unwilling to take a quantum leap to a federal state. The French and Dutch rejections of the Constitutional Treaty prove the case in point. Many of the hallmarks of a federal state—a large central budget funded through direct taxation or giving the power of constitutional amendment to the legislatures or legislators of the constituent states (as opposed to their governments)—are unimaginable. There is no united political movement or demos pushing for a European federation.

To be sure, as the history of the EU shows, there can be federalism without a federation. The euro and European Central Bank (ECB) are nothing if not federative elements. Thus, we find another apparent contradiction: the idea of a federal Europe—a nightmare to Eurosceptics—is both a utopian pipe-dream and a practical reality in some areas of policy. But if it ever arrives, a United States of Europe will not arrive in the near future. In some ways, political agreement on the 2007 Reform Treaty, as an alternative to the Constitutional Treaty, was a major setback to those who support a federal Europe.

A final, *functional* model of the future is a mix between the previous two. It is in essence what the new EU Treaty represents. More than either the intergovernmental or federal variants, the functional model favours continuity in European integration and is sceptical of radical change. It embraces a largely functional path of integration, which is practical and utilitarian rather than decorative or symbolic. It accepts that the EU does not yet (and may never) operate in policy areas such as child care and most forms of taxation. It accepts that the Community method of decision-making, with powers shared between the EU's institutions, is inappropriate (at least initially) for some areas where European cooperation makes sense, including defence and border controls. The functional model might even accept a 'core Europe' in some areas of policy, as occurred in early eras with Schengen or the Eurozone, with some EU states forging ahead with cooperative agreements that others could not support on the assumption that outsiders might become insiders later on. But the functional model also values power-sharing for its own sake. It thus favours pragmatic cooperation that extends to all EU members based on strengthening the current institutional triangle between the Commission, Council, and EP—with the ECJ adjudicating disputes between them.

A basic assumption underpinning this model is that the EU—warts and all—has worked to further the greater good of European citizens. But form should follow function, not vice versa as in the federal vision. The functional model represents a path that has been followed from the earliest beginnings of European integration in the 1950s. It may well live on in the EU of the future simply because, in the past, it has worked: most say reasonably and some say remarkably, even if a minority says not at all.

Conclusion

The reality of European integration is naturally more complex than the simple models that we have just outlined. French EU policy illustrates this point. On some federal projects—such as the euro—France has been instrumental. At the same time France has given intergovernmentalists many reasons to be happy by putting a halt to further European integration: in 1954 by blocking the European Defence Community, in 1966 by refusing to move to QMV, and in 2005 by rejecting the constitution. On foreign and security policy France has been an advocate of the Community method, thus revealing its affinity for a Europe that is a more 'functional' global actor.

The EU has always been a combination of these three models. It is more than an ordinary international organization, but less than a state. It is likely always to be a multilevel system in which the supranational, national, and regional co-exist. It is a unique and original way of organizing cooperation amongst states, whose governments (if not always their citizens) genuinely see themselves as members of a political union.

The EU of the future will probably remain an experimental system, always in flux, with plenty of scope to be reformed and competing ideas about how to do it. It will continue to be, above all, an exercise in seeking consensus and trying to achieve unity, where it makes sense, out of enormous diversity. As such, how it really works will never match one vision of how it should work.

▌ APPENDIX: Chronology of European Integration*

1945 May	End of World War II in Europe
1946 Sept.	Winston Churchill's 'United States of Europe' speech
1947 June	Marshall Plan announced
	Organization for European Economic Cooperation established
1949 Apr.	North Atlantic Treaty signed in Washington
1950 May	Schuman Declaration
1951 Apr.	Treaty establishing the ECSC signed in Paris
1952 May	Treaty establishing the European Defence Community (EDC) signed
Aug.	European Coal and Steel Community launched in Luxembourg
1954 Aug.	French parliament rejects the EDC
Oct.	Western European Union (WEU) established
1955 May	Germany and Italy join NATO
June	EC foreign ministers meet in Messina to relaunch European integration
1956 May	Meeting in Venice, EC foreign ministers recommend establishing the European Economic Community (EEC) and the European Atomic Energy Community (Euratom)
1957 Mar.	Treaties establishing the EEC and Euratom signed in Rome
1958 Jan.	Launch of the EEC and Euratom
1961 July	The UK, Denmark, Ireland, and Norway apply to join the EEC
1962 Jan.	Agreement reached on the Common Agricultural Policy
1963 Jan.	French President Charles de Gaulle vetoes the UK's application; de Gaulle and German Chancellor Konrad Adenauer sign Elysée Treaty
July	Signing of Yaoundé Convention between EEC and eighteen African states
1964 May	EEC sends single delegation to Kennedy Round negotiations on tariff reduction in General Agreement on Tariffs and Trade (GATT)
1965 July	Empty Chair Crisis begins
1966 Jan.	Empty Chair Crisis ends with Luxembourg Compromise
1967 May	The UK, Denmark, Ireland, and Norway again apply for EEC membership
July	The executive bodies of the ECSC, EEC, and Euratom merge into a Commission
Nov.	De Gaulle again vetoes the UK's application
1968 July	The customs union is completed eighteen months ahead of schedule
1969 Apr.	De Gaulle resigns
July	The UK revives its membership application
1970 Oct.	Council agrees to create Euopean Political Cooperation (EPC) mechanism
	Luxembourg's Prime Minister Pierre Werner presents a plan for Economic and Monetary Union (EMU)

1972 Oct.	Meeting in Paris, EC heads of state and government agree to deepen European integration
1973 Jan.	The UK, Denmark, and Ireland join the EC
Oct.	Following the Middle East War, Arab oil producers quadruple the price of oil and send the international economy into recession
1975 Feb.	Lomé Convention (superceding Yaoundé Convention) agreed between EEC and 46 African, Caribbean, and Pacific (ACP) states
Mar.	EC heads of state and government inaugurate the European Council (regular summit meetings)
June	In a referendum in the UK, a large majority endorses continued EC Membership
July	Member states sign a treaty strengthening the budgetary powers of the European Parliament and establishing the Court of Auditors
1978 July	Meeting in Bremen, the European Council decides to establish the European Monetary System (EMS), precursor to EMU
1979 Mar.	Member states launch the EMS
June	First direct elections to the European Parliament
1981 Jan.	Greece joins the EC
1985 June	The Commission publishes its White Paper on completing the single market
1986 Jan.	Portugal and Spain join the EC
Feb.	EC foreign ministers sign the Single European Act (SEA)
1987 July	The SEA enters into force
1988 June	EC and Comecon (East European trading bloc) recognize each other for first time
1989 Apr.	The Delors Committee presents its report on EMU
Nov.	The Berlin Wall comes down
1990 Oct.	Germany is reunited
1991 Dec.	Meeting in Maastricht, the European Council concludes the intergovernmental conferences on political union and EMU
1992 Feb.	EC foreign ministers sign the Maastricht Treaty
June	Danish voters reject the Maastricht Treaty
1993 May	Danish voters approve the Maastricht Treaty, with special provisions for Denmark
Nov.	The Maastricht Treaty enters into force; the European Union (EU) comes into being
June	Copenhagen European Council endorses eastern enlargement
1994 Apr.	Hungary and Poland apply to join EU
1995 Jan.	Austria, Finland, and Sweden join the EU
1995 Mar.	Schengen Agreement implemented by seven EU member states
1995–6	Eight additional Central and Eastern European countries apply to join the EU
1997 June	European Council agrees Amsterdam Treaty, which creates post of High Representative for the CFSP
Oct.	EU foreign ministers sign the Amsterdam Treaty
1998 Mar.	The EU begins accession negotiations with five Central and Eastern European countries, plus Cyprus

	UK and France agree St Malo Declaration on European defence
June	The European Central Bank is launched in Frankfurt
1999 Jan.	The third stage of EMU begins with the launch of the euro and the pursuit of a common monetary policy by eleven member states
Mar.	The Commission resigns following the submission of a report of an independent investigating committee; the Berlin European Council concludes the Agenda 2000 negotiations
May	The Amsterdam Treaty enters into force
Dec.	The European Council signals 'irreversibility of eastern enlargement'; recognizes Turkey as a candidate for EU Membership
2000 Feb.	The EU begins accession negotiations with the five other Central and Eastern European applicant countries, plus Malta
Dec.	Meeting in Nice, the European Council concludes the intergovernmental conference on institutional reform
2001 Feb.	EU foreign ministers sign the Nice Treaty
June	Irish voters reject the Nice Treaty
2002 Jan.	Euro notes and coins enter into circulation
Feb.	Convention on the 'Future of Europe' opens
2003 Feb.	The Nice Treaty enters into force
June	The Convention on the Future of Europe promulgates a Draft Constitutional Treaty
Oct.	An intergovernmental conference opens to finalize the Constitutional Treaty
2004 May	Cyprus, the Czech Republic, Estonia, Hungary, Latvia, Lithuania, Malta, Poland, Slovakia, and Slovenia join the EU
June	The intergovernmental conference reaches agreement on the Constitutional Treaty
Oct.	National leaders sign the Constitutional Treaty in Rome
2005 May	French voters reject the Constitutional Treaty
June	Dutch voters reject the Constitutional Treaty
	The European Council launches a year-long 'period of reflection' on the stalled Constitutional Treaty
Oct.	The EU opens accession negotiations with Turkey
2006 June	The European Council decides to prolong the 'period of reflection' and calls on Germany to find a solution to the constitutional impasse during the country's presidency in the first half of 2007
2007 Jan.	Bulgaria and Romania join the EU
	Slovenia adopts the euro
Mar.	EU leaders celebrate the 50th anniversary of the Rome Treaty at a ceremony in Berlin and release a Declaration on the Future of Europe
June	European Council agree mandate for new 'Reform Treaty' to replace Constitutional Treaty
July	Intergovernmental Conference opens to agree details of Reform Treaty

*Compiled by Desmond Dinan

GLOSSARY

Several of the terms below are defined and elaborated in more detail in the concept boxes of each of the chapters. Where this is the case, the box number is provided.

The EU also has its own official EU glossary which can be found at: http://europa.eu/scadplus/glossary/index_en.htm

Absorption capacity (see Box 9.1) Refers to the EU's ability to integrate new members into its system.

Accession (see Box 9.1) The process whereby a country joins the EU and becomes a member state.

Acquis communautaire (see Box 4.1) Denotes the rights and obligations derived from the EU treaties, laws, and Court rulings. In principle, new member states joining the EU must accept the entire *acquis*.

Assent procedure (see Box 3.5) Decision-making procedure used to establish the European Parliament's approval of major decisions such as the accession of new member states.

Asylum (see Box 7.1) Protection provided by a government to a foreigner who is unable to stay in their country of citizenship/residence for fear of persecution.

Benchmarking (see Box 6.1) The use of comparison with other states or organizations with the aim of improving performance by learning from the experience of others.

Biometric technology (see Box 7.1) Allows measurements of unique physical characteristics to be taken and stored digitally in passports, visas, or databases.

Cabinet The group of staff and advisers that make up the private offices of senior EU figures, such as Commissioners.

Candidate countries (see Box 9.1) Refers to a country whose application is confirmed by the EU but is not yet a member.

Charter of Fundamental Rights (see Box 8.1) Adopted by the Council at the Nice Summit in 2000 but not legally binding, the Charter seeks to strengthen and promote the fundamental human rights of EU citizens.

Civil society (see Box 5.1) The collection of groups and associations (such as private firms and non-governmental organizations) that operate between the individual and state.

Co-decision procedure (see Box 3.5) Under this decision-making procedure the European Parliament formally shares legal responsibility for legislation jointly with the Council of Ministers.

Cohesion policy Introduced after the first enlargement in 1973, its aim has been to reduce inequality among regions and compensate for the costs of economic integration.

Community method (see Box 6.4) Used especially in areas where common EU policies replace national policies (such as the internal market) the community method is a form of supranational policy-making in which the Union's institutions wield considerable power. Usually contrasted to the intergovernmental method.

Conditionality (see Box 9.1) Means that accession is conditional on fulfilling the criteria for membership.

Constitutional charter (see Box 8.1) The name the European Court of Justice has given to the

Treaties' constitutional elements which amount to an uncodified or informal constitution enshrined in custom, law, and treaties.

Constitutionalism (see Box 8.1) Respect for the rules and values in a constitution, including the protection of fundamental rights.

Constructivism A school of thought drawing on cultural and sociological studies and emphasizing the non-rational 'social construction' of the collective rules and norms that guide political behaviour.

Consultation procedure (see Box 3.5) Decision-making procedure whereby the Council seeks the opinion of the European Parliament but need not heed that opinion.

Cooperation procedure (see Box 3.5) Decision-making procedure whereby the European Parliament may request a second opportunity to amend or reject legislative proposals.

Coreper (the Committee of Permanent Representatives) The most important preparatory committee of the Council, Coreper is composed of heads of the Permanent Representation (EU ambassadors) and their supporting delegations maintained by each member state in Brussels. (See also **Perm Reps.**)

Demandeur (see Box 4.1) French term often used to refer to those demanding something (say regional or agricultural funds) from the EU.

Democratic deficit (see Box 8.1) Refers broadly to the belief that the EU lacks sufficient democratic control. Neither the Commission, which proposes legislation, nor the Council, which enacts it, is directly accountable to the public or national parliaments.

Demos From the ancient Greek, refers to 'the people', 'populace', or 'citizen body'.

Direct effect Established in the 1963 *van Gend en Loos* case, the doctrine has become a distinguishing principle of Community law. Under direct effect Community law applies directly to

individuals (not just states) and national courts must enforce it.

Directive (see Box 6.1) The most common form of EU legislation. It stipulates the ends to be achieved but allows each member state to choose the form and method for achieving that end.

Directorates General (DGs) The primary administrative units within the Commission, comparable to national ministries or Departments. There are about twenty DGs, each focusing on a specific area of policy such as competition or trade.

Economic and Monetary Union (EMU) A package of measures designed to harmonize the economic and monetary policies of participating member states. It includes the free movement of capital and convergence of monetary policies. Its most visible element is a single currency—the euro—adopted in 1999 with notes and coins circulating in 2002. By 2008 fifteen member states were members of EMU.

Elysée Treaty (1963) A treaty of friendship signed between Germany and France signalling greater political cooperation.

Empty Chair Crisis (see Box 2.2) Protesting the Commission's plans to subject more decisions to Qualified Majority Voting, French president De Gaulle pulled France out of all Council meetings in 1965 thereby leaving one chair empty.

Europe Agreements Signed in the early 1990s, these cooperation agreements between the EU and several east European countries were viewed as a first step towards accession. The agreements cover economic cooperation, cultural exchanges, and some foreign policy coordination.

European Defence Community (EDC) A French-inspired, American-backed proposal for a European army. Tabled in 1950, the plan collapsed following its rejection by the French National Assembly in 1954.

Europeanization (see Box 4.1) The process whereby national systems (institutions, policies, governments) adapt to EU policies and integration more generally, while also themselves shaping the European Union.

Europol The European Police Office designed to improve the effectiveness with which police forces across the EU could cooperate across national borders.

European Political Cooperation (EPC) The precursor to the Common Foreign and Security Policy (CFSP), the EPC was launched in 1970 as a way for member states to coordinate their foreign policies and speak (and sometimes act) together when national policies overlapped.

European Security and Defence Policy (ESDP) The effort to give the EU a defence capability, such as through the creation of a Rapid Reaction Force or multinational 'battle groups'.

Eurozone (see Box 6.1) The countries that are part of the Economic and Monetary Union (EMU). By 2008 fifteen member states belonged to the Eurozone.

Federalism (see Box 6.1) Principle of sharing power and sovereignty between levels of governance, usually between central or federal level, and substate (state, provincial, Länder) level.

Flexible integration (see Box 4.1) Also called 're-inforced' or 'enhanced cooperation', flexible integration denotes the possibility for some member states to pursue deeper integration without the participation of others. Examples include EMU and the Schengen Agreement.

Framework decision (see Box 7.1) Legislative 'blueprints' used to harmonize national criminal law.

Free trade area (see Box 2.4) An area in which restrictive trading measures are removed and goods can travel freely among its signatory states. These states retain authority to establish their own tariff levels and quotas for third countries.

GDP (gross domestic product) An index of the total value of all goods and services produced by a country, not counting overseas operations

Globalization (see Box 1.5) The process by which the world becomes increasingly interconnected and interdependent because of increasing flows of trade, ideas, people, and capital.

GNP (gross national product) An index of the total value of all goods and services produced by a country, including overseas trade. Most common measure of a country's material wealth.

Governance (see Box 1.5) Established patterns of rules, principles, and practices that enable a community to be governed even without a government or ruler. The term is usefully applied to the EU because of its lack of identifiable government.

Human trafficking (see Box 7.1) The criminal enterprise of transporting people (mainly women and children), who are often enslaved for profitable exploitation.

IGCs (Intergovernmental Conferences) Conferences bringing together representatives of member states to hammer out deals and consider amendments to the treaties, or other history-making decisions such as enlargement.

Integration, European (see Box 1.5) The process whereby sovereign European states relinquish (surrender or pool) national sovereignty to maximize their collective power and interests.

Integration, negative Integration through market-building and the removal of obstacles to trade. Less ambitious than positive integration.

Integration, positive Integration through the active promotion of common policies which effectively replace national ones.

Intergovernmentalism (see Box 1.5) Process or condition whereby decisions are reached by specifically defined cooperation between or among governments. Sovereignty is not directly undermined.

Internal market More than a free trade area, an internal market signifies the free trade of goods, services, people, and capital. Also known as the single market.

Legitimacy The right to rule and make political decisions. More generally, the idea that 'the existing political institutions are the most appropriate ones for society' (Lipset 1963).

Liberal intergovernmentalism A theory of European integration which argues that the most important decisions taken concerning the EU reflect the preferences of national governments rather than supranational institutions.

Lobbying (see Box 5.1) An attempt to influence policy-makers to adopt a course of action advantageous (or not detrimental) to a particular group or interest.

Luxembourg Compromise (see Box 2.2) Agreed in 1966 to resolve the 'Empty Chair Crisis', this informal agreement established that when a decision was subject to Qualified Majority Voting (QMV), the Council would postpone a decision if any member states felt 'very important' interests were under threat.

Market (Box 6.1) A system of exchange bringing together buyers and sellers of goods and services.

Marshall Plan (1947) (see Box 2.2) A US aid package of $13 billion to help rebuild West European economies after the war.

Multilevel governance (see Box 1.5) A term denoting a system of overlapping and shared powers between actors on the regional, national, and supranational levels.

Neofunctionalism A theory of European integration which suggests that economic integration in certain sectors will provoke further integration in other sectors, and can lead to the formation of integrated supranational institutions.

New institutionalism As applied to the EU, a theoretical approach that suggests that institutions, including rules and informal practices, can mould the behaviour of policy-makers (including national officials) in ways that governments neither plan nor control.

Non-tariff barriers (see Box 6.1) Regulations, such as national standards, that increase the cost of imports and thus have the equivalent effect of tariffs.

Path dependency The idea (developed especially by new institutionalists) that once a particular policy path or course of action is taken, it is extremely difficult to turn back because of the 'sunk costs' (time and resources already invested). Used to explain why even those policies that have outlived their usefulness remained unreformed.

'Perm Reps' Eurospeak for the Permanent Representatives (EU ambassador) and the Permanent Representations (similar to embassies) of each member state. Together the 'Perm Reps' from each of the member states make up Coreper.

Petersberg tasks A series of security tasks designed to strengthen European defence capability and the EU's role as a civilian power. These tasks include humanitarian, rescue, and peacekeeping operations as well as tasks involving combat forces in crisis management.

Pillars A shorthand term for describing the 'Greek temple' architecture created by the Maastricht Treaty, with the first pillar (the pre-existing European Community) and the second (foreign and security policy) and third (justice and home affairs) pillars together constituting the 'European Union'. If ratified, the Reform Treaty would collapse the EU's pillars into one institutional structure.

Policy networks Clusters of actors, each of whom has an interest or stake in a given policy sector and the capacity to help determine policy success or failure. Scholars applying this notion argue that analysing such networks can reveal a great deal about day-to-day decision-making in the EU.

Public policy (see Box 6.1) A course of action (decisions, actions, rules, laws, and so on) or inaction taken by government in regard to some public problem or issue.

Qualified Majority Voting (QMV) (see Box 2.2) Refers to the most commonly used voting method in the Council of Ministers. Under this system each member state is granted a number of votes roughly proportional to its population.

Rapporteur (see Box 5.1) The Member of the European Parliament responsible for preparing a report in one of the Parliament's committees.

Schengen Agreement (see Box 2.2) An agreement stipulating the gradual abolition of controls at borders. By 2008 fifteen EU member states were signatories as were Norway and Iceland. The UK and Ireland have not signed, and Denmark has opted out of certain aspects.

Schuman plan A plan proposed by the French Foreign Minister, Robert Schuman, in 1950 to combine the coal and steel industries of Germany and France, thus making war between them impossible. It eventually became the basis for the European Coal and Steel Community, launched by the 1950 Treaty of Paris.

Screening (see Box 9.1) In the context of enlargement, screening occurs at the start of negotiations when the applicant and the Commission examine the *acquis* to see if there are particular problems to be resolved.

Separation of powers (see Box 8.1) The constitutional principle according to which different governmental functions (executive, legislative, and judicial) should be exercised by different agencies.

Single market (See internal market.)

Sovereignty (see Box 1.5) Refers to the ultimate authority over people and territory.

Subsidiarity (see Box 2.2) The idea that action should be taken at the most efficient level of governance, but as close to the citizens as possible.

Supranationalism (see Box 1.5) Above states or nations. Supranationalism means decisions are made by a process or institution which is largely independent of national governments. The term supranationalism is usually contrasted with intergovernmentalism.

Third countries Refers to non-EU countries, often in the context of trade relations.

Tour de table (see Box 4.1) In the Council of Ministers a 'tour around the table' allows each delegation to make an intervention on a given subject.

Transitional period (see Box 9.1) Refers to a period in which application of some of the rules may be phased in or delayed after accession.

Transparency In the EU this refers to the process of making EU documents and decision-making processes more open and accessible to the public.

Transposition (see Box 7.1) The act of amending national law to meet the specifications of EU legislation.

Venue shopping (see Box 5.1) The activities of an interest group searching or 'shopping' for a decision setting most favourable or receptive to their policy claims.

The Glossary was compiled with the assistance of Louise Maythorne, University of Edinburgh

REFERENCES

Allott, P. (2002), *The Health of Nations: Society and Law Beyond the State* (Cambridge and New York: Cambridge University Press).

Armstrong, K., and Bulmer, S. (1998), *The Governance of the Single European Market* (Manchester and New York: Manchester University Press).

Aspinwall, M., and Greenwood, J. (1998), *Collective Action in the European Union: Interests, and the New Politics of Associability* (London: Routledge).

Aspinwall, M., and G. Schneider (2000), 'Same Menu, Separate Tables: The Institutionalist Turn in Political Science and the Study of European Integration', *European Journal of Political Research* 38/1: 1–36.

Avery, G. (2004), 'The Enlargement Negotiations', in F. Cameron (ed.), *The Future of Europe, Integration and Enlargement* (London: Routledge): 35–62.

——— (2005), *The External Action Service: The Viewpoint of the European Commission* (Berlin: presentation to Symposium of the Europäische Akademie).

Barysch, K., Everts, S., and Grabbe, H. (2005), *Why Europe Should Embrace Turkey* (London: Centre for European Reform).

Baumgartner, F. (2007), 'EU Lobbying: A View from the US', *Journal of European Public Policy* 14/3: 482–8.

Baun, M., Dürr, J., Marek, D., and Šaradín, P. (2006), 'The Europeanization of Czech Politics', *Journal of Common Market Studies*, 44/2: 249–80.

Baylis, J., and Roper, J. (2006), (eds.) *The United States and Europe: Beyond the Neo-Conservative Divide?* (London and New York: Routledge).

Bindi, F. with Cisci, M. (2005), 'Italy and Spain: A Tale of Contrasting Effectiveness in the EU', in S. Bulmer, and C. Lequesne, (eds.), *The Member States of the European Union* (Oxford and New York: Oxford University Press): 142–63.

Biscop, S. (2005), *The European Security Strategy: A Global Agenda for Positive Power* (Aldershot and Burlington, VT: Ashgate).

Bonneau, C., and Striko, T. (2006), 'The US Supreme Court', in G. Peele, C. Bailey, B. Cain, and B. Guy Peters (eds.), *Developments in American Politics 5* (Basingstoke and New York: Palgrave Macmillan): 107–23.

Booker, C. (1996), 'Europe and Regulation: The New Totalitarianism', in M. Holmes (ed.), *The Eurosceptical Reader* (New York: St. Martin's Press): 186–204.

Börzel, T. (2005), (ed.), 'The Disparity of European Integration: Revisiting Neofunctionalism in Honour of Ernst Haas', Special Issue of *Journal of European Public Policy*, 12/2.

Bretherton, C., and Vogler, J. (2006), *The European Union as a Global Actor*, 2nd edn. (London and New York: Routledge).

Bulmer, S. (1998), 'New Institutionalism and the Governance of the Single European Market', *Journal of European Public Policy* 5/3. 365–86.

Bulmer, S., and Lequesne, C. (2005a), 'The EU and its Member States: An Overview', in S. Bulmer, and C. Lequesne, (eds.), *The Member States of the European Union* (Oxford and New York: Oxford University Press): 1–24.

—— —— (2005b), *The Member States of the European Union* (Oxford and New York: Oxford University Press).

Burchill, S., Linklates A., Devetak, R., Donnelly, J., Paterson, M., Reus-Smit, C., and True, J. (2005), *Theories of International Relations* (Basingstoke and New York: Palgrave).

Cafruny, A., and Ryner, M. (eds.) (2003), *A Ruined Fortress? Neoliberal Hegemony and Transformation in Europe* (Oxford and Lanham MD: Rowman & Littlefield).

Caporaso, J. (1996), 'The European Union and Forms of State: Westphalian, Regulatory or Post-Modern?' *Journal of Common Market Studies* 34/1: 29–52.

—— (2001), 'The Europeanization of Gender Equality Policy and Domestic Structural Change', in M. Green Cowles, J. Caporaso, and T. Risse (eds.), *Transforming Europe: Europeanization and Domestic Change* (Ithaca, NY: Cornell University Press): 21–43.

Carlsnaes, W. (2006), 'European Foreign Policy', in K. E. Jørgensen, M. A. Pollack, and B. Rosamond (eds.), *Handbook of European Union Politics* (London and Thousand Oaks CA: Sage): 545–60.

—— Sjursen, H., and White, B. (eds.) (2004), *Contemporary European Foreign Policy* (London and Thousand Oaks CA: Sage).

Checkel, J. (1999), 'Social Construction and Integration', *Journal of European Public Policy* 6/4: 545–60.

—— (2004), 'Social Constructivisms in Global and European Politics; A Review Essay', *Review of International Studies* 30/2: 229–44.

—— (2006), 'Constructivism and EU Politics', in K. E. Jørgensen, M. Pollack, and B. Rosamond, (eds.) *Handbook of European Union Politics* (London: Sage): 57–76.

Closa, C., and Heywood, P. S. (2004), *Spain and the European Union* (Basingstoke and New York: Palgrave).

Coen, D. (2004), 'Environmental and Business Lobbying Alliances in Europe: Learning from Washington?', in D. Levy and P. Newell (eds.), *Business in International Environmental Governance: A Political Economy Approach* (Cambridge, MA: MIT Press): 197–22.

Coen, D. (2007), 'Empirical and Theoretical Studies in EU Lobbying', *Journal of European Public Policy* 14/3: 333–45.

—— and Richardson, J. (2007), *Lobbying in the European Union: Institutions, Actors and Issues* (Oxford and New York: Oxford University Press).

Commission (1992), *Europe and the Challenge of Enlargement*. Prepared for the European Council, Lisbon, 26–7 June 1992. Commission Bulletin of the European Communities, Supplement 3/92 . Brussels, 24 June 1992.

—— (2001), 'Interim report from the Commission to the Stockholm European Council: Improving and Simplifying the Regulatory Environment', COM (2001) 130 final, Brussels, 7.3.2001.

—— (2006a), 'Allocation of 2005 EU Expenditure by Member State', Available at: http://ec.europa.eu/budget/library/documents/revenue_expenditure/agenda_2000/allocrep_2005_en.pdf

—— (2006b), *Enlargement Two Years After: An Economic Evaluation*, European Economy no. 24 (Brussels: DG for Economic and Financial Affairs) Available at http://ec.europa.eu/economy_finance/publications/occasional_papers/2006/ocp24en.pdf

_____ (2006c), *European Commission Press Release* IP/06/1230 (21/09/2006) (Bruxelles: Commission).

_____ (2006d), *General Budget of the European European Union for the Financial Year 2006. The Figures* (Luxembourg: Commission).

_____ (2006e), *Progress in Notification of National Measures Implementing Directives* Available at http://ec.europa.eu/community_law/eulaw/pdf/mne_country_20060831_en.pdf

_____ (2007a), 'Distribution of Officials and Temporary Agents by Directorate General and Category (all budgets)' *Statistical Bulletin*, Jan 2007 http://ec.europa.eu/civil_service/docs/bs_dg_category_en.pdf

_____ (2007b), *The Official EU Languages*. Available at: http://ec.europa.eu/education/policies/lang/languages/index_en.html

_____ (2007c), Translation Directorate General 'Frequently Asked Questions' at: http://ec.europa.eu/dgs/translation/navigation/faq/faq_facts_en.htm

Cooper, R. (2004a), 'Hard Power, Soft Power and the Goals of Diplomacy', in D. Held and M. Koenig-Archibugi, *American Power in the 21st Century* (Oxford and Malden MA: Polity): 168–80.

_____ (2004b), Untitled in *EU Security and Defence Policy: the First Five Years (1999–2004)* N. Gnesotto (Paris: Institute for Security Studies).

Corbett, R., Jacobs, F., and Shackleton, M. (2007), *The European Parliament*, 7th edn. (London: Cartermill).

Cowles, M. G., and Curtis, S. (2004), 'Developments in European Integration Theory: The EU as "other" ', in M. G. Cowles and D. Dinan, *Developments in the European Union II* (Basingstoke and New York: Palgrave): 296–309.

Dannreuther, R. (ed.) (2004), *European Union Foreign and Security Policy: Towards a Neighbourhood Strategy* (London and New York: Routledge).

_____ and Peterson, J. (eds.) (2006), *Security Strategy and Transatlantic Relations* (London and New York: Routledge).

De Grauwe, P. (2002), *Economics of Monetary Union*, 5th edn. (Oxford: Oxford University Press).

Dinan, D. (2004), *Europe Recast: A History of European Union* (Boulder, CO: Lynne Rienner Publishers and Basingstoke: Palgrave).

_____ (ed.) (2006), *Origins and Evolution of the European Union* (Oxford and New York: Oxford University Press).

Douglas-Scott, S. (2002), *The Constitutional Law of the European Union* (Harlow: Longman/Pearson Educational).

Duchêne, F. (1994), *Jean Monnet: The First Statesman of Interdependence* (New York: Norton).

Dyson, K. (ed.) (2002), *European States and the Euro: Europeanization, Variation, and Convergence* (Oxford and New York: Oxford University Press).

_____ and Featherstone, K. (1999), *The Road to Maastricht: Negotiating Economic and Monetary Union* (Oxford and New York: Oxford University Press).

Earnshaw, D., and Wood, J. (1999), 'The European Parliament and Biotechnology Patenting: Harbinger of the Future?' *Journal of Commercial Biotechnology* 5/4: 294–307.

Egan, M. (2001), *Constructing a European Market: Standards, Regulation, and Governance* (Oxford: Oxford University Press).

Eilstrup-Sangiovanni, M. (2006), 'The Constructivist Turn in European Integration Studies', in M. Eilstrup-Sangiovanni (ed.) *Debates on European Integration. A Reader* (Basingstoke and New York: Palgrave): 393–405.

Eising, R. (2007), 'The Access of Business Interests to EU Institutions: Towards Elite Pluralism?' *Journal of European Public Policy* 14/3: 384–403.

Elman, C., and Elman, M. F. (eds.) (2003), *Progess in International Relations Theory* (Cambridge and London: MIT Press).

Emerson, M. (ed.) (2005), *Democratisation in the European Neighbourhood* (Brussels: Centre for European Policy Studies).

EPIC (2007), 'European Neighbourhood Policy', Special Issue of *European Political Economy Review*, 7 (summer), available online at: http://www.lse.ac.uk/collections/EPER.main.htm

Eurobarometer (2007) *Standard Barometer 67, First Results* Spring 2007 (Brussels: European Commission). Available at: http://ec.europa.eu/public_opinion/archives/eb/eb67/eb_67_first_en.pdf

Eurostat (2002), *News Release 13/2002* 29 January, 2002 (Luxembourg: Eurostat).

―――― (2006), *News Release 63/2006* 18 May, 2006 (Luxembourg: Eurostat).

―――― (2007), *Statistics in Focus. Population and Social Conditions*, 41/2007. (Luxembourg: Eurostat). Available at: http://epp.eurostat.ec.europa.eu/cache/ITY_OFFPUB/KS-SF-07-041/EN/KS-SF-07-041-EN.PDF

Everts, S. (2002), *Shaping a Credible EU Foreign Policy* (London: Centre for European Reform).

Falkner, G. (2000), 'How Pervasive are Euro-Politics? Effects of EU Membership on a New Member State', *Journal of Common Market Studies* 38/2: 223–50.

Farrell, M. (2007), 'From EU Model to External Policy? Promoting Regional Integration in the Rest of the World', in S. Meunier, and K. McNamara (eds), *Making History: European Integration and Institutional Change at Fifty* (Oxford and New York: Oxford University Press): 299–316.

Galtung, J. (1973), *The European Community: A Superpower in the Making* (London: George Allen & Unwin).

Geddes, A. (2006), 'The Politics of European Union Domestic Order', in K. E. Jørgensen, M. A. Pollack, and B. Rosamond (eds.), *Handbook of European Union Politics* (London and Thousand Oaks: Sage): 449–62.

George, S. (1998), *An Awkward Partner: Britain in the European Community*, 3rd edn. (Oxford and New York: Oxford University Press).

Gillingham, J. (1991), *Coal, Steel and the Rebirth of Europe, 1945–1955* (Cambridge: Cambridge University Press).

―――― (2003), *European Integration, 1950–2003* (Cambridge: Cambridge University Press).

Ginsberg, R. (2001), *The European Union in International Politics: Baptism by Fire* (Boulder, CO and Oxford: Rowman & Littlefield).

Goergen, P. (2006), *Lobbying in Brussels: A Practical Guide to the European Union for Cities, Regions, Networks and Enterprises* (Brussels, D&P Services).

Goetz, K. H. (2005), 'The New Member States and the EU: Responding to Europe', in S. Bulmer and C. Lequesne (eds.), *The Member States of the European Union* (Oxford and New York: Oxford University Press): 254–84.

Grabbe, H. (2006), *The EU's Transformative Power: Europeanization through Conditionality in Central and Eastern Europe* (Basingstoke and New York: Palgrave Macmillan).

Green Cowles, M., Caporaso, J., and Risse, T. (eds.) (2000), *Transforming Europe: Europeanization and Domestic Change* (Ithaca, NY: Cornell University Press).

Greenwood, J. (2003), *Interest Representation in the EU* (Basingstoke: Palgrave).

Guiraudon, V., and Jileva, E. (2006), 'Immigration and Asylum', in P. M. Heywood, E. Jones, M. Rhodes, and U. Sedelmeier, *Developments in European Politics* (Basingstoke and New York: Palgrave): xx.

Haas, E. (1958), *The Uniting of Europe: Political, Social, and Economic Forces* (Stanford, CA: Stanford University Press).

_____ (1964), *Beyond the Nation-State: Functionalism and International Organization* (Stanford, Calif: Stanford University Press).

_____ (2001), 'Does Constructivism Subsume Neo-functionalism?' in T. Christiansen, K. E. Jørgensen, and A. Weiner (eds.), *The Social Construction of Europe* (London and Thousand Oaks CA: Sage): 22–31.

Hagemann, S., and De Clerck-Sachsse, J. (2007), *Decision-making in the Council of Ministers before and after May 2004*, Special CEPS Report (Brussels: Centre for European Policy Studies).

Hayes-Renshaw, F. (2006), 'The Council of Ministers' in J. Peterson, and M. Shackleton, (eds.), *The Institutions of the European Union*, 2nd edn. (Oxford: Oxford University Press): 60–80.

_____ and Wallace, H. (2006), *The Council of Ministers*, 2nd edn. (Basingstoke: Palgrave).

Heisbourg, F. (2004), 'The "European Security Strategy" is Not a Security Strategy', in S. Everts *et al*. *A European Way of War* (London: Centre for European Reform): 27–39.

Heisenberg, D. (2007), 'Informal Decision-Making in the Council: The Secret of the EU's Success?', in S. Meunier, and K. McNamara (eds), *Making History. European Integration and Institutional Change at Fifty* (Oxford and New York: Oxford University Press): 67–88.

Henderson, K. (ed.) (2005), *The Area of Freedom, Security, and Justice in the Enlarged Europe* (New York: Palgrave Macmillan).

_____ (2007), *The European Union's New Democracies* (London and New York: Routledge).

Hill, C. (1998), 'Closing the Capabilities-expectations Gap?', in J. Peterson and H. Sjursen, *A Common Foreign Policy for Europe? Competing Visions of the CFSP* (London and New York: Routledge): 91–107.

_____ (2004), 'Rationalizing or Regrouping? EU Foreign Policy since 11 September 2001', *Journal of Common Market Studies* 42/1: 143-63.

_____ (2006), 'The European Powers in the Security Council: Differing Interests, Differing Arenas', in K. V. Laatikainen and K. E. Smith, *The European Union at the United Nations* (Basingstoke and New York: Palgrave).

_____ and Smith, M. (eds.) (2005), *International Relations and the European Union* (Oxford and New York: Oxford University Press).

Hoffmann, S. (1966), 'Obstinate or Obsolete: The Fate of the Nation-state and the Case of Western Europe', *Daedalus* 95/3: 862–915 (reprinted in S. Hoffmann (1995), *The European Sisyphus: Essays on Europe 1964–1994* (Boulder, CO and Oxford: Westview Press).

_____ (1995), *The European Sisyphus: Essays on Europe 1964–1994* (Boulder, CO, and Oxford: Westview Press).

Holmes, M. (ed.) (2001), *The Eurosceptical Reader*, 2nd edn (Basingstoke: Palgrave).

Hooghe, L. (2001), *The European Commission and the Integration of Europe* (Cambridge: Cambridge University Press).

_____ and Marks, G. (2001), *Multi-Level Governance and European Integration* (Lanham and Oxford: Rowman & Littlefield).

_____ and Marks, G. (2003), 'Unraveling the central state, but how? Types of multi-level governance', *American Political Science Review*, 97/2: 233–43.

House of Lords (2004), *Daily Hansard* 10 May 2004. Available at: http://www.publications.parliament.uk/pa/ld200304/ldhansrd/vo040510/text/40510w02.htm

House of Lords (2006), *The Further Enlargement of the EU: Threat or Opportunity?* European Union Committee, Report with Evidence, HL Paper 273 (London: Stationery Office Ltd.). Available at http://www.publications.parliament.uk/pa/ld200506/ldselect/ldeucom/273/273.pdf

Howorth, J. (2007), *Security and Defence Policy in the European Union* (Basingstoke and New York: Palgrave).

IMF (International Monetary Fund) (2006), *Direction of Trade Statistics Quarterly*, June 2006 (Washington, DC: IMF).

Jeffrey, C. (2006), 'Social and Regional Interests: The Economic and Social Committee and Committee of the Regions', in J. Peterson, and M. Shackleton, (eds.), *The Institutions of the European Union*, 2nd edn. (Oxford: Oxford University Press): 312–30.

Joerges, C., Mény, Y., and Weiler, J. H. H (eds.) (2000), *What Kind of a Constitution for What Kind of Polity?* (Florence: European University Institute).

Jordan, A. (ed.) (2005), *Environmental Policy in the European Union*, 2nd edn. (London and Sterling, VA: Earthscan Publications).

Jørgensen K. E. (2006), 'Overview: the European Union and the World', in K. E. Jørgensen, M. A. Pollack, and B. Rosamond, *Handbook of European Union Politics* (London and Thousand Oaks CA: Sage): 507–25.

_____ Pollack, M., and Rosamond, B. (eds.) (2006), *Handbook of European Union Politics* (London and Thousand Oaks CA: Sage).

Journal of European Public Policy (2007), Special issue on 'Empirical and Theoretical Studies in EU Lobbying', 14/3.

Judge, D., and Earnshaw, D. (2002), 'No Simple Dichotomies: Lobbyists and the European Parliament', in *Journal of Legislative Studies* 8/4: 61–79.

Kassim, H., Peters, B. G., and Wright, V. (eds.) (2001), *The National Co-ordination of EU Policy: The European Level* (Oxford and New York: Oxford University Press).

Kaunert, C. (2007), 'Without the Power of Purse or Sword?: The European Arrest Warrant and the Role of the Commission', *Journal of European Integration* 29/4: xx.

Kennedy, T. (2006), 'The European Court of Justice', in J. Peterson, and M. Shackleton, (eds.), *The Institutions of the EU*, 2nd edn. (Oxford and New York: Oxford University Press): 124–43.

Kok, W. (2003), *Enlarging the European Union, Achievements and Challenges* (Florence: Robert Schuman Centre for Advanced Studies, European University Institute). Available online at http://www.iue.it/RSCAS/Research/Enlargement/

Krasner, S. (1984), 'Approaches to the State', *Comparative Politics* 16/2: 223–46.

Kurzer, P. (2001), *Markets and Moral Regulation: Cultural Change in the European Union* (Cambridge and New York: Cambridge University Press).

Laatikainen, K. V., and Smith, K. E. (eds.) (2006), *The European Union at the United Nations: Intersecting Multilateralisms* (Basingstoke and New York: Palgrave Macmillan).

Laffan, B. (1989), 'While You are Over There in Brussels Get Us a Grant: The Management of the Structural Funds in Ireland', *Irish Political Studies* 4/1: 43–58.

_____ (2006), 'Financial Control: The Court of Auditors and OLAF', in J. Peterson, and M. Shackleton, (eds.), *The Institutions of the European Union*, 2nd edn. (Oxford: Oxford University Press): 210–28.

Laffan. B., O'Donnell, R., and Smith, M. (2000), *Europe's Experimental Union: Rethinking Integration* (London and New York: Routledge).

Landmarks (2006), *The European Public Affairs Directory* (Brussels: Landmarks sa/nv).

Laursen, F. (ed.) (2002), *The Amsterdam Treaty: National Preference Formation, Interstate Bargaining and Outcome* (Odense: Odense University Press).

Lefebure, P., and Lagneau, E. (2001), 'Media Construction in the Dynamics of Europrotest', in D. Imig and S. Tarrow (eds.), *Contentious Europeans: Protest and Politics in an Emerging Policy* (Oxford and Lanham MD: Rowman & Littlefield): 187–204.

Lenschow, A. (ed.) (2002), *Environmental Policy Integration: Greening Sectoral Policies in Europe* (London and Sterling, VA: Earthscan Publications).

Leonard, M. (2005), *Why Europe Will Run the 21st Century* (London and New York: Harper Collins).

Leonard, D., and Leonard, M. (eds.) (2001), *The Pro-European Reader* (Basingstoke: Palgrave).

Lewis, J. (2003), 'Institutional Environments and Everyday EU Decision Making: Rationalist or Constructivist?' *Comparative Political Studies* 36/1–2: 97–124.

Lindberg, L. (1963), *The Political Dynamics of European Economic Integration* (Stanford, CA: Stanford University Press).

_____ and Scheingold, S. A. (1970), *Europe's Would-Be Polity: Patterns of Change in the European Community* (Englewood Cliffs, NJ: Prentice-Hall).

Lipset, S. M. (1963), *Political Man* (London: Mercury Books).

MacCormick, N. (2005a), 'The Health of Nations and the Health of Europe', *The Cambridge Yearbook of European Legal Studies* 7: 1–16.

_____ (2005b), *Who's Afraid of a European Constitution?* (Exeter: Imprint Academic).

McNamara, K. (2005), 'Economic and Monetary Union', in H. Wallace, W. Wallace, and M. Pollack (eds.), *Policymaking in the European Union*, 5th edn. (Oxford: Oxford University Press): 41–60.

Majone, G. (1999), 'The Regulatory State and its Legitimacy Problems', *West European Politics* 22/1: 1–13.

_____ (2005), *Dilemmas of European Integration: the Ambiguities and Pitfalls of Integration by Stealth* (Oxford and New York, Oxford University Press).

Manners, I. (2002), 'Normative Power Europe: A Contradiction in Terms?' *Journal of Common Market Studies* 40/2: 235-58.

_____ (2006), 'Normative Power Europe Reconsidered', *Journal of European Public Policy* 13/2: 182–99.

Martin, A., and Ross, G. (eds.) (2004), *Euros and Europeans: Monetary Integration and the European Model of Society* (Cambridge: Cambridge University Press).

Mayhew, A. (1998), *Recreating Europe: The European Union's Policy towards Central and Eastern Europe* (Cambridge: Cambridge University Press).

Mearsheimer, J. J. (2001), *The Tragedy of Great Power Politics* (New York and London: Norton).

Meunier, S., and McNamara, K. (eds.) (2007), *Making History: European Integration and Institutional Change at Fifty* (Oxford: Oxford University Press).

Milward, A. (1984), *The Reconstruction of Western Europe, 1945–51* (Berkeley: University of California Press).

—— (1992), *The European Rescue of the Nation-state* (London and Berkeley: Routledge and University of California Press).

—— (2000), *The European Rescue of the Nation-State*, 2nd edn. (London: Routledge).

Monar, J. (2006), 'Justice and Home Affairs', *Journal of Common Market Studies* 44/1: 101–18.

Moravcsik, A. (1993), 'Preferences and Power in the European Community: A Liberal Intergovernmentalist Approach', *Journal of Common Market Studies* 31/4: 473–524.

—— (1998), *The Choice for Europe: Social Purpose and State Power from Messina to Maastricht* (Ithaca, NY and London: Cornell University Press and UCL Press).

—— (2001), 'Despotism in Brussels? Misreading the European Union', *Foreign Affairs* 80/3: 114–22.

Morgan, G. (2005), *The Idea of a European Superstate* (Princeton and Oxford: Princeton University Press).

Morgan, R., and Bray, C. (1986), *Partners and Rivals in Western Europe: Britain, France and Germany* (Hampshire: Gower Press).

National Geographic (2005), 'Lost in Translation?' available at: http://news.nationalgeographic.com/news/2005/02/0222_050222_translation.html

Nelsen, B., and Stubb, A. (eds.) (2003), *The European Union: Readings on the Theory and Practice of European Integration*, 3rd edn. (Boulder: Lynne Rienner and Basingstoke: Palgrave).

Norman, P. (2003), *The Accidental Constitution* (Brussels: Euro Comment).

Nugent, N. (2004), *European Union Enlargement* (Basingstoke and New York: Palgrave).

—— (2006), *The Government and Politics of the European Union*, 6th edn. (Basingstoke and Durham, NC: Palgrave and Duke University Press).

Nuttall, S. (2000), *European Foreign Policy* (Oxford and New York: Oxford University Press).

Nye Jr., J. S. (2004), *Soft Power: The Means to Success in World Politics* (New York: Public Affairs).

O'Donnell, R. (2000), *Europe: The Irish Experience* (Dublin: Institute of European Affairs).

OECD (2005), *National Accounts—Volume IV—General Government Accounts* (Paris: OECD).

Occhipinti, J. (2003), *The Politics of EU Police Cooperation: Toward a European FBI?* (Boulder Co.: Lynne Rienner).

—— (2005), 'Policing Across the Atlantic: EU–US Relations & Transnational Crime-Fighting', *Bologna Center Journal of International Affairs*, May.

_____ (2007), 'Justice and Home Affairs: Immigration and Policing', in M. Smith, K. Weber, and M. Baun (eds.), *Governing Europe's Neighbourhood: Partners or Periphery?* (Manchester and New York: University of Manchester Press).

Papadimitriou, D., and Phinnemore, D. (2007), *Romania and the European Union* (London and New York: Routledge).

Patten, C. (2001), 'In Defence of Europe's Foreign Policy', *Financial Times*, 17 October. Available at: www.ft.com

Patten, C. (2005), *Not Quite the Diplomat: Home Truths About World Affairs* (London and New York: Allen Lane/Penguin).

Peers, S. (2006), *EU Justice and Home Affairs Law*, 2nd edn. (Oxford: Oxford University Press).

Peterson, J. (1995), 'Decision-Making in the EU: Towards a Framework for Analysis', *Journal of European Public Policy* 2/1: 69–73.

_____ (2004), 'Policy Networks', in A. Wiener and T. Diez, *European Integration Theory* (Oxford: Oxford University Press): 117–33.

_____ (2006), 'The College of Commissioners', in J. Peterson, and M. Shackleton (eds.) *The Institutions of the European Union*, 2nd edn. (Oxford: Oxford University Press): 81–103.

_____ and Bomberg, E. (1999), *Decision-Making in the European Union* (Basingstoke and New York: Palgrave).

_____ and Pollack, M. (eds.) (2003), *Europe, America, Bush* (London and New York: Routledge).

_____ and Shackleton, M. (eds.) (2006), *The Institutions of the European Union*, 2nd edn. (Oxford: Oxford University Press).

Pierson, P. (1996), 'The Path to European Integration', *Comparative Political Studies* 29(2): 123-63.

Pollack, M. (2004), 'New Institutionalism', in A. Wiener and T. Diez, *European Integration Theory* (Oxford: Oxford University Press): 137–56.

Preston, C. (1997), *Enlargement and Integration in the European Union* (London: Routledge).

Puchala, D. J. (1972), 'Of Blind Men, Elephants and International Integration', *Journal of Common Market Studies* 10/3: 267–84.

Redmond, J. (2007), 'Turkey and the EU: Troubled European or European Trouble?' *International Affairs* 83/2 (London: Chatham House): 305–17.

Rees, W. (2006), *Transatlantic Counter-terrorism Cooperation: The New Imperative* (London and New York: Routledge).

Rieger, E. (2005), 'Agricultural Policy: Constrained Reforms', in H., Wallace, W., Wallace and M. Pollack (eds.) *Policy-Making in the European Union*, 5th edn. (Oxford: Oxford University Press): 161–90.

Rifkin, J. (2004), *The European Dream* (Cambridge: Polity Press).

Risse, T. (2004), 'Social Constructivism', in A. Wiener and T. Diez (eds.), *European Integration Theory* (Oxford: Oxford University Press): 159–75.

Rometsch, D., and Wessels, W. (1996), *The European Union and Member States: Towards Institutional Fusion?* (Manchester: Manchester University Press).

Rosamond, B. (1999), *Theories of European Integration* (Basingstoke and New York: Palgrave).

_____ (2005), 'The Uniting of Europe and the Foundation of EU Studies: Revisiting the Neofunctionalism of Ernst B. Haas', *Journal of European Public Policy* 12(2): 237-54.

Rosenfeld, M. (1994), 'Modern Constitutionalism as Interplay Between Identity and Diversity', in M. Rosenfeld, (ed.), *Constitutionalism, Identity, Difference and Legitimacy: Theoretical Perspectives* (Durham and London: Duke University Press): 3–38.

Roth, K. (2007), 'Europe must Pull its Weight on Human Rights', *Financial Times* 12 January. Available at: www.ft.com

Sandholtz, W., and Stone Sweet, A. (1998), *European Integration and Supranational Governance* (Oxford: Oxford University Press).

Sasse, G., and Thielemann, E. (eds.) (2005), 'Migrants and Minorities in Europe', Special Issue of *Journal of Common Market Studies* 43/4.

Sbragia, A. (2001), 'Italy Pays for Europe: Political Leadership, Political Choice, and Institutional Adaptation', in M. Green Cowles, J. Caporaso, and T. Risse (eds.), *Transforming Europe: Europeanization and Domestic Change* (Ithaca, NY: Cornell University Press): 79–96.

Scharpf, F. W. (1999), *Governing in Europe: Effective and Democratic?* (Oxford and New York: Oxford University Press).

Schimmelfennig, F. (2004), 'Liberal Intergovernmentalism', in A. Wiener and T. Diez, *European Integration Theory* (Oxford and New York: Oxford University Press): 75–96.

_____ and Sedelmeier, U. (eds.) (2005), *The Politics of European Union Enlargement: Theoretical Approaches* (London: Routledge).

Settembri, P. (2007), 'The Surgery Succeeded. Has the Patient Died? The Impact of Enlargement on the European Union', Paper Presented at the Global Fellows Forum, NYU Law School, New York: 5 April 2007. Available at: http://www.nyulawglobal.org/fellowsscholars/documents/gffsettembripaper.pdf

Short, C. (2000), 'Aid that doesn't help', *Financial Times*. 23 June. Available at: www.ft.com

Siedentop, L. (2000), *Democracy in Europe* (Harmondsworth Allen Lane/Penguin Press).

Sjursen, H. (ed.) (2006), 'What Kind of Europe? European Foreign Policy in Perspective', Special Issue of *Journal of European Public Policy* 13/2.

Smith, K. E. (2003), *European Union Foreign Policy in a Changing World* (Oxford and Malden MA: Polity).

_____ (2005), 'Enlargement and European order', in C. Hill and M. Smith (eds.), *International Relations and the European Union* (Oxford and New York: Oxford University Press): 270–91.

Smith, M. E. (1997), 'What's Wrong with the CFSP? The Politics of Institutional Reform', in P.-H. Laurent and M. Maresceau (eds.), *The State of the European Union Volume 4* (Boulder CO and Essex: Lynne Rienner and Longman): 149–76.

_____ (2003), *Europe's Foreign and Security Policy* (Cambridge and New York: Cambridge University Press).

_____ (2004), 'Institutionalization, Policy Adaptation and European Foreign Policy Cooperation', *European Journal of International Relations* 10/1: 95–136.

_____ Crowe, B., and Peterson, J. (2006), 'International Interests: The Common Foreign and Security Policy', in J. Peterson and M. Shackleton, *The Institutions of the European Union* (Oxford and New York, Oxford University Press): 252–69.

Spence, D. (ed.) (2005), *The European Commission*, 3rd edn (London: John Harper).

Steyn, M. (2006), *America Alone: The End of the World as We Know It* (London and New York: Regnery Publishing).

Stubb, A. C.-G. (2002), *Negotiating Flexibility in the European Union: Amsterdam, Nice and Beyond* (Basingstoke and New York: Palgrave).

Sullivan, M. P. (2001), *Theories of International Relations: Transition vs. Persistence* (Basingstoke and New York: Palgrave).

Tonra, B. (2001), *The Europeanisation of National Foreign Policy: Dutch, Danish and Irish Foreign Policy in the European Union* (Aldershot and Brookfield VT: Ashgate).

_____ and Christiansen, T. (eds.) (2004), *Rethinking European Union Foreign Policy* (Manchester and New York: Manchester University Press).

Torreblanca, J. I. (2001), *The Reuniting of Europe: Promises, Negotiations and Compromises* (Aldershot: Ashgate).

Wagner, W. (2006), 'Guarding the Guards. The European Convention and the Communitization of Police Co-operation', *Journal of European Public Policy* 13/8: 1230–46.

Wallace, H. (2000), 'The Policy Process', in H. Wallace and W. Wallace (eds.), *Policy-Making in the European Union* 4th edn. (Oxford and New York: Oxford University Press): 39–64.

_____ (2005), 'Exercising power and Influence in the European Union: The Roles of Member States', in S. Bulmer and C. Lesquene (eds.), *The Member States of the European Union* (Oxford and New York: Oxford University Press): 25–44.

_____ Wallace, W., and Pollack, M. (eds.) (2005), *Policy-making in the European Union*, 5th edn. (Oxford and New York: Oxford University Press).

Wallace, W. (2002), 'Where does Europe End? Dilemmas of Inclusion and Exclusion', in J. Zielonka (ed.), *Europe Unbound, Enlarging and Reshaping the Boundaries of the European Union* (London: Routledge): 78–94.

Waltz, K. N. (2002), 'Structural realism after the Cold War', in G. J. Ikenberry (ed), *America Unrivaled: the Future of the Balance of Power* (Ithaca NY and London: Cornell University Press): 9–67.

Weiler, J. H. H. (1999), *The Constitution of Europe* (Cambridge: Cambridge University Press).

Wendt, A. (1992), 'Anarchy is What States Make of It: The Social Construction of Power Politics', *International Organization* 46/3: 391–426.

Wendt, A. (1999), *Social Theory of International Politics* (Cambridge: Cambridge University Press).

Wessels, W. (1997), 'The Growth and Differentiation of Multi-Level Networks: A Corporatist Mega-Bureaucracy or an Open City?', in H. Wallace and A. Young (eds.), *Participation and Policy-making in the European Union* (Oxford: Clarendon Press): 17–41.

_____ Maurer, A., and Mittag, J. (eds.) (2003), *Fifteen Into One? The European Union and its Member States* (Manchester and New York: Manchester University Press).

White, B. (2001), *Understanding European Foreign Policy* (Basingstoke and New York: Palgrave).

Wiener, A., and Diez, T. (eds.) (2004), *European Integration Theory* (London: Oxford University Press).

Wissels, R. (2006), 'The Development of the European Neighbourhood Policy', in *Foreign Policy in Dialogue* 7/19 (Trier: University of Trier). Available at http://www.deutsche-aussenpolitik.de/newsletter/issue19.pdf

Woll, C. (2006), 'Lobbying in the European Union: From Sui Generis to a Comparative Perspective', *Journal of European Public Policy* 13/3: 456-69.

Young, A. R. (2002), *Extending European Cooperation: the European Union and the 'New' International Trade Agenda* (Manchester and New York: Manchester University Press).

Zielonka, T. (ed) (2002), *Europe Unbound: Enlarging and Reshaping the Boundaries of the European Union* (London and New York: Routledge).

Zito, A. (2000), *Creating Environmental Policy in the European Union* (Basingstoke and New York: Palgrave).

▮ INDEX

A

abortion policy, Ireland 116, 121
accession 73–6, 180, 189–90
  chronology of enlargement 185
  new member states 53, 151–2,
    187
  see also enlargements
Accession Treaties 164, 183, 186
Achen 216
Acquis communautaire 72, 75–6,
  151, 194, 198
Action Committee for the United
  States of Europe 28
Adenauer, Chancellor
  Konrad 25–6, 39
Afghanistan 139, 155, 188, 211,
  215–16
  EU missions 204
  US policy goals 219
Africa 139, 153, 204, 211
African, Caribbean and Pacific
  states (ACP) 34, 209
Agence Europe 85, 98
agenda 230
Agenda 2000; 38
agriculture 61, 116, 132, 134, 192
Agriculture and Fisheries
  Council 51
aid and development 7, 208–11
Airline security 144
Al Qaeda 139
Albania 74, 154, 189, 192, 196–7
alcohol control policy in Finland
  and Sweden 116, 121, 123
Algeria 155, 194
Allot, P. 173
Amsterdam Treaty (1997) 6, 16,
  36–8, 48–9, 139, 142–5,
  151, 170, 213, 215
  provisions Box 9.2; 183, 196
Andorra 153, 197
Anglo-Saxon tradition 81
Arab–Israeli conflict 203
Argentina 30, 203
Armenia 193–4, 197
Armstrong, K and S. Bulmer 12,
  65
Asia 153

Asia Minor 196
Asia Pacific Economic Cooperation
  (APEC) 30
Asian Tsunami 211
Aspinwall, M.
  and G. Schneider 13
  and J. Greenwood 108
Association of South-East Asian
  Nations (ASEAN) 30
asylum and refugee policy 140,
  151, 155–6
Australia 30, 116, 153
Austria 54, 77, 80, 117, 132
  accession (1995) 17, 38, 74,
    82, 181–2, 185, 187
  Kurier 98
  Länder 80
  Turkish membership 193
Avery, G. 215
Azerbaijan 193–4, 197

B

Balkans 155, 189–90, 199,
  204–5, 210
  wars 37, 141
  see also Western Balkans
Baltic (EU) states 153
Barnier, Michel 162
Barroso, José Manual 47, 59, 170,
  225
Barysch, K. et al 192
'Battle of Paris' 25
Baumgartner, F. 108
Baylis, J. and J. Roper 217
Belarus 194–5, 197
Belgium 10, 74–7, 82, 117,
  150
  Council of Ministers 54, 80
  Dernière 98
  Laeken meeting of European
    Council (2001) 161
  Presidency 148
  Schengen Agreement 25
Benelux states 26, 75, 141
Berlin
  relocation of capital 75
  Wall, fall of (1989) 36
Bindi, F. and M. Cisci 75

biometric
  data on visa applicants Box 7.1;
    144, 152
  technology 140
Biscop, S. 217
Black Sea region 192
Blair, Tony 218
Booker, C 124
Borrell, Josep 210
Börzel, T. 227
Bosnia 74, 192, 213, 216
Bosnia Herzegovina 74, 189,
  196–7
Brazil 30, 95
Bretherton, C. and J. Vogler 218
Brunei 153
Brussels 85, 96, 98, 103, 224, 229
  lobbying, Box 5.2; 96–7
  Rond Point Schuman 85
  see also Belgium
budget, for research, regional and
  social spending 99, 102, 130
Bulgaria 47, 54, 77–8, 82
  accession EU (2007) 17, 38,
    74, 185
Bulmer, S. and C. Lequesne 88
Bundesbank 36, 66
Bunia (Congo) 215
Burchill, S. et al 216
Bush, President George
  W. 214–15, 219
BusinessEurope 95, 108
Buttiglione, Rocco 59, 170

C

Cafruny, A. and M. Ryner 208
California 211
Cameroon 212
Canada 116, 147, 153, 188, 197,
  212, 226
  North American Free Trade
    Agreement (NAFTA) 30
Canary Islands 153–4
CAP *see* Common Agricultural
  Policy (CAP)
capital, movement of 116
Caporaso, J. 132
Carlsnaes, W. 202

Carribbean countries 153
Caspian Sea 196
Cassis de Dijon case (1979) 62
Catalonia 174
Central America 153
Central and Eastern Europe 182,
    187–9, 194, 203
  applications to join EU 38
  competition policy 125
  EU aid programmes 210–11
  EU borders 213
  passport-free zone 141–2
Centre for European Policy
    Studies 96
CFSP *see* Common Foreign and
    Security Policy (CFSP)
Charter of Fundamental Rights 9,
    39
  Box 8.1; Nice Treaty
    (2001) 161, 164–6
Chechnya 210
Checkel, J. 13, 88
chemical industry 95, 106, 132
child care 121
China 30, 106, 202, 205–6, 212,
    231
Chirac, President Jacques 119,
    210
Christian Democrats 59
Christian religion 196
Churchill, Winston 24–5
CIA 149
civil liberties groups,
    terrorism 148
civil servants working
    overtime 125
civil society 93, 133
climate change 50, 69, 230
Coal and Steel Community 27, 31
Cockfield, Lord 47
Coen, D. 97
Cohesion Fund 78–9, 130
cohesion policy 38, 79, 128–32,
    181, 192
Cold War 22, 24–6, 36–40, 139,
    141, 188, 215
College of Commissioners 46–7,
    50, 170
Commission 5, 8, 15, 40, 46–50,
    87–8, 170, 196, 198
  accession negotiations 183–4
  administrative (the
    bureaucracy) 46, 60
  advisory groups 89

bilateral economic
    agreements 212
business case studies 106
cabinet appointments 47
Common Foreign and Security
    Policy 68, 213
competition policy 125–6
consultations 101
development policies 96
Directorates-General
    (DGs) 47–8, 126
drafting legislation 105, 108
drug-trafficking 148–9
Economic and Monetary
    Union 36
enlargement 189
European Court of Justice
    (ECJ) 120
European Parliament (EP) 37,
    103, 171
external embassies and
    international
    organizations 96–8
guardian of the treaties 167
Hague Programme 145
influence 65
international trade talks 32
internet consultations 106
Jacques Delors 35
legal right of initiative 64
legislative initiative 169
lobbying 101–2, 107–8
mergers 125–6, 212
NGOs 101–2
policies, Box 3.1; 50–1
political fortunes 34
portfolio assignments 47
powers 33, 48, 167
President 47, 60, 170, 218
resignation (1992) 37, 61
scope and capacity 226
second and third pillars 37,
    141
size and role 40, 68
terrorism 148
Treaty of Accession 186
Treaty Reform and conferred
    powers 48
unelected nature 170–1
Commissioners 32, 46–7, 61, 68,
    78, 100, 170
  for Competition 126
  for development and trade
    policy 218
  for External Affairs 214

Committees
  of Agricultural Organizations in
    the EU (COPA) 95
  of Independent Experts 168
  of Permanent Representatives
    (Coreper) 32, 52, 55–7,
    143
  of the Regions (CoR) 66, 80,
    100, 162
Common Agricultural Policy
    (CAP) 31–2, 38, 99, 102,
    128–9, 132, 169, 207
  spending breakdown,
    Table 6.2; 128, 130
Common Foreign and Security
    Policy (CFSP) 4–6, 17, 37,
    65, 78, 83, 98, 168–9, 181,
    203–4, 207, 213–15, 217
  pillars 171
Common Market *see* European
    Economic Community
    (EEC)
'*Compared to What?*' 8
competition policy 125–6, 135
Competitiveness Council 51
conditionality, Box 9.1; 180
constitution 16, 80, 98, 163
  patriotism 174
Constitutional Charter 161,
    163–4
  Box 8.1; 160
Constitutional Treaty
    (2004) 15–16, 39, 76, 84,
    98, 156, 161, 163, 175, 198,
    214–15, 224, 230–2
  Box 1.4; 8–9
  rejection by French and Dutch
    voters (2005) 67, 161, 163,
    215, 230–2
Convention on the Future of
    Europe (2003– 4) 9, 39, 84,
    161–3
  Box 8.2; 160–3, 165
Cooper, R. 215, 219
Copenhagen criteria (1993)
    Box 9.2; 182–3, 189, 196,
    198
Coreper *see* Committee of
    Permanent Representatives
    (Coreper)
Corporate Europe
    Observatory 102
Costa v *ENEL* (1964) 62
Cotonou agreement 209–10

Council of Ministers 5, 8, 32,
    34–5, 37, 39, 46, 50–8, 64,
    67, 83–4, 89, 109, 196–7
  applications for
    membership 186
  Belgium regional ministers 10
  Charter of Fundamental
    Rights 165
  co-decision procedure 167–9
  competition policy 125–6
  Convention on the Future of
    Europe 161
  Copenhagen (1993) 183
  criminal law 148
  decisions Box 3.3; 53, 56, 166
  EU enlargement 88
  Foreign Ministers (High
    Representative) 213–15, 218
  framework decision 172
  Framework Decisions
    (FDs) 172
  interest groups 100
  Intergovernmental Conferences
    (IGCs) 35, 84
  intergovernmentalism 171–3
  Länder ministers 80
  legislative powerhouse 171
  Lisbon (2000) 123
  national delegations 100
  national preferences 85
  power Box 8.4; 174
  Presidency 9, 56–7, 83, 89,
    182–4, 214
  REACH Regulation on
    Chemicals 106
  Secretariat 51–2
  summits
    (2000) 75
    Box 3.7; 64, 166
    Lahti (Finland) (2006) 210
  terrorism 148
  tours de table 72, 84
  transposition 120
  Treaties 50–1, 65
  Treaty Reform and conferred
    powers 48–9
  views 64
  voting 78, 225, 228
    Table 3.2; 53–5
  working groups 89
  see also qualified majority voting
    (QMV)
Court of Auditors 66
Court of First Instance 61
Cowles, M.G. and S. Curtis 217

crime-fighting 139, 145–51
criminal law 139
  and counter-terrorism 148–51
Croatia 74, 77, 98, 153, 196–7
  accession (2005) 38, 185, 190,
    192
customs union 31–2, 35, 209
Cyprus 38, 54, 74, 78, 117, 150
  accession (2004) 38, 82, 185
  Turkish Republic of
    Northern 193
Czech Republic 54, 74, 76–7,
    81–2, 185

D

Dannreuther, R. 212
  and J. Peterson 217
de Gaulle, President Charles 25,
    31–4, 39
de Vries, Gijs 149
death penalty 124
defence cooperation 75
defence policy 45–69, 86
Delors, President Jacques 35–6,
    40, 226
Delors Report (1989) 36
demandeur Box 4.1; 72
democratic deficit 161
  Box 8.1; 160
demos 173–4
Denmark 54, 77, 80–3, 98, 117,
    151
  accession EC (1973) 17, 34,
    74, 78, 185, 187
  Maastricht Treaty referendums
    (1992) and (1993) 37
d'Estaing, President Valéry
    Giscard 73, 162
diplomats 204, 215
Dohan Round of WTO
    negotiations 128, 209
drugs 148–50
Duchéne, F. 27

E

Eastern European countries 141,
    199
  see also Central and Eastern
    Europe
Economic and Monetary Union
    (EMU) 31, 36–7, 72, 117,
    126–7, 135

Economic and Social Committee
    (ESC) 66, 100, 162
Economist 56
ECSC see European Coal and Steel
    Community (ECSC)
Ecuador 153
EDC see European Defence
    Community (EDC)
education 121
Egypt 194
Eilstrup-Sangiovanni, M. 13
Fising, R. 101, 108
Elman, C. and M.F. Elman 216
Elysée Treaty (1963) 73
emissions trading scheme 50
'Empty Chair Crisis' 25
energy policy 95, 121, 133, 230
enlargements 17–18, 73, 89,
    179–200
  (1995) 78, 185
  (2004 and 2007) 17, 78, 88,
    187–90, 193, 198, 225
  aspirant countries 198
  chronology of Box 9.3; 185
  fatigue 198
  Figure 4.1; 73–4
  forgotten 193–4
  institutional impact, Box 3.9;
    67–8, 100, 127
  problems 109
  transformative power 182
Enlightenment, experience of
    the 196
environment 65, 95–6, 102, 106,
    116–17, 205
  and social policy 80, 132
equal pay 132
Erhard, Ludwig 29
Estonia 54, 74, 77, 82, 185, 210
euro 7, 34, 75, 83, 127, 195, 230,
    232–3
Euro-Mediterranean
    Partnership 194, 209
Eurobarometer (2007) 82
Eurodac database 155
Europe 175, 196–9, 230–1
European
  anthem 224, 231
  citizens 232
  democracy 173–4
  intergovernmental
    organizations 196–7
  NGOs 99
  non-profit organizations 95–6
  organizations Box 9.7; 196–7

European (*continued*)
power internationally 218
refugee crisis 141
regulation, national
approaches 83
security strategy Box 10.4; 217
European Arrest Warrant
(EAW) 144, 149–50, 173,
212
Box 8.4; 150, 171–2
European Atomic Energy
Community (Euratom) 16,
25, 28
European Candle
Manufacturers 94
European Central Bank (ECB) 36,
66, 127, 135, 232
European Chemical Industry
Council 94
European Citizen Action Service
(ECAS) 96, 99
European Coal and Steel
Community (ECSC) 11,
15–16, 26–8, 31–3, 64–5
European Commission *see*
Commission
European Community (EC) 4–5,
23, 28–33, 39
Charter 23
commercial policy 32, 126,
208–9
Box 10.1; 208–9
enlargements
(1973) 34, 78, 129
(1980s) 78
(1990) 185
foreign ministers meeting
(1966) 25
Humanitarian Aid by region,
Figure 10.1; 211
including Economic and
Monetary Union 37
law 33, 164, 168
overseas territories
provisions 25
powers 25
six founding states (1952)
(Germany, France, Italy,
Netherlands, Belgium and
Luxembourg) 17, 73–4, 164,
187
Turkey 231
European Community
Humanitarian Office
(ECHO) 211

European Consumers
Organization (BEUC) 96, 99
European Convention on Human
Rights (ECHR) Box 8.3;
164–5
European Court of Justice (ECJ) 5,
10, 15, 25, 33, 46, 61–4, 87,
142–3, 167–8, 212–13
Charter of Fundamental Rights
of the European Union 165
Constitutional Charter 161,
164
first pillar 152, 168
foreign and security policy 67
human rights 164
infringement cases 157
institutional triangle 232
interpretations of primacy and
direct effect 164
Maastricht Treaty third
pillar 141
passenger name records 144
single market 116
Table 3.1; 48–9
Treaty Reform and conferred
powers 49
US Supreme Court 63
European Defence Community
(EDC) 27–9, 31, 33, 203,
233
European Development Fund
(EDF) 209
European Economic Area
(EEA) 180, 193–4
Box 9.1; 180, 187
European Economic Community
(EEC) (Common Market) 4,
11, 31, 78, 126
establishment (1956) 29
founders 187, 202
European Environmental
Bureau 99
European Evidence Warrant
(EEW) 150
European Food Safety
Authority 132
European Free Trade Association
(EFTA) 30
European Lift Components
Association 94
European Monetary System
(EMS) 34, 75
European Neighbourhood Policy
(ENP) 142, 144, 154–5,
194–5, 198, 212

Figure 9.1; 190–2
European Ombudsman 162
European Parliament (EP) 5,
32–3, 40, 46, 51, 58–61, 87,
144
accountability to voters 171
applicant states 224
bargaining power 64
co-decision procedure 37,
106–8, 143, 152, 167–9
Common Foreign and Security
Policy 68
democratic
decision-making 175
elections 8, 61, 106, 170,
174
by universal suffrage 167
first direct (1979) 34
EU 9, 35, 37, 88
influence 65
intergroups 103
Justice and Home Affairs
proposals 143
law-making 169
linguistic challenges 8
lobbying 103
members (MEPs) *see* MEPs
national parties 59
powers 33, 67
Box 3.4; 59–61
President 170
proposed biotechnology
patenting directive 105
rapporteur 93, 108
Box 5.1; 171
REACH Regulation on
Chemicals 106
role 61, 142, 183
seats 78
second and third pillars 37,
141
services directive 59
standing Committees 59
on Civil Liberties, Justice and
Home Affairs 143
Treaty of Accession 183, 186
Treaty Reform and conferred
powers 49
European Police College
(CEPOL) 146
European Police Office (Europol)
Box 7.5; 145
European Policy Centre 96
European Political Cooperation
(EPC) 34, 203, 213, 217

European Public Affairs
    Consultancies Association
    (EPACA) 102, 104
European Public Health
    Alliance 96
European Refugee Fund
    (ERF) 155
European Report 139
European Security and Defence
    Policy (ESDP) 15, 37, 204,
    213, 215–16
European Security Strategy
    (ESS) 217
European Trade Union
    Confederation (ETUC) 95,
    108
European Union (EU) 35–8, 116
    absorption capacity Box 9.1;
        180, 198
    adjudication 120–3, 166
    administrative spending 129
    Agreements 188–9
    assent procedure 60
    background 1–21
    benchmarking, Box 6.1; 117,
        121
    borders 139, 151–6, 193,
        195–6, 198, 212–13
    budget 61, 79–80, 88, 96,
        98 9, 102, 128, 192
        bargaining Box 6.2; 118 19
        breakdown of spending
            Figure 6.1; 128–9
    candidate countries 77–8, 180,
        189, 191, 211
    citizenship 174–5
    co-decision procedure 167–70,
        174
        see also Council of Ministers;
            European Court of Justice;
            European Parliament
    Community method
        of decision-making 142, 232
            Box 6.4; 122, 133–4, 167,
            204
    comparative politics
        approach 12, 227–8
    constitutionalism 15, 167–8,
        174
        and democracy in the
            EU 159–76
        without a
            Constitution 161–3
    constructivism 13–14, 88, 218,
        229

consultation procedures 60
conventions, two kinds
    Box 8.3; 165
cooperation procedure 60
    Box 3.6; 35, 62, 183
creation (1992) 4
decision gridlock, Box 4.3;
    88–9
decision-making 89, 92–3,
    100, 109, 198, 205, 229
    citizen participation 135
    modes for enlargement 182
democratic deficit 37, 108
dependence on Russian
    energy 205, 210
determining features 73–86
directives 117
    draft 101
    proposed biotechnology
        patenting 105
    services (2006) 81
    software patenting 103
dumping of foreign goods 95
economy 78–81, 117, 123 4,
    205, 213
EU-level training initiatives 156
explaining 226–9
federal states (Germany, Austria
    and Belgium) 80
foreign capitals, missions
    in 214–15
four freedoms (free movement
    for people, goods, services
    and money) 116, 139, 165
functional constitution 160–1,
    231–2
global actor 94–8, 201–21
global power 202
governance 174, 223
    multilevel 87, 130, 225
        Box 1.5; 10–11, 17
    of a state 10, 160
hierarchy 228
history 23
information and alliances 105
integration 4, 6, 10, 15, 23, 28,
    32, 46, 72–5, 86, 116, 135,
    156, 175, 181, 189, 227–8,
    233
    history 39
    interpreting Box 2.1; 23
    negative and positive 207
    preference 81–4
    theories of (Table 1.1)
        13–14, 98

international power 204
joining singly or together
    Box 9.6; 188, 190
large states 76–7
limits for 195–6
managing business 86
medium states 76–7
micro states 76–7
mini-states 197
    see also Andorra; Holy See;
        Liechtenstein; Monaco;
        San Marino
Minister for Foreign Affairs
    (MFA) 9, 214 15
    and national budgets Table 6.1;
        118–19
    and NATO, double race to
        membership 188
    negotiations 86
    net contributors club 80
    organized interests 92–111
        overview, Table 5.1;
            93–4
    path dependency 12, 87
    policies 50, 77, 88, 130
        comparing types 133–4
            Table 6.4; 133–4
        competencies Box 6.3;
            120–1
        in national
            administrations 86
        networks 13–14, 87, 105,
            228
        and politics 92
        process, three modes
            Box 6.4; 121–6
    political system 87
    political union 36
    readmission (deportation)
        agreements 154–5
    recalcitrate states 224
    Russia Box 10.2; 209 10
    secure constitutional
        foundation 230–1
    sharing power and seeking
        consensus 224–5
    small countries 57, 76–7, 204,
        207
    sociological/cultural
        approach 13–14, 229
    soft power 219
    states, four clusters 76–7
    structures 66–7, 80
    studying 4
    subsidies 80

European Union (EU) (continued)
three-pillar structure 141, 157,
168–9, 171, 173, 203, 231
Box 1.2; 4–6, 16, 37
first 37, 143, 152, 168,
212–13
third pillar 139–45, 156
transformative power 192
unitary states 80
European Voice 65, 98, 210
European Youth Forum 96
Europeanization 156
Box 4.1; 72, 84
Europol 144–5, 147, 149, 154,
157
and Federal Bureau of
investigation (FBI) Box 7.5;
147
Europol Drugs Unit 147
Europolitics 98
Eurosceptics 232
Eurozone (Germany, France and
Italy) 117, 127, 232
Box 6.1; 124
Everts, S. 204
Exchange Rate Mechanism
(ERM) 34
experimentation and
change 14–18, 223–4
external
embassies and international
organizations 96–8
internal policies 211–12
spending 129
External Action Service 214–15
External Affairs Council 57
extradition 144
ExxonMobil 102

F

families 121, 157
Farrell, M. 224
Federal Bureau of Investigation
(FBI), Box 7.5; 147, 149
federalism 24, 117, 231–3
Europe 230–2
nation-states 225–6, 232
Financial Times 75, 98, 125, 130,
135, 219
Finland 77, 80, 86, 117, 120
accession EU (1995) 17, 38,
74, 82, 181–2, 185, 187
alcohol control policy 121, 123
Council of Ministers 54

EU Council Presidency 57,
173, 210
fisheries policy 194
food and drink sector 69, 95,
99
foreign intelligence services 149
foreign policy 45–69, 78, 121,
202–6, 208–16, 231
decisions Box 10.3; 212–14
three systems Table
10.1l 205–6
three-pillar structure, second
pillar 37, 140–1, 213
Framework Decisions (FDs) 140,
143, 148, 172
France 23, 27, 74, 76–7, 82, 95,
120
Assemblée Nationale 167
budget 119
CAP spending 130
chemical industry 106
constitution 166
Constitutional Treaty
referendum (2005) 9, 37, 39,
67, 161, 198, 215, 230–3
Council of Ministers 54
Economic and Monetary
Union 117
economic and security
interests 25
EU policy 233
foreign policy leadership 206
Fourth Republic 31
geographical and political
priorities 195
global perspective 204
intergration 83
intervention in Bunia
(Congo) 215
interventionalist EU 81
Le Monde 98
Maastricht Treaty 37
overseas departments 196
potential members 198
President of the Republic 57,
167, 173
Qualified Majority Votes 25
regions 96
Schengen Agreement
(1985) 25, 141, 152
terrorism 148–9
Turkish membership 193
veto on admissions (1963) 185
world's poorest countries 208

Franco-German relations
22–6, 31, 36, 39–40, 73,
75
free trade agreements 208
Free Trade Area (FTA) 30
Friends of the Earth Europe 102
Frontex (Frontièrieures) 154

G

Galtung, J. 203
Gaza 216
gender equality 116–17, 132
General Affairs and External
Relations Council
(GAERC) 51–2
Box 3.2; 52
General Agreement on Tariffs and
Trade (GATT) 29, 32
General Electric 126
Genetically Modified Organisms
(GMOs) 132
Geneva Convention (1951) 140,
155
Georgia 194, 197
German Federal Constitutional
Court 164
Germany 23, 25–6, 74, 76–7, 80,
98, 187, 226
Berlin 75
budget 119
CAP spending 130
central bank (Bundesbank) 36,
66
Chancellor 170
chemical industry 106
constitution 166
constitutional 'Basic Law'
(1949) 164
Constitutional Treaty 9
Council of Ministers 54
Council Presidency (2007) 58,
231
Economic and Monetary
Union 36, 117
economy 26, 28, 81
EU legislation 132
European Arrest Warrant 150,
172
European competitiveness 40
Federal Republic of
(FRG) 23–5
Frankfurter Allgemeine
Zeitung 98

geographical and political
  priorities 195
global perspective 204
governance 225
integration 83
Länder 80, 96–7
liberalization of trade 29
Maastricht Treaty 37
MEPs 106
NATO 28
political assertiveness 40
post war 24, 206–7
Prüm Convention 145
Qualified Majority Votes 25
regions 24–6, 100
remilitarization 28
reunification 75, 185, 187
Schengen Agreement
  (1985) 25, 141
sexual harassment 132
terrorism 148–9
Turkish membership 193
see also Franco-German
  relations
Ginsberg, R. 203
globalization Box 1.4; 10, 24, 39
Goetz, K.H. 81
'goldplating' policy Box 6.5; 125
Gorbachev, Mikhail 203
governmental organizations 94
Grabbe, H. 182, 188
Greece 35, 74, 76–8, 82, 120,
  132
  accession (1981) 17, 35, 78,
    190
  accession applications, (1975
    and 1979) 181–2, 185, 190
  cohesion status 78
  Council of Ministers 54
  Economic and Monetary
    Union 117
  Eurozone 127
  refugee status 155
Greek Cypriots 193
Greenpeace 96
Groups
  of Eight (G-8) 214
  of Six (G-6) 157
Guadeloupe 196
Guiraudon, V. and E. Jileva 152
Gulf War 203

H

Haas, Ernst 11, 13, 23, 217

Hagemann, S. and J. De
  Clerck-Sachsse 57, 78, 88
The Hague
  Europol and Eurojust 145
  Programme Box 7.4; 144–5,
    156
Hallstein, Walter 32
Hayes-Renshaw, F. and H.
  Wallace 55, 56
health
  care 121
  patient groups 105
Heisbourg, D. 217
Heisenberg, D. 88
Herzog Convention 165
Herzog, President Roman 165
Hill, C. 205, 218
  and M. Smith 202
Hoffmann, S. 11
Holy See (Vatican See) 153, 197
home affairs policy 86
Honeywell 126
Hong Kong 153–4
Hooghe, L and G. Marks 10, 17,
  87
House of Commons 166
House of Lords 78
'How it Really Works' 8
human rights 96, 164–6, 202
Human Rights Watch 96, 202
human trafficking 140
humanitarian and development
  aid 98
Hungary 54, 74, 76–7, 82, 185

I

Iceland 30, 188, 194, 196–7,
  199, 211
  EU border management 151
  European Economic Area
    (EEA) 180, 193
  Schengen Agreement 25
immigration 50, 151–5, 157
Indonesia, Asia Pacific Economic
  Cooperation (APEC) 30
industrial markets 32
industrial relations 121
institutionalism 12–14, 87, 227,
  229
institutions 12, 15, 38, 45–69,
  92–3, 133–5, 146, 174–5,
  197, 227–8
  accountability 170–1
  bodies, Box 3.8; 64, 66

distribution of functions 167
  enlargement 182
  infrastructure 145
  key 171
  and member states 225
  national preferences 85
  paradox 182–4
  powers 164, 181, 224
  reform 230
  staff 109
  supranational 11–12, 87, 133
  Treaty Reform and conferred
    powers, Table 3.1; 9, 48–9,
    58
  triangle between Commission,
    Council and EP 232
  see also Commission; Council;
    Court; European Parliament
Intergovernmental Conferences
  (IGCs) 15, 35, 156, 173,
    182–3, 230
  (1990) 36–7
  (1996– 7) 142
  (1997) Amsterdam 16
  (2000) 37–8, 84
  (2003) 39
  (2007) 231
  Box 4.2; 83–4
  European Council 35, 84
intergovernmentalism 10, 13–14,
  23, 33, 67, 87, 133–4,
  171–5, 209, 229, 231
  member states 227
  method of policy-making 122
internal market 35, 129, 208
international
  associations 95
  law 62
  NGOs 99
  relations approaches 11–12
  trade 28–9, 46, 116
International Fund for Animal
  Welfare 96
International Organizations
  (IOs) 96–7, 226
International Relations (IR) theory 13
Interpol 147
introduction 3–21
Iran 193, 205, 213–14, 219
Iraq 155, 193, 202, 207,
  216–19
Ireland 26, 77, 82
  abortion policy 116, 121
  accession EC (1973) 17, 34,
    74, 78, 185, 187

Ireland (*continued*)
cohesion status 78–9
Council of Ministers 54
Economic and Monetary Union
36? 117
EU border manaement 151
Nice Treaty referenda, (2001)
and (2005) 37
Schengen Agreement 25
terrorism 148
UK free-travel zone 151
Islam 192–3
Israel 153, 194
Italy 74–7, 82, 106, 120, 132,
195, 204
CAP spending 130
Council of Ministers 54
Economic and Monetary
Union 117
EU aerial and marine
support 154
European Arrest Warrant 150
Lampedusa 153
Mezzogiorno 78
Qualified Majority Votes 25
terrorism 148–9

J

Japan 30, 98, 106, 153
Jeffrey, C. 100
Jenkins, Roy 34
Joint Terrorism Task Forces 149
Jordan, ENP 194
Jørgensen, K.E. 202, 213, 216–17
Judge, D. and D. Earnshaw 108
jurisdiction 120–3
justice 86
Justice and Home Affairs
(JHA) 4–6, 17, 37, 138–9,
145–6, 203, 212
Council 152–3, 155
democratic deficit 142
intergovernmentalism 173
legislation 157
pillars of EU 141, 143, 168–9,
171
policy making 142, 152, 156,
173
Box 7.2; 142–3
terrorism 148
Justus Lipsius 85

K

Kaunert, C. 150
Kazakhstan, OSCE 197
Kerr, Sir John 162
Key concepts and terms, Boxes
1.5; 6, 8, 10
5.1; 93, 99, 108
6.1; 116–17, 120–1, 124
7.1; 140, 143, 148, 151
8.1; 161
9.1; 180, 182, 186–7, 198
key policies 115–37
Kissinger, Henry 214
Kohl, Chancellor Helmut 73
Korean War (1950) 28
Kosovo 192, 215
Krasner, S. 12
Kyrgyzstan 197

L

Laatikainen, K.V. and
K.E.Smith 202
labour, movement of 116
Laffan, Brigid
and Alexander Stubb 71–91
et al. 224
Landmarks 94–6
languages 73, 97
Box 1.7; 8, 17–18, 50
Latvia 54, 74, 77, 82
accession (2004) 185
law-making 75, 139
laws 33, 62, 120
and obligations 75–6
Lebanon 194
Lefebure, P. and E. Langneau 98
legal system 33, 37–9, 62
legislation 7, 46, 53, 101, 157,
169
Box 3.5; 59–61
on criminal procedure 150
versus execution 119–20
legitimacy 22, 61, 228
Leonard, M. 219
Lewis, J. 13, 55–7
Libya 155, 194–5
Liechtenstein 30, 180, 193, 197
Lindberg, L. 23
and S.A. Scheingold 11
Lithuania 54, 74, 77, 185
Lobby Control 102
lobbying 92–111

in Brussels and Washington,
Box 5.2; 96–7
Commission 101–2
REACH Regulation on
Chemicals 106–7
Local Authorities 66
Lomé agreement (1975) 34
London terrorist attacks 152, 212
Luxembourg 33, 57, 74, 82, 103,
120, 229
Council of Ministers 52, 55
Economic and Monetary
Union 117
Prüm Convention 145
Reform Treaty (2007) 163
Schengen Agreement 25
see also European Court of
Justice
Luxembourg Compromise 25, 33

M

Maastricht Treaty (1992) 4–5,
36–7, 39, 48–9, 207
Article 36 Committee
(CATS) 143
asylum policy 155
Committee of the Regions 66
Common Foreign and Security
Policy (CFSP) 203, 213
criteria 127
Economic and Monetary
Union 31, 126
EU pillars 37, 139, 141, 152,
168–9
European Court of Justice 62
Europol 145
foreign and security policy 204
intergovernmentalism 173
Justice and Home Affairs
(JHA) 203
Länder ministers 80
post-Maastricht period 37
Qualified Majority Voting
(QMV) 214
Treaty on European Union 16,
165
Macau 153–4
MacCormick, N. 174
Macedonia (FYROM) 74, 77, 190,
196–7
accepted as candidate (2006)
Box 9.1; 38, 192
application for
membership 185, 190

civil war (2001) 213
Madrid terrorist attacks
    (2004) 148–9, 212
Majone, Giandomenico 124, 225
Malaysia 153
Malta 25, 55, 74, 82, 117, 120,
    153–4
    accession (2004) 38, 185
Manners, I. 215–16, 218
market
    Box 1.3; 7, 117
    building 124–7, 133–4
    correcting and cushioning
        policies 128–34
    institutions 24
Marshall Plan (1947) 25
    Box 2.2; 24–5, 37
Martinique 196
Mearsheimer, J.J. 216
Mediterranean states 78, 181,
    190, 210
member states 53, 71–91,
    151–2, 227
    after (2004) 204
    and candidate countries by size,
        Table 4.1; 77
    explaining engagement 86–8
    founders 75, 81
    Gross Domestic Product (2005),
        Table 4.2; 78–9
    Gross National Income 7,
        78–80
    institutions 225
    interaction 85
    path to Box 9.4; 186
    potential 189–92, 197, 199
    power 224
    relations with 87, 226–7
    support for, Table 4.3; 81–3
MEPs (Members of the European
    Parliament) 12, 32–3, 58–9,
    68, 96, 100–1, 103, 105, 162
    control of 171
    power 142
    terrorism 148
    votes 228
Mercosur (Southern Cone
    Common Market) 30
Merke, Angela 210
Meunier, S. and K. McNamara 87,
    228
Mexico 30, 98, 208
Microsoft 126, 134
Middle East 192, 204, 210, 219
migration 45–69, 139

military 204, 215
Milward, Alan 11, 23
Ministries of Foreign Affairs 86
Mitterrand, President François 36,
    73, 181
Moldova 194, 197
Mollet, Guy 25
Monaco 153, 197
monetary policy 116–17, 133,
    135
Monnet, Jean 26–8, 202
Montenegro 74, 190, 192, 196–7
Moravcsik, Andrew 11–12, 23,
    87, 174, 216, 227
Morgan, G. 218
Morocco 153–5, 194
multinationals 95, 229
Munich, Olympic Games, terrorist
    attack (1972) 141
Mutual Legal Assistance 144

N

names 4
    Box 1.1; 4, 16
national
    business organizations 95
    chambers of commerce 95
    concepts of identity,
        sovereignty 10, 22, 174, 204,
        227
    and EU policies, differences
        between 118–23
    fingerprints and DNA data 145
    foreign policies 202, 206–7
    governments 135, 172
    interests 23–4
    nationhood 174
    pension systems 132
    preferences 83
    representatives 85
    visa and asylum policy Box 7.1;
        139–40
National Geographic 18
NATO *see* North Atlantic Treaty
    Organisation (NATO)
Neighbourhood Policy 199
Nelsen, B. and A. Stubb 13
neofunctionalism 11, 13–14,
    217, 227
Nestlé 95
Netherlands 29, 74–7, 80, 82,
    117, 150

Constitutional Treaty rejection
    (2005) 37, 39, 67, 75, 161,
    198, 215, 230–2
    Council of Ministers 54
    EU legislation 132
    European Arrest Warrant 150
    Schengen Agreement 25
New Zealand 153, 196
9/11/2001; 148–50, 156, 212,
    217
1970s, difficult decade 34–5
Nice
    European Council (2000) 25,
        53, 75, 161, 164
        Charter of Fundamental
            Rights of the European
            Union 165
        Table 3.2; 25, 53–5
    Treaty (2001) 16, 37–9, 48–9,
        53, 57–8, 76, 84, 142, 198,
        215, 230–1
        Charter of Fundamental
            Rights of the European
            Union Box 8.1; 161,
            164–6
        European Commission 198
        trade in services 126
Non-Governmental Organizations
    (NGOs) 18, 96, 99, 101–2,
    108–9, 162, 202
non tariff barriers 117
Nordic states
    accession 81
    see also Finland; Sweden
North Africa 196, 210
North American Free Trade
    Agreement (NAFTA)
    (1992) 30, 124
North Atlantic Treaty Organisation
    (NATO) 32, 188, 203, 213,
    215, 226
    EU relationship 188
    European security 192
    Germany 28
    membership 28, 187–8, 190,
        193
        Box 9.5; 187–8
    peacekeeping force 215–16
    Yugoslavia 190
North Korea 205, 216, 219
North Rhine Westphalia 96–7
Norway
    EU border management 151
    European Economic Area 180,
        193

Norway (continued)
    European Free Trade
        Association 30
    European intergovernmental
        organizations 196–7
    membership application 34,
        185, 199
        Box 9.3; 193–4
    NATO membership 188
    referenda (1972 and 1994) 34,
        38, 185
    Schengen Agreement 25
nuclear diplomacy towards
    Iran 205
Nugent, N. 50, 212
Nuttall, S. 213
Nye Jr. J.S. 219

O

Occhipinti, J. 144, 146
occupational health and
    safety 116–17
Official Journal 94
Open Method of Coordination
    (OMC) 121–3
Organization for European
    Economic Cooperation
    (OEEC) 28–9
Organization for Security and
    Cooperation in Europe
    (OSCE) 196–7, 203
Organized Crime Threat
    Assessment 147

P

Pacific Rim countries 30
Palestine Authority 194
pan-European
    associations 92, 94–5, 101,
        105
    policy 99
Paraguay 30
Paris Treaty (1950) 15, 164
Paris–Bonn axis 73
passarelle 142
Passenger Name Record
    (PNR) 144
passports 144, 157
Patten, Commissioner Chris 205,
    207, 210–11
pensions 121

Permanent Representation 55, 84,
    86
Petersberg tasks 215
Peterson, J. 11–12, 59, 170, 228
    and E. Bomberg 12, 133
    and M. Pollack (2003) 202
    and M, Shackleton 69
pharmaceuticals 105, 133
Philippines, Asia Pacific Economic
    Cooperation (APEC) 30
Pierson, , P. 12, 228
Pineau, Christian 25
Poland 54, 76–7, 81–2, 195,
    204, 224
    accession (2004) 185
    cohesion funds 130
    Council of Ministers 76
    European Arrest Warrant 150,
        172
    Ukraine as member 197–8
Police Chiefs Task Force
    (PCTF) 146
police cooperation 78
policies
    internal security 138–58
    process 64, 86
policy-making 81, 85, 89, 93, 122
Political and Security
    Committee 215, 217
Pollack, M. 12, 65
poor regions, Table 6.3; 129–31
Portugal 77, 82, 117, 120, 132
    accession (1986) 17, 35, 74,
        78, 181, 185, 187, 190
    anti-terrorism laws 148
    cohesion status 78
    Council of Ministers 54
    dictatorial regime 26, 35
Post-War Settlement 24–31
poverty 78, 121
power-sharing and
    consensus 14–18, 19, 64,
        66–7
powers, checks and balances,
    separation of 166–7
practical significance Box 1.3;
    6–7
prison administration 121
private
    economic interests 94–5
    organizations 94
    stakeholders 135
Procter & Gamble 95
Prüm Convention (2005) 143,
    145, 157

public
    health 96, 121
    interest bodies 94–6
    policy 12–13, 117, 228
Puchala, D.J. 4
Putin, President Vladimir 195,
    210

Q

Qualified Majority Voting
    (QMV) 25, 35, 37–40, 53,
        56, 83, 142–3, 145, 152,
        214, 225, 231, 233
    Box 2.2; 33, 53
    Council of Ministers 66, 174

R

Rapid Reaction Forces 215
REACH (Registration, Evaluation,
    Authorization, and
    Restriction of Chemicals)
    Regulation on Chemicals,
    lobbying 105–7, 132
    Box 5.4; 105, 132, 168
Redmond, J. 192
Rees, W. 214
Reform Treaty (2007) 5, 9, 16, 39,
    47–9, 51, 53, 59–60, 75, 81,
    84, 143, 145, 156–7, 198,
    215, 230–1
    institutional reforms 218
    Justice and Home Affairs 157
    Qualified Majority Voting 25
    recalcitrate states 224
refugees see asylum and refugee
    policy
region-to-region agreements 209
regional and economic integration,
    Box 2.4; 30–1, 224
regions
    governments 92, 99
    representatives 96–7
relations
    between Russia, China, and
        India 231
    with neighbours Box 10.2;
        209–10
    with US 219
Renaissance 196
Rice, Condoleezza 218
Rieger, E. 128
Rifkin, J. 219

Risse, T. 229
role in world politics 230
Romania 54, 74, 76–8, 82
    accession EU (2007) 17, 38,
        185
    Commissioners 47
Rome Treaties (1957) 4, 16, 23,
        25, 31, 33, 48–9, 61, 124,
        126, 164, 196, 203
Rosamond, B. 11
Rosenfeld, M. 160
Roth, K. 202
Ruhr problem 24–6
Russia 187–8, 197, 212
    Box 10.2; 209–10
    energy supplies 205, 210
    European intergovernmental
        organizations 197
    Neighbourhood Policy 195
    relations with China and
        India 231
    relations with EU 154, 198,
        209–10
    see also Soviet Union

S

San Marino 153, 197
Santer Commission 168, 211
Santer, President Jacques 37, 168
Sarkozy, Nicolas 81
Scandinavian member states 26,
        132
Schengen Agreement (1985) 25,
        72, 83, 141, 143, 151–2,
        154, 195
    Box 2.2; 36, 139
    zone 141, 147, 151–4
Schengen Information System
        (SIS) 151–2
Schmidt, Chancellor Helmut 73
Schuman Plan (1950) 26–8
    rhetoric versus reality, Box 2.3;
        26
Schuman, Robert 26
scope and capacity 17–18, 223,
        225–6
Scottish executive 80
screening Box 9.1; 180
Second World War 22–3
security challenges 139
security policy 67, 121
separation of powers Box 8.1;
        161, 166–7
Serbia 74, 190, 192, 196–7

Settembri, P. 88
Seville, Council of Ministers
        (2002) 154–6
sexual harassment 132–3
Shipping security 144
Short, C 211
Siedentop, L. 173
Singapore 153
Single European Act (SEA)
        (1986) 16, 33, 35, 39, 48–9,
        60, 141, 181, 183, 203
single market 15, 62, 167, 212
    programme (1992) 35–6, 75,
        78, 99
Situation Center (CitCen), foreign
        intelligence services 149
Slovakia 54, 74, 77, 82, 185
Slovenia 57, 77–8, 117, 153, 170
    accession (2004) 74, 185, 192
Small and Medium-sized
        Enterprises (SMEs) 106
Smith, K.E. 212
Smith, M.E. 207, 217
social, educational, and
        environmental
        programmes 102
social regulation 81
Socialists 59
Solana, General Javier 213–14,
        217
Somalia 139
South Africa 203, 206, 208
South America 30, 153
South Korea 153
Soviet Union 153
    collapse (1989) 139, 187,
        203
Spaak, Paul-Henri 25
Spain 76–7, 82, 98, 117, 120,
        132, 170, 210
    accession (1986) 17, 35, 74,
        78, 181, 185, 187, 190
    bullfighting policy 116
    CAP spending 130
    cohesion funds 130, 788–9
    Council of Ministers votes 54
    dictatorial regime 26, 35
    EU aerial and marine
        support 154
    geographical and political
        priorities 195
    illegal immigrants 153
    referenda on Constitutional
        Treaty 163
    regions 96

terrorism 148–9
    see also Madrid
Spinwatch 102
Sri Lanka 154
Stability and Association Process
        (SAP) 192
Stability and Growth Pact
        (SGP) 127
Stability Pacts (1993) 213
Statewatch 173
Strasbourg 103, 229
    see also Court of Human Rights
Strategic Committee on
        Immigration, Frontiers and
        Asylum (SCIFA) 143
Stubb, A.C-G. 213
subSaharan Africa 155
subsidiarity 25
    Box 2.1; 80, 175, 232
Sullivan, M.P. 216
supranationalism 10–11, 23, 26,
        33, 39, 67, 87, 169–73, 209,
        214–15
supremacy doctrine 164
Sweden 77, 80, 82, 117, 155, 170
    accession (1995) 17, 38, 74,
        181–2, 185, 187
    alcohol control policy 116, 121,
        123
    Council of Ministers 54
Switzerland 30, 153, 194, 225
    European intergovernmental
        organizations 196–7
    membership application 185,
        193–4, 199
    neutrality 26, 194
    Schengen agreement 151
Syria 193–4

T

Tajikistan 197
Tampere Programme 145, 148,
        154–5
taxation 169, 232
technology, new and old
        techniques 105–7
Tehran (Iran) 213–14
terrorism 139, 141, 145–51, 152,
        212, 217
    EU and US Box 7.6; 147–9
Thatcher, Margaret 34, 36, 47,
        119
theory and conceptual
        tools 10–12

Thessaloniki, Council of Ministers
    (2003) 163
third countries 96–9
third world development 208
Times 98
Tobacco Advertising, Directive on
    (2000) 168
tobacco companies 95
Tonra, B. 207
    and T. Christiansen 202, 218
tours de table 72, 84
trade
    associations 99
    Box 1.3; 7
    policy 204, 216
transatlantic
    cooperation Box 7.3; 144, 214
    trade dispute 'Chicken War' 32
transitional periods Box 9.1; 180
transparency 37, 83, 102, 109
transport policy 31
transposition 120, 140, 148
travel documents 144
treaties 46, 62, 67–8, 72, 85, 87,
    92, 223–4
    Box 1.6; 16
    Council 50–1, 65
    institutions 93
    modification 83, 229–30
Treaty Establishing the European
    Community (TEC) 16
Treaty of European Union
    (TEU) 9, 16
    Article 48; 84
Treaty reform 228
Trevi Group 141, 156
Tunisia 194
Turkey 74, 77, 95, 98, 153,
    192–3, 196–9
    application for membership
        (1987) 17, 185, 192, 231
    Association Agreement with
        EU 192
    NATO membership 188
    relations with EU 209
Turkmenistan 197

U

Ukraine 154, 194, 197–9, 209,
    212
United Kingdom (UK) 76–7, 95
    accession
        (1973) 74, 78, 81, 185

and competing visions of
    Europe, Box 2.5; 31–2
applications (1961; 1963
    and 1967) 32–4, 185, 187
America's Grand Design 32
budget 119
Cabinet 166, 170–1
Charter of Rights 165
chemical industry 106
Confederation of British
    Industry 95
constitution 163
Council of Ministers 54
EC early difficulties 34
Economic and Monetary
    Union 117
EU border management 151
European Arrest Warrant 150
European Free Trade
    Association 30
global perspective 204
House of Commons 167
and Ireland free-travel zone 151
liberalization of trade 29
Maastricht Treaty 37
ministers 166
national sovereignty 26
net contributors club 80
Parliament 171
Permanent
    Representation 99–100
Prime Minister 167, 170–1
Qualified Majority Votes 25
recalcitrate states 224
regions 78, 96, 100
reluctant Europeans 81
Schengen Agreement 25
shared sovereignty 24
support for EU membership 82
supranationalism 25
terrorism 148–9, 152, 212
Times 98
trade preferences for
    Commonwealth countries 32
view of EU 207
United Nations (UN) 226
    National Security Strategy
        (NSS) 217
    peacekeeping force 193
    reform 202
    Universal Declaration of Human
        Rights (1947) 165
    Yugoslavia 190
United States of Europe 24–5,
    232

United States (US) 95, 116
    Asia Pacific Economic
        Cooperation (APEC) 30
    Attorney General 147
    budget 119
    chemicals industry 106
    Congressional Research
        Service 97
    constitution 166, 230
    Container Security
        Initiative 144
    Department of Homeland
        Security 149
    Director of National
        Intelligence 149
    European conflicts 37
    firms foreign direct
        investments 125–6
    foreign policy 206
    Genetically Modified
        Organisms 132
    global power 202
    governance 225
    Grand Design 32
    influence 22, 24
    Interpol 147
    military 215, 217, 219
    National Security Council 217
    NATO 188
    North American Free Trade
        Agreement (NAFTA) 30
    OSCE 197
    Patriot Act 149
    Supreme Court, European Court
        of Justice 63
    terrorist attacks 147–9, 212
    visa list 153
    Visa Waiver Program
        (VWP) 144
Ural Mountains 196
urban regeneration 121
Uruguay 30
Uzbekistan 197

V

Van Gend en Loos case (1963) 62
venue shopping 93, 108
Vietnam 95
Visa Information System (VIS) 152
visa lists, white and black Box 7.7;
    152–3
visa policy 152
Vitorino, Antonio 162

W

Wales 174
Wallace, H. 67, 195
Waltz, K.N. 216
Warsaw, Frontex
    (*Frontièrieures*) 154
Washington, lobbying 96–7
Washington Treaty 26,
    188
    see also NATO
wealth influences 80
Weiler, W.H.H. 62–3, 160,
    212
Wendt, Alexander 218
Wessels, W. 99
West Africa 65

Western Balkans 190,
    192
    European perspective 38
    see also Albania;
        Bosnia-Herzegovina; Croatia;
        Macedonia; Montenegro;
        Serbia
Western European Union
    (WEU) 28
where do we go from here 229–33
White, B. 205
widening versus deepening 180–2
Woll, C. 97
Work safety directive
    (2001/45/EC) 125
Working Time Directive
    (2003/88/EC) 125

World Trade Organization
    (WTO) 124, 128, 209, 226
World Wide Fund for Nature
    (WWF) 96
world's poorest countries 208–10

Y

Young, A.R. 212
Yugoslavia 190, 203
    ex-Yugoslavia 139, 153, 155–6,
    187

Z

Zaventem (Brussels airport) 85